FORGING
UNITY
OUT OF
DIVERSITY

FORGING UNITY OUT OF DIVERSITY

THE APPROACHES OF EIGHT NATIONS

EDITED BY

ROBERT A. GOLDWIN, ART KAUFMAN, AND WILLIAM A. SCHAMBRA

American Enterprise Institute for Public Policy Research
Washington, D.C.

CHICAGO RESEARCH AND TRADING GROUP, LTD.
440 SOUTH LA SALLE STREET
CHICAGO, ILLINOIS 60605

Distributed by arrangement with

UPA, Inc.
4720 Boston Way   3 Henrietta Street
Lanham, MD 20706   London WC2E 8LU England

Library of Congress Cataloging-in-Publication Data

Forging unity out of diversity / Robert A. Goldwin, Art Kaufman,
    William A. Schambra, editors.
        p.   cm.—(AEI studies)
    ISBN 0-8447-3653-8 (alk. paper).   ISBN 0-8447-3652-X (pbk. : alk.
paper)
        1. Constitutional law—Congresses.   2. Cultural relations—
Congresses.   I. Goldwin, Robert A., 1922–   .   II. Kaufman, Art.
III. Schambra, William A.   IV. American Enterprise Institute for
Public Policy Research.   V. Series.
K3165.A55   1983
342'.029—dc19
[342.229]   88-7733
                                                                 CIP

AEI Studies 471

Printed in the United States of America

Contents

Introduction

That all human beings are fundamentally equal is a central tenet of modern constitutionalism and essential to all systems of political liberty. To assert that we are all equal means, necessarily, that we are all equally human, sharing one and the same human nature. This view is widely held and advanced, sometimes as fact, sometimes as aspiration, and denied or disputed mostly by those who are thought to be benighted or bigoted, or both. The universality of human nature, the oneness of humankind, is a vital part of modern democratic thought.

And yet wherever we look in the world we see mankind divided into tightly bound groups by differences of race, religion, language, or nationality, differences so important that the bonds of loyalty they engender often override all other considerations, including even the obligations of national citizenship.

Whether or not we are "all brothers and sisters under the skin," two indisputable, and indisputably linked, facts are evident everywhere: first, that there is a powerful, natural, fraternal bond among persons who share the same religion or race or language or nationality; second, the corollary fact, that that same inclusive bond commonly has the effect of excluding those who are different and engendering hostility toward "outsiders."

In almost all countries with diverse populations—and almost all countries around the world do have significant diversity—we see not the "domestic tranquility" spoken of in the preamble of the Constitution of the United States, but domestic hostility between fellow citizens of the same nation-states: Protestants and Catholics in Northern Ireland, Muslims and Christians in Lebanon, Jews and Muslims in Israel, blacks and whites in the United States, Dutch speakers and French speakers in Belgium, Armenians and Azerbaijanis in the Soviet Union, Serbs and Albanians in Yugoslavia, Greeks and Turks in Cyprus, Hausas and Ibos in Nigeria, Hutus and Tutsis in Burundi,

1

English speakers and French speakers in Canada, Sikhs and Hindus (and Muslims and Hindus) in India, Castilian speakers and Catalan speakers (and, of course, the Basques) in Spain, Sinnhalese and Tamils in Sri Lanka, Malays and Chinese in Malaysia—and this list does not come close to being exhaustive.

The varied constitutional problems posed by diversity, and the ways eight nations have sought to forge national unity in the face of it, form the subject of this volume. Eight very different kinds of constitutions are presented, analyzed, and discussed; they are constitutions of nations from different regions and with different histories and political systems, but they all have in common a significant diversity of races, religions, languages, or nationalities: Belgium, Canada, India, Malaysia, Spain, Switzerland, the United States, and Yugoslavia. As even this small but carefully representative selection of countries demonstrates, with very few exceptions anywhere in the world the populations of modern nations are heterogeneous. The nation-state may be the dominant political group in international life, but experience almost everywhere in the world reveals that the most powerful human loyalties are to groups other than the nation-state. Within these groups of ethnic, racial, religious, lingual, even geographic identity, there are almost always high degrees of cohesiveness and dedication to community. But there is, on the other hand, also hostility between such groups which tends to the disintegration of the larger community.

Diversity therefore presents a problem for constitution makers. Citizens who are members of groups significantly different from others of the population can reasonably have grave concerns: fear for their physical safety, concern that they will not be allowed to participate in the political, social, and economic life of the nation, and fear that they will be restricted in the practices that are characteristic of their special way of life. To address these fears, many constitutions have special provisions, usually addressed directly to groups by name, assuring them of participation in the national life and guaranteeing freedom of religion or use of language, or promising preferences in education or employment on the basis of nationality or race. The dilemma such provisions pose, however, is that they raise the differences within the population to a constitutional status and tend thereby to identify, emphasize, and perpetuate the divisions within society.

As readers will see, the most unusual constitution of a diverse population is that of the United States. It deals with the problem of diversity by seeming to ignore it; that is, although the population even at the time of the Founding was unusually diverse, the fact of

2

differences of race, language, religion, and national origin is not mentioned at all in the Constitution. The strategy of silence seems to have as its aim unity by assimilation, by emphasizing the equality of all individuals as individuals, without reference to group identification, whereas almost all other constitutions seem to concentrate on protecting the rights of members of groups identified as such.

* * *

The way in which this volume emerged says much about the way serious study of constitutionalism can contribute to addressing many of our most pressing political problems. AEI's bicentennial project, "A Decade of Study of the Constitution," begun in 1979, undertook a series of conferences and volumes on the United States Constitution, but it soon became apparent that a proper commemoration of the world's first written national constitution would be incomplete without attention to the issues, problems, and principles of constitutionalism generally. Thus, we began to think about the ways in which constitutionalism had served other nations in addition to the United States.

Since more than half of the existing constitutions in the world today have been written within the last fifteen years, we realized that living constitution writers—in a number far exceeding any other time in history—could be brought together to report on and discuss their countries' constitution-making experiences. Therefore, we conducted our first international conference in 1983 on the writing of constitutions, at the Supreme Court with the Chief Justice of the United States as host and honorary chairman.

Almost all of the authors of the papers for that conference (contained in this book's companion volume, *Constitution Makers on Constitution Making: The Experiences of Eight Nations*) had played leading roles in the writing of their constitutions. Each author had an instructive story to tell about how the framers of his country's constitution confronted specific issues in special circumstances.

The concluding session of that conference was devoted to identifying the key themes and issues that had come to light in the course of the conference. One of the most august constitution writers present, the late Constantine D. Tsatsos, former president of Greece, made the following observation:

> [H]uman rights . . . are the basic preconditions for democracy, but in those cases where historical conditions lead to the formation of confederate or federal states there arise highly difficult and complicated problems. Communities of

different national origin, or communities burdened with different history, want general unity and individual autonomy simultaneously. Between absolute unity and absolute autonomy there are many gradations. This problem, which is so complicated and which leads to so many constitutional varieties, could be a subject for another conference like this one.

We could not have agreed more, and soon afterwards AEI organized a second international conference on constitutionalism—this one focusing on the theme of "unity and diversity"—and this book results from that conference.

As with the companion volume on constitution making, each chapter in this book contains a major paper on the constitutional experience of a country, a shorter commentary on that paper by a fellow countryman writing from a different perspective, and edited portions of the transcript of discussion. The discussion selections greatly enrich the volume, we believe, because along with the authors themselves, the additional participants in the conference came from more than twenty countries in every corner of the world—Asia, Africa, West Europe, East Europe, Central America, South America, and North America. They include Supreme Court judges, appeals court judges, a solicitor general, parliamentarians, and professors from universities in Mexico City, Fribourg, Jerusalem, Paris, Cairo, Belgrade, Toronto, Kuala Lumpur, Jakarta, Delhi, and Brussels. They also include about a dozen Americans from many disciplines and diverse backgrounds.

There are numerous people to whom we owe a great debt of gratitude for both the successful undertaking of the conference and publication of this volume. First and foremost, we thank the Honorable Warren E. Burger, then Chief Justice of the United States, who was host to the conference, making the conference rooms and support staff of the Supreme Court building available to us, and whose presence and hospitality ensured the necessary atmosphere conducive to teaching and learning.

We also acknowledge the assistance of Richard Ware and David B. Kennedy of the Earhart Foundation; Charles Z. Wick, director, the U.S. Information Agency; John Hedges who, until his untimely death, coordinated bicentennial programs at USIA; Michael Schneider, Mark Blitz, Ray Harvey, Albert Ball, Kathy Plowman-Super, and their colleagues at USIA; M. Peter McPherson, director of the U.S. Agency for International Development; Beverly Farrell and Travis Horel also at AID; Philip Merrill; Mark Cannon, Bradford Wilson, Marjorie Vaughan, and their colleagues in the Office of the Chief Justice of the United States; John C. Whitehead, Gerald

Hellman, Suzanne Butcher, and their colleagues at the Department of State; then acting Archivist of the United States Frank Burke and his staff; then Attorney General of the United States Edwin Meese III; Gary McDowell of the Department of Justice; then acting chairman of the National Endowment for the Humanities John Agresto and his colleagues; Ingeborg Wichmann and her team of simultaneous interpreters; Katy Breen, Larry Foust, Cecil Moore, and their staffs at AEI; and for his consistent, unwavering support of the project, William J. Baroody, Jr., then president of AEI.

ROBERT A. GOLDWIN
ART KAUFMAN
WILLIAM A. SCHAMBRA

1

The Indian Constitution: An Experiment in Unity amid Diversity

Fali Sam Nariman

Geographical and Cultural Unity. India's diversity begins with its geography. The subcontinent—which today includes the modern nations of Pakistan, Bangladesh, Sri Lanka, and, of course, India—is a separate geographical entity bounded by high mountains in the north and great oceans to the west, south, and east. In this great land mass of nearly 2 million square miles live more than one-fifth of all humanity. Until about fifty years ago the subcontinent could be approached only by sea or through the narrow passes in the northwest. Protected by natural barriers, it formed historically a cul-de-sac; successive migratory waves of invaders were halted and intermingled with the indigenous residents to such an extent that radically distinct categories of people became hard to identify. Language and religion, rather than ethnic origin, became the primary distinguishing features of the myriad peoples of India.

Within the subcontinent, in the triangle narrowing down from the everlasting snows of the Himalayas to the eternal sultry heat of Cape Comorin (Kanyakumari), where the Arabian Sea and the Bay of Bengal meet the Indian Ocean, are distinct and varied geographical areas. The great mountain ranges in the north and west, containing some of the world's highest peaks, are very sparsely populated but include some of the holiest places long revered by the Hindus.[1]

The Indo-Gangetic Plain lies below the Himalayan ranges. Scorching hot in summer and bitterly cold in winter, this vast heartland of India is formed by the three rivers of the north: the Indus, the Ganges, and the Brahmaputra. The plain is one of the most densely populated regions of the world; but, in this land of sharp contrasts, this same region also includes the desolate salty marshlands of the Rann of Kutch in the west (where the onagers roam), more than

100,000 square miles of dune-covered deserts of Rajasthan, and the vast swamps of the Sunderbans in the east at the mouth of the Ganges (the habitat of the Bengal tiger).

In the northeastern mountain ranges, much lower than the Himalayas, live the colorful hill tribes of Sino-Tibetan origin. A range of hills in central India (the Central Highlands) separates the southern two-thirds of the subcontinent. This hill region, having its own distinctive economy, is peopled by the descendants of the ancient hill tribes of India. South of this is the large Deccan Plateau, which has metamorphosed rocks of the earliest period; here lies most of India's mineral wealth.

Further south the land has been occupied for centuries by dark-skinned Dravidians. They were already a civilized people when the fair-skinned Aryans from the north invaded their land. To this day the Deccan (the southern part of the peninsula of India) is still essentially Dravidian in stock, customs, language, and literature.

Writing in the quiet seclusion of a British prison in 1944 (during his ninth term of imprisonment for revolting against the British), Jawaharlal Nehru contemplated "the variety and unity" of India:

> The diversity of India is tremendous; it is obvious: it lies on the surface and anybody can see it. It concerns itself with physical appearances as well as with certain mental habits and traits. There is little in common, to outward seeming, between the Pathan of the Northwest and the Tamil in the far South. Their racial stocks are not the same, though there may be common strands running through them; they differ in face and figure, food and clothing, and, of course, language. . . . The Pathan and Tamil are two extreme examples; the others lie somewhere in between. All of them have still more the distinguishing mark of India. It is fascinating to find how the Bengalis, the Marathas, the Gujaratis, the Tamils, the Andhras, the Oriyas, the Assamese, the Canarese, the Malayalis, the Sindhis, the Punjabis, the Pathans, the Kashmiris, the Rajputs, and the great central block comprising the Hindustani-speaking people, have retained their peculiar characteristics for hundreds of years, have still more or less the same virtues and failings of which old tradition or record tells us, and yet have been throughout these ages distinctively Indian, with the same national heritage and the same set of moral and mental qualities. There was something living and dynamic about this heritage which showed itself in ways of living and a philosophical attitude to life and its problems. Ancient India, like ancient China, was a world in itself, a culture and a civilization which gave shape to all things. Foreign influences poured in and often influenced

that culture and were absorbed. Disruptive tendencies gave rise immediately to an attempt to find a synthesis. Some kind of a dream of unity has occupied the mind of India since the dawn of civilization. That unity was not conceived as something imposed from outside, a standardization of externals or even of beliefs. It was something deeper and, within its fold, the widest tolerance of beliefs and customs was practiced and every variety acknowledged and even encouraged. . . .

In ancient and medieval times, the idea of the modern nation was non-existent, and feudal, religious, racial, and cultural bonds had more importance. Yet I think that at almost any time in recorded history an Indian would have felt more or less at home in any part of India, and would have felt as a stranger and alien in any other country. He would certainly have felt less of a stranger in countries which had partly adopted his culture or religion. Those, such as Christians, Jews, Parsees, or Moslems, who professed a religion of non-Indian origin or, coming to India, settled down there, became distinctively Indian in the course of a few generations. Indian converts to some of these religions never ceased to be Indians on account of a change of their faith. They were looked upon in other countries as Indians and foreigners, even though there might have been a community of faith between them.[2]

Drafting a Constitution for Independent India. Nehru was the main architect of the Constitution of independent India and its first prime minister. But when he wrote the quoted passage, he was speaking of undivided India, of British India—the home of more than fourteen major languages (and thirty-three main dialects) belonging to four language families wholly unrelated to one another. The Indian National Congress, of which he was president, regarded India as a single country and its diverse inhabitants as one people. The rival political organization, the Muslim League, considered India to be occupied by two nations, the Hindus and the Muslims; in the late 1940s, the league pressed its demands for territorial adjustments to establish what later became the Islamic State of Pakistan.

Eventually, in June 1947, a scheme was devised that enabled the Muslims to have Pakistan if they wanted; since this was ultimately acceptable to the Indian National Congress, the Indian Independence Act of 1947 was passed by the British Parliament. It provided that on August 15, 1947, there would be two dominions in the subcontinent of India: the Dominion of India and the Dominion of Pakistan. The predominantly Muslim areas (East Bengal,[3] West Punjab, Sind, Baluchistan, and the northwestern provinces) went to Pakistan. The remainder, which included Madras, Bombay, West Bengal, the United Provinces (Uttar Pradesh), East Punjab, Bihar, the Central Provinces and Berar, Orissa, and Assam, became a part of India. So did a majority of the Indian states: prepartition India comprised not only British India but more than 550 separate units under the suzerainty of individual Indian rulers or princes who owed allegiance to the British Crown. A few of these Indian states, or princely states, like Hyderabad and Kashmir, were as large as the United Kingdom while some were minute holdings of only a few thousand square yards.

The main feature that distinguished the Indian states from the provinces in prepartition India was that the states had not been annexed by the British paramount power. They had no status internationally; the exclusive power to conduct their foreign relations lay with the British government. Pledging loyalty to the British Crown, the ruler of each Indian state was an absolute monarch; all laws flowed from his edicts. In turn, the British government granted the ruler safety from external attack and internal revolt. Forty-five percent of the area of prepartition India (or 600,000 square miles) was in the princely states, and about one-fourth of the total population resided in them. They were scattered throughout the subcontinent. Their geographical distribution, however, did not coincide with any ethnic, religious, or linguistic division. The peoples of the provinces of British India and of the Indian states suffered alike from successive waves of invasion and foreign domination. Close ties of cultural affinity, as also of blood and sentiment, bound the people of the states and of the provinces together.

With the passing of the Indian Independence Act of 1947 by the British Parliament, the suzerainty (better known as "paramountcy") of the British Crown in relation to Indian states lapsed, and the two dominions were free to negotiate with them.[4] Most of the rulers of the Indian states signed instruments of accession to the government of India. Some smaller states were merged into the former provinces and became Part A states in the Constitution of India of 1950; some were grouped together into viable units and designated Part B states; a few became chief commissioner's provinces (later union territories) administered directly by the central (or union) government.[5] The state of Sikkim in the strategic northeast stayed out.[6]

The Indian Independence Act of 1947 meant the removal of British control. A Constituent Assembly was established in December 1946 and set to work immediately. Its participants were elected by members of the lower houses of the provincial legislatures of the provinces forming part of British India on the basis of one member for every 1 million of the population. Representation of the princely states was fixed on the same basis: one representative to 1 million people. Special representation was given to Muslims and in the East Punjab to the Sikhs. The debates in the Constituent Assembly run to ten large volumes. Almost every page of them reflects the members' anxious awareness of the stupendous task involved in drafting independent India's first written constitution: the need to forge political unity out of a multilingual, multireligious assortment of people at varied stages of development.

Competing Claims of Diversity and Unity

The Constitution of India of 1950—one of the longest ever fashioned for an independent country—was proclaimed on January 26, 1950. It contained 395 articles and eight schedules occupying, in the official edition, 251 pages. "Too long, too detailed and too rigid" was the laconic comment of Sir Ivor Jennings, the constitutional historian of the Commonwealth.[7] Its length was due not merely to the size of the country but also to the problems of accommodating, in a federal parliamentary constitution, the points of view of representatives of peoples speaking different languages and observing varied faiths, all striving at the same time to transform a rigid, hierarchical social order into an egalitarian society. The Chapter on Fundamental Rights (Part III) owed much to the standard-setting Charter of the United Nations and the almost contemporaneous Universal Declaration of Human Rights of 1948.

The Constitution is divided into twenty-two parts dealing with various aspects of the country's governance. In some places it suffers from excessive emphasis on detail, which could have been left to ordinary legislation, and often shows a hybrid mixture of different, almost conflicting, concepts. India is a land of contrasts—the Ganga (the Ganges) is revered and worshiped by millions as India's most sacred river; yet it is very polluted—and in a land of conflicting ideas and ideals, it is not surprising that the basic document of governance is replete with incongruities.

• With more than thirty main indigenous languages and dialects from which to choose, the Constitution recognized English as one of two official languages.

• Among the fourteen regional languages listed in the Eighth Schedule was Sanskrit, which, like Latin, is a dead language, spoken only in prayer.

• The Preamble to the Constitution proclaimed India a secular republic; yet the Chapter on Fundamental Rights recognized and protected India's six main religions and nearly 200 "religious persuasions."[8]

• The right to equality was guaranteed, and the state was prohibited from discriminating against any citizen on grounds of race, religion, caste, or place of birth, but the Constitution recognized and encouraged compensatory discrimination in favor of socially and educationally backward classes of citizens; however, economic backwardness arising out of dire poverty was not recognized as a basis for preferential treatment in educational institutions or in employment by the state.

• While adopting adult suffrage as the basis for periodic elections to Parliament and state assemblies and abolishing special electoral rolls based on race, religion, caste, or sex, the Constitution provided for the reservation of seats in the House of the People and in the legislative assembly of every state for Scheduled Castes and Scheduled Tribes (for centuries the outcastes of Hindu society).

Despite these seemingly disparate and contradictory provisions necessitated by social, historical and political considerations, if there is one overriding concept discernible in the Indian Constitution, it is the concern for the unity of the nation.

Common Citizenship as a Bond of Unity

The ideal of a unified, independent India mentioned in the Preamble to the Constitution, which inspired the provisions for common citizenship, posed few problems.[9] British India was already politically one unit. With the lapse of paramountcy and the loss of protection by the British Crown, the inhabitants of the Indian states became virtually stateless. This condition contributed directly to the relatively smooth absorption of almost all the Indian states into the union of India. The Constitution provided a common citizenship not only for the former inhabitants of British India but also for those of the former Indian states. With their accession to India, the territory of these states became a part of the territory of India. Every person domiciled in India who was born (or either of whose parents was born) in India or who had ordinarily been a resident in India since 1945 was deemed to be a citizen of India (Part II, Article 5). The Constitution guaranteed to every citizen the right to move freely throughout India and to reside and settle in any part of India (Article 19[1][d] and [e]).[10]

Common citizenship meant nondiscriminatory participation in the political life and affairs of the country. Communal representation in legislative bodies and separate electorates for separate communities (introduced by the British in 1909) were abolished. There was to be one general electoral roll for every territorial constituency (Article 325), and every adult citizen of India was entitled to be registered as a voter at every election of the House of the People (the lower house of Parliament) and of the assembly of the state in which he or she resided (Article 326). Anyone—Hindu, Muslim, Sikh, Christian, Buddhist, Jain, Parsee—who was a citizen could be elected to any office in the land, including the highest. Each decennial census (after 1951) has found that more than 80 percent of the Indian people profess some form of the Hindu religion; the Muslims constitute about 11 to 12 percent of the population and the Sikhs less than 2 percent. Since 1950 there have been seven presidents of India; three have been Muslims (one of them acting president), and the present incumbent is a Sikh.

Problems of Language, the Growth of Linguistic States, and Special Provisions for Linguistic Groups

If the provision of a common citizenship raised few or no problems, the next step—that of a common language—presented manifold difficulties and occasioned acrimonious debates in the Constituent Assembly. The languages spoken by the majority of the people of India fell into two major, unrelated language families: in the north the Sanskrit-based Indo-Aryan languages (Assamese, Bengali, Gujarati, Hindi, Marathi, Oriya, Pahari, and Punjabi); in the south the Dravidian languages (Kannada, Malayalam, Telugu, and Tamil).[11]

Then there was the language of the conquerors. Under the Moghul rule (which preceded the British), Persian was the court language, but with the fall of the Moghul Empire, Persian was replaced by Urdu.[12] With the establishment and consolidation of British rule, English came to be adopted as the language in which official correspondence was carried on at higher levels throughout the country. Higher education was also imparted in English, and English became increasingly the language linking the intelligentsia of the country. It was also the language of the superior courts (the high courts and the Federal Court of India). It served as a force for national unity and for the development of a national consciousness.

Competing claims were made in the Constituent Assembly for recognition of one or another language as the official language. Feelings ran high. To assuage them Gandhiji suggested the adoption of Hindustani—a mixture of Hindi and Urdu—as the common language, its use being recognized in both the Devnagari and the Urdu scripts. But Hindustani was not acceptable to the people of the south.

The Constituent Assembly commenced its debate on the official language and on recognition of regional languages in a tense atmosphere; more than 300 amendments to the Language Resolution were offered. Language, which contributed to the diversity and cultural richness of India, was now threatening to divide it. Statesmanship compelled a compromise, and this compromise is reflected in the language clauses of the Constitution.[13]

The official language of India was declared to be Hindi in the Devnagari script, but English was to continue in use for all official purposes for an initial period of fifteen years, extendable by Parliament (Article 343).[14] This period for the concurrent use of English was extended indefinitely with the enactment by Parliament of the Official Languages Act of 1963. Accordingly, since 1950 both Hindi and English have been official languages of the union of India. Both are used to transact business in the houses of Parliament (the House of the People and the Council of States) and for all official communications between the union government and the government of a state that has not adopted Hindi as its national language (see Article 346). The official language in each state was left to be decided by the state legislatures—each could adopt the regional language or Hindi (Article 345). In 1950 the states were multilingual; several languages were spoken in different regions of each state. Therefore, the Constitution provided that the president be empowered to direct that a language be recognized officially throughout a state when a substantial portion of that state's population who spoke the language so demanded (Article 347).

The territorial division of states in 1950 was a legacy from the past, a result of historical accident; the demarcation was determined partly by the sporadic growth of British power in India and partly by the process of integration of 550 princely states into India. Shortly after the Constitution came into effect, a demand arose for a rational reorganization of states on linguistic and cultural bases, the provisions of Article 347 notwithstanding. It was first conceded (in 1953) in the case of the Telugu-speaking areas of Madras and Mysore states, which in 1956 were merged with the Telugu-speaking areas of the former state of Hyderabad to form India's first and largest linguistic state, Andhra Pradesh, in the south.

This new state had to contend with many growing pains. Shortly after its formation, people of the same stock, united by a common language, again threatened to divide. There were demands—and violent demonstrations—for the formation of a separate state for the Telangaha region, which was economically and culturally more backward than the rest of Andhra. Happily, the problems were contained, and disruption of the state was averted, but only after a constitutional guarantee that in matters of public employment and education equitable opportunities would be provided for the people of the Telangaha region (Article 371-D, introduced in 1973). Andhra is a reminder that a feeling of being oppressed and outflanked by the more fortunate can transcend, and even disrupt, bonds of racial and linguistic affinity.

On the recommendation of a distinguished commission presided over by a sitting judge of the Supreme Court of India, the territories of other existing states were readjusted by law, and the readjustment of territorial boundaries to fit the linguistic and cultural similarities of inhabitants of various areas has continued. In northeastern India an attempt was made to enforce a regional language. The composite state of Assam, as defined by the Constitution, included the hill and tribal areas. In their zeal to promote unity among diverse elements in the state, the Assamese insisted that theirs should be the only recognized regional language. This alienated the people of the hill area. "Nothing gives rise to so much anger, hostility and even hatred," writes a distinguished civil servant with firsthand experience in the northeastern region, "as the apprehension of cultural aggression and it is this apprehension that has been at the root of unrest in India's Northeastern frontiers since British withdrawal."[15] The result was the formation of smaller, nonviable northeastern states and union territories—the new state of Meghalaya and the Union territories of Mizoram and Arunachal Pradesh—which were once part of Assam. Today India (which is described in the opening article of the Constitution as "a Union of States") includes twenty-two linguistic states and nine union territories directly administered by the central government.

Each linguistic unit has adopted its own regional language—at times more than one. Hindi is the regional language in the five northern states (Bihar, Haryana, Madhya Pradesh, Rajasthan, and Uttar Pradesh); Urdu in Jammu and Kashmir;[16] Punjabi in Punjab; Hindi and Gujarati in Gujarat; Pahari in Himachal Pradesh (a hill state carved out of the former state of East Punjab); Marathi in Maharashtra (whose principal city is Bombay); Oriya in Orissa; Assamese in Assam; Bengali in Tripura and West Bengal; Manipuri in Manipur; English (along with Lepcha, Bhutia, and Nepali) in the eastern hill state of Sikkim; English and Khasi in Meghalaya and in the tribal and mountainous state of Nagaland; and English and Mizo in the union territories of Mizoram[17] and Arunachal Pradesh.

In the south the regional language is Telugu in Andhra Pradesh; Kannada in Karnataka (the former state of Mysore); Malayalam in Kerala and in the offshore union territory of Lakshadweep (the Lac-

CHICAGO RESEARCH AND TRADING GROUP, LTD.
440 SOUTH LA SALLE STREET
CHICAGO, ILLINOIS 60605

cadive Islands); and Tamil—the oldest Dravidian language—in Tamil Nadu (originally, the state of Madras). In the former Portuguese possession of Goa on the west coast, the languages of administration are Konkani and Marathi; and in the former French enclaves of Pondicherry and Mahe on the east coast, French, English, Tamil, Telugu, and Malayalam are used for official purposes.

This proliferation of regional languages has prompted India's constitutional historian to remind its citizens of the biblical story of the Tower of Babel and why it was never built.[18] The reminder is timely. But the Founding Fathers anticipated this trend and laid the constitutional groundwork for strengthening the official language of the union. Article 351 imposes a duty on both Parliament and the central government to promote and strengthen the Hindi language, drawing sustenance from, but not interfering with, the fourteen other main languages specified in the Eighth Schedule. It also directs that a commission be constituted every ten years to make recommendations for the progressive use of the Hindi language for the official purposes of the union (Article 344).

Because of a desire not to disturb the broad pattern of the judicial system introduced by the British, all proceedings in the Supreme Court of India (the highest court) and in the high courts located in the states were to be (and are) conducted in English. Bills introduced in, and all acts passed by, the Parliament and state legislatures were also to continue to be in English (Article 348). A provision authorizing the use of Hindi in the high courts when the state legislature so decides and the president concurs has been availed of in two high courts (the High Court of Uttar Pradesh and the High Court of Rajasthan), where proceedings are now conducted both in English and in Hindi.

In providing for the principal languages spoken in India, the constitutional draftsman apparently overlooked the innumerable "mother tongues," languages spoken in homes in various parts of India.[19] By a constitutional amendment in 1956, special obligations were imposed on states and local authorities throughout India to provide adequate facilities for instruction in the mother tongue at the primary stage of education for children belonging to linguistic minorities (Article 350-A).

Safeguards for Linguistic Groups and the Problems of Regionalism and Linguistic States

The constitutional safeguards for linguistic groups are found in Articles 29 and 30. Any group of citizens having a distinct language, script, or culture has a fundamental right to conserve it (Article 29[1]) and thus maintain its cultural identity. Likewise, no citizen can be denied admission on grounds of language, religion, race, or caste into any educational institution maintained by the state or receiving aid out of state funds (Article 29[2]). Since language, script, and culture can only be preserved and promoted through education, Article 30 guarantees to linguistic minorities "the right to establish and maintain educational institutions of their choice." These rights are absolute and, like all other fundamental rights, are enforceable through the established superior courts.

In 1952 a small linguistic minority known as Anglo-Indians, who managed many reputable schools in Bombay, were adversely affected when the state government passed an order forbidding state-aided schools that used English as a medium of instruction to admit pupils other than Anglo-Indians or citizens of non-Asian descent.[20] Anglo-Indians could maintain and administer their schools and teach in English but only to Anglo-Indians; if they admitted other Indians, they forfeited state aid unless, of course, they switched to Hindi as the medium of instruction. The object was laudable—to encourage the use of the official language (itself a constitutional prescription under Article 351)—nonetheless, the order was struck down as violating Article 29(1) and 29(2) because Anglo-Indians had a distinct language (English) that they had the right to conserve and because the direct effect of the order was to prevent Indians from entering Anglo-Indian schools, on grounds of race and language.[21]

The Supreme Court of India has also emphasized that included in Article 29(1) is the right to agitate, even politically, for the protection and preservation of a particular language and for one that is not necessarily a regional or a state-recognized language.[22] With the reorganization of states into linguistic units, a constitutional amendment in 1956 provided for the appointment of a special officer for linguistic minorities. His duty is to investigate all matters relating to constitutional safeguards for linguistic minorities and to report to the Parliament and to concerned state governments (Article 350-B).

Differing views have been held on the utility and effect of the regrouping of states on linguistic and cultural bases and on ensuring separate educational and cultural opportunities to linguistic groups. They have led in recent years to regional, fissiparous, and at times secessionist tendencies. To counteract them, the Constitution was amended in 1963 to introduce the overriding concept of the sovereignty and integrity of India. Basic individual freedoms guaranteed under Article 19 (of free speech, peaceful assembly, forming associations or unions, moving freely throughout India, residing and settling in any part of India, and practicing any profession, occupation, trade, or business) are now subject to laws imposing reasonable restrictions on the exercise of these rights in the interests *(inter alia)* of "the sovereignty and integrity of India"—in other words, in the wider interests of the unity of India.

Then, in accordance with recommendations of the National Integration Council, amendments were introduced in the general penal law to make it an offense for anyone to promote or attempt to promote feelings of enmity or hatred among religious, social, or language groups or communities. The divisive force of language has also been contained by the Supreme Court of India in its role as interpreter of the Constitution. States had plenary power over education until 1976.[23] When the state of Gujarati enacted a law prescribing Gujarati as the exclusive language of instruction in the universities in the state, the Supreme Court invalidated the law. It held that although the subject matter of education was within the exclusive jurisdiction of the state, legislation respecting "co-ordination and determination of standards in the institutions for higher education" included prescription of the language of instruction in Indian universities. The substance of the state law touched on a matter reserved exclusively for legislation by Parliament and was therefore beyond the competence of the state legislature.

Despite judicial and constitutional attempts at containment, linguistic factionalism has fostered a pervading spirit of regionalism. Language differences are the most significant aspect of the diversity of India. They are part of regional identity, but they help to perpetuate regional distinctiveness and encourage regional loyalty. In the *State of the World Atlas* India is described as a country with "a significant linguistic conflict." It is not an unrealistic comment.

Accommodating Religions in a Secular Republic

India is also a religiously pluralistic society. The majority of its people (82.6 percent in the census of 1981) profess the Hindu religion; almost the same percentage did so when Europeans (the French, the Portuguese, and the British) first came to India. Within its borders are also found followers of all the major religions of the world. From the matrix of Hinduism have emerged three other great world religions—Jainism, Buddhism, and Sikhism. Christianity came to India many centuries before it reached Europe. One of the twelve original apostles of Jesus, St. Thomas, visited India in A.D. 56, converted a large number of Hindus, was martyred in Mylapore, and lies buried in Madras. Judaism and its adherents (though very few) also found a home and refuge in India. The ancient synagogue in Cochin, in the state of Kerala, built in 1568, bears testimony to the Indian rulers' tolerance of those of alien faiths.

Next to the several cults of Hinduism, however, the main religion is Islam. It has been on Indian soil since A.D. 650, a few years after the Prophet's death, when Arab traders settled on the western seacoast of Malabar (now part of the state of Kerala). Their descendants are so Indianized that they speak the same language as their Hindu brethren and read the Koran only in Malayalam. Forced conversion in Europe and Central Asia in the Middle Ages effectively destroyed the identity of religious minorities. Not so in India. The Ismaili Khojas (followers of the Aga Khan), the Cutchi Memons, and the Bohras were all originally Hindus; they were converted to Islam about 500 years ago during the invasions of Mohamed of Gazni and his successors. Devout Muslims, they practice the religion of Islam but for centuries have retained part of their original identity. Until statutory law intervened in 1938, they were governed by Hindu law in matters of inheritance and succession.

Religion in India not only means the profession of faith but also encompasses places—temples, gurudwaras, mosques, churches, and synagogues. It includes idols and deities and offerings to them, bathing places, graves, tombs, and properties attached to and owned by religious institutions. All this—faith, worship, ritual, and the secular activities of religious groups—had to be provided for in the Constitution, in the Chapter on Fundamental Rights, beyond the reach of legislative or executive interference.

There is no provision similar to the First Amendment of the Constitution of the United States of America, prohibiting the establishment of religion by law, but there is no state religion. That was clarified in 1976 by a constitutional amendment that added the word "Secular" to the Preamble. In the "Sovereign, Socialist, Secular Democratic Republic of India" no religious instruction can be provided in any educational institution wholly maintained out of state funds (Article 28[1]), nor can any person be compelled to pay taxes to be used for the promotion or maintenance of any particular religion or religious denomination (Article 27). Similarly, no person attending any educational institution recognized by the state or receiving aid out of state funds can be compelled to take part in any religious instruction imparted in that institution or to attend any religious worship conducted in it without his or his guardian's consent (Article 26[3]).

At the same time all persons (not merely citizens) are equally entitled to freedom of conscience and the right freely to profess, practice, and propagate their religion (Article 25). All religious de-

19

nominations (there were 183 of them in the 1981 census) and even particular sects have the fundamental right to establish and maintain institutions for religious and charitable purposes, to manage their own affairs in matters of religion, and to own, acquire, and administer their properties in accordance with law (Article 26).

The freedom to practice religion and the freedom to manage religious affairs are not, however, absolute; they are subject to public order, morality, and health. The clauses on freedom of religion were modeled on Article 44 of the Constitution of Ireland. The Supreme Court of India has repeatedly stressed the breadth and the limits of this freedom. Religion includes forms of worship and all religious practices that are (or are believed by the faithful to be) an integral part of the religion;[24] even the right of the head of a religious denomination to excommunicate any of its members on religious grounds has been upheld.[25] But the right to "propagate" religion does not include the right of conversion to another faith, since Article 25 guarantees freedom for all religions, not for any particular one.[26] Although every religious denomination enjoys complete autonomy in deciding what rites and ceremonies are essential according to its tenets, the right to manage the properties of a religious institution has always been regarded as a secular matter that can be regulated by law.[27]

Protection of Minority Rights by the Constitution and the Courts

The Objectives Resolution, moved by Jawaharlal Nehru at the first sitting of the Constituent Assembly on December 13, 1946, contained a pledge that in the Constitution "adequate safeguards shall be provided for minorities, backward and tribal areas and other backward classes."[28] Accordingly, Article 30(1) of the Constitution guaranteed to all minorities, whether based on religion or on language, the right to establish and administer educational institutions; the state was prohibited from discriminating against any educational institution on the ground that it was under the management of a religious or linguistic minority (Article 30 [2]). When the right to acquire and hold property was deleted from the Chapter on Fundamental Rights by a constitutional amendment in 1978, an exception was made for minority educational institutions. Under Article 30(1A) their property could be compulsorily acquired for public purposes only if the state ensured that the amount fixed or determined by law for the acquisition was such as would not restrict or abrogate the right guaranteed under Article 30(1).

When Sikkim became a part of India in 1975, special provisions had to be made for the protection of its original inhabitants. With the waves of immigration of the Nepalese into Sikkim over the course of a hundred years, the Bhutia-Lepchas (the indigenous population) had become a minority in their own country. This ethnic group was ensured equal representation in the Sikkim assembly.[29]

Despite declarations of constitutional rights, minorities in society cannot find adequate protection in the normal political process; they need the protection of courts. The courts in India, when dealing with minority rights, have tended to conceptualize their role as that of a political party in opposition.[30] Almost every time that minorities have approached the Supreme Court complaining of infraction by state or central legislation, the challenge has been upheld. In 1958 the court thwarted an attempt by the Communist-controlled government of Kerala to take over the management of Christian schools. In an advisory opinion given by the Supreme Court (on a reference by the president under Article 143 of the Constitution), large parts of the Kerala Education Bill were declared unconstitutional.[31]

Since the state governments found it increasingly difficult to regulate educational standards, the highest court was asked in 1974 to constitute a larger bench to reconsider its previous decisions. Certain provisions of the Gujarat University Act of 1949 laid down conditions for affiliation of colleges in Gujarat with the Gujarat University. They applied to all educational institutions, including those run by minorities, and they provided that teaching and training in all colleges affiliated with the university would be conducted and imparted by teachers appointed only by the university. Since the provisions interfered with the right of minorities "to establish and administer educational institutions of their choice"—a right guaranteed under Article 30—they were challenged by the Ahmedabad St. Xavier's College Society (managed by Jesuits).

The court, sitting *en banc* (nine judges participating), struck down the offending provisions as inapplicable to colleges run by minorities.[32] Mr. Justice K. K. Mathew read into the article the right of parents to determine which school their children should be sent to for study: "The fundamental postulate of personal liberty excludes any power of the State to standardize and socialize its children by forcing them to attend public schools only." Mr. Justice Khanna gave the reason why minority interests were so zealously protected by the courts:

> The safeguarding of the interest of the minorities amongst sections of the population is as important as the protection of the interest amongst individuals of persons who are below the age of majority or are otherwise suffering from some kind of infirmity. The Constitution and the laws made by

21

civilized nations, therefore, generally contain provisions for the protection of those interests. It can, indeed, be said to be an index of the level of civilization and catholicity of a nation as to how far their minorities feel secure and are not subject to any discrimination or suppression.

The ambit of the constitutional protection for minorities has been considerably extended by the judicial interpretation given to the term "minorities." Members of a reformed Hindu sect (Arya Samaj) were held to be entitled, under Article 30(1), to the fundamental right to establish and administer educational institutions in the state of Punjab (where Sikhs and not Hindus are in a majority).[33] In India, because of its size, minority status is determined by state, not by country.[34]

Accommodating Equality in a Sea of Untouchability and Backwardness

The Legacy of the Past. The provisions relating to "the Right of Equality" in the Constitution (Articles 14 to 18) reflect the grim reality of a developing country, slowly emerging out of a rigid, caste-bound social system. "The spirit of the Age" Nehru once wrote, "is in favor of equality, but practice denies it almost everywhere." In keeping with the spirit of the age, the Constitution guarantees to all persons the equal protection of the laws and prohibits the state (which includes all lawmaking and law enforcement bodies) from denying to any person equality before the law (Article 14). Equality of opportunity is ensured to all citizens in matters relating to employment or appointment to any office under the state (Article 16[1]); the state cannot discriminate (either generally or in matters relating to public employment) against any citizen on grounds of religion, race, caste, sex, or place of birth (Articles 15[2] and 16[2]); and no citizen can be denied admission into any educational institution maintained by the state or receiving aid out of state funds on grounds of religion, race, caste, or language (Article 29[2]).

Nothing in these provisions, however, prevents the state from making special provisions for what the Constitution regards as "weaker sections of Society": for them protective discrimination is recognized and encouraged as a fundamental duty of the state. Article 46 (in Part IV, Directive Principles of State Policy) enjoins the state to "promote with special care the educational and economic interest of the weaker sections of the people and in particular of the Scheduled Castes and the Scheduled Tribes"; it directs the state to "protect them from social injustice and all forms of exploitation." The beneficiaries of preferential treatment are indicated clearly in the Constitution:

• Women and children are exceptions to the general rule against any form of discrimination (Article 15[3]).

• Scheduled Castes, Scheduled Tribes, and socially and educationally backward classes of citizens are also exceptions to the general rule against discrimination (Articles 15[4] and 16[4]). The Scheduled Castes (or "untouchables") are the largest of these groups. The Constitution enables the state to make special reservations in educational institutions and in public services for backward classes of citizens and to ensure that they are adequately represented insofar as is consistent with maintaining efficient administration (Article 335). It also provides for representation in Parliament and in state assemblies for Scheduled Castes and Scheduled Tribes and a proportional reservation of seats for them in the lawmaking bodies of the nation (Articles 330 and 331). These provisions for representation were initially intended to operate for ten years but have been extended periodically by constitutional amendments. As the Constitution now stands, they will be in effect until 1990.

Preferential treatment for women and children is easily explained. In every society children are treated differently from adults. Women constitute nearly 50 percent of India's population; the majority of them have been an oppressed class. The personal and customary laws of the Hindus and Muslims imposed special disabilities and constraints on them.[35] "Na stree swatjamtramarhati," said Manu the lawgiver: The woman does not deserve independence. In a male-dominated society women were looked on as chattels, useful only for marriage and the bearing of children. The institution known in Roman law as the perpetual tutelage of women was, as Sir Henry Maine pointed out, carried to its logical conclusion in India.[36]

Why have safeguards and special provisions for "Scheduled Castes," "Scheduled Tribes," and "Backward Classes"? For treating adult male citizens differently there must be a reason, for, as Isaiah Berlin said in a famous essay on the subject, "the assumption is that equality needs no reason, only inequality does." The answer lies in our history. The reason for the unequal and preferential treatment of these categories in the Constitution is that these groups have been disadvantaged for centuries, many of them beyond the pale of law—Scheduled Castes and Scheduled Tribes even beyond human compassion. For more than 2,000 years, "untouchables" and "tribals" were treated as if they were less than human beings, a treatment rationalized by the argument that they and their children were inherently inferior in ability to those born into superior stations in life. As Marc Galanter says in his excellent treatise on the subject: "India embraced equality as a cardinal value against a background of elaborate, valued and clearly perceived inequalities."[37] In other words, when drafting the Constitution, we were atoning for the past.

What was the past? We must go back over two milleniums. The Aryans were the first invaders of the land inhabited by the serpent-worshiping Nagas and other ancient tribes in the north and by the Dravidians in the south. The Aryans subjugated India without pretending to elevate it. They wanted land and pasture for their cattle; slowly they made their way eastward along the Indus and the Ganges until all Hindustan was under their control. Outnumbered by a subject people whom they considered inferior, the Vedic Aryans sought to preserve their racial identity. In a couple of centuries, however, they were assimilated and absorbed. The first caste division was not by status but by color (as Will Durant reminds us).[38] It separated the fair Aryans with long noses from the dark, broad-nosed Dravidians: "It was merely the marriage regulation of an endogamous group." But that was only how it started.

As the India pictured in the Vedas (2000–1000 B.C.)[39] changed to the conditions described in the great Hindu epics of the Mahabarata and the Ramayana (1000–400 B.C.),[40] occupations became hereditary and more specialized, and caste divisions were more rigidly defined. First were the Kshatriyas (or fighters), who considered it a sin to die in bed. But as conditions of war gave way to peace and as religion and ritual (largely an aid to agriculture in the face of incalculable elements) grew in importance and complexity, requiring proficient intermediaries between men and gods, the Brahmins consolidated their position. They alone knew the ancient Sanskrit (the oldest in the European group of languages); they alone could recite the Vedas. They were able to recreate the past and form the future in their own image, molding each generation into one with greater reverence for the priests, building for their caste a prestige that in later centuries gave them the supreme place in Hindu society.

Below the Brahmins and Kshatriyas were the Vaishyas—farmers and traders. These three castes (or varnas) were regarded as twice born, the second birth (or regeneration) consisting in the study of the Vedas and in the performance of sacraments. The twice-born status was denied to the fourth varna, the Shudras—or the working class—who made up most of the population. Over the years a fifth category long unrecognized in theory, the outcastes, emerged—unconverted native tribes, captives of war, and men reduced to slavery as punishment. This small group of the casteless formed the nucleus of what has become the world's largest minority: the untouchables (euphemistically described as "the Scheduled Castes").

It was not as if the caste principles on which Hindu society was organized were never questioned from within. The religious hegemony of the Brahmins was contested by the Kshatriya nobleman who founded Buddhism. This new religion rejected the predetermination of status by birth and the hierarchical ranking of castes. It became the religion of the kings who ruled India for nearly 900 years. Embraced by the Emperor Ashoka (273–232 B.C.), Buddhism gained a foothold in the subcontinent. For more than 200 years it posed a real threat to Hinduism. But then it became riddled with schisms and sects and was influenced by Hindu pantheistic beliefs. Generations of Hindu culture proved too much for this ascetic, nontheistic religion. Buddha was slowly absorbed into the Hindu pantheon as one of the incarnations of the God Vishnu.[41] During the reign of Harsh-Vardhan (A.D. 606–648)—the last Buddhist king—the great casteless religion was stamped out in the land of its birth. The oriental scholar Sir Charles Eliot has described the denouement in an expressive phrase: "Brahmins killed Buddhism by a fraternal embrace."[42]

The Hinduism that replaced Buddhism was an amalgam of faiths and ceremonies that had four common characteristics; it recognized the caste system; it reaffirmed the leadership of the Brahmins; it accepted the law of karma (destiny) and the transmigration of souls; and it replaced with new gods the deities of the Vedas. Caste came back into its own and with it the antithesis of "pure" versus "impure." The untouchables—Hindu outcastes—grew in number, particularly with the introduction of new occupations. By the latter part of the Middle Ages India was more advanced in agriculture, handicrafts, and commerce than many other countries. To the traditional division of society into four main castes (Brahmins, Kshatriyas, Vaishyas, and Shudras) were added an almost indefinite number of occupational castes (in the thousands). The criteria for the hierarchical status of high or low multiplied a thousand-fold with new occupations. For each new activity it was the Brahmins who determined which aspects were low or impure, and the number of outcastes increased even further.

Muslim rule brought some changes into Indian society, but neither the new language of the courts (Persian) nor the religion of the new rulers (Islam) made any difference to the traditional division of labor organized through specialized groups ranked in hierarchical order. Caste and untouchability flourished during Muslim rule.

Only during British rule were the first attempts made at emancipation. The new economic order brought in by the conquerors from the West altered the design of a social system that had retained a remarkable continuity for centuries. Moreover, with English education more people became acquainted with modern European and American history, with their concepts of equality and fraternity. The beneficiaries of the British system of education, mainly the children of high-caste Hindu families, grew up questioning the principles on which their society was organized. A few cosmetic changes were introduced, such as the Caste Disabilities Removal Act of 1850, but it was a dead letter. Social consciousness had not yet been aroused.

Then, at the beginning of this century, Gandhi introduced into the independence movement two new concepts: peaceful non-cooperation with the British (nonviolent Satyagraha) and a plea for a better deal for the outcastes. Gandhi lived among them and described them as Harijans (children of God). In the liberal spirit of the age, the name stuck. It brought an increasing awareness to the Indian mind of the shame of untouchability. Among the more enlightened of the higher castes a movement started to do something to relieve the lot of the depressed classes. To uplift them was regarded as an act of compassion, a voluntary righting of the wrongs of many years. But as the benefits of Western-style education permeated downward, the bright young men in the society of outcastes also spearheaded a movement that was based not on compassion but on right. The leader of this movement—and its most eloquent member—was Dr. B. R. Ambedkar, a Harijan; he was, along with Nehru, one of the principal architects of the Constitution of India.

Atonement for the Past. This, then, was the legacy that we inherited with independence. Aware of the generations of accumulated and accentuated group inequalities, the Constituent Assembly adopted a constitutional policy of deliberate preferential treatment for the historically disadvantaged peoples. First untouchability was abolished and its practice in any form forbidden (Article 17).[43] The Untouchability Offences Act of 1955 (renamed in 1967 the Civil Rights Act) adopted legal sanctions in aid of the constitutional prohibition. All temples and religious institutions were constitutionally "thrown open" to the untouchables (Article 25[1][b]). A form of apartheid, long practiced by the twice-born classes against the untouchables, was abolished, and all citizens became entitled to equal access to shops, restaurants, hotels, and places of entertainment and to the use of wells, tanks, bathing places, roads, and places of public resort (Article 15[2]).

Untouchability was not merely a stigma, however; it was an attitude of mind. Mere constitutional declarations were not enough. It was against this background that the Constitution recognized, promoted, and encouraged special treatment in educational and employment opportunities for the Harijans and the less fortunate classes. It enabled Parliament and the states to make special provisions through ordinary law for the advancement of Scheduled Castes, Scheduled Tribes, and other backward classes—those who by reason of their occupational background were socially and educationally backward. Provisions could be made, without infringing the equality clauses, for reservation of seats in educational institutions and of posts at almost all levels of public services. Although the Constitution does not pre-scribe the number, reservations up to (and at times exceeding) 50 percent have always been upheld by the Supreme Court of India as not violating the clauses guaranteeing equality to all (Articles 14, 15[1], and 15[2]) or the meritocratic principles they embody.[44]

The Constitution prescribed an agency and a method for desig-nating Scheduled Castes and Scheduled Tribes. The president (that is, the central government, since all executive action of the government of India is taken in the name of the president) was empowered to specify the castes, races, or tribes that, for the purposes of the Consti-tution, would be deemed to be Scheduled Castes or Scheduled Tribes within any particular state or union territory (Articles 341 and 342). Once promulgated, these lists could be changed only by an act of Parliament.

The Scheduled Castes Order promulgated by the president in 1950 (with amendments introduced over the years) proceeded pri-marily on the basis of untouchability, measured by the incidence of social disability combined with economic, occupational, educational, residential, and religious tests.[45] The Scheduled Tribes Order of 1950—amended over the years—listed backward tribes in need of preferential treatment.

The scheme of Scheduled and Tribal Areas (under the Govern-ment of India Act of 1935) was adopted in the Constitution (Part X, Article 244 and 244[A], and the Fifth and Sixth schedules). These designated areas were to be administered as a special responsibility of the governor of the state in consultation with tribal committees and councils.

The provisions for Scheduled Tribes in the Constitution were intended to preserve their separate identities. The aim was a balanced improvement of their condition with such a degree of assimilation as would preserve their distinctiveness and give them a measure of autonomy. Primitive cultures react sharply to alien interference. Expe-rience has shown that indigenous tribal communities are prepared to adapt themselves to change only on their own terms and in their own time. The constitutional policy for Scheduled Castes has been to overcome their disabilities and disadvantages by preferential treat-ment, to eliminate their distinctiveness by enabling them to share the advantages for lack of which they are still a class apart from other, advantaged citizens of Hindu society.

While the categories of Scheduled Castes and Scheduled Tribes have been constitutionally determined, the "other backward classes" (OBCs) also designated for preferential treatment (Articles 15[4] and 16[4]) were left undefined. They are therefore to be determined by the states and by government agencies. The absence of any identifiable and constitutionally prescribed test has led to much bitterness and dissatisfaction, especially in recent years. Although commissions appointed under Article 340 to investigate and report on the socially and educationally backward classes have made recommendations, they have not always been uniform, nor have they been accepted. The first Backward Classes Commission submitted its report in 1955, listing 2,939 castes as "socially and educationally backward." The report was not accepted by the central government since no objective tests were laid down for identifying OBCs. The government was opposed to the adoption of caste as a criterion for backwardness; it would have preferred the application of an economic or means test.

The second Backward Classes Commission (better known as the Mandal commission), in its report submitted in 1980, rejected the application of a means test in view of the language of Article 340; that article and the reservations envisaged in Article 15(4) applied only, it said, to "socially and educationally backward classes," not to economically backward classes. The commission concluded that, in view of the permanent stratification of society in a hierarchical caste order, low ritual caste status had a direct bearing on a person's social backwardness.

The commission produced some startling figures. It estimated, from census data, that socially and educationally backward classes (both Hindu and non-Hindu) constituted as much as 52 percent of the population of India, excluding the Scheduled Castes and Scheduled Tribes, which accounted for an additional 22.5 percent. It also reported that the representation of other backward classes in government services and public employment was only 13 percent and their representation in "plum" jobs (Class I posts) a meager 4.7 percent. Statistics, when skillfully presented, dispel complacency. The backward classes were agitated.

Meanwhile, the state of Karnataka set up its own commission to investigate and report on backward classes in the state. This commission (named, after its chairman, the Havanur commission) ignored the principle of caste in the concept of social backwardness and devised a new test, that of poverty coupled with isolation. This test cut across the caste system and included as backward classes several groups of temple functionaries (who belonged to higher castes) as well as some Kshatriyas. At the same time it excluded some groups in the traditionally low castes on the grounds of their economic advancement. The state of Karnataka accepted the report and made reservations in accordance with it. As expected, the state action was challenged in the High Court of Karnataka and later in the Supreme Court of India.

Meanwhile a commission in Gujarat, appointed to recommend identifying tests for the socially and educationally backward classes in the state, submitted its report to the government of Gujarat. This commission (known as the Rane commission) also ignored castes and subcastes in listing the socially and educationally backward classes. It concluded that, for an initial period of ten years, it should be assumed that those who belonged to the lower castes or subcastes but who were individually and financially well off did not suffer from any social and educational backwardness. The financial criterion adopted was an annual family income over Rs. 10,000; those with family incomes less than that figure would become beneficiaries of Articles 15(4) and 16(4) of the Constitution. The government's acceptance of this recommendation and its decision to increase the percentage of reservations from about 30 percent to nearly 50 percent sparked a series of riots in the state in the summer of 1985. The decision has generated a new conflict over reservation that threatens to spread beyond Gujarat. The swelling numbers of the backward classes, by the improvident fertility of those having nothing to lose, have further aggravated the problem.[46]

Against this background the decision of the Indian Supreme Court in the Karnataka case (*K.C. Vasanth Kumar* v. *State of Karnataka,* May 8, 1985, unreported) was disappointing. Called on to give guidelines for determining other backward classes (for purposes of the state's reservation policy), the five justices spoke in different voices, responding without any unanimity on the main points of contention. The justices were divided on whether reservation of more than 50 percent was permissible; on whether castes should form the basis—or at least an important element—for determining social and educational backwardness; and on whether in jobs requiring high expertise and skill a policy of reservation, detracting from merit, was possible.

On one point, however, they were all agreed. They were agreed and alarmed about a new trend, that of privileged groups among underprivileged classes monopolizing for themselves the preferential benefits intended for the class. Mr. Justice Chinnappa Reddy dwelt on the degrading spectacle:

The paradox of the system of reservation is that it has engendered a spirit of self-denigration among the people. Nowhere else in the world do castes, classes or communities queue up for the sake of gaining the backward status. Nowhere else in the world is there competition to assert backwardness and to claim "we are more backward than you." This is an unhappy and disquieting situation, but it is stark reality.

Mr. Justice D. A. Desai, who made a fervent plea for the recognition of poverty as a true criterion for backwardness, said that if a survey were made about the benefits of preferred treatment among the undefined economically and socially backward classes, "it would unmistakably show that the benefits of reservations are snatched away by the top creamy layer of the backward castes."

This consideration prompted the chief justice of India, C. J. Chandrachud, to recommend that a test of economic backwardness be applied not only to the other backward classes but also to Scheduled Castes and Scheduled Tribes. He stated that the policy of reservations in public employment, in education, and in legislative bodies should be reviewed once every five years. That would help the state to rectify the distortions arising out of the implementation of the reservations policy; it would also help the people (backward and other) to vent their views in a continuing public debate on the practical effects of that policy.

Conclusion

A contemporary assessment of the record of the first thirty-five years in the working of any constitution is bound to be faulty. It lacks perspective. It does not have the historical advantage of time and distance. But as we see it today, the Indian experiment of unity amid diversity has so far succeeded only partially.

The difficulty of language was almost insurmountable in the early years; it has not been resolved. It has been contained through a spirit of accommodation, by constant attempts at a synthesis; consensus has been the distinguishing feature of Indian culture.

We have achieved greater success in our treatment of minorities. Thirty-five years under the Constitution have ensured for religious and linguistic minorities and for religious denominations of every kind a freedom from state interference that is truly remarkable. The freedom these groups enjoy in the Indian polity is unsurpassed among developing, pluralistic societies.

We have not yet solved our main problem, however. We have not resolved the complexities that lie buried in the great but elusive doctrine of equality. To what extent should the claim based on merit and on the fundamental right of equality be ignored? How far does the Constitution, truly interpreted, direct us to go? How soon are we to atone for the oppression of centuries? Should we go on equalizing downward? and for how long?[47] These questions surface periodically. The underrepresentation of the underprivileged in public employment remains highly disproportionate, and, as Ralph Bunche once said, "Inalienable rights cannot be enjoyed posthumously."

Still, we cannot ignore the groundswell of public opinion: an increasing resistance to the view that the sins of generations of forefathers in the higher castes should be expiated here and now—in a couple of generations. Even the Hindu law's theory of "pious obligation" requires the Hindu son to meet the financial obligations only of his father, not of the forebears of his father. The judges, who have the final word in all constitutional matters, have not been very helpful. They have interpreted the compensatory discrimination clauses differently at different times. They have on occasion prodded and energized governments to live up to the constitutional commitment to alleviate the lot of the downtrodden, but the ground rules have kept fluctuating. Marc Galanter, a sympathetic critic, has explained why:

> In an area of law founded on the constitutional embrace of conflicting principles, it should not be expected that courts would provide an enduring synthesis that transcends and encompasses them and settles disputed issues with finality. Rather, we would expect—if the courts are at all representative of the larger society—some ambiguity and vacillation.[48]

Amid all the controversy and vacillation one thing is certain: as long as poverty continues to stalk the land and gross disparities between the rich and poor remain, the ideal of an egalitarian society envisaged in our basic document of governance will remain a dream. Whatever the nation's karma, the founding fathers cannot be faulted for a lack of idealism, nor can Providence. Truly, it is not in our stars but in ourselves that we are thus. It is not because of our Constitution but despite its provisions that we have failed to achieve what were naively assumed (in 1950) to be achievable goals.

We have abolished untouchability and outlawed backwardness in the Constitution of India. Alas, many of us have not eliminated it from our hearts.

Notes

1. The term "Hindu" is used in a theological sense, not in a national or racial sense; there is no such race as "Hindu." It is not the inhabitants of Hindoostan who are Hindus, but only those who profess the Hindu religion.

Etymologically, the word "Hindu" is derived from Sindhu (literally, large mass of water, used to describe the mighty Indus). The Persian invaders described all northern India as Hindoo-stan, the Land of the Rivers. It is out of this derived Persian term "Hindu" that the invading Greeks coined "India." See Will Durant, *The Story of Civilization*, vol. I, pp. 392–93.

2. Jawaharlal Nehru, *The Discovery of India* (Calcutta: Signet Press, 1946), pp. 61–62.

3. In March 1971 East Bengal broke away from Pakistan and formed the separate state of Bangla-Desh. The imposition of Urdu in the Arabic script proved the breaking point. Muslims, the majority of the people of East Bengal, spoke and wrote in Bengali (an Indo-Aryan language).

4. With the lapse of paramountcy, the princes were (as described by Malcolm Muggeridge) "finally bereft of all authority, little lost pools of sovereignty, left behind on a barren shore, by a receding tide of history."

5. For a fuller account of the Indian states, see Shiva Rao, *The Framing of India's Constitution*, chap. 18; and the White Paper on Indian States issued by the government of India in July 1948.

6. The British Indian state of Sikkim was under a hereditary ruler called the chogyal. With the lapse of paramountcy Sikkim became a protectorate of India. In 1974 the Sikkim assembly passed the Government of Sikkim Act, establishing a fully responsible government and seeking representation for the people of Sikkim in India's parliamentary system. By a constitutional amendment (1974), Sikkim was given the status of an "associate state," entitled to send two representatives to the two houses of Parliament. The chogyal resented this and sought international intervention, which prompted the Sikkim assembly to pass a resolution abolishing the institution of chogyal and expressing a desire to become part of India. The decision was approved in a referendum by an overwhelming majority. Sikkim was admitted to the union by the Thirty-sixth Amendment to the Constitution in 1975 and became the twenty-second Indian state.

7. Sir Ivor Jennings was the chronicler of the Westminster-type constitutions of the new countries that were emerging (after World War II) after the breakup of the British Empire. He helped draft some of these constitutions, including the first constitution of Ceylon.

8. The six major religions listed in the latest census (1981) are Hindus, 82.6 percent of the population; Muslims, 11.4 percent; Christians, 2.4 percent; Sikhs, 2.0 percent; Buddhists, 0.7 percent; and Jains, 0.5 percent. Those having no religion—or no religion stated—constitute only 0.01 percent of the population. The census lists 183 "other religions and persuasions" (from Abutani, a small religious cult in the northeastern state of Arunachal Pradesh, to one of the world's oldest religions, Zoroastrianism, whose adherents in India, the Parsis, number only 71,630). Since the 1971 census the number of Hindus has increased 24.2 percent, of Muslims 30.6 percent, of Christians 16.8 percent, of Sikhs 26.2 percent, of Buddhists 22.5 percent, and of Jains 23.7 percent.

9. The Preamble of the Constitution resolved to constitute India into a sovereign democratic republic, to secure to all its citizens justice, liberty, and

equality, to promote fraternity, and to ensure "the dignity of the individual and the unity of the Nation."

10. Under the Citizenship Act of 1955, which supplements Part II of the Constitution, Indian citizenship is acquired by birth, descent, registration, or naturalization.

11. There are also two minor language groups. The tribes in India's central hill regions (in Bihar, Chota Nagpur, Orissa, and Central India) speak Mundu, a language belonging to the Austro-Asiatic family. The other branch language of the family (Mon Khmer or Khasi) is spoken by the Khasis in northeastern India and by the Nicobarese in the Andaman and Nicobar islands stretching across the Indian Ocean in the south. The inhabitants of the northeastern mountain areas, who have had a longstanding connection with the people of Tibet and Southeast Asia, have developed their own language dialects, which are Sino-Tibetan. The Sino-Tibetan family is represented in India by two branches: Thai-Chinese and Tibeto-Burman. The latter includes Manipuri, the regional language of the state of Manipur.

12. The name "Urdu" is derived from "Zaban-E-Urdu-Muala," which means the language of "the exalted camp," that is, the camp or court of the ruling sultan of Delhi. It was with the Sultanate of Delhi in A.D. 1206 that Muslim (or Afghan) rule took hold in India. After that a large part of India was dominated by a succession of Muslim dynasties, the longest being the Moghul. The Moghul Empire was tottering by 1750 but lingered for a hundred years and was wiped out by the British after the suppression of the Indian Mutiny in 1857.

13. A detailed and well-documented account of the forces at play is given in Glanville Austin, *The Indian Constitution: Cornerstone of a Nation*, pp. 264–307.

14. Among the various dialects of Hindi, the dialect chosen as official Hindi was the standard Khariboli, originally spoken in Delhi and in western Uttar Pradesh.

15. Nari Rustumjee, *Imperilled Frontiers* (London: Oxford University Press, 1983).

16. Urdu and Hindi have the same grammar and the same basic vocabulary. They differ mainly in the script: Urdu is written in the Persian-Arabic script and Hindi in the Nagari (or Devnagari) script. Urdu has a large admixture of Persian and Arabic words; Hindi (particularly official Hindi) is enriched with Sanskrit words.

17. The Mizos are a distinct linguistic ethnic and cultural unit of hill tribes. They came under the influence of British missionaries in the nineteenth century, and many of them were converted to Christianity, with which came English and education. The missionaries introduced the Roman script for the indigenous Mizo language.

18. See H. M. Seervai, *Constitutional Law of India*, 3d ed., vol. 2, p. 2148. The unifying and dividing force of language has rarely been portrayed more vividly than in the account of the Tower of Babel (in Genesis XI): Once upon a time all the world spoke a single language, and men decided to build a city with a tower with its top in the heaven. The Lord saw the city and tower they

were building, and he said: "Here they are, one people with a single language, and now they have started to do this, and henceforward nothing they have a mind to do will be beyond their reach. Come, let us go down and confuse their speech, so that they will not understand what they say to one another." Their speech was confused, they did not understand one another, they were dispersed over the surface of the earth, and their city and tower remained unbuilt.

19. The last census listed 1,652 "mother tongues," but only thirty-three of them were spoken by groups of people numbering more than 100,000.

20. The Anglo-Indians were people who could trace their ancestry in 1950 to an English parent or grandparent. They were a preferred class during British rule. Since they were a minority, the reservations for them in posts (railway, customs, postal, and telegraph services) and the facilities of state educational grants were continued for a decade (Articles 336 and 337). In addition, they have two reserved seats in the House of the People and in assemblies in states that have sizable Anglo-Indian communities (Articles 331 and 333). They are quickly losing their identity as a separate group; most of them have assimilated into Indian society and are now indistinguishable from other Indians.

21. State of Bombay v. Bombay Education Society, AIR 1954 SC 561.

22. Jagdev Singh v. Pratap Singh, AIR 1965 SC 182.

23. By constitutional amendment this area of legislation was removed from the exclusive State List and placed in the Concurrent List. The matters enumerated in the Concurrent List (List III—Seventh Schedule) can be legislated on both by Parliament and by state legislatures. In the event of a conflict, legislation by Parliament prevails.

24. Commissioner of Hindu Endowments v. L. T. Swamine, AIR 1954 SC 853. The court refused to follow Davis v. Beason 133 US 333, 342, where the Supreme Court of the United States held that cults and forms of worship of a particular sect were not matters of religion. In holding that matters of religion included acts done in pursuance thereof, the Supreme Court of India preferred the views of the High Court of Australia interpreting S. 116 (the religious freedom clause) of the Australian Constitution (Latham CJ. in Adelaide v. Commonwealth 66 CLR 127).

25. Saifuddin Saheb v. State of Bombay, AIR 1962 SC 853 (a much criticized decision).

26. Rev. Stanislaus v. State of Madhya Pradesh, AIR 1977 SC 908. The decision runs counter to the intent of the draftsmen. In the draft article approved by the Minorities Sub-Committee (and later by the Constituent Assembly), the right to propagate religion was deliberately added so as to guarantee to proselytizing religions (like Christianity and Islam) the right to preach religion with the object of conversion. See Rao, *Framing of India's Constitution*, p. 261.

27. Durgah Committ Ajmer v. Syed Husain Ali, AIR 1961 SC 1402; Nathdwara Temple Case, 1963 SC 1638.

28. *Constituent Assembly Debates* (Official Series), vol. I, pp. 58–60.

29. Article 371 F(f), introduced by the Constitutional Act of 1975 (Thirty-sixth Amendment).

30. As in other jurisprudences. See Chief Justice Stone's famous footnote in U.S. v. Carolene Products Co., 304 US 144: "Judicial deference to legislative wisdom must not be allowed to undercut the normal democratic processes by legislators to display 'prejudice against discrete and insular minorities.'"

Professor Upendra Baxi, in his introduction to a collection of essays by Justice K. K. Mathew, *Democracy, Equality, and Freedom* (Eastern Book Company), describes in detail the role of the Supreme Court of India in regarding minority rights as one of the "preferred freedoms."

31. Re: Kerala Education Bill, AIR 1958 SC 956.

32. St. Xavier's College v. State of Gujarat, AIR 1974 SC 1389.

33. D. A. V. College Jull v. State of Punjab, AIR 1971 SC 1737.

34. The extent to which religions and religious beliefs are accommodated and protected in the secular republic of India is illustrated in a recent judgment by the Supreme Court (C.A. 870 of 1986—Bijoe Emmanuel & Ors v. State of Kerala—judgment d/-Aug. 11, 1986) concerning Jehovah's Witnesses, of whom there are only a few thousand in India, mostly in Kerala. Their children attend schools. When the national anthem, "Jana Gana Mana," is sung during the daily assembly, they have stood respectfully but have refused to sing, not because of the words or the thoughts expressed in the anthem but because of the tenets of their religious faith. No one has thought them disrespectful.

They were left in peace and to their beliefs until July 1985, when a member of the legislative assembly noticed that three children of the sect did not sing "Jana Gana Mana" at the morning assembly in a particular school. He thought it unpatriotic and raised a question in the local assembly. A commission of inquiry was appointed and reported that the children were law-abiding, showed no disrespect to the national anthem, and stood in respectful silence when it was sung but did not sing. On the instructions of the inspector of schools, the three children were expelled.

When administrative remedies proved to be of no avail, the children, through their parents, filed a writ in the High Court of Kerala seeking a restraint order against the authorities' preventing them from attending school. The court rejected their plea. They came in appeal to the Supreme Court, which in August 1986 reversed the verdict of the high court.

The court held that the children did not join the singing of the national anthem in the morning assembly because of their conscientiously held religious faith, which did not permit them to join in any rituals except prayers to Jehovah. The court noted: "Jehovah's Witnesses wherever they are, do hold religious beliefs which may appear strange, even bizarre to us, but the sincerity of their beliefs is beyond question." The court held that their expulsion violated the fundamental right to freedom of conscience and freedom to profess, practice, and propagate religion guaranteed under Article 25(1) of the Constitution.

The justices directed the authorities to readmit the children to the school and permit them to pursue their studies without hindrance. At the end of their judgment, they encapsulated the attitude of the highest court in matters of genuine religious faith: "We only wish to add: our tradition teaches tolerance; our philosophy preaches tolerance; our Constitution practices tolerance; let us not dilute it."

35. Their social condition has improved vastly thanks to the spate of statutory enactments. Indigenous movements for their emancipation have helped to create an increasing awareness among women of their rights and facilities available for enforcing them.

36. "In India," Maine wrote in 1861, "the system survives in absolute completeness, and its operation is so strict that a Hindoo Mother frequently becomes the ward of her own son." H. S. Maine, *Ancient Law* (London: Oxford University Press, 1950; first published 1861), p. 127.

37. Marc Galanter, *Competing Equalities: Law and the Backward Classes in India* (Oxford University Press, 1984). See also Louis Dumont, *Homo Heirarchicus: An Essay on the Caste System* (Chicago: University of Chicago Press, 1970).

38. Durant, *Story of Civilization*, vol. I, p. 398. The early Hindu word for caste was *varna* (color). The Portuguese later translated it as *casta*, from the Latin castus: pure.

39. The word "veda" means knowledge: literally, a book of knowledge. Of the many Vedas that existed, only four have survived: the *Rig-Veda*, or *Knowledge of the Hymns of Praise*; the *Sama-Veda*, or *Knowledge of the Melodies*; the *Yajur-Veda*, or *Knowledge of the Sacrificial Formulas*; and the *Atharva-Veda*, or *Knowledge of the Magic Formula*. Each of these is divided into four sections: the Hymns; the Brahmanas, or Manuals of Ritual, Prayer, and Incantation for the Priests; the Aranyakas, or "forest-texts" for hermit saints; and the Upanishads, which describe the mysteries of the unintelligible world. They are the oldest extant commentaries on the philosophy and psychology of the human race.

40. These great epics are the most famous and best-loved of ancient Hindu literature. The Mahabharata resembles the *Iliad*, being the story of a great war fought by gods and men and occasioned partly by the loss of a beautiful woman by one nation to another. The Ramayana resembles the *Odyssey* and tells of the hero's hardships and wanderings and his wife's patient waiting for reunion with him.

41. Brahmins even adopted Buddhist practices as their own; under pressure of the ethics of renunciation preached by Buddhism (and Jainism), a majority of the Brahmins changed to a vegetarian diet and "renounced" all forms of meat. Since then they have regarded caste Brahmins who ate meat as impure. The caste system conceptualized "purity." (See Dumont, *Homo Hierarchicus*, pp. 55–56.)

42. Sir Charles Eliot, *Hinduism and Buddhism*.

43. This article and others (Article 15[2]) free access to public places; Article 23(1), prohibition of forced or bonded labor, and Article 24, prohibition of employment of children in factories, mines, or hazardous occupations, are primarily directed against individual groups and citizens and accordingly are enforceable against them.

44. In M. R. Balaji v. State of Mysore, AIR 1963 SC 649, the Supreme Court struck down a total reservation of 68 percent of the seats (for all backward classes, including Scheduled Castes and Scheduled Tribes) for admission into medical colleges, on the ground that it encroached excessively on the merit principle. Similarly, in T. DeVadasan v. Union of India, AIR 1964 SC 179, the court (by a majority) struck down a carry-forward rule of reservation in central government services that operated in a given year to the detriment of more meritorious candidates. It reserved 64 percent of all the posts for Scheduled Castes and Scheduled Tribes. In later cases, however, the Supreme Court upheld percentages exceeding fifty. Thus, in the State of Kerala v. N. M. Thomas, AIR 1976 SC 490, a majority of the court (of seven judges) upheld the temporary promotion of lower division clerks in the Registration Department of the state of Kerala as not violating Article 16(1) despite a further exemption granted to them from the requirement of passing certain tests that resulted in the promotion of thirty-four of fifty-one candidates of the reserved categories in a given year (more than 50 percent). Similarly, in AVSK Sangh v. Union of India, AIR 1981 SC 298, a bench of three judges upheld the carry-forward rule in the context of reservation of posts in government-owned railways so that appointments and promotions of posts should not in any given year substantially exceed 50 percent. In a very recent decision, Vasant Kumar v. State of Karnataka (delivered on May 9, 1985), the Constitution Bench refused to invalidate reservations for backward classes (including special groups of impoverished citizens) that, together with the traditional reservations for Scheduled Castes and Scheduled Tribes, totaled over 65 percent. Thus the 50 percent maximum first suggested in Balaji has not been adhered to as a hard-and-fast rule.

45. The Scheduled Castes Order applies only to Hindus (and a part of the Sikhs), the traditionally depressed classes of India being the Hindu outcastes. Those among them who have embraced Buddhism, Jainism, Islam, or the Christian religion and members of other non-Hindu religious groups do not qualify for preferential treatment as Scheduled Castes, although they may qualify under the other constitutionally recognized (but undefined) category, other backward classes (OBCs).

46. The population growth in India has been quite staggering. According to the latest census, the population rose from 533 million in 1971 to 665 million in 1981. India's prime minister, Rajiv Gandhi, has gone on record as saying that although population control was both a social and a political problem, "we must see that politics has one view, that of reducing the population" (*Times of India*, May 14, 1983).

47. In fact, at least two judges (of five) on the Constitution Bench in Vasant Kumar v. State of Karnataka (decided on May 8, 1985) were in favor of a reservations policy having a time limit. "Otherwise," as one of them said, "concessions tend to become vested interests."

48. Galanter, *Competing Equalities*, p. 539.

Commentary

P. K. Tripathi

At the outset it is perhaps significant that the present Constitution of India, in a sense, stands on the ashes and ruins of an attempt to solve a problem of diversity.

When the Constituent Assembly first met on December 9, 1946, to draw up the Constitution of India, the members of the assembly belonging to the Muslim League party boycotted it. They had been insisting on their demand for a separate nation to be called Pakistan and for a separate Constituent Assembly to draw up its constitution.[1] The Congress party, which claimed to represent all the people of India, irrespective of caste or creed, and which stood for a united, secular, democratic India, would not concede to a partition of the country. It soon became clear, however, that the Muslim League was adamant. It issued a call for "direct action" to force acceptance of its demands, as a consequence of which communal riots and senseless killings occurred in several parts of the country.[2] Ultimately, on June 3, 1947, the Congress party conceded on the Mountbatten proposals that established the procedure for ascertaining the will of the people in areas in which the Muslim League had influence. Commending these proposals to the nation, Jawaharlal Nehru ruefully observed:

> It is with no joy in my heart that I commend these proposals to you, though I have no doubt that this is the right course. For generations we have dreamt and struggled for a free, independent and united India. The proposal to allow certain parts to secede if they so will is painful for any of us to contemplate. Nevertheless, I am convinced that our present decision is the right one. . . . The united India that we have labored for is not one of compulsion and coercion but a free and willing association of free people.[3]

This is not to say that the Congress party did not have a good following among the Muslims of India. Several prominent Muslim leaders were congressmen; and in the Northwest Frontier Province (NWFP), with more than 90 percent Muslim population, there had always been a Congress government until after the Congress party agreed to the partition of India and to a referendum in the NWFP to let the people decide whether they would join one or the other of the dominions. The choice was indeed unreal because the NWFP was separated from India by the territory of West Pakistan. The fact remains, however, that in most of the provinces of British India the Muslim League had a massive political following and it was able to win almost all the seats in their assemblies reserved for the Muslims.[4]

It is important even today for India to know, or at least to speculate, why Muslims throughout India (except in the NWFP and Baluchistan) were so massively in favor of having a separate Muslim state of Pakistan and were unwilling to stay in a United India. Most of them living in the provinces where Muslims were not in a majority must also have known that they were, in any case, to continue to stay in India rather than move into the new state of Pakistan. Did they expect to be discriminated against and subjected to humiliation or hardship in India merely because they would be in a minority? If any such fears or misgivings guided their choice, do they now feel they were mistaken? After all, under the Constitution of India, their rights have been secured, and they have been sharing the highest offices of trust and importance in the country, including the office of the president of India, governorships of states, membership in the union and state cabinets, and judgeships in the Supreme Court and the high courts of India.

The Congress party, and Indians generally, blame Muslim distrust on the policy of the British government, which was deliberately directed toward creating and exacerbating differences between the Hindus and the Muslims of undivided India; this was the policy of a foreign power designed to divide and rule. This explanation is not altogether inaccurate. The Muslim League, by and large, seldom embarrassed the British government by boycotting British goods or by demonstrations, protests, and Satyagrahas against British legislative or administrative action, or by demanding that they should quit India.[5] In turn, the British government pampered the Muslim League by granting to Muslims separate electorates and reservation of seats in the legislatures and in government services. By contrast, the Hindus often put off the British officers by their orthodoxy, especially in matters of food and even dress. They appeared to be guilty of a superciliousness of belief and conduct, which is unpardonable to a subject people. On the whole, British and Muslim officers mixed together better than either of them with Hindus.

If Muslim mistrust of a non-Muslim majority was a creation of the British and survived because of British rule in India, these problems should now have faded, especially with the constitutional guarantees and democratic governments functioning in India. If there are other, persisting reasons for the distrust, however, efforts must be made to identify them and to strengthen the bonds of common citizenship between the communities. In India, where even today there are more Muslims than in the whole of Pakistan, the importance of this strategy cannot be overstated.

In this context the constitutional policy of reservations in government posts and educational institutions, which waters down the principle of equality and which I shall detail later, seems to be clearly counterproductive and dangerous.

The British Legacy

Whether the British were responsible for the tensions between Muslims and Hindus in India, their presence and rule were not an unmitigated evil. One of the good things that could be attributed to contact with them is the consciousness of India as a political entity and a nation in the modern sense.

It is indeed true that from ancient days India has been more than a mere geographical entity and that the people of the Indian subcontinent (including today's Pakistan and Bangladesh) have inherited a common cultural heritage, which, in Nehru's words, "showed itself in ways of living and a philosophical attitude of life and its problems." It is also true that this oneness is not impaired by the differences of language, religion, and physical characteristics among the peoples of the subcontinent. Even so, before the advent of British rule, the Indians did not seem to regard their subcontinent as a political entity. Apart from the fact that the idea of the nation-state is comparatively recent—even in Europe where it originated (at least in its present form)—it is still noteworthy that Indians did not feel bothered, before the British arrived, by the lack of a single, ruling government. Indians themselves conceived of India not as a political or administrative entity, as already stated, but as some kind of cultural universe. When one prince in this universe attacked another, or had more territory under his sway than another, or when one dynasty or the other rose to power or disappeared from the political scene, this universe was not swayed or shaken. In fact, even when invaders with a different religion or culture came from outside, mostly from the northwest, not much perturbed this universe. Of course, new architecture, new philosophies, and new weapons and techniques of warfare made their presence felt, but they only enriched the cultural texture of that universe, without damaging it or impairing its vigor and beauty.

The British were different from other invaders in at least two significant ways. Unlike most invaders from outside India, the British came from the east. True, their earliest settlement was at Bassein, near Bombay, but their first military victory and territorial acquisitions were made in Bengal, where the authority of the dying Moghul Empire was probably feeblest. From the battle of Plassey in 1765, which gave them their first territorial possession and military victory in the Gangetic delta, to the defeat of the Sikhs and acquisition of Punjab in 1848, the British swept over the plains of north India, vanquishing in the meanwhile the Marathas and the sultans of the south as their only other rivals for power.

Even throughout this whole period, however, Indians did not generally understand British victories to be different from the victories of any other indigenous power, like the Moghuls or the Marathas. Indians did not clearly appreciate the military and political implications of conquest by a highly organized, capitalist nation motivated by the search for captive markets; nor did they understand that British generals and governors were fundamentally different from the Indian nawabs and rajahs, the British being employees of the East India Company (later on, of the British government) who had to serve their employer faithfully, or be replaced if found unsuitable for their jobs.

The revolt of the Indian army and rulers against the British in 1857 was indeed a brave, united attempt to overthrow British rule, but it is doubtful that much understanding of the nature of the British government and of the totality of its political and military interests was behind that effort. It is also not likely that the revolt would have contributed much toward establishing a "national" government in India, had it succeeded in driving the British out.

The truth, therefore, seems to be that with all its richness of culture, intellectual attainments, and wisdom, toward the end of the seventeenth and the beginning of the eighteenth century India was behind the Western world, particularly England, in understanding and manipulating the new ideas and methods of political organization and in marshaling the resources of the people—ideas and methods that were to control the destiny of mankind in the coming centuries. Nationalism as an inspiring concept was one of those new ideas. In fact, the cultural universe that was India was not exposed at all to these new developments taking shape in Europe. It was only when the British established their foothold in India and when the Indian mind reconciled itself to subjugation by the British government, that the phase of grasping these new developments, new ideas, and new forces began.

The consciousness of India as a nation and the dream that it should be organized as a free, strong nation-state began to take shape as a result of Western contact generally, but particularly as a result of Western education in the colleges and universities established by the British themselves in India and the education Indians began to receive in English and other European universities. This spirit of nationalism was crystalized and steeled by the struggle for India's independence that spread over more than half a century. India's ardent desire for independence from British rule was the desire of a nation to be born.

Western Values in India

Like modern science which, though Western in origin, is nonetheless indispensable and beneficial for all mankind, nationalism, democracy, egalitarianism, rule of law, and the like are ideas that are also Western in origin but that are universal in their validity and their potential for human good. The Western countries learned these ideas and values from one another, with no single nation credited with all these ideas, or all scientific knowledge, by itself. Far from being a matter of shame or inferiority, for a non-Western people to learn these ideas and to acquire the knowledge of science from the West is a measure of the elevation of its mental and moral base, because not all peoples have been able to learn and acquire them with equal ease or readiness. In fact, one aspect of Mahatma Gandhi's greatness as a leader of humanity was that he readily perceived the moral values underlying the institutions of democracy and rule of law and that he had the insight and wisdom to realize that those same moral values were central to the concepts of truth and nonviolence intrinsic in India's philosophical thought and culture for centuries. As a result, Western institutions of democracy and rule of law were connected to the values of truth and nonviolence and could therefore draw succor from India's own cultural heritage.[6] Perhaps because some such assimilation was not possible elsewhere, these values have not survived in several other Afro-Asian lands.[7]

Fundamental Constitutional Rights

The roles of democracy, rule of law, and justiciable, fundamental rights or civil liberties in dealing with the diversity of a population cannot be overstated. In a society in which the individual has the fullest opportunity to air his grievances and to organize public opinion to redress them without fear of vengeance from those in power— or in a society wherein a single individual can challenge, in the name of his rights (or his view of his rights), the whole nation represented in its parliament and may even succeed in upholding his own will against the will of the entire nation—being in a minority, or even being alone, is not a great disadvantage. Thus, the democratic structure of the Constitution of India, the provision in it of justiciable fundamental rights, and the easy and comparatively inexpensive procedure for approaching the high courts and the Supreme Court for the enforcement of these rights are the most important guarantees of tolerance and respect for diversity.[8] These institutions are not provided just on paper in India's Constitution; they are living, pulsating, and vigilant institutions. Thousands of cases are presented to the high courts every year challenging the validity of acts of the Parliament and state legislatures, as well as rules, regulations, orders, or directions issued by the central and state governments; and hundreds of them succeed. The Indian citizen is acutely aware that laws and governmental orders must conform to the Constitution, and I wonder if anything brings him more pleasure than to have a law or an order declared invalid or unconstitutional.

Running a government so unquestionably under the law and so vigilantly watched by the citizens and the judiciary obviously requires great self-discipline on the part of all those who wield power. Constitutional and legal restraint is ultimately based on the moral quality of the people concerned. This moral quality was first developed in the West, but for *any* nation to develop it is a matter of pride and accomplishment. This quality in a people, is the greatest assurance and protection to minorities and dissenters. It is not only the most civilized but also the most effective way of dealing with diversity. Given this quality, the laws and even the Constitution can be altered to give further accommodation to minorities and dissenters where needed.

Exceptions to Equal Treatment

One unfortunate legacy the British left in India was the practice of making reservations for various castes and communities in educational institutions (especially in institutions imparting professional and technical education, such as medical and engineering colleges), in government employment, and in the legislatures.[9] As already mentioned, they even went so far as to set up separate constituencies for the communities, so that only Muslims voted to fill Muslim seats in the legislatures, and so on.[10] This policy exacerbated the differences among the castes and communities in India and weakened the sense of national unity.

In the Constitution of India communal representation for the communities was dropped without hesitation. Moreover, by making provision for equality for all persons before the law (Article 14), by prohibiting discrmination (generally) among the citizens on the basis of "religion, race, caste, sex or place of birth" (Article 15), by prohibiting discrimination among citizens in the matter of admission to state-run or state-aided educational institutions on the basis of "religion, race, caste or language" (Article 29-2), and by prohibiting discrimination among citizens in the matter of state employment on the basis of "religion, race, caste, sex, descent, place of birth, or residence" (Article 16), the Constitution adopted the principle of equal treatment for all persons and citizens. This rendered diversities of caste, religion, or community irrelevant in the relations between the individual and the state.

This healthy principle, however, was compromised by an exception, made even in the original Constitution, permitting reservations in state employment "in favour of any backward class of citizens which, in the opinion of the State, is not adequately represented in the Services under the State."[11] And within about a year after the Constitution went into effect, a similar provision qualified the equal right for admission to educational institutions.[12]

As the principal paper by F. S. Nariman explains in great detail, the courts in India have made a valiant effort to keep to a minimum the inroads made by these permissive provisions on the right to equality. In the Supreme Court opinion written by Mr. Justice Bhagwati (who became chief justice of India) in the case of *Dr. Pradeep Jain* v. *Union of India*,[13] the court restricted reservations in educational institutions on the basis of residence to an upper limit of 70 percent of the seats available after the other reservations had been accounted for. The court has also laid down a sort of timetable for gradually reducing those reservations. The basis of this effort has been the general equality provision of Article 14, and the court has subordinated other constitutional provisions to this general provision—a strategy and reasoning that some may regard as controversial.

Be that as it may, the point remains that India does not seem to have understood the vital significance of the egalitarian principle to the working of democratic and free institutions, and pressure groups seem to have succeeded in protecting their private interests at the cost of something vital to the unity and integrity of the nation.

In truth, equality is indispensable to freedom and democracy. The only exception that can be made with any justification is some preferential treatment for the people of the Scheduled Castes and Scheduled Tribes.[14] These groups have been kept subjugated, outside the fringes of humanity itself. They cannot free themselves from the psychological and material damage done to them for centuries. A positive and unorthodox social effort is needed to pull them back into the orbit of normal human living and thinking. Educational facilities and job reservations for them may be a necessary strategy, justified by their very exceptional history and circumstances. Even while extending preferential treatment to these people, however, it must always be remembered that an exception to the general principle of equality is being made, that it is to be withdrawn as soon as circumstances permit, and, what is more, that in no case is this exception to be made an excuse for others.

Thus, another exception in favor of "backward classes"[15] is just the exception that destroys the rule. If backwardness exists, it should be removed by proper means and methods, not by compromising a great constitutional principle. Once concession for backwardness is made, we slide down the road to communal and caste reservations and separate electorates. There is no rational or effective check along the way. Therefore, India must ask itself whether it really understands the meaning of equality and its place in the fabric of a free society. It must choose between reservations for "backward classes" or for "sons of the soil" (residence), on the one hand, and a free and just society on the other. Eventually, India will have to choose between a united India, and an India subdivided into communities that have only hatred for one another. This dilemma can be resolved only by a constitutional amendment; the courts cannot do much except to show the way, as they have already done.

Religion and Party Politics

India has handled the problem of religious diversity with similar inaptness in the conduct of elections. The Constitution guarantees freedom of conscience and the freedom to profess, practice, and propagate religion to every person.[16] It also guarantees to every religious denomination the freedom to manage its own affairs in the matter of religion.[17] And, as is expected, the courts guard these fundamental rights with their usual vigor and alertness.

It is unfortunate, however, that in India, religion is permitted to vitiate politics, because political parties may be organized exclusively on the basis of religion. A political party whose sole membership is a religious group naturally promotes only the narrow communal interests of a religious minority; how else would a candidate solicit the votes of such a group? This has led to problems: recently, for instance, the Muslim fundamentalists in Kerala sought to dispense Muslim criminal justice in defiance of the law of the land and to punish a Muslim woman for offenses that could never have been proved in the law courts through fair procedure. This phenomenon of "religious" political parties is also responsible for the Punjab problem, which we hope is nearing solution for the time being.

A political party organized on a communal basis is the total negation of democracy and free government. Such a party avowedly does not stand for the country and therefore has neither the desire nor the capacity to do any good for the country. It can only fan the fires of communalism and, in a country like India, prey upon the ignorance and religious emotions of the people to secure their votes. Modern India cannot afford to permit the destructive activities of communal politics.

Defense and Commerce

I conclude with a word about defense and trade or commerce, which, in modern times, have drawn disparate neighboring communities together to form federations and to come under a single powerful government; the United States of America is the most illustrious and inspiring example.

The British demonstrated how an India under a single government could organize a strong defensive capability and how trade and commerce could flourish under such a government. They spread the network of railways and roads throughout the length and breadth of the country, which not only facilitated troop movements and commerce but also brought the people from different parts of India together.

The Constitution of India has, expectedly, given full protection to trade and commerce against any local restraints or impediments. In fact, it has given a kind of duplicate protection that has bred its own problems. It has, on the one hand, put interstate trade under the exclusive jurisdiction of the union government,[18] after the example of the United States, and it guarantees to the citizen the fundamental right to carry on any occupation, trade, or business.[19] On the other hand, as in Australia, it has separately guaranteed that "trade, commerce and intercourse throughout the territory of India shall be free."[20] In fact, this guarantee goes much further than that in section 92 of the Australian Constitution since the latter refers only to interstate trade, whereas the Indian guarantee has been phrased and judicially interpreted to extend also to internal trade within a state.[21]

Commerce rubs off the bristles of diversity better than anything else and so does a defense system where men and women from all communities and groups learn to live, fight, and die for common ideals and interests.

Notes

1. The British government announced its final decision to hand over the government of India to the Indians and to call a Constituent Assembly of Indian representatives to draw up the Constitution of India on May 16, 1946. The announcement was made in a plan presented to Indian leaders by the cabinet mission sent by the British prime minister to India for facilitating the transfer of power.

See B. Shiva Rao, *The Framing of India's Constitution*, vol. I (New Delhi: Indian Institute of Public Administration, 1966), pp. 208 and the following.

The Congress party finally accepted this plan on June 25 (Shiva Rao, p. 278).

The Muslim League finally announced its decision to dissociate from the Constituent Assembly on November 21, 1946 (Shiva Rao, p. 325).

The Constituent Assembly held its first meeting, without the participation of the representatives of the Muslim League, on December 9, 1946 (Shiva Rao, p. 393).

2. Ibid., p. 525 and the following.

3. Ibid., p. 527.

4. See charts and details in ibid., chapter 61.

5. Even the "direct action" launched by Mr. Jinnah and the Muslim League during the last few months of British rule in India was directed against Hindus only.

6. For the success of Gandhi's effort to take the values and ideas of freedom and democracy to the grass roots of Indian society generally, see Tripathi, "Free Speech in the Indian Constitution: Background and Prospect," *Yale Law Journal*, vol. 67 (1957–1958), p. 384.

7. See Rupert Emerson, *Representative Government in South East Asia* (Cambridge, Mass.: Harvard University Press, 1955).

8. In India, a petitioner for the enforcement of a "fundamental right" may either approach the high court (Article 226) or he may directly approach the Supreme Court (Article 32) as he chooses.

9. Government of India Act, 1935, section 61, read with Schedule V.

10. Ibid.

11. Clause (4) of Article 16, Constitution of India.

12. Constitution (First Amendment) Act of 1951, section 2.

13. *All India (Law) Reporter* 1984 SC 1420.

14. See Constitution of India, Part xiv.

15. See Constitution of India, Articles 15 and 16.

16. Constitution of India, Article 25.

17. Ibid., Article 26.

18. Constitution of India, Schedule VII, List I (Union List), entry 42.

19. Constitution of India, Article 19(1)(g).

20. Constitution of India, Article 301.

21. See Automobile Transport Ltd. v. State of Rajasthan, AIR 1962 SC. 1406.

Discussion

ROBERT GOLDWIN: If we did not have the living example of present-day India before our eyes and if we did not have the evidence that it does exist as a political entity, would we not be justified in doubting that such a nation could survive? After all, it has hundreds of different languages and ethnic groups spread over a vast territory; a huge population, millions of them very poor; a long history of domination by foreign rulers; and a uniquely divisive hierarchical social system. With all these extraordinary obstacles to unity, would we not be justified in doubting the probability, even the possibility, that such a political entity could long survive as one nation?

But we do have the evidence before our eyes, and that leads me to the question I propose we now consider: what accounts for Indian nationhood? What holds India together as one nation? How can we explain Indian national unity?

FALI NARIMAN: After thirty-five years at the bar, I am as puzzled as anyone about how this nation works. But if there is an explanation, perhaps India's unity could be attributed principally to two things: first, an amazing spirit of tolerance among a vast variety of people; and second, the judicial system, particularly the judges in the highest court, the Supreme Court of India.

Another part of Mr. Goldwin's question was, After so many years of subjugation by various invaders, how did we acquire a sense of nationhood? Professor Tripathi's commentary is very instructive here, for he notes one of the anachronisms of India: a country with thirty-three principal languages and about a hundred different religions nonetheless deliberated about its constitution in English. Although this was the language of a conqueror, we never regarded it as such, because through this language we were all educated and came to know and cherish the freedom that those in the West know and cherish. For instance, one of the textbooks prescribed for me as an undergraduate was Burke's *Reflections on the Revolution in France*, and in a postgraduate course, the Bombay University prescribed Alexis de Tocqueville's *Democracy in America*.

The British made one big mistake as a colonial power: they taught the same things in the colonies that they taught themselves at home. People learned about and were impressed by the refusal of John Hampden to pay his ship's money to a tyrannical king, the success of the barons in forcing King John to sign the Magna Carta, and the pronouncements of a host of distinguished jurists—including a famous judge who said that the air of England is so free that the slaves must be released. As a result, the colonized peoples became nationalists, and they, too, cherished freedom.

So if someone wants to know how we acquired a sense of nationhood, he must look to the English language, what it taught us— the rudiments of Western-style education—and the two persons who perhaps are the very embodiment of what went into the Constitution. One was a typical Brahmin, a Kashmir Brahmin, Jawaharlal Nehru, who was an elitist, brought up in the lap of luxury; his father was one of the greatest lawyers of his time. And from the other end of the spectrum came Dr. Ambedkar, a man of the scheduled castes, the largest oppressed minority in the world, who was self-educated. Both of them were and are regarded today as the fathers of the Indian Constitution.

Since 1950, a written constitution with a bill of rights has become more and more important to us, particularly to the minorities in our country. The proliferation of religions in our country derives principally from the numerous avenues for redress of grievances. I speak not only of court processes. One of the articles in our Constitution grants minorities the right to establish and administer educational institutions of their choice. The Supreme Court has bent over backward to give minorities a near monopoly on everything that happens within their own institutions. Virtually no regulatory law governing other universities or schools applies to these institutions, apart from the prescription of the syllabus. They are free to appoint their own professors, principals, and headmasters and to instruct their own people however they wish. That is one of the safeguards that the Constitution provides and that, I am happy to find, the Supreme Court has so far upheld.

Perhaps that is one of the reasons why, with this diverse conglomerate of people with different religions, languages, and views, India nonetheless has a certain cultural unity. It cannot easily be described, but those who have been there probably realize it. As the film *Gandhi* shows, too, it might have been a different India, or even a different subcontinent, but for the vision of that man. One of the stories Lord Mountbatten tells in his memoirs is that when the British Christians suggested dividing the subcontinent into Moslem and non-Moslem parts, Gandhi told Mountbatten, "Give the prime ministership of India to Mr. Jinnah; let him be prime minister." He knew that this political issue was ephemeral, concerning only fifteen or twenty years in the life of a subcontinent or a country that has lasted 3,000 years and will, we hope, last 3,000 more. Unfortunately events proved otherwise, and we now have a divided subcontinent, which during the past ten years was subdivided further, with the appearance of Bangladesh.

Most Indians have this sense of unity, however, along with the spirit of tolerance, which I would say is the hallmark of the major religion of the country. Hinduism was responsible for that horrible institution known as untouchability, which still persists, although it is officially abolished by the Constitution. But at the same time it is one of the most amorphous of religions—so much so that even after Buddhism had flourished for 900 years in our country, it was subsequently completely assimilated by Hinduism. Buddha became simply an incarnation of Vishnu, another god; today barely 2 percent of the population of India professes Buddhism. Hinduism has thus contributed a great deal to the tolerance with which we regard most of the religions in our part of the world.

As to whether we will survive, I think we should. We do have problems that make survival questionable, of course. At the moment we live in unity, though it is not particularly tranquil. We have a lot of problems, among which our linguistic problems are paramount. But I think we have accommodated the religious problems. Each religion is free to do whatever its faith directs. The government is very reluctant to interfere with any aspect of religion.

I belong to a faith that is very ancient but that has very few adherents today: the Zoroastrian faith, one of the oldest monotheistic religions. We are now about 100,000 in the world. When it was proposed to extend the Adoption Act to people in our community, a group of us opposed it and sent a delegation to the prime minister. Mrs. Gandhi assured us that unless we came up with a formula that all of us could accept, nothing would be imposed.

Perhaps we have to grow into this diversity and unity, and this is what we are now trying to do. Surviving the first thirty-five years was quite important and is an indicator that we might perhaps get through.

P. K. Tripathi: I consider the problem of unity and diversity in India to have been created and solved by our history. As Mr. Goldwin put it in his question, if this kind of commonwealth or government were created out of nothing today, then probably such a thing would be impossible. Why does it exist? Because it has been through the process of history.

I look at the problem in the reverse of the usual way, maintaining that the diversity in India has evolved out of an original unity. And, as the commentator on the American essay, Professor Pangle, has said, diversity is not to be eliminated and probably should be not only encouraged but created. Diversity is freedom. From a religious point of view, diversity began developing because people started questioning the interpretation of the sacred writings. Some interpreted them differently. Although there may have been attempts to prevent them from doing so initially, those attempts did not succeed. So in India there developed a tradition of differing with the orthodox doctrine and of tolerating the differences.

We never try to solve our problems by suppressing or eliminating diversity, and that has been our weakness and our strength. Suppression is not our way of doing things. We respect diversity, we encourage it, and we think we can all flourish together. There have been problems with this, of course. Immediately after the British left, we had a great bloodbath; hundreds of thousands of people died in the partition. But eventually when we had the opportunity to draw up our own constitution, it was not sectarian. We did not make India a Hindu or a Moslem state. We made it a secular democratic state, and we gave minorities not only the right to survive, but the right, for instance, to profess and propagate different religions.

The British contact, like all contacts with foreign rulers, had its unpleasant side. But to forget the unpleasant side for a moment, I think India benefited vastly in many ways. The British created a network of railways and communications, and they demonstrated that India could be ruled by one government under one constitution. That became part of our education. When I was born, there was one India, and today there is one India, with the difference only that Pakistan is separate. So with that tradition, I do not foresee any problems with the existence of India as one nation. And now new unifying interests have developed, for instance, commerce. Commerce cannot survive if there are too many political boundaries obstructing its course, so in our Constitution the power to legislate commerce is given exclusively to the national parliament.

Defense is also a unifying interest. Although to the people of India the creation of Pakistan was a sorrow because we were not able to accommodate the wishes of all groups or inspire them with confidence, still, the fear of war with Pakistan, Bangladesh, or China is another very great cohesive force. So long as Pakistan exists—and

51

long live Pakistan—we will remain united. As long as external threats are there and we are surrounded by peoples hostile to us, the unity of India is not endangered. The unity is fostered by these dangers.

ALBERT BLAUSTEIN: I would argue that the main cohesive force for nationhood in the world today is a combination of colonialism and priorities. It has been over a century since the nations of Europe met in Berlin to divide Africa. No one in his right mind would divide Africa today the way it was divided then, along lines that broke through tribal unities. But when Haile Selassie met with the other nations at the beginning of the Organization of African Unity, he said, "Let's keep the colonial boundaries, because if we don't we will just start fighting over this one issue." I think today that the nation of India realizes what its priorities are and that if it were to divide itself linguistically or along other "logical" lines, it would be impossible to work out any kind of accommodation.

Unity in India, I suggest, was forged primarily by the British. It was a *fait accompli*, bringing the Indians together. So to what my colleagues have said about India and tolerance, I want to add the importance of unity created by colonialism, conquest, and war.

KEITH KYLE: I agree with Mr. Blaustein that what caused the unity of India was, very simply, British rule. Mr. Nariman refers in passing to India's federal, parliamentary-type constitution. There are certain difficulties with that system that were most apparent during and after the recent state of emergency. The British parliamentary system on which the Indian is modeled is an informal system that does not depend upon written constitutions. But a federal system, of all systems, is a system that most depends upon written constitutions. The combination therefore is a difficult one to visualize.

Furthermore, the Indian states do not conform to the definition of the states in this country. The federal units are not buttressed in India as the federal units are buttressed here. And in the absence of this, we saw rather serious questions arise during the emergency. Indeed, the state of emergency threw light upon several problems with the Indian Constitution, and I did not find that question adequately discussed in either of these two papers.

Many people asked themselves, when the state of emergency had been introduced, how it was possible to introduce this kind of thing under the parliamentary system. What was safeguarding the people's rights? A full answer has not yet been given to that question. It has been, as it were, postponed, because Mrs. Gandhi decided voluntarily to return to parliamentary elections, and there was a change of party in office.

This again is one of the difficulties of operating a parliamentary system in India. Under normal political conditions, there is not a two-party system in India. In conditions unaffected by the trauma of an emergency, there is no party other than the Congress party, which operates as a truly national party.

This was one result of partitioning India on a religious basis. It had two effects: one, Pakistan was created, where the only unifying principle was the Moslem religion. This left India being by definition that party of the subcontinent that was not the Moslem state. The Janata party was subsequently handicapped because of its association with Hindu nationalism, which was not normally tolerable, and it only came into office because of the extraordinary circumstances of the state of emergency and the emotions thereby aroused.

MR. TRIPATHI: I agree with one very important observation of Mr. Kyle's. As an Indian, I am very much worried about the monolithic structure of the Congress party and the absence of a healthy two-party system.

When we became independent, Gandhi suggested that the Congress party be dissolved and other parties formed. If we had done that, we would have more or less the same kind of party system as the United States or Britain has. Unfortunately, the other idea prevailed— that for a period, to maintain stability, the Congress party should remain as it was. It is important for those outside India to understand that the only other really powerful party in 1950 was the Communist party. For the first few years after independence, there was a fierce struggle between the Congress party with its ideals of democracy and rule of law and the Communist party with its ideas about a different form of government. Fortunately, from my point of view, the Communist party today has an ever-diminishing following.

MR. KYLE: Another important issue raised in these papers is the question of affirmative action and positive discrimination. The papers show the difficulties one is liable to encounter when one pursues these ideas to their logical extreme. When so many groups of people are benefited by positive discrimination, then a backlash arises from the majority group, which feels itself hopelessly discriminated against.

This is a very real problem. It is a dilemma we face in Britain at the moment. Until rather recently, there had been general opposition to the idea of positive discrimination. But lately, local government units in some big cities have started providing what they say is affirmative action to ensure that blacks, immigrants, and other ethnic minorities get a reasonable number of jobs in the public service. Some suggest that we also need affirmative action in the private sector. This whole matter is very delicate in Britain at the moment, because people are ready and want to do something. Yet by looking at India, people can see the dangers that might be encountered with affirmative action.

ENOCH DUMBUTSHENA: There is no doubt in my mind that one of the factors that contributed to the unity of India was the presence of a colonial power able and determined to govern that nation, even if Indians did not want to be governed. It has always been during colonial occupation that different classes of the indigenous population began to work together. And then, as we have seen in every country that has attained independence, soon after independence is achieved, the unity breaks up. This dissolution started in India as soon as it was clear that independence would come about, and that is the reason we have Pakistan. In the case of my own country we had unity right up to the doors of Lancaster House in London, where the state of Zimbabwe was born, and immediately after the doors of Lancaster House were closed, the patriotic front broke down.

I have little knowledge of India, but I am a great admirer of Indian democracy. Although I do not admire it uncritically, I do admire the fact that it has made its bill of rights work. One reason is that India can still boast a class structure—a class structure that has contributed significantly to the continued existence and unity of India—because to implement a bill of rights an educated class must exist that appreciates the essence of the rights entrenched in a constitution. Without that class, a bill of rights means absolutely nothing to the rulers and to the followers. This class, then, is one contributory factor to the unity of India.

India does not present a homogeneous society. In the Commonwealth it has perhaps the greatest number of people who live in poverty. At the conference of appellate judges in India in March 1984, the chief justice of India said that the number of poor people in India had doubled since independence. In the years to come that problem may lead to the undoing of India and all that the Indians have achieved up to now. I am not quite sure I agree with Mr. Kyle's contention that positive discrimination is not desirable. In my own country, positive discrimination was necessary to create a balance, for instance, in the employment of blacks in industry and the public service, because those areas were previously closed to blacks.

THOMAS FLEINER: The authors of these papers do not seem to think that federalism as a constitutional structure may be a way to create unity. Does a parliamentary system permit real dualism or separation of power between state and union? Is not local authority well developed in India, and does this not help make it possible to achieve unity while preserving much diversity?

NATHAN GLAZER: Let me return for a moment to the original question. It is surprising that no one has spoken of Indian culture, specifically Hindu culture, as one of the unifying elements in India. Hinduism is, after all, described in one of the papers as being the religion of 83 percent of the people. This is responsible for India's sacred geography. Despite the limitation of linguistic and other groups to separate parts of the country, all groups think of India as a geographical unity in terms of Indian myth and in terms of the practical role of Indian religion today. So people from the north go all the way south to visit Kanya Kumari, and people from the south go all the way north to visit the sources of the Ganges and other sacred spots. There is a unifying geography.

And there are many other unifying religious elements. In the myths or epics, the characters travel all over India. Wherever a person goes in that nation, people say, "Rama stopped here," or someone else did something there. And the epics are translated into all the languages of India; these ancient translations are accepted as standard in each area.

This raises a question: can India's commitment to secularism be sustained, along with the very powerful unifying element of Hinduism? In the United States, of course, we want to be secular, too, but we keep slipping into observations of Christianity, which are then very often struck down by the Supreme Court. It is possible this doesn't happen in India because Hinduism is a different kind of religion, but I wonder if this is not a potential problem for India.

The second question is really informational. I was confused in these papers about how one sets up scheduled castes and other backward classes. Were the authors suggesting that it would be proper to define a group—any group—as meriting aid if its average income was below a certain amount, or were they suggesting that aid should be directed to people on the basis of individual characteristics?

MR. NARIMAN: To take the last question first, the scheduled castes— so called because they were treated in a separate schedule under the Government of India Act—and the scheduled tribes, which were even more backward than the scheduled castes, were all treated as outcasts in Hindu society. They now have a certain guaranteed representation in the state assemblies and parliament, as well as a certain guaranteed representation, about 22 percent, in the various public services.

The Constitution leaves these categories to be defined by presidential order. So far no one has disagreed that there has to be, as the Chief Justice of Zimbabwe said, some atonement for what has happened for over a thousand years. These groups have been kept back, and we are now atoning by giving them special representation, not only initially in the services but also in promotions.

The problem has arisen with another group of people, called "other backward classes," or OBCs. These are persons or groups for whom special provision may be made, notwithstanding the equality clause, because they are socially and educationally backward; the word "economically" is not used in the Constitution. The OBCs are not defined in the Constitution, and they are not left to be defined by the president—they are left to be dealt with by each state separately. Clearly undue preferences are shown for some of these so-called other backward classes, and a recent Supreme Court judgment has pointed out the inequity of a system of unguided reservations (or quotas) for this group. It found that among those socially and educationally backward, some are much less backward than others, and yet they take the same benefits, at a cost to their own group.

MR. TRIPATHI: I fully support Mr. Nariman's view. The scheduled castes and scheduled tribes have lost the will to bring themselves up and to return to society. That is why we make reservations for them. But these reservations for the backward classes are unhealthy and meaningless. As Mr. Nariman has said in his paper, there is an unhealthy competition among them to show who is more backward.

We have one real problem, then, and one fake problem. A genuine case exists for the scheduled castes, but there is no justification for allowing this exception to proliferate.

MR. NARIMAN: You have to realize the problem. A commission reported that apart from scheduled castes and scheduled tribes, which make up 22 percent of the population, the other backward classes— genuinely backward classes: socially, educationally, and therefore economically backward—make up an additional 52 percent of the population. And yet their representation in the services, for one reason or another, was as low as 20 percent.

JACQUES VANDERLINDEN: I think that is absolutely universal. Look at the Belgian Parliament: it is a parliament of men, of wealthy, aged, and learned men. Are we going to decide that, because it does not reflect at all the social structure of the Belgian population, that, for instance, women have been mistreated?

MR. BLAUSTEIN: In regard to treatment of minorities, the Irish Constitution of 1937 created the first constitutional distinction between policy goals and judicially enforceable human rights. The Indian Constitution carried this distinction to the farthest extreme, because it distinguishes between directed principles of state action—literacy, jobs, women's rights, and so forth—on the one hand and a group of judicially enforceable rights on the other. And when this issue came before the Indian Supreme Court in an early case, it stated that in that particular conflict it would enforce the equality provision over the policy provision. Thereupon an amendment was added to the Constitution, stressing that even though equality was important, the Constitution does not proscribe special rights for the disadvantaged.

We have struggled with this conflict of principles in America through the judicial process. And our Canadian brethren will tell us that, having witnessed this confusion in America, they, in their new Constitution, delineated special rights and privileges for backward people, without having three different classes as they have in India.

I believe very strongly, with my colleague Mr. Vanderlinden, that if a nation follows policies favoring groups like the Indians in Canada or the untouchables in India, that is one thing. But to carry such policies much farther creates one muddle after another.

MR. NARIMAN: I want to address the point about the parliamentary system and the federal structure. Federalism in India is anachronistic, unlike Canadian or American federalism. Our judges have called it a quasi-federal structure, "quasi" because there were not originally independent states that subsequently merged together, as in Australia. Our states were for the most part administrative areas or provinces originally. The federal concept was adopted only because the Government of India Act, essentially the first constitution passed in 1935 by the British Parliament, needed it to accommodate the Indian states— the states of the maharajas and so on—which were supposed to accede to the Indian union. As it turned out, none of them did accept the union, and therefore federalism was really a dead letter at the outset. Nonetheless, we had a ready-made federal suit to put on, and so marched out as a federal parliamentary-type structure. Professor Kyle was correct in saying that in a Westminster model, a federal system just does not work.

But today, when opposition parties control some of the states in our country, we are finding that the federal suit we donned is a convenient method by which to try to accommodate different policies. Of course, we still have a centrist bias—in the Supreme Court as well—so conflicts have occurred between the center and the states. In all of them, the states have lost. The center has always come out on top because the judges genuinely believe that a strong center is important. Even the judges have not accommodated themselves to a truly federal structure. We might find a little more life in this quasi-federal structure, however, as opposition political parties come to control some of the states.

RUTH BADER GINSBURG: May I ask Mr. Nariman to tell us a little more about India's judges? From his paper, it appears that the Supreme Court exercises constitutional review of legislation and executive acts with a vengeance. Is there any concern about a body of judges exercising that high role?

No doubt Mr. Nariman is familiar with the discomfort in this country when lifetime-appointed judges override the legislature, the elected representatives of the people.

MR. NARIMAN: There is quite a lot of controversy about activist judges in our country. In fact, quite recently two ministers of Mrs. Gandhi's government launched a tirade against several judgments by the Supreme Court, saying "What do these seventeen nonelected men know? Do they know more than the elected members of Parliament?"

In our framework, the Constitution is supreme. What the judges say the Constitution is, therefore, prevails. They have even struck down constitutional amendments, which possibly has not been done anywhere else in the world, because they allegedly violated the basic structure of the Constitution.

In its investigative role, the court has also probed various types of inequities, as in bonded labor and the like. It has improved prison conditions by appointing commissioners to go into prisons, for instance. It has done an enormous amount of work that might actually be beyond its constitutional power, strictly speaking. I applaud the court for going ahead, because one must do something.

HERMAN BELZ: I have heard much talk today about reservations (or quotas) of jobs in India. Does it work well? Are the people qualified, and do they perform services as they ought to?

MR. NARIMAN: They have minimal qualifications. There is a lot of dissatisfaction, because reservations occur not only at the hiring stage but even in promotions. For instance, there is a reservation of 22 percent in the engineering profession for scheduled classes. But these candidates, once admitted, do not then have to prove competence and compete with other engineers. The Supreme Court has said that even at the stage of promotion they have that 22 percent niche right up to the top. So after twenty years a hopelessly incompetent chief engineer might block a very competent junior deputy chief engineer. We are atoning, as I said, but how much should we atone for?

MR. GOLDWIN: Our discussion of India raises two massive issues that will be pertinent to our discussions of other nations.

First, for years India has had a system of preferences for certain well-defined groups—and others are working hard to get themselves defined as deserving of preferential treatment. Yet we are told that the numbers living in poverty have doubled since independence. Does a system of preferences, then, really address the basic problem?

Second, although the character of the Indian people—namely, their great openness and tolerance—is said to have contributed to national unity, India is a place where violence on an overwhelming scale takes place. The difficulties before the separation of India and Pakistan have been described as a bloodbath, and also more recently bloody rioting occurred after the assassination of Mrs. Gandhi.

We are thus left with certain very difficult questions. In one form or another, however, although these problems are particular to India, something very much like them applies to many other countries as well.

2

The Constitution
and American Diversity

Nathan Glazer

The American Constitution is very likely the briefest national constitution in existence; it is the oldest written constitution in current use;
and its vitality, far from declining with the years, decades, and centuries, continues to expand, at least if measured by the amount of
litigation brought under it, the number of important issues of public
life decided by it (as interpreted by the Supreme Court and lower
federal courts), and the volume of analysis given to it in scholarly
articles and books. Concerning many key institutions and areas of
American life the Constitution is silent. It is largely a procedural
document, setting up the machinery of a federal government composed of separate states. This government replaced a weaker union of
the thirteen states under the Articles of Confederation, which the
leaders of the nascent nation found inadequate.

The functions of government at the time of its framing were
almost entirely in the hands of local units of government and the
states. The former English colonies had become states with the Declaration of Independence in 1776 and had written constitutions for
themselves. English traditions of government dominated, though the
penchant for written constitutions was an American innovation.
Thus, following the English pattern, a very large share in government
was held by local, self-governing units, towns, and counties. The
United States was already a very diverse country—diverse in religion,
in race, and in ethnic background. Little of this diversity, however,
was reflected in the Constitution that was written by the Constitutional Convention in Philadelphia in 1787. If it was thought of at all—
and as I shall show in some limited degree it was—this diversity was
conceived of as being within the proper sphere of the states, as were
almost all the functions of government except for defense, the national currency, and interstate commerce.

The type of diversity that most concerned the framers of the

Constitution was not that of race, religion, and ethnicity, but rather a diversity of political units—of the states that made up the United States and that had sovereign powers under the Articles of Confederation that then bound them together.[1] It was a weak bond, permitting damaging hostilities between the states and giving little power to the national government. That weakness was the reason the Constitutional Convention was called. The key issues for the Constitutional Convention were: What powers would the states be required to give up to the national government? What powers would they retain? How would the new federal government prevent large states from imposing their will on the small?

Because the Constitutional Convention dealt more directly with these problems, it paid little attention to diversities of race and ethnicity. Because it was creating a union of preexisting states, it had little reason to address race and ethnicity, for the states controlled these matters. Thus, southern states had elaborate codes regulating slavery and the rights of free blacks. Some states had established religions. (Using the contemporary meaning of establishment, probably all had established religions.) The states varied greatly in the degree to which they were themselves heterogeneous. Indeed, a study of the role of the Constitution in governing American heterogeneity might better begin with the fifty state constitutions than with the national Constitution. Nevertheless, in the Constitution of 1787, even more in the Bill of Rights of 1789, and most significantly in the amendments that followed the Civil War (thirteen, fourteen, and fifteen in 1865, 1868, and 1870), key provisions play a great role in governing American diversity today.

Several kinds of diversity characterized the United States at the time of the writing of the Constitution (which was 180 years after the beginnings of permanent English colonization on the eastern shores of North America). The United States was already more diverse in religion than any nation in Europe. Massachusetts had been created by dissenters from the state religion of England, who hoped to create a holy commonwealth in New England in which state and church were closely merged and in which a single orthodoxy prevailed. For a while they succeeded. But quite rapidly dissenters arose from within the community created by dissenters, and new dissenters—Baptists and Quakers—arrived from England. One of these dissenters, driven out, founded Rhode Island, a more liberal colony. Offshoots of Massachusetts in Connecticut and New Hampshire tried to preserve the Massachusetts pattern, but revivals sweeping through New England (and the other colonies) in the eighteenth century multiplied sects and variant divisions in New England religion. Religion—or religions—flourished in America (it is the birthplace of the Mormons, the Christian Scientists, the Seventh Day Adventists, and many other new religions). The Middle Colonies were even more diverse than New England: New York had been founded as New Amsterdam by the Dutch, Pennsylvania had been founded as a refuge for Quakers— and others—by William Penn, and Maryland had been founded as a refuge for Catholics by an English Catholic nobleman.

Virginia, founded before Massachusetts, began without the intention of providing a home for dissent or diversity. The white population of the South remained more homogeneous in religion and ethnic background than that of New England and the Middle Colonies. But it was also affected by religious revivals. Old churches split, new ones were founded, and the monopoly of established churches was broken.

It was in the South that the gravest form of diversity in American history was first established: diversity of race created by the importation of Negro slaves. Nor did black and white exhaust the roster of American races. There was a large but indeterminate population of American Indians in every colony, around the fringes of settlement and beyond. (Asians did not appear in the United States for another sixty years or more.)

In addition to religious and racial diversity, there was ethnic diversity. The Anglo-Americans, the dominant group by far, were divided and included Scots, Welsh, and Scotch-Irish; there were also Dutch, German, French, Irish, Jews, and many more.

The Middle Colonies in particular showed a mix of ethnic groups. Jews arrived early in New Amsterdam. Pennsylvania became a home to persecuted German sects, and its German population became so large that it aroused the concern of Benjamin Franklin. (Pennsylvania still today provides, in the Amish, one of the most remarkable examples of how ethnic and religious distinctiveness can be preserved in the contemporary United States—though not without the aid of the Constitution, as we shall see.)

It is convenient to consider American diversity under the headings of religion, race, and ethnicity; yet this division should not suggest any sharp distinction among the three. Two or three of these elements might be linked together to characterize a single group, creating something like the national groups found in other diverse and multiethnic societies. The German speakers of Pennsylvania were not only Protestants speaking German, they were of distinct sects in which nationality and religion were merged together, to the point where the maintenance of the German language was a religious duty.

Jews were Jews not only by religion, they also considered themselves a people. Not only were blacks distinguished by race from other southern Protestants, in time they developed distinctive churches. Links between ethnic group and religion remained strong in the mass migrations of the nineteenth century, in which each Scandinavian immigrant group brought its own type of Lutheranism, and the Irish were indissolubly linked to the Catholic church, and indeed controlled it to the point where German and Polish Catholics tried to break away to create their own variants.

We can detect, if not nations in the America of 1787, quasi-nations. But nowhere was a concentration or a quasi-nation within a state of the United States so great that it could raise the fear, in the minds of the Founding Fathers or their successors, that parts of the union would break away or demand greater autonomy because of a distinctive religious, racial, or ethnic group concentration. The South, it is true, was a separate section, but only because of slavery. When secession became a reality in American life because of the unsolvable conflict over slavery, it was not because a section defined by religion, race, or ethnicity different from the rest was breaking away, it was because southern Americans, speaking the same language and professing the same religions as northerners of the same Anglo-American stock, decided that the preservation of their peculiar institution demanded a separate country.

This point is important to keep in mind because it makes the problem of Constitution and diversity in the United States quite different from what it is in India, Belgium, Canada, Yugoslavia, or other states in which distinct ethnic groups, speaking their own languages, and professing their own religions, can be marked off by territorial boundaries. Thus the careful delineation of the powers and roles of the states in the Constitution had no bearing on the question of the autonomy of religious, racial, or ethnic groups. It was always possible, of course, that in time immigrants from one or another country might come to dominate a state, such that its political autonomy and constitutional powers could be used to foster a distinctive language, culture, or religion. One can imagine such possibilities in American history (the French Canadians in Maine, the Germans in Wisconsin, or the Mexicans in New Mexico), but it never came to pass except in the most moderate ways, such as the Spanish bilingualism of New Mexico. We see this fear today, hardly voiced but muttered, as a heavy immigration of Mexicans into the Southwest continues. One can imagine constitutional issues arising in the future (one already has, in the demand for an amendment to the Constitution making

English the national language, which would probably limit the official use of Spanish in the Southwest and elsewhere). But 200 years of life under the Constitution has not yet raised this question sharply.

There is one exception: the Mormons. The adherents of this new religion (founded by the prophet Joseph Smith of New York) in 1847 were led by Brigham Young beyond the frontier of settlement to found a state in which they would be secure from the persecution of their neighbors. Utah was thus settled by one religious group, a group so distinctive in its beliefs and customs that it may well be considered a near-nation.[2] This coincidence of religion, people, and state was to create problems for the United States and the Constitution—but it was the only case.

Framing the Constitution

Little of the existing religious, racial, and ethnic diversity of the American people was reflected in the Constitution, and no grand plan was laid down for any diversity that might be expected in the future. The Constitution had nothing to say about the ethnic diversity of the United States. Written in English, for example, there is no requirement that English be the national language, or any protection for any other language. Indeed, there is no reference to language.

The United States, despite its ethnic, religious, and racial diversity, was overwhelmingly still a country of Anglo-Americans, and its leadership was almost exclusively Anglo-American. The founders did not expect this to change. Among the framers of the Constitution there was no person from any other ethnic group, numerous as they were in different parts of the states. The Constitution had nothing to say about the immigration that was to transform the United States— and continues to transform it to this day—to the point where the Anglo-Americans became one ethnic group among many. In one pregnant passage, however, enumerating the powers of Congress (Article I, section 8), Congress is authorized "to establish a uniform Rule of Naturalization." The framers could hardly have expected the mass and diverse immigration that lay in the future. Indeed, immigration was not substantial for fifty years after the adoption of the Constitution, and when Tocqueville toured the United States in 1836–1837, it was still, to him, the country of the "Anglo-Americans" (his term). The diversity that caused him and Beaumont to fear for the future was that represented by Indians and blacks.

Congress began almost immediately to legislate the control of naturalization. But it was not at all clear it had power to regulate immigration. The first Congress passed a resolution (in 1788) recommending to the states "that they pass proper laws for preventing the transportation of convicted malefactors from foreign countries into the United States." E. P. Hutchinson comments, "Although an expression of national concern, the resolution was also a tacit recognition of state jurisdiction over immigration; almost thirty years was to pass before Congress ventured to legislate on the subject."[3] When it did, some protested. Nevertheless, Congress cautiously entered this area to regulate the transportation of immigrants to protect their health and safety. The courts struck down state efforts to control immigration, and in 1876 "the Supreme Court declared unconstitutional the state laws imposing head taxes and gave its opinion that under the Constitution power over immigration lies in the hands of the Federal government."[4] Under this power, Congress restricted immigration for the first time by limiting the entry of Chinese in 1882. The power to control the growth of American population through immigration has, under this interpretation, rested securely with the federal government.[5]

That this was to continue to be a country of immigration was implied in other provisions of the Constitution: those specifying that a member of the House of Representatives had to be a citizen for at least seven years, a senator a citizen for nine years, and the president a "natural born citizen," or someone already a citizen at the time of the adoption of the Constitution (Article I, sections 2 and 3, and Article II, section 1).

The Constitution had more to say about religious diversity: indeed, religion was the central source of diversity among the Anglo-Americans. In the constitutional text there is only one provision: "no religious test shall ever by required as a qualification to any office or public trust under the United States" (Article VI, section 3). But there was more in the Bill of Rights, the first ten amendments to the Constitution that were demanded by a number of states as a condition for ratification. What was said was brief: "Congress shall make no law respecting an establishment of religion, or prohibiting the free exercise thereof." It is the first section of the First Amendment and has had enormous consequences.

Because these phrases continue to govern whatever in any way may be done in legislation and administrative action affecting religion in the United States, and because they play a role in highly controversial current issues, the history of the formulation and adoption by Congress of these phrases in 1789 has been subjected to meticulous and controversial analysis by scholars and judges.[6] Rarely have any words, aside perhaps from some in sacred scriptures, been subjected to such a volume of analysis. Cynics and advocates of free interpretation of the Constitution insist that what the Supreme Court does today, and indeed what it should do, is not and should not be bound by the intentions of the framers of the Constitution: how could these intentions be relevant to such questions as the legitimacy of school prayer or a state law requiring a moment of silence in schools, when public schools hardly existed at the time of the framing of the Constitution—when indeed religious practices in schools of any kind were unchallenged and taken for granted?

Nevertheless, whatever the positions of the cynics and the free interpreters, the Supreme Court does pay attention to the intentions of the framers, even if, in the minds of many critics, it distorts them. Its authority, after all, comes only from its mandate to interpret that 200-year-old document, and if there is a revolution, it will not be the justices who discard the Constitution (or they will discard it only while insisting they are interpreting it). The fact is they continue to engage in detailed historical analysis to defend their decisions or dissents. This may be the tribute hypocrisy pays to naiveté, but the tribute is paid. Fortunately or unfortunately, even serious historical examination demonstrates enough different strands of intention behind these phrases on religion to justify the justices' taking diametrically opposed positions on issues in dispute.

A brief consideration of the intentions behind the religious clauses of the First Amendment is warranted because it reveals just what the situation was in regard to religious diversity and its relation to government at the time. Laurence Tribe summarizes the consensus of historical research as follows:

> [At] least three distinct schools of thought . . . influenced the drafters of the Bill of Rights: first, the evangelical view (associated primarily with Roger Williams) that "worldly corruptions . . . might consume the churches if sturdy fences against the wilderness [of the secular world] were not maintained"; second, the Jeffersonian view that the church should be walled off against the state in order to safeguard secular interests (public and private) "against ecclesiastical depredations and incursions"; and third, the Madisonian view that religion and secular interests alike would be advanced best by diffusing and decentralizing power so as to assure competition among sects rather than dominance by anyone.[7]

These are basic political and philosophical orientations. There was also a current, pragmatic reason for these provisions: "At least some evidence exists that, for the framers, the establishment clause was intended largely to protect state religious establishments from national displacement."[8] A footnote continues:

Until 1844, New Jersey limited full civil rights to Protestants. Pennsylvania and Maryland required belief in God of public office holders, Maryland until 1961. Connecticut taxed for the support of the Congregational establishment until 1818. The Massachusetts constitution, until 1833, authorized towns to maintain ministers where voluntary contributions were inadequate; New Hampshire did so until the twentieth century.[9]

If this was part of the original intention, it plays no role in constitutional analysis and litigation today, because against the plain text ("*Congress* shall make no law. . .") the Supreme Court has "incorporated" over the past fifty or sixty years the provisions of the Bill of Rights, including the "establishment" and "free exercise" clauses, so as to make them applicable to the states, and almost all litigation under these clauses applies to state action.

Regarding race, the Constitution had more to say in 1787, and far more to say in the key amendments, the Thirteenth, Fourteenth, and Fifteenth, adopted after the Civil War. The Constitution itself had to deal with the problem of Negro slavery. Slaves then made up one-fifth of the population, almost entirely concentrated in the South. In some northern states slavery was illegal and in all repugnant to large groups (as it was then repugnant to many leaders of southern opinion, too). How could a Constitution designed to govern slave and nonslave states deal with this issue? Through compromise: Congress was denied the right to forbid the importation of slaves for twenty years, until 1808, after which it was allowed to (Article I, section 2). Fugitive slaves could not escape to freedom but would have to be returned (Article IV, section 2). But the key compromise dealt with how slaves were to be taken into account for purposes of representation in Congress. If they were fully counted, the South would dominate the United States. If they were not counted at all, the South feared northern power. The compromise: "Representatives and direct taxes shall be apportioned among the several states . . . according to their respective numbers, which shall be determined by adding the whole number of free persons . . . and excluding Indians not taxed, three-fifths of all other persons" (Article I, section 2).

The word slave is not used here or in any other part of the Constitution: After all, its preamble speaks of its objective as "to secure the blessings of liberty to ourselves and our posterity." The avoidance is largely a result of discomfort in the face of slavery, and indeed hostility to it: "The Constitution strikingly but subtly reveals the Convention's hostile view of slavery: the word slave never appears in it. Fugitive slaves are euphemistically referred to as 'Persons held to Service of Labor' (Article I, section 9). As Patterson of New Jersey said in another connection, 'They had been ashamed to use the term "slaves" and had substituted a description' [July 9]. The Convention did not want the Constitution stained with the word after the thing itself had long last disappeared."[10]

To summarize, in the original Constitution of 1787 and its first ten amendments we find only the merest phrases and clauses referring to the diversity of Americans, then already great, and to become, through immigration and religious creativity, even greater in the nineteenth and twentieth centuries. The power to naturalize (and by extension to govern immigration) was put in the hands of Congress; Negro slavery was given protection and recognition—but power to ban the importation of slaves was given to Congress; there would be no religious test for office, no national establishment of religion, but the free exercise of religion was constitutionally protected. This is clearly a slim base on which to build the great diversity of religious, racial, and ethnic groups that flourish today in the territory of the United States under conditions of freedom that are equaled by few other nations. How did this come about?

The first seventy years of life under the new Constitution did not give many hints of this development. Immigration began to swell in the 1840s, bringing in great numbers of Irish Catholics and Protestant and Catholic Germans and arousing in response a nativist reaction, anti-immigrant and anti-Catholic, which was to recur again and again in American life. Anti-Catholic passions led to mob violence here and there, but this was still a matter for local government and states: the national government played no role in the protection of religious rights. But political freedom and diversity meant that in many places where Irish or Germans were numerous they could play important roles in local and state government. Free blacks had only ambiguous protection under the Constitution; their rights were meager in the North and nonexistent in the South, where almost all blacks were held in perpetual slavery, with the protection of the Constitution. Chinese began to make their appearance in California after the discovery of gold in 1849 but were treated almost from the beginning, in custom and state law, as a lesser breed with few rights. Indians were pushed across the Mississippi and were occasionally subjected to genocidal war. Certainly the Constitution was no great protector of diversity during the first third of its history. But even then the conditions were being set that were to make it the formidable instrument of protection it was to become.

Writing the Constitution to Protect Diversity

A constitution is words; it requires something more to give it life. The American Constitution was given this life by the Supreme Court. What was involved was a subtle mixture of arrogance and humility. The judiciary, after all, as Alexander Hamilton wrote in *The Federalist*, expounding and defending the Constitution that was being put to the states for adoption, was "the least dangerous" branch of the government that was being proposed, with "no influence over the sword or the purse." Yet it established itself as the interpreter of the Constitution, the final interpreter. There was no redress from its decisions except the complex process of amendment, and between 1804 and 1865 no amendment to the Constitution was added. But the Court was generally careful not to engage in actions that might produce a response from Congress or the president that demonstrated how truly without power it was. Its true power was public acceptance; and that acceptance was gained step by step, despite conflicts with a series of strong presidents who sometimes defied it. In a series of major decisions, the Supreme Court, under Chief Justice John Marshall, succeeded in establishing itself as the supreme arbiter of the Constitution and the laws under it, taking the power to declare acts of Congress and of state legislatures unconstitutional, and the power to override the state courts. But it rarely touched issues of diversity: these were securely within the province of the states. No case dealing with religion or ethnicity came before it.

Even on the great issue that was tearing the country apart, slavery, the Court held its distance—for a while. Eventually, after a number of cautious decisions touching on slavery, it was tempted into one that was far too sweeping. Under Chief Justice Roger Taney, Marshall's successor, in the *Dred Scott* decision of 1856, it asserted that Negroes are not and could not be citizens in the meaning of the federal Constitution and that Congress had exceeded its power in banning slavery in territories (parts of the country not yet states and under congressional authority). Negroes were, the court asserted, without any of the rights given to "persons" or "citizens" by the Constitution. The storm that broke on this decision was one of the key events leading to the election of Abraham Lincoln, the southern secession, and the Civil War and seemed to portend the end of the Court as supreme arbiter of Constitution and law. But as Robert McCloskey writes:

Taney and his colleagues had built better than he knew. On the foundations Marshall had bequeathed, the Taney Court had fashioned a system of jurisprudence and a judicial image; and the nation had learned to accept one and admire the other. . . . This achievement had been endangered by the audacious assumption in *Dred Scott* that the judiciary could solve the major problem facing America. But the public habit of reverence was strongly ingrained by those years of painstaking cultivation, and not even this calamity could stamp it out altogether. . . .[11]

The *Dred Scott* decision was not overruled extraconstitutionally by Congress or the president: acting within the Constitution (but only because the southern states had been militarily crushed and occupied), Congress, in three amendments, freed the slaves, protected their rights, gave them citizenship and the vote, and added to the Constitution, with the approval of the states, the amendments that form, along with the religion clauses, the basic protection for diversity in the United States.

It is of course not only a written Constitution that gives rights. It needs an interpreter or interpreters, and that was the role of the Supreme Court. It needs too the support of the other branches of government, and in the course of a complex history in which Congress and president often defied the Court (and in measure still do), that was gained, as McCloskey points out. Beyond that it needs, as the ultimate guarantor of the rights of the Constitution, the acceptance of the people. The Constitution, after all, derives from the people: "That all lawful power derives from the people and must be held in check to preserve their freedom is the oldest and most central tenet of American constitutionalism."[12] Just as an army can overthrow a constitution and its guarantees, so can a Congress or president if it takes the power and is willing to wield it, and so can the people: they can reject its basic principles and wield their majority power against the rights of individuals and minority groups. Indeed, the central tension in the protection of diversity in the United States is not that between states and a federal judiciary or between a federal judiciary and the legislative or executive power: it is that between the passions and prejudices of popular majorities and constitutional guarantees. These passions can be directed against races, religions, or ethnic groups. The history of the United States offers the spectacle again and again of an aroused people restricting the liberties of minorities, either through mob rule or through the legislative power of the states. The Supreme Court, particularly during the past sixty years, has generally defended those liberties—and has made its will prevail. Should we take it then that we need a judicial elite acting against the people to protect group rights? Certainly the common themes of the story of nativism, racism, and religious prejudice in the United States suggest this: yet it is the people who in the end accept the judicial determination. If they refuse, the Court will bend or be helpless.

In other words, were the American people not willing to accept these rights, even if it took quite a while to come to this acceptance— and the education of public opinion, as well as the courts, was necessary to induce it—minorities could have no rights in America. And when the people, or some substantial portion of them, set their minds adamantly against granting rights, rights have been withdrawn. So while we must examine a constitution to see what rights are given and how they are developed, we must simultaneously be aware of a political process in which sovereign states, an independent Congress, and an independent executive interact with a judiciary interpreting the Constitution, and we must be aware of a public opinion from which all these powers, except that of the judiciary, derive.

It is common to speak of Congress and the presidency as the majoritarian branches of government, and the judiciary as nonmajoritarian, because Congress and the president are elected, and the judiciary is not. But this is to make the distinction too sharp. Congress often stands against public opinion, as measured by public opinion polls and other tests. Thus, for example, the defenders of the right to free abortion continually refer to the support of public opinion; Congress nonetheless remains steadily restrictive in limiting this right, insofar as its powers permit (by restrictions on money for medical programs that might be used for abortion, for example). The president far more commonly stands against public opinion: in some of the issues with which we are concerned, such as immigration, presidents have generally, for a hundred years or so, been more open and less restrictive than Congress. It was the presidents in power at the time who opposed congressional restrictions on Chinese immigration in 1879, on Japanese immigration in 1906–1907, and restriction of Europeans on grounds of literacy in 1915.[13] (At the times in question, it was not possible to test public opinion directly, but the presidents opposed Congress, the most popular branch of government.)

Even the nonelected Court cannot stand forever against a popular will. It is appointed, but appointed by elected presidents. The point is that we cannot explain the protection of diversity through a written Constitution and a Supreme Court alone: we will concentrate on these, but it will be necessary to refer constantly to the independent actions of the states, of Congress and the president, and of the people.

71

Ensuring Equal Treatment and Independence. With the Thirteenth, Fourteenth, and Fifteenth Amendments to the Constitution, all the provisions bearing on diversity in the Constitution are complete: no amendment since deals with these issues, and thus to the remarkably few words of the original Constitution and the First Amendment we have to add only a few more. The key provisions:

> Neither slavery nor involuntary servitude, except as a punishment for crime whereof the party shall have been duly convicted, shall exist within the United States. . . . (Amendment Thirteen, 1865)

> All persons born or naturalized within the United States, and subject to the jurisdiction thereof, are citizens of the United States and of the State wherein they reside. No State shall make or enforce any law which shall abridge the privileges or immunities of citizens of the United States; nor shall any State deprive any person of life, liberty, or property, without due process of law; nor deny to any person within its jurisdiction the equal protection of the law. (Amendment Fourteen, 1868)

> The right of citizens of the United States to vote shall not be denied or abridged by the United States or by any State on account of race, color, or previous condition of servitude. (Amendment Fifteen, 1870)

Each of these amendments provides that Congress shall have power to enforce its provisions by appropriate legislation.

The key phrases of the Fourteenth Amendment—"privileges and immunities," "due process," and "equal protection"—have served as the basis for constitutional decisions reaching into every corner of American life. The volume of analysis by constitutional lawyers exceeds by far that devoted to even the religion clauses: much of American constitutional law, it seems, is reduced to argument over the meanings and reach of these key phrases—what they permit the states to do, what they permit Congress to do, what they permit officials at all levels of government to do, and what they offer in the way of protections to "persons" (more than citizens) of every color or nationality or ethnic origin, of any age or condition or sex.[14]

It is on the basis of these provisions that the races, ethnic groups, and religious groups of the United States are ensured equal treatment and independence in a vast range of activities—education, religion, philanthropy, political action. But these provisions did not immediately reveal their meaning. They should have, one would think: the congresses that framed them between 1865 and 1870 also wrote many laws to enforce them and also could have been consulted as to their meaning and scope (though that is not the way constitutional adjudication is conducted). But the Supreme Court was more conservative than the radical Republican congresses that wrote these provisions and more solicitous of the rights of the states, even the states lately in rebellion and controlled by the white majorities that had participated in that rebellion. Thus the Court found reasoning to declare the protections of these amendments and the acts enforcing them for the most part ineffective. This was of monumental practical importance for southern American blacks, since it kept them in a position of legal inferiority, deprived of the vote, for 100 years after the Civil War. The due process scope of the Fourteenth Amendment was extravagantly expanded to protect business and property against state action, a peculiar use of an amendment designed to protect the rights of former slaves and a racial minority. But this reasoning on due process and equal protection is now legally without effect. The Supreme Court began a process of reinterpretation of these amendments sixty years ago, and the amendments have given Congress for the past twenty years, and the Court for the past thirty, almost unlimited powers to protect the interests of minorities.

The effective nullification of the Fourteenth and Fifteenth Amendments and of the legislation implementing them was not simply a matter of an exotic interpretation by a conservative Supreme Court: rights come from the people, and the American people generally, and white southerners in particular, did not want to grant equality to blacks. As John Hope Franklin writes:

> Neither the Fourteenth Amendment nor the radical legislation embodied in Congressional Reconstruction was sufficient to protect the Negro in his political and civil rights. Southern resistance was stiff and effective . . . the ex-Confederates went grimly about the task of nullifying [radical reconstruction legislation] in every possible way. By violence, intimidation and ingenious schemes of economic pressure . . . they began to "redeem" their state governments. Neither the Fifteenth Amendment nor the Ku Klux Klan Acts [passed by Congress to prevent the physical intimidation of blacks by white supremacist organizations] could stem the tide.[15]

The Supreme Court generally endorsed the stratagems by which white supremacy was restored. How effective the white supremacists would have been had the Court stood against them is an indeterminate question: It would have needed the support of presidents and congresses unwilling to grant it. The Civil Rights Act decision of 1883 denied that Congress had power to protect blacks from a host of private and municipal and indeed state actions that limited them. The *Plessy* v. *Ferguson* decision of 1896 accepted the rights of the states to pass legislation separating the races, which the southern states did in every sphere of life, including education.

Quite early, however, the Supreme Court widened the scope of the Fourteenth Amendment, written to protect the freed slaves, to reach out to other minorities. In *Yick Wo* v. *Hopkins* (1886) the Supreme Court struck down a California statute that appeared fair on its face but was applied only to Chinese. A 1906 decision (*Hodges* v. *United States*, 203 U.S. 1) declares of the Thirteenth Amendment that "Slavery or involuntary servitude of the Chinese, the Italian, the Anglo-Saxon are as much within its compass as slavery or involuntary servitude of the African." Thus the amendments were not totally without force: but their power did not extend far enough to protect blacks in the South, and in much of the North and West (though the powers granted to states by the Constitution and Supreme Court permitted liberal northern states such as Massachusetts to provide a considerable degree of legal equality and protection), or to protect Chinese and Japanese from the racist legislation and practices of California.

The American people were in a remarkably restrictive mood regarding rights of minorities, whether racial, religious, or ethnic, from the turn of the century on. To the antiblack legislation and practices of the South, and the anti-Asian legislation and practices of California (some of which met the opposition of the Supreme Court), was added a general nativism. This movement was principally in response to the largest waves of immigration ever to arrive in the United States, during the last decade of the nineteenth century and the first two of the twentieth. The immigrants, in addition to their huge number, were predominantly Catholics and Jews rather than Protestants, southern European and eastern European rather than from the more traditional sources of immigration (Great Britain, Ireland, Germany, Scandinavia), and they settled in the great cities rather than in rural areas. A powerful movement to restrict immigration arose. Chinese immigration had already been restricted in 1882, Japanese in 1907, but restrictionists also demanded a reduction in immigration from southern and eastern Europe. During World War I, nativism and xenophobia reached very high levels. In the early 1920s, restrictionists succeeded, and immigration to the United States was reduced drastically. Immigration from Asia was completely banned, and from Europe it was sharply reduced, with immigrants from southern and eastern Europe limited to tiny quotas.

The nativist forces were antiforeign, anti-Catholic, anti-Semitic. They called for a more rapid homogenization of the American population and disliked the extensive system of nonpublic religious schools, primarily Catholic and Lutheran, created by minorities in the United States. Much state legislation was passed requiring education in English only and limiting the private schools favored by religious and national minorities. It was at this point, when restrictions were imposed on the ability of ethnic and religious groups to maintain their culture and schools, that the Supreme Court began to find in the sparse phrases of the Constitution new protections for diversity. In *Meyer* v. *Nebraska* it struck down a Nebraska state law prohibiting the teaching of foreign languages in schools before the eighth grade. In *Pierce* v. *Society of Sisters* it struck down an Oregon statute requiring all children to attend public schools:

> This limitation on state power was found to derive from the "liberty" guaranteed by due process in the Fourteenth Amendment, with particular emphasis upon the teacher's liberty to pursue a vocation and the liberty of parents and the school of their choice to conclude a contract for the education of their children.[16]

These decisions stand as a charter granting an important if minimal protection to the right of groups to educate their children as they see fit.

In the 1920s, 1930s, and 1940s one detects a greater willingness on the part of the Supreme Court to consider restrictions on the states in the defense of civil liberties and civil rights. Thus, it began to "incorporate" the protections of the Bill of Rights into the Fourteenth Amendment on the ground that the vague phrases "due process" and "equal protection" included some of these fundamental rights. And so one finds the First Amendment rights of speech, press, assembly, petition, free exercise of religion, and nonestablishment of religion all accepted by the Supreme Court as rights that the states, as well as the Congress, must recognize.[17] Even the rights of blacks, so trodden down in the South, began to receive protection from the Supreme Court in the 1920s, in particular the right to vote.[18] In the postwar era, decisions favoring black claims in voting and education, came faster and faster, culminating in the historic *Brown* v. *Board of Education* decision of 1954, which declared "separate but equal" in educational arrangements unconstitutional and gave a momentous push to the process of unraveling the whole system of caste legislation and practice in the South. In major civil rights legislation dealing with education, voting, jobs, public facilities, and housing—the Civil Rights Acts of 1957, 1964, 1965, 1968, and 1972—Congress began again, after a long hiatus that had lasted since the 1870s, to legislate to protect civil rights. This legislation was intended primarily to protect the civil rights of blacks, but it also banned discrimination on grounds of race, color, national origin, and language.

Individual versus Group Rights

The constitutional protection of diversity in the United States today presents a picture not of rights inadequately and insufficiently established but one of rights clashing with each other. We are at the end of a period of great expansion of both group rights and individual rights, which began with the *Brown* decision of 1954 and the Civil Rights Act of 1965. An enormous expansion of constitutional law has resulted, without the need to add any more words to the Constitution. But that expansion has raised some difficult problems as to the freedom and liberty and rights of groups, problems it seems intimately implicated in the very decisions and acts that expand rights.

Before attempting to find solutions to the problems that have arisen, it is necessary to understand that the provisions of the Constitution referred to here, and of almost all the legislation that implements them, defend *individual* rights. This is true of the clauses dealing with the free exercise of religion, the nonestablishment of religion, religious tests for office, the guarantee of due process, and the equal protection of the laws. These are all matters of the defense of an individual's claim: every case sets an individual against an agent of government or a level of government. The rights that are protected may indeed be hardly connected with the life of any group, religious, ethnic, or racial. They may be rights to individual conscience unconnected to any group belief or loyalty or culture: the right to be an atheist and yet hold public office; the right to have a personal opposition to war and not to be subjected to the draft.

Despite the language that frames them, however, all these clauses refer, by implication, to the rights of groups, religious, racial, and ethnic. Similarly, the rights that follow the free exercise and establishment clauses in the First Amendment are individual rights. (Congress may also not make a law "abridging the freedom of speech, or of the press; or the right of the people peaceably to assemble, and to petition the government for a redress of grievances.") But clearly groups lay claim to those rights (particularly political groups), and those rights serve to protect group freedoms. The connection between individual rights and group rights is, however, complex: the interests of a group and of the individuals that make it up are not identical, and conflict between them is indeed possible. Religious, racial, ethnic, and political groups (parties, movements) in the United States are voluntary, with no power of state action. They may find it necessary on occasion to defend themselves against the state; but at the same time the individuals within them, despite their voluntary character, may find it necessary to defend themselves against the group.

The rights of an individual may thus also be threatened by one of those diverse groups whose freedom of action we want to preserve in our diverse society. Religious groups have no state power, but they have the power that comes from the ownership of property, strength of organization, and the ability to mold the opinions and actions of adherents. In all these ways, they have the power to act against the interests of individuals. The civil liberties and civil rights we have discussed in a somewhat amalgamated fashion may thus stand against each other. Individual conscience may stand against group power—and against group conscience.

One of the major cases settling the limits of state power against the group also raises the question of group power over the individual. It arises in the context of education, as so many cases involving group rights and limits do. In *Wisconsin* v. *Yoder*, the question was raised whether the state of Wisconsin could require the children of members of the Old Order Amish religion and the Conservative Amish Mennonite religion to attend school until the age of sixteen, as state law required. The issue was not whether they would have to attend a public school—that was settled by *Pierce* v. *Society of Sisters* in 1925. But the law required that they have schooling of some kind. Parents of children not in school were tried and convicted of violating the compulsory-attendance law and fined. They argued in their defense that under the "free exercise of religion" clause of the First Amendment, incorporated into the Fourteenth, they had the right to refuse to send their children to high school beyond the age of fourteen or fifteen. They believed that their children's attendance at high school, public or private, "was contrary to the Amish religion and way of life. They believed that by sending their children to high school, they would not only expose themselves to the censure of the church community, but, as found by the county court, endanger their own salvation and that of their children" (*Wisconsin* v. *Yoder*, 406 U.S. 205 (1972)). The Supreme Court upheld the right of the Amish to keep their children out of school.

But what of the rights of the children? Justice William O. Douglas in dissent argued they would have to be taken into account:

> If the parents in this case are allowed a religious exemption, the inevitable effect is to impose the parents' notion of reli-

gious duty upon their children. Where the child is mature enough to express potentially conflicting desires, it would be an invasion of the child's rights to permit such an imposition without canvassing his views. . . . Religion is an individual experience.

The American voice and one American dilemma is heard in that last sentence. "Religion is an individual experience," yes, but religion is even more a group experience. The *Yoder* case brings up the issue of group versus individual rights in an exceptional situation, that of a small religious group whose family life is exemplary and highly admired. The situation arises in other contexts, where the group does not enjoy such high public repute. In the many cases of parents whose children have joined new sects that separate them from their families, should the parents be allowed to forcibly retake possession of the children in an effort to change their views?

The United States remains a country of continual group creation, particularly in the sphere of religion. It has spawned thousands upon thousands of sects, some of which have become strong and respectable. The free exercise of religion does not give them unlimited rights—the Supreme Court stood with Congress in denying to the Mormons, for example, the right to polygamy under the free exercise clause, and polygamy was stamped out by force.

As American diversity expands under the impact of 600,000 immigrants a year, primarily from Asia and Latin America, issues in which individual rights clash with the maintenance of group authority—and thus with the opportunity to maintain "diversity"—will undoubtedly become more complex. Consider the implications of an increase, for example, in the Muslim population. The problem here is less one of polygamy than one of the rights of women and female children. American law now, in its expansion of the rights of women, has made it difficult to maintain single-sex schools. Indeed, in the public sector schools, this is all but impossible. What then if Muslims raise the same claims as the Old Order Amish in order to protect their female children?

But we need not go to such exotic possibilities to see the clash between group rights and individual rights, state versus group, and group versus group exhibited. The individual rights of the Constitution envisage as the chief danger an abstract state enforcing uniformity on diverse individuals (or by extension, on groups and peoples) and being held back by constitutional restraints. The state is restrained by these protections from interfering with a community, racial, religious, or ethnic, that participates in a certain way of life, holds certain beliefs, or engages in some organizational activity. But the state also embodies, to some degree, such a community. A school district, a village, a town, even a city may not be marked by the diversity common to the United States in general. Its homogeneity may be ethnic or religious or racial. Its expression, through public action, of a religious or group practice or belief, raises another kind of conflict between community and individual—or between community and community. When one community has the power to pass laws or to compel uniform behavior, an individual or another community may resist. The present thrust of constitutional law strongly limits the state. Neither the state (nor an individual school district, school, or teacher) may require a prayer, or the reading of the Bible, or the placing of the Ten Commandments on the school walls. Those who want to do these things claim their action is supported by the "free exercise" of religion guaranteed by the First Amendment, or perhaps by the state's duty to uphold conventional and universal morality. Those who oppose such free exercise claim it is an example of the "establishment of religion" prohibited by the same amendment.

Supporters of religion in the schools claim their motives are the same as those of the Amish in withdrawing their children from the secular and godless and hedonistic high school: to raise responsible and dutiful children. Even when an action is voluntary (such as a moment of silence for meditation or voluntary prayer), the law authorizing it has been held unconstitutional under the establishment clause. There is an answer to those who wish to exercise their religious practices in the school—withdrawing their children from the public school and placing them in a private religious school, where prayer is not only permitted, but if they so wish, prescribed. But there is a cost to such an action—a cost to the "free exercise" of religion, which in other contexts may not be impeded.

Much of the most fiercely disputed constitutional litigation in the United States today revolves around the question of what a religious, ethnic, or racial community may do to protect its values and its way of life. American diversity and American constitutional protection make it very difficult to do this. How far may a community go, for example, in restricting the sale of pornography, the exhibition of pornographic movies, and the like? They fall under the protection of the First Amendment to some extent, but to an extent far greater than communities, as represented in municipalities and other local governments, would like to allow. How much respect may a community grant its churches? May it reach the point of allowing a church to deny the sale of liquor in its neighborhood? The state of Massachusetts said yes, but the Supreme Court said no. Some major American religions oppose the sale of alcohol and public drinking; combined with other reformers they were able, remarkably, to pass the Eighteenth Amendment to the Constitution prohibiting the making or sale of "intoxicating liquors." Were they imposing their religious views on the American people (violating the "establishment" clause)? Were they, by placing restrictions on the religious practices of Jews and Catholics, limiting "free exercise"? These issues became constitutionally moot because prohibition was embodied in an amendment to the Constitution itself. It created such problems that it was repealed in 1933 by the Twenty-First Amendment. The new amendment, however, left full powers to control the transportation and importation of intoxicating liquors with the states, and thus we have today's crazy-quilt of regulation from state to state and from community to community.

Since the mid-1970s the "fundamentalist" or evangelical trend in American religion has experienced a strong revival, particularly in Southern Baptism, but reaching in varying degrees into most of the major Protestant denominations. In the 1920s, two key demands of the fundamentalists were that evolution not be taught in schools in opposition to the Biblical account of creation and that liquor be prohibited. They lost on both counts, and fundamentalism was subsequently considered a backwater of American life that would not become nationally significant again. But it has, by focusing on new issues—issues in large measure created by a liberal and progressive trend in constitutional interpretation, which defends the rights of individuals against locally dominant groups that try to implement their views through state and local legislation. The prohibition of school prayer, of restrictions on abortion, of support to private schools (since they are mostly religious, they would violate the establishment clause), the defense of student rights against school-imposed discipline, and the defense of "sexual preference" (the rights of homosexuals and lesbians) all are part of this progressive tendency. As a result, a true *kulturkampf* now rages in the United States, and the Constitution offers no guidance as to how it may be resolved.

The issue of the protection of diversity is also raised by a set of conflicts pitting individual rights against group rights, those dealing with the attempt to overcome discrimination against blacks (and some other minority groups) through constitutional and legal prohibition of such practice. The problem here is not so much the protection of a specific culture or religion. A regime of discrimination and prejudice against blacks and Asians coexisted with the maintenance by those groups of associations, churches, language schools, or whatever else they wished. Indeed, the complaint of blacks was that through segregation they had rather more of their own schools and churches than they wished: they wanted to overcome discrimination and prejudice so as to enter the mainstream of American life. They did so through new interpretations of the Constitution and laws against discrimination, again based on the equal rights of individuals without regard to color, race, or national origin. Once again, the laws try to deal with prejudice and discrimination against groups by defending the rights of individuals. The rights in question are to education in an unsegregated and integrated setting, to jobs and promotions, to rental and purchase of housing, and to access to public facilities without discrimination on grounds of race, color, or national origin. All these changes of course had implications for ethnic and racial diversity.

Consider, for example, the first consequence of effective integration of the segregated black schools of the South. As two different school systems were merged into one, black principals, administrators, and teachers were dismissed, found to be "excess." Whatever capacity existed to create an education in some way directed to or reflecting the culture of the segregated group disappeared. If blacks had been more interested in entering white churches, the black church, another key protection of diversity for the black group, would have declined as well.

But other groups—and their ability to maintain their diversity— were also affected. The fierce conflicts that developed over school busing were largely over diversity, though they were not often presented in the constitutional or scholarly or even popular literature as a conflict of this type. The *Brown* decision declared segregation by race in education unconstitutional, as denying the equal protection of the laws. But what right did the decision guarantee? Was it the right to admission to any school without racial restriction, or was it the right to an educational setting with a majority of the majority race and a more than token number of persons of one's own race? The argument for the latter was that if very few persons of the protected race chose a given school setting, segregated schooling continued (through intimidation or otherwise), and no further examination was required judicially as to why. And if too few members of the majority race were present, that also demonstrated that segregation persisted. Under such circumstances, the Court ruled that children could be assigned to school by race, but did not explain why certain proportions of a minority group and a majority group were necessary in each school (perhaps to overcome their self-consciousness as a minority, to provide them with the power to demand better education, and so on).

In line with Supreme Court decisions, assignment of minority and majority children to schools by race became common. Some children content with their schools were assigned to other schools to create a racial balance in each school. These children could be from communities that desired their children to remain close to their homes and that preferred them to be educated among those of their own group. The Chinese children and Mexican-American children of San Francisco, for example, were bused to provide an integrated setting for blacks.[19] In some cases, these efforts to achieve balance and to integrate made it more difficult for communities to maintain close ties among themselves and their identity as distinct communities. The Constitution does not defend the right to maintain separate ethnic or cultural communities, yet if we are sympathetic to community maintenance we cannot be indifferent to the idea of sending children to schools outside their community simply to create a nonblack majority in those schools.

Although these measures were developed primarily to implement the rights of blacks, many blacks doubted that this kind of dispersion was what they wanted for the education of their children.[20] Indeed, some preferred the schools blacks maintained during the period of segregation, in part because they *were* black community institutions.[21]

This issue of community and its relationship to school integration could be raised in a different way. Communities differ in values, orientation, and behavior. It may well be that the primary objective in school assignment should be to mix communities so all can learn about each other. But if some of their differences relate to the use of language, or sexual attitudes, or religious attitudes, the parents in some communities will wish to protect their children and reject homogenization, or they may simply reject integration on racial grounds. Many private schools (so-called segregation academies) have been created in response to judicial desegregation decisions. Sometimes it is perfectly clear that the only reason such schools have been established is to keep the races separate; in other cases motives are more mixed and may indeed be predominantly religious or moral, such as because public schools cannot provide religion or because they do not impose a traditional discipline. Private schools are often established directly by churches and meet on church property. Are they entitled to tax exemption as schools? Or does the fact that they have no or few minority children demonstrate that they segregate racially and should not be eligible for tax exemption?

There is no question that conservative communities in the United States now feel threatened by the expansion of civil rights and civil liberties and that liberal communities feel threatened by the mobilization of the traditionalists. On one side, the expansion of rights may be seen as giving the greatest possible freedom to the individual—and in that freedom individuals can create the subcommunities they desire, whether traditional or radical, conventional or unconventional. On the other side, this expansion may be, and indeed is, seen as the arrogant extension of values and behavior that threaten traditional communities, so that they cannot protect their schools and their neighborhoods from intrusions they find offensive, and that prevent them from providing a protected environment for their children. This was the claim Yoder made in refusing to comply with the compulsory attendance laws of the state of Wisconsin; it is a claim now raised by the large section of the American population that adheres to traditional values. As a result, other individuals and communities characterized by liberal and progressive values believe their lifestyles are threatened. The conflict breaks out anywhere: when New York City insists that the institutions that provide its social services must not discriminate against homosexuals, and the Catholic church, which provides such services, says its religion cannot allow it to accept this prohibition; when communities and states seek means to get around the Supreme Court's constitutionalization of abortion; when communities and neighborhoods seek ways to keep out adult theaters or to ban books with explicit sexual language from their school libraries. And the list can be extended.

American diversity today is well protected. Association on religious, racial, and ethnic bases flourishes widely, with the protection of the Constitution. Individual choice to express this diversity raises few problems: at the margin, law can be invoked against extreme and dangerous claims made on grounds of race, religion, or ethnicity, but this is rare. But diversity is a matter of more than individual choice: it is a matter of communities seeking some type of control, whether voluntary or state, to defend their values, their distinctiveness, and their ideals. In so doing, they may deny individual rights or use state power to try to oppress other groups. There are no simple answers to such problems. A generally divided Supreme Court is the best we can do in setting legal norms. The system works, and it can be changed if enough people think it is not working, as we see in present movements to amend the Constitution to make English the national language, to return control of abortion to the states, and to prevent the Supreme Court from making decisions on school prayer.

Where diversity prevails, there will always be conflict. The hard questions are how to hold it within the bounds of law and of the Constitution and how to solve its problem in ways that are more widely accepted.

Notes

1. In American constitutional law, "diversity" refers to differences among the laws of the states, not to the diversity of religion, race, and ethnicity.
2. See Sidney E. Ahlstrom, *A Religious History of the American Peoples* (New

Haven, Conn.: Yale University Press, 1972), p. 508, quoting Thomas O'Dea, *The Mormons.*

3. E. P. Hutchinson, *Legislative History of American Immigration Policy, 1798–1965* (Philadelphia, Pa.: University of Pennsylvania Press, 1981), p. 11.

4. Ibid., p. 75.

5. Ibid.

6. See the dissent of Justice Rehnquist to the decision in Wallace v. Jaffree, June 4, 1985, *U.S. Law Week,* June 4, 1985, pp. 4679–86.

7. Laurence Tribe, *American Constitutional Law* (Mineola, N.Y.: The Foundation Press, 1978), p. 816.

8. Ibid., p. 819.

9. Ibid.

10. Martin Diamond, Winston Mills Fisk, and Herbert Garfinkel, *The Democratic Republic* (Skokie, Ill.: Rand McNally, 1966), pp. 50–51.

11. Robert G. McCloskey, *The American Supreme Court* (Chicago: University of Chicago Press, 1960), pp. 99–100.

12. Tribe, *American Constitutional Law,* p. 1.

13. John Higham, *Strangers in the Land* (New Brunswick, N.J.: Rutgers University Press, 1955), pp. 104–5, 191.

14. Tribe's *American Constitutional Law* devotes 187 pages to "due process" and 236 pages to "equal protection."

15. John Hope Franklin, quoted in Derrick A. Bell, Jr., *Race, Racism, and American Law* (Boston: Little, Brown, 1973), pp. 198–99.

16. Tribe, *American Constitutional Law,* p. 902.

17. Ibid., pp. 567–68.

18. Derrick A. Bell, Jr., *Shades of Brown* (New York: Columbia University, Teachers College Press, 1980), p. 125.

19. David Kirp, *Just Schools: The Ideal of Racial Equality in American Education* (Berkeley, Calif.: University of California Press, 1982).

20. Bell, *Shades of Brown.*

21. Thomas Sowell, "Black Excellence—the Case of Dunbar High School," *The Public Interest,* no. 35 (Spring 1974).

Commentary

Thomas L. Pangle

Our age is one in which imperatives of technology, as well as of economics and politics, tend to rule out political systems that are not capable of embracing enormously diverse populations. Can populations of great size and heterogeneity be governed effectively by truly democratic means? Or is the regimentation imposed by despotic, bureaucratic authority—benevolent or no—inevitable and essential if there is to be law and order, strong national defense, and productive economic development? Outside the geographic and cultural bounds of North America and Western Europe, there is but shaky evidence for the viability, let alone the flourishing, of legally regulated, openly contested popular government that protects the political and civil rights of individual citizens, especially those in dissent. The seemingly almost unmanageable diversity—ethnic, racial, but above all religious and economic—of many nations in the so-called third world (but also of the Soviet and Chinese empires) is often said to be a major reason for this lamentable historical record. It makes sense to ask whether the designers of the American republic confronted anything like the problem confronted by nations trying to establish democracy today: could their thoughts, which guided an amazingly successful republican founding, provide us with any helpful guidance?

An adequate answer to this question requires studying the Constitution itself as well as the history, including the history of constitutional law, *after* the ratification and the first, formative generation of the Republic. We ought not, of course, suppose that history followed a path preordained by what the Founding Fathers said and did. But we need also to bear in mind that that subsequent history was largely derived from the basic moral and political principles articulated, defended, and thought through during the founding and immediately thereafter. Especially during the ratification debates that took place in the fall and spring of 1787–1788, a level of reflection was reached that, in depth and breadth, has rarely been matched in the recorded history of statesmanship. If we look back solely through the familiar optic of our own era, or through the perhaps distorting lens of more recent history, and do not try to see those original debates as they were seen by their greatest protagonists, we will fail to open ourselves to the full challenge of the Founders' debate and thought about the fundamental problems of democracy.

In my judgment we need to begin by questioning the supposition that because the most visible issues in the Constitutional Convention were those concerned with the relation between the states and the new federal government, the Convention paid little attention to diversities of religion, race, and ethnicity. In trying to understand the problems the Convention faced, I believe we cannot do better than to orient ourselves by James Wilson's great speech in the Pennsylvania ratifying debates, November 24, 1787. Wilson begins by characterizing the Convention delegates' conception of the massive problem they faced as follows:

> Their views could not be confined to a small or a single community, but were expanded to a great number of states; several of which contain an extent of territory, and resources of population, equal to those of some of the most respectable kingdoms on the other side of the Atlantick. . . . Numerous states yet unformed, myriads of the human race, who will inhabit regions hitherto uncultivated, were to be affected. . . . It was necessary, therefore, to form their calculations on a scale commensurate to a large portion of the globe. . . . The United States contain already thirteen governments mutually independent. . . . Their soil, their climates, their productions, their dimensions, their numbers are different. In many instances a difference and even an opposition subsists. . . . [W]ill any member of this honorable body be surprised, that such a diversity of things produced a proportioned diversity of sentiment? Will he be surprised that such a diversity of sentiment rendered a spirit of mutual forbearance and conciliation indispensably necessary to the success of the great work?[1]

Wilson does go on to speak of the problem of designing a proper balance between federal and state governments; but this is not the first or even the second of the great challenges he describes, and it is not a problem that, according to Wilson, ever posed much difficulty in principle: "It was easy," he says, "to discover a proper and satisfactory principle on this subject." The only thorny problem was applying the easily-discovered correct principle. But what then were the truly baffling or puzzling issues of principle with which the Convention wrestled? The issue Wilson speaks of as paramount, the only issue he in fact calls very important, is that which arises "from comparing the extent of the country to be governed, with the kind of government which it would be proper to establish in it." As Wilson proceeds to explain,

It has been an opinion, countenanced by high authority (Montesquieu, *Spirit of the Laws* Bk. 8, chap. 20), "that the natural property of small states, is to be governed as a republick; of middling ones, to be subject to a monarch; and of large empires, to be swayed by a despotick prince; and that the consequence is, . . . the spirit of the state will alter in proportion as it extends or contracts its limits." This opinion seems to be supported, rather than contradicted, by the history of the governments in the old world. Here then the difficulty appeared in full view. On one hand, the United States contain an immense extent of territory, and, according to the foregoing opinion, a despotick government is best adapted to that extent. On the other hand, it was well known, that, however the citizens of the United States might, with pleasure, submit to the legitimate restraints of a republican constitution, they would reject, with indignation, the fetters of despotism. What then was to be done? . . . Permit me to add, . . . that the science even of government itself seems yet to be almost in its state of infancy. . . . The ancients, so enlightened on other subjects, were very uninformed with regard to this.[2]

Wilson's vision of a mammoth future nation, a nation whose "springs of opposition were so numerous and strong,"[3] a nation whose prospect of free government is denied by all past political experience and theory, is echoed and given an added dimension by Benjamin Rush, in his essay on the need for a federal university (1788). There he remarks that the English language spoken in American dialects is probably destined to "be spoken by more people in the course of two or three centuries, than ever spoke any one language at one time since the creation of the world"; he goes further: the influence of American English together with American Spanish "upon manners, commerce, knowledge and civilization" will be of a magnitude that eludes "the utmost grasp of the human understanding."[4]

It was in large measure because they conceived America as destined to be so gargantuan and heterogeneous a society that some of the most thoughtful Founders felt a national university was essential. Presidents Washington, Jefferson, Madison, and John Quincy Adams all sent messages to Congress calling for a truly national university. "Amongst the motives to such an Institution," Washington declared in his message of December 7, 1796, "the assimilation of the principles,

87

opinions, and manners of our Country men . . . well deserves attention. The more homogeneous our citizens can be made in these
particulars, the greater will be our prospect of permanent Union."[5]

In a similar vein, Madison in his message of 1810 stressed that
"by assimilating the principles, the sentiments, and the manners, of
those who might resort to this temple of science, to be redistributed,
in due time, through every part of the community, sources of jealousy
and prejudice would be diminished, the features of national character
would be multiplied, and greater extent given to social harmony."[6]
Nor did the concern for educational reform as a remedy for the
perceived threats from diversity stop at the federal or university level.
Rush's observations in an essay of 1798 are again illuminating:

> I conceive the education of our youth in this country to be
> peculiarly necessary in Pennsylvania, while our citizens are
> composed of the natives of so many different kingdoms in
> Europe. Our schools of learning, by producing one general,
> and uniform system of education, will render the mass of the
> people more homogeneous, and thereby fit them more easily
> for uniform and peaceable government.[7]

A careful study of the writings on civic education of Wilson,
Jefferson, and Rush would provide much food for thought about how
education, strategically directed, can ameliorate the problems diversity poses for democracy; and I will return in closing to some more
specific remarks on the contents of those writings. But for most of the
leaders of the founding generation (with the notable exceptions of
Rush and Jefferson), education policy was *not* the principal locus of
thought about the problems of diversity. The relentless—but of course
unsuccessful—call for a national university signified a great concern
rather than revealed the way that concern was dealt with. In order to
grasp the much more important, or major, strand in the Founders'
well-spun web of thoughts about diversity, we need to turn to the
single most incisive theoretical writing of the Founders, James
Madison's famous *Federalist* No. 10.

This essay, together with its remarkable prelude, Hamilton's
Federalist No. 9, identifies the threat of oppression and disintegration
arising from diversity as the most worrisome feature of popular government: "The friend of popular governments never finds himself so
much alarmed for their character and fate as when he contemplates
their propensity to this dangerous vice." Madison speaks of this
problem as the problem of "faction" or of "party." The choice of
terminology is significant. Madison sees and tries to understand the
problem of diversity in political, rather than social terms; he sees

diversity as a problem calling for political science and theory, not sociology or social theory. In this he is the heir to the entire preceding history of philosophy, from Aristotle to Montesquieu. For all its profound disagreements, this tradition is unified in holding that the social phenomena are shaped by the political—in insisting that the political variables are the most truly independent of all the social variables. It seems to me that this approach gives Madison a depth of insight and a clarity that is lacking in much of our discussion of the problem of diversity. Madison, one may say, represents the common-sense or citizen's perspective, which sees that religious groups, for example, become problematic for a society only if, or to the extent that, they gain political power and enter the political arena.

Guided by this emphatically civic mode of theorizing, Madison treats religious diversity as a far more serious problem than linguistic or ethnic or racial diversity. In fact, he does not explicitly or specifically discuss these latter as potentially dangerous manifestations of diversity. Instead, he focuses on economic diversity on the one hand (what nowadays would often be called class conflict), and on diversity arising from opinion combined with passion on the other. Exactly what does he mean to refer to by identifying this second sort of diversity? First and foremost, diversity in religion; second, diversity in what we might call ideology ("a zeal for different opinions . . . concerning government, and many other points, as well of specula-tion as of practice"); third, diversity growing out of attraction to competing and magnetic political figures ("an attachment to different leaders ambitiously contending for pre-eminence and power"); and, fourth, a diversity rooted in passionate loyalty to what we might call charismatic individuals, martyrs, or heroes ("an attachment to . . . persons of other descriptions whose fortunes have been interesting to the human passions"). (This last is clearly closely tied to, but in Madison's judgment not identical to, religious diversity.)

If we reflect critically on this rather complex typology, we begin to see an implicit answer, I believe, to the question of why Madison leaves racial, ethnic, and linguistic diversity in the background. Madison seems to have believed that these and other sorts of diversity usually become politically dangerous or problematic only when they are activated by politically ambitious or charismatic leaders or when they are linked to economic, religious, or ideological diversity. If this is true, then the political danger of diversity can be adequately dis-posed of without focusing on (though not by ignoring) these other types of diversity.

If we next ask, prompted by the text, why Madison might have supposed uplifting charisma, religious and ideological opinion, and economic interest were the truly durable and intense grounds for strife, the following answer suggests itself. Human beings as a species have three overriding and lifelong concerns: physical security and comfort, dignity, and eternal salvation. Only the differences and diversities that seriously affect these three concerns are by nature, or inescapably, of the utmost urgency for mankind.

Yet Madison was by no means inclined to suppose that deadly discord can always be traced to these permanent sources. Madison judged mankind as constitutionally prone to conflict, even in the absence of seemingly sensible grounds: "So strong is this propensity of mankind to fall into mutual animosities that where no substantial occasion presents itself the most frivolous and fanciful distinctions have been sufficient to kindle their unfriendly passions and excite their most violent conflicts." This fundamental insight into human psychology, an insight based on Madison's study of recorded history and on the insight's proven explanatory power in the everyday life he saw around himself, forms the very bedrock of the political theory of *The Federalist* and of the Founders generally. Because they were so convinced of humankind's natural and inexpugnable unsocial sociability, the Founders, with Madison their great spokesman, rejected any attempt to deal with the danger of faction and diversity by "removing the causes" of such diversity. That is to say, they rejected as unnatural, as necessarily requiring continual coercive violence, the vision of a homogeneous, unfactionalized, or uncompetitive society.

In rejecting any hope or attempt to create a society without inner conflict and contradiction, the Founders attacked head-on what they saw as the two great failed alternative sources of inspiration for dreams of social harmony. The first was the tradition of political theology, growing out of the apparent demands of the monotheistic and universalistic religions based on revelations inaccessible to unassisted sense perception and reason. These great movements based on the Bible claimed to bring to mankind the ultimate truth about human fulfillment, including especially the truth about law and its relation to morality. Yet that truth was in crucial respects unevident to human reason, the only natural human faculty that gives mankind access to shared or universal truth. As a result, argument between competing claimants to divine revelation, argument over the true content of divine law, seemed difficult if not impossible to arbitrate.

The American people originated, in large part, from minorities fleeing the effects of religious warfare and persecution sponsored by the supposedly divinely anointed heads of Christendom (and, indirectly, Islam). The Founders were therefore quite confident that official toleration and judicial protection, of at least Christian religious diversity, was, in principle, a prime desideratum among almost all ranks of Americans in 1787. But would it remain so in practice, as hard cases occurred and new sects emerged? Would it remain so even in principle, if a large (perhaps majoritarian) sect were to come into being, in a generation distantly removed from the direct experience of the bitterness of religious warfare and the fanaticism of religious persecution? Nathan Glazer observes in this volume, "the central tension in the protection of diversity in the United States is not that between states and a federal judiciary, or a federal judiciary and the legislative or executive power: it is that between the passions and the prejudices of popular majorities and constitutional guarantees." This tension was a source of worry clearly implied in the sober sentences of *Federalist* No. 10, and more fervently expressed by Jefferson.[8]

The worry was deepened and compounded, especially for Hamilton and Madison, when they reflected on the second great source of inspiration for attempts to remove the causes of factional strife. At the time of the American Founding, the classical civic republic, which reached its historical apogee in Greece and Rome but was reborn in various versions in northern Italy, Switzerland, Germany, and Holland, still remained a powerful paradigm—and more than that. Before the establishment of the United States, as we have heard James Wilson stress, there simply was no historical example of any republican political system of a sort other than the small communitarian republic, the polis. In other words, although political theorists like Montesquieu and Spinoza had laid down the blueprints for a new "commercial" and liberal republicanism, republicanism remained largely synonymous, practically speaking, with classical, illiberal republicanism. That republicanism, as Montesquieu taught, being based on direct rule by all citizens working together, had to remain very small and had to demand from its citizens the unnatural "virtues" of awesome conformity, severe self-abnegation, and strict communal censorship. Liberty, in the classical republican sense, was understood to be inconceivable without true equality and fervent fraternity. But only persons who shared the same religious beliefs, the same education, the same family habits, the same economic status and condition—only persons who had grown up as and remained a small group on intimate terms, sharing the same decisive experiences of joy and sorrow—could look upon one another with an authentic sense of brotherhood. Only in such social conditions could human beings be regularly expected to conceive of themselves as merely parts of a more important social whole.

The framing of the American Constitution and the devising of the unprecedented *liberal* republicanism of the United States entailed nothing less than a deep and fully thought through theoretical break with the entire previous history of this republican political theory and practice. At the very heart of that theoretical revolution was the new idea that competitive diversity is natural to man, and that diversity can potentially play a creative role in a new kind of republicanism.

While the authors of *The Federalist* still venerate, to some degree, the heroic classical aspirations evoked by Plutarch (their chosen pen name, after all, is Publius), they reject the model of the classical republic not only because of its inapplicability to and inappropriateness for America but, more importantly, because it is in the final analysis against nature and hence inherently disastrous. They in fact seize upon the history of the classical republics as powerful empirical evidence for their thesis that humanity is by nature too diverse—above all, in its "different and unequal faculties of acquiring property"—to be able to sustain for any length of time the sort of fraternity and solidarity required by the civic republican model. The turbulent histories of Athens, Rome—and later of Florence and Venice—disclose an uncheckable tendency for such republics to become riven with conflict between rich and poor; the conflict eventually leads to greater and greater predominance of the poor, acting as a mob, which soon falls under the spell of demagogues and military despots. Under this sort of administration, commerce is constantly interrupted or distorted, the securities of individuals and minorities are destroyed, virtue is replaced by hypocrisy and fanaticism, a mockery is made of the rule of law, and prudent management of foreign as well as domestic policy gives way to whimsical short-term emotionalism.

> It is impossible to read the history of the petty republics of Greece and Italy without feeling sensations of horror and disgust at the distractions with which they were continually agitated, and at the rapid succession of revolutions by which they were kept in a state of perpetual vibration between the extremes of tyranny and anarchy. . . . If it had been found impracticable to have devised models of a more perfect structure, the enlightened friends to liberty would have been obliged to abandon the cause of that species of government as indefensible.[9]

What is the "model of a more perfect structure" devised by the American Founders to save the cause of republican government? Its bedrock is Madison's famous argument in *Federalist* No. 10, an argument that turns the propositions of the classical republic on their heads. In effect, Madison says: Let us abandon the goals of direct political participation, strong civic solidarity, and close mutual surveillance of manners and morals; for if we do so, we can cease to wring our hands over the unprecedented extent and diversity of the new republic. Instead, we can (and should) welcome the conditions that foster a vast manifold of divided, cross-cutting, and competing interests, spread over so large a geographic area as to make their combination somewhat difficult.

First, the development of such a mosaic of factions renders highly unlikely the formation of a majority faction:

> Extend the sphere and you take in a greater variety of parties and interests; you make it less probable that a majority of the whole will have a common motive to invade the rights of other citizens; or if such a common motive exists, it will be more difficult for all who feel it to discover their own strength and to act in unison with each other. . . . The influence of factious leaders may kindle a flame within their particular States but will be unable to spread a general conflagration through the other States. A religious sect may degenerate into a political faction in a part of the Confederacy; but the variety of sects dispersed over the entire face of it must secure the national councils against any danger from that source. . . .

Second, an extended republic allows—and what is even better, requires—representative as opposed to direct democracy. Through representative institutions, government is removed from the direct hands of the mass, inevitably made mob-like by its collective talk and action, and placed instead in the hands of the mass's delegates, chosen in open and contested elections. Thus the popular will remains supreme, but it becomes a will "refined and enlarged." By limiting the people's expression of their views to occasional election campaigns, a seriousness and weightiness greater than that found in ceaseless assemblies may be induced. The delegates selected will be answerable to their opponents and to their constituents in the next election, and yet compelled to compromise and deliberate with other delegates with competing programs; each delegate will therefore be checked in two directions, and constrained to synthesize the local with a broader national interest, arising from the process of give and take. National majorities and majority parties will surely be formed, but they will tend to be majority coalitions rather than majority factions; "parties" will take on a new, nonideological, nondoctrinal character. All this requires, of course, that the national or federal government and its policy making be clearly supreme in dignity and importance over the state government; and the one great worry Madison had about the new Constitution was that it still left too much political scope and power in the hands of the states.

In his praise of representative government in *Federalist* No. 10, Madison also expresses the hope that delegates chosen from relatively large districts would tend to be men of better education and more capacious minds and hearts than the average. But he stresses at the same time that the new republic cannot rely on great statesmanship: "enlightened statesmen will not always be at the helm." What this means becomes clearer when *Federalist* No. 10 is read in the context of *The Federalist* taken as a whole; then it becomes clear that for Madison and Hamilton the "extended republic" is not by itself sufficient to guarantee adequately prudent and liberal government. To be safe and effective, republican government must be not only extended and representative but also regulated by the famous system of internal "checks and balances" or the "separation of powers." And here a new and paradoxical dimension of the problem of diversity rears its unexpected head: America from this point of view is revealed to be *not sufficiently diverse.*

To understand this aspect of the problem of diversity as it confronted the framers, we must return again to Montesquieu, who is the classic proponent of the theory of separation of powers as the key to free and strong government. This is not the place to trace in all its rich details Montesquieu's theorizing on this subject; it suffices to delineate one key strand. For Montesquieu, the separation, checking, and balancing of the three functions of government (lawmaking, administration, and judicial judgment) depends on and is interwoven with an institutional representation of different and competing permanent classes or estates (especially the royal family and court; the clergy, the nobles, the urban bourgeoisie, the rural gentry, etc.). Montesquieu's model of a successful system is England, with its House of Lords, House of Commons, popular jury system, established Church of England, and royalty. But the United States is to be a nation without most of these inegalitarian lynchpins of permanently competitive diversity. In the United States, every branch and institution of government, including the judiciary, is to be beholden, in the last analysis, to the majority or "the great body of the people." (As Nathan Glazer remarks, "It is the people who in the end accept the judicial determination. If they refuse, the Court will bend or be helpless.") Moreover, in the new American form of republic, every branch of government is filled with persons of the same or of very similar class background—the middle class, or what came to be called the bourgeoisie. Does this not mean that the United States is, after all, threatened by a coalescence within government, or, more seriously, by a "tyranny of the majority" in society? Montesquieu had argued that a system like the English had very little need of classical virtue, because the clash of permanently distinct, proud, and selfish class interests, fomented and channeled through the institutional separation of powers, would forestall the development of majority or minority tyranny. But in America, where the majority holds sway everywhere, does there not persist a need to imbue the all-powerful people at large with certain virtues, such as self-restraint, patriotism, and reverence for law and for key moral principles or notions of human rights underlying the law? The Founders felt these questions rather acutely (partly because they were continually reminded of them by some of their opponents, antifederalists like Patrick Henry).

They responded in part by trying to devise purely institutional substitutes for the class or estate differentiation found in Montesquieu's England. Thus the presidency and each house of the legislature are assigned modes of selection intended to make their constituencies distinct. Of course, the most important of these institutional measures (the electoral college and the indirect election of the Senate) could not withstand the pressures of the demands of popular sovereignty, and the intended effect, though not entirely nullified, has been very considerably diminished. The result has been a nation in which "public opinion"—that moody, amorphous monster—has a sway unprecedented in human history and probably unforeseen by the Founders. The classic analyst of this frighteningly homogenizing force in liberal democratic society is of course Alexis de Tocqueville, who discovered and described how the soft tyranny of leveling egalitarianism corrodes the very soul of the atomistic and highly conformist individual who inhabits the new mass liberal democracy.

Tocqueville never denied that American society manifests an extraordinary apparent diversity or, as Nietzsche would say, motleyness. But he insisted that the endlessly changing intellectual fashions, religious trends, and experimentation with what are today revealingly termed lifestyles masks a fundamental absence of deeply rooted distinctions or convictions. Worst of all, he believed, the citizens of the new democracy suffer a loss of capacity for any action and thought that would truly oppose or challenge the reigning democratic dogma and its insistence on turning *vox populi* into *vox dei*. American democracy is the historical incarnation of the principles of the modern philosophic tradition initiated by Descartes; that tradition teaches men to see everyone and every opinion as equal, to distrust all received authority, and to rely solely on one's own individual judgment.

The unintended consequence is the erection of a new authority, far less subject to challenge than any previous source of moral authority. In Tocqueville's penetrating words:

> The nearer men are to a common level of uniformity, the less are they inclined to believe blindly in any man or any class. But they are readier to trust the mass, and public opinion becomes more and more mistress of the world. . . . The citizen of a democracy comparing himself with the others feels proud of his equality with each. But when he compares himself with all his fellows and measures himself against this vast entity, he is overwhelmed by a sense of his insignificance and weakness. The same equality which makes him independent of each separate citizen leaves him isolated and defenceless in the face of the majority. So in democracies public opinion has a strange power of which aristocratic nations can form no conception. It uses no persuasion to forward its beliefs, but by some mighty pressure of the mind of all upon the intelligence of each it imposes its ideas and makes them penetrate men's very souls.[10]

Nowhere—not in politics, not in journalism, not in higher education, not in the arts—do Americans exhibit or encounter truly antidemocratic ways of living and thinking. The only permitted radicalism is a more democratic way of living and thinking, more democratic radicalism. The predominant so-called values (another revealing new term) of egalitarianism, relativism, scientism, commercialism, secularism, and individualism reign unchallenged, except by backward kooks and fringe elements held up to scorn by all right-thinking, "progressive" opinion leaders. Because modern democrats encounter no living, respectable challenges to democratic prejudice (of the sort Tocqueville himself encountered from the predemocratic and rapidly disappearing European aristocracy), they gradually lose the ability to defend or argue for their own fundamental egalitarian or democratic principles; they do not truly know those principles because they do not experience the debate from which they originally grew and do not see the sharp alternatives that alone can define any principled position.

If the most farsighted among the Founders anticipated very much of this Tocquevillian analysis, they did not bring such gloomy thoughts to the fore. They were evidently much more concerned with the traditional threats to nascent liberal democracy. In fact, they can be said to have quietly but deliberately sought to quench some of the radical diversity in fundamental opinion whose absence Tocqueville was later to regret.

If we turn back to *Federalist* No. 10 with the questions we have learned to ask regarding how or to what extent Madison intended American public opinion to express not just a mosaic of diverse interests but some distinctive, and even exclusive, general tone, we begin to appreciate perhaps the deepest level of his position. For it is not true that Madison treats all important sources of faction or interest as equal in value; he clearly favors, or treats as more sensible, faction founded on economic interest. This point emerges much more frankly in one of Madison's earlier rehearsals of the argument presented in *Federalist* No. 10. In a private letter to Thomas Jefferson (Oct. 24, 1787), Madison draws the same fundamental distinction he draws in *Federalist* No. 10, between factions based on economic condition and factions based on opinion and passion; but he goes on to characterize this distinction as follows:

A distinction of property results from that very protection which a free government gives to unequal faculties of acquiring it. . . . In addition to these *natural* distinctions, *artificial* ones will be founded, on accidental differences in political, religious, or other opinions, or an attachment to the persons of leading individuals. However *erroneous* or *ridiculous* these grounds of dissension and faction may appear to the enlightened Statesman or the benevolent philosopher, the bulk of mankind who are neither statesmen or philosophers, will continue to view them in a different light. (Emphasis added.)

Economic diversity is rooted in nature; religious and other merely opinionated diversity is so littled rooted in reality that it may well appear ridiculous to the wise man, especially when he is speaking to another such in a private letter. From this we can better understand Madison's most important remark in *Federalist* No. 10: "The protection of these faculties [the faculties of men from which the rights of property originate] is the first object of government." It is man's economic life, expressed in his pursuit of property and the inalienable right to the protection of private property, that is paramount in the new republic. Or as Madison also says in *Federalist* No. 10:

A landed interest, a manufacturing interest, a mercantile interest, a monied interest, with many lesser interests, grow up of necessity in civilized nations, and divide them into different classes, actuated by different sentiments and views. The regulation of *these* various and interfering interests forms the principal task of modern legislation, and involves the spirit of party and faction in the necessary and ordinary operations of government. (Emphasis added.)

Madison's argument for the fostering of diversity is by no means, then, an unqualified endorsement of all sorts of diversity. The fostering of diversity is controlled and limited by the fostering of a more basic homogeneity, which is intended to set some rather distinct bounds to American diversity. The liberation of acquisitiveness, the encouragement of the free market for private enterprise, the preoccupation with material welfare and security in this life, are meant to sap some of the vigor of age-old religious, philosophic, and moralistic sources of overweening pride, inhuman fanaticism, and discriminatory strife. Natural human competitiveness, selfishness, and self-assertiveness are not to be repressed or denied, but channeled into peaceful and productive avenues redounding to the benefit of all. It was this spirit or hope that later allowed Thomas Jefferson to express the confident expectation that by the second half of the nineteenth century Unitarianism would "become the general religion of the United States" (Letter to James Smith, Dec. 8, 1822).

The faculties for acquiring property are indeed unequally distributed among men, and hence considerable inequalities in wealth will result; but these inequalities can be prevented from leading to oligarchy or a renewal of traditional class conflict. The access to property is to be opened up as much as possible to all, and tax and inheritance laws (for example, the abolition of primogeniture) are to ensure a considerable redistribution of wealth and of opportunity over the generations. This aspect of the Founders' thought is given unusually bold expression in a famous passage from Noah Webster's contribution to the ratification debates:

> *Virtue,* patriotism, or love of country, never was and never will be, till men's natures are changed, a fixed, permanent principle and support of government. But in an agricultural country, a general possession of land in fee simple, may be rendered perpetual, and the inequalities introduced by commerce, are too fluctuating to endanger government. An equality of property, with a necessity of alienation, constantly operating to destroy combinations of powerful families, is the very *soul of a republic.*"[11]

Yet Webster's statement is *un*representative in the ease or alacrity with which it jettisons reliance on civic virtue. Most of the Federalists and Founders were more uneasy than Webster seems to have been about this feature of their new republican theory. They were troubled by the depressing awareness that the cultivation of commercialism and individualism was at odds with the requirements of public spirit and patriotic devotion. And it was this disquiet that led a number of them back, after the Founding, to the theme of moral and, yes, even religious education. For when they speak of a national university or a new educational policy as a means of "assimilating" the opinions and morals of the new citizenry, they emphasize that they seek not mere sameness, not just homogenization as such, but rather sameness in civic virtue. They feel keenly, in other words, the need to promote actively—through government sponsorship—the growth of specific traits of character in the young: some strength or source of self-transcendence that would enable them to bear economic hardship without whining and undergo military service without flinching; a capacity for judging and deliberating that would prepare them to assume the responsibilities of sober, vigilant, but patriotic political partisans in a country where national and public interests are not overshadowed by the restricted interests of groups.

Not long after the Convention, Thomas Jefferson stressed that "It is the manners and spirit of a people which preserve a republic in vigour. A degeneracy in these is a canker which soon eats to the heart of its laws and constitution."[12] In the years after ratification, the concern that Jefferson expressed came to preoccupy the leaders of the Founding generation more and more. Two especially pregnant utterances may appropriately close our discussion:

> I beg leave to remark, that the only foundation for a useful education in a republic is to be laid in Religion. Without this there can be no virtue, and without virtue there can be no liberty. . . . Such is my veneration for every religion that reveals the attributes of the Deity, or a future state of rewards and punishments . . .[13]

> I have been zealous—I hope I have not been altogether unsuccessful—in contributing the best of my endeavors towards forming a system of government; I shall rise in importance, if I can be equally successful—I will not be less zealous—in contributing the best of my endeavors towards forming a system of education likewise, in the United States. . . . What are laws without manners? How can manners be formed, but by a proper education? The ancient wisdom of the best times did always make a just complaint, that states were too busy with their laws; and too negligent in point of education.[14]

Notes

1. James Wilson, quoted in Randolph Adams, ed., *Selected Political Essays* (New York: Alfred Knopf, 1930), pp. 163–64.
2. Ibid., pp. 166–68.
3. Ibid., p. 164.
4. R. Hofstadter and W. Smith, *American Higher Education: A Documentary History*, 2 vols. (Chicago: University of Chicago Press, 1961), p. 154.

5. Ibid., p. 158.

6. Ibid., p. 177.

7. Ibid., p. 170.

8. Thomas Jefferson, quoted in W. Peden, ed., *Notes on the State of Virginia* (Chapel Hill, N.C.: University of North Carolina Press, 1954), p. 161.

9. Alexander Hamilton, *Federalist* No. 9.

10. Alexis de Tocqueville, *Democracy in America*, trans. G. Lawrence, ed. J. P. Mayer (New York: Doubleday Anchor, 1969), vol. II, part 1, p. 435.

11. Herbert J. Storing, *What the Anti-Federalists Were For* (Chicago: University of Chicago Press, 1981), p. 46.

12. *Notes on the State of Virginia*, p. 165.

13. Benjamin Rush on Republican education, 1798, in Hofstadter and Smith, *American Higher Education*, p. 170.

14. James Wilson in a lecture introducing the study of law, University of Pennsylvania, 1790, in Adams, ed., *Selected Political Essays*, p. 208.

Discussion

ROBERT GOLDWIN: Mr. Glazer refers to the slim base upon which the great diversity of religious, racial, and ethnic groups flourishes in the territory of the United States—the slim base being those very few references to race or religion in the Constitution of the United States. As he points out, a power to naturalize, a prohibition against religious tests for office, provisions having to do with establishment of religion and the free exercise of religion, and the now-obsolete references to slavery, constitute that base. Is that slim base an effective way to preserve diversity without endangering unity?

NATHAN GLAZER: I do not believe it is the sort of approach one can recommend to new nations, with diverse populations, that are writing constitutions. Politically, I suspect it is impossible. Once the nations know about these issues of conflict, they will want to use constitutional law to establish some conditions and protections.

In the American case, the slim base is not the result of the great foresight of the Founding Fathers, looking ahead, seeing all this diversity, and concluding that the less they said about it, the better. They expected the states to take care of those things. As a result the Constitution is very sparse and general and not only in connection with the protection of minorities. The interstate commerce clause is an example; from it we have the enormous mass of regulation, requirements, controls on labor, laws affecting the organization of workers, and the like.

THOMAS PANGLE: I am inclined to disagree a little with Professor Glazer. It is not so much the case that the Founding Fathers looked ahead and saw, or failed to see, great diversity. I think they looked behind and saw terrible religious warfare springing from the worst kind of diversity. The image of that warfare—conveyed to them not only through history but also through the texts of Montesquieu, Hume, Smith, and Hobbes—was an extraordinarily vivid animus behind the American Constitution.

Furthermore, they had had very recent experience with religious quarrels. In referring to the state constitutions, Professor Glazer is right that those were an important part of the experience that the convention looked back to. The most important recent such experience had been the 1780 Massachusetts Constitutional Convention, in which a constitution was drawn up that included an established religion. No other clause caused such animosity, such concern, or such severe debate, both in the convention—at which John Adams, Samuel Adams, and John Hancock were all in attendance—and outside, throughout the hinterland of Massachusetts. It was a tinderbox, and people sensed they were up against something frightening—the possibility of the sort of political scene that had been in the not-so-distant past very dangerous.

From their reading and experiences, the Founders concluded that they must try to create a country where the focus was shifted from groups to individuals—or from religious sects to individuals and families—who would coalesce into diverse groups, through something we could call a free market of ideas as well as of goods. Therefore, the best way to protect a harmless diversity—a genuine but nonsectarian or nonideological diversity—is to cultivate a social arena in which individuals can come together freely, protected by a state but not directed by a state, and from that let grow the spontaneous coalescence of groups, sects, and the like. But it was very clearly understood by the Founding Fathers that to accomplish this, they had to deemphasize the role of religion in the life of the society. Not that they were atheists or against religion, but they were very interested in shifting the focus of human beings' lives from the other world to this world, from salvation to comfortable self-preservation, from theology to science.

It is a remarkable fact that the only reference to rights in the original Constitution is the guarantee of the patent right to inventors. From the beginning technology was thus a central concern in the original Constitution. The Founders wanted to ensure that this would be a country devoted to the cultivation of scientific enterprise aimed at the public good; the Founding Fathers thought this change in the mood, tone, or outlook of the people was fundamental. This object was not, however, something accomplished by writing it into the Constitution. The achievement of scientific innovation is the result of the framework of the Constitution and the reliance on political leadership to guide the country in the right direction.

RUTH BADER GINSBURG: Our Constitution says very little about rights, but I think the spirit of the time is indicated more by the Declaration of Independence than by the Constitution. There we find the famous words, "We hold these truths to be self-evident that all men are created equal, that they are endowed by their creator with certain unalienable rights." The rights were there, but they were natural rights. The Bill of Rights was therefore framed in terms of prohibitions upon government. It does not declare that people have the right to freedom of speech and of press. It says that "Congress shall make no law. . . ." The right, then, was inherent in the human status, and the state was told to leave those rights untouched.

I should add that the three amendments that came after our Civil War are critical to the notions of equality and due process that have dominated the Supreme Court's jurisprudence in the current century. The Court dealt very little with individual rights before the twentieth century and those post-Civil War amendments. In answer to the question that was posed, How can rights be preserved when the Constitution says so little? I think that constitutional review by courts, especially in the context of those amendments, has a lot to do with it.

MR. GOLDWIN: Judge Ginsburg, when we discussed the Indian Constitution, we had an example of a constitution that deals with problems of diversity in great detail; the Indians also have an active court system—perhaps even more activist than ours. But if everything can be done on a slim base—that is, without detail—the question becomes, Is that a more effective way of coping with diversity, or is it better to have it all spelled out, as in the Indian Constitution?

MS. GINSBURG: I don't think these things are transportable. What fits our society is not necessarily right for another society. Every modern constitution is much more detailed than ours. Our kind of document, moreover, would not fit very well with a system that has no judicial review, where the constitution is a set of goals or aspirations at least as far as individual rights are concerned and not positive law enforceable in court.

MR. GOLDWIN: I will pose one more question. It seems to me that in a society where the intention is assimilationist—that is, where the idea is to have as few distinctions as possible and where every individual is considered primarily as an individual as in the United States—by being silent or almost silent about such distinctions, the Constitution is most in accord with that spirit. In contrast, where a constitution dwells on the differences in order to give various groups preferences or guarantees and assurances of representation and protection, the tendency is to emphasize, strengthen, and perpetuate the differences and so is divisive. Whether intentional or not, the unusual silence of the U.S. Constitution may be a way of avoiding these difficulties.

Ms. GINSBURG: I do not think the silences are surprising for an eighteenth-century constitution. In the twentieth century, things are done differently. The UN fundamental rights documents, for instance, include a whole aspect that is totally excluded from our Constitution. We have a minimal statement of political rights, but there are no economic rights delineated, as in the UN document. And some of the constitutions around the world speak of a right to work, a right to housing, and a right to food and the basic necessities of life. None of that is in our Constitution. There are simply different notions of what a constitution is supposed to do and whether they should state judicially nonenforceable goals for society to achieve incrementally.

Meanwhile, I have a question for Dr. Glazer. I see, as a very large problem for the United States toward the end of this century, a large population increase through immigration, not from the traditional source, namely, Europe, but mostly from Latin America. Do we have constitutional means to deal with those problems?

MR. GLAZER: I don't think we have to change the Constitution to deal with that problem. In the end, and even in the beginning, the assimilative powers of American society are very strong. Cubans, for example, have run for the mayoralty of Miami, and we can expect many more Mexican-American and Cuban-American office holders.

I think we should avoid putting too many obstacles in the way of this assimilative power. One such obstacle, for example, is the requirement that federally supported programs aimed at children from families that do not speak English be conducted in the home language. We should not impose that requirement everywhere. It creates new kinds of interest groups and begins to keep the group away from an assimilation they might otherwise undergo. We should not erect divisions where our history suggests they would tend to decline.

Minority groups now have many more rights as groups than they used to have, and we are thus in a more delicate position. In theory, minority groups could conceivably maintain their own language, assert a right to a certain percentage of representatives, or the like. A right inevitably creates an interest. If there is a right to a certain number of black or Hispanic representatives, there will be an interest pushing that right, and the interest becomes stronger as a result. A right to education in a foreign language creates an interest for the teachers who will teach it and the administrators who will run the program. I hope we are less generous with rights where they create the kind of interest that prevents what I think, on the whole, has been a thorough assimilation in the United States.

JOSE SORZANO: I wonder whether Judge Ginsburg, in referring to the increase in the Hispanic population of the United States, really means to describe it as a problem or whether she means to use the terminology used by Professor Glazer that it is a challenge. I came to this country twenty-four years ago, and, like my brethren in Miami, I think we have done rather well in this system because of both the written and the unwritten Constitution of the United States. The way of life has allowed us to move up the social scale of the United States to attain some position of respectability. If that has been the case, it has been so simply because our rights have been protected by the Constitution.

Ms. GINSBURG: I regard the immigration of Hispanics as the greatest challenge we will face this century, because these new groups want to belong to this nation and yet to keep their own culture and heritage. The earliest waves of immigrants from Europe had children who wanted to reject the parents' background quickly and become Americanized. That is not quite so for the Hispanic group, and that is certainly a challenge.

EDWARD BANFIELD: Mr. Glazer's paper lists quite accurately the very considerable diversities that existed in the American colonies at the time of the founding, but I suggest that this diversity was generally overlooked or minimized by the founders. They perceived the American colonies as Anglo-Saxon, Anglo-American, or Anglo-Protestant. In *The Federalist* No. 1, the author congratulates Americans on being descended from common ancestors, having a common religion, and having fought a bloody war together. Americans perceived themselves as a common people at the end of the revolution, and it is of interest, in relation to the chairman's question, that *The Federalist* No. 1 sees fit to play on the unity, rather than on the diversity, of the public.

MR. PANGLE: What Mr. Banfield says about the beginning of *The Federalist* Papers is an important point and supports ideas in Professor Glazer's paper. It is true that after the Revolution Americans did feel themselves very much one people, but I think they felt it was a fragile unity. In *The Federalist* Nos. 7, 8, and 9, for instance, Hamilton conjures up a vision of wars among Pennsylvania, Virginia, and New York—a vision of horrible fratricide. He says, in effect, God forbid that we should ever come to this, but if we fail to do something politically, war will be inevitable. There was a sense of unity at the time, but also a sense of fragility along with it, based on the Founders' deeper understanding of human nature and its antagonistic character.

To disagree somewhat with Judge Ginsburg, I think economic rights were absolutely crucial during the founding period. This is clearer in the Revolution than it is in the Constitution. It is important to remember that the battle cry of the American Revolution was "no taxation without representation"; it clearly involved property rights. That slogan, which of course comes directly out of Locke's *Second Treatise*, is a cardinal article of natural law, according to him. It points to the concern for property rights and the belief that representative government was the best way to protect them. The notion that the courts would protect economic rights emerged quite a bit later.

It is important for our discussion to remember that the Bill of Rights—which also refers to property rights in one way or another—was a list of amendments, not proposed by the Constitutional Convention. In fact, the idea of such a Bill of Rights was opposed in *The Federalist* by Madison and Hamilton. This opposition stemmed from their worry about the role of the courts and the possible loss of popular government. They were also worried that if rights were listed and the list were not complete, people could contend afterwards that if a right were not in the Constitution, it would not be a right. Can rights be written in stone, so to speak? That was part of their worry.

THOMAS FLEINER: One great aspect of the American Constitution is that it established a democracy permitting diversity through the different states. In the French Revolution several years later, the French conjoined democracy with unity. The experience of the French Revolution was much more influential in Europe. From this point of view, then, diversity was an issue in the writing of the Constitution, with respect to the different constitutional systems of the states.

MR. GOLDWIN: On the issue of assimilation versus diversity, there is a way that the two things in the United States seem to me to be compatible. All kinds of ethnic institutions are present in the United States, thousands of foreign-language newspapers and magazines, and school districts where scores of different languages are spoken by the students. And so some preservation of diversity is definitely taking place. But none of it is politically significant, because it occurs in the context of quite rapid, effective assimilation. Both things are therefore possible, as long as diversity loses its political significance, as Mr. Pangle put it much earlier. As Madison explains in *The Federalist*, the way we are constituted has a strong assimilating effect upon people coming from all over the world. They can be allowed and even encouraged to keep these differentiating customs and ways of life, because in the final analysis, they are Americans, just like everybody else.

VOJISLAV STANOVCIC: I have heard that there is a revival of "tribalism" in the United States. How far has this gone, and what are the reasons for this revival?

MR. GLAZER: I think we are past the peak of tribalism, which occurred in the early 1970s. (And I am not sure the word tribalism is right.) What happened was that, in response to the civil-rights revolt, black power, and the self-assertion of Hispanic-Americans, Asian-Americans, and American Indians, some leadership groups among European ethnics tried to get something from government along the lines of what the other groups were getting. They pushed for the passage of an Ethnic Heritage Act, for example.

Another aspect of the revival was that discrimination had declined to such an extent there was no longer an inhibition on expressing ethnic origin. No one would lose anything by saying he is an Italian-American or a Polish-American or a Jewish-American. I do not see tribalism as a major tendency today.

There *is* something of a fundamentalist religious revival in the United States, it is true. But strangely enough, in the 1980s it has a less ethnic character than it had in the 1920s. In the 1920s, American fundamentalism was very clearly the fundamentalism of Anglo-Saxons in the South and the Midwest, and perhaps some other ethnic groups, but it was rather antiforeign and definitely antiblack and anti-Catholic. Today, the fundamentalist revival does not have that character at all. It does not emphasize ethnic character; it emphasizes religious and moral elements and asserts that all groups are welcome to join—and to some extent they do.

DANIEL ELAZAR: What we are experiencing in the United States today is more like what is usually called "life style pluralism," which allows everything in one sense but insists upon the permanency of nothing. It is, in a sense, the ultimate individualism. But in any case, it brings to mind Mr. Pangle's discussion about the tolerance of diversity, as long as it does not have certain kinds of political effects.

There are two particularly important characteristics of this new diversity. One is that it is the least territorial of all American diversities. Earlier diversities were in some respects spread over a variety of territories, but by and large diversity in the United States in the past was more territorial than not, even if not nearly as territorial as European diversities.

The other thing this pluralism points up is the difference between culture and political culture in the United States. In the 1830s, there was a renewed discussion about the need for a common political culture for the United States. This was illustrated most forcefully and perhaps least influentially at the time by Abraham Lincoln in the "Young Men's Lyceum" Address. He was echoing a common theme: diversity is possible, providing the political culture is the same and the civil religion is the same. That remains the most important point to consider in thinking about American diversity: that life style diversities of a wide range—far wider than early Americans might have ever anticipated—are possible. Although it may have seemed for a brief period that the political culture was unraveling, it is clear that it is "rewoven" now. Disintegration is not perceived as much threat to the polity, because all is held together by a shared political culture.

COMMENT: Regarding the dangers of detailed provisions in constitutions versus vague protections, if the Constitution of the United States were to be redrafted at this stage, would express provisions be put in to account for the diversity in population, bearing in mind the experience of the Malaysian, the Indian, and many other modern constitutions?

MR. PANGLE: If the Founders were to come back to life today, I think they would remain true to their original convictions and not invest minorities with rights written into the Constitution. The hope would still be for assimilation into a political culture, as Professor Elazar was saying. Such a political culture is the real glue of the society; it allows great diversity of other kinds of culture, but it serves as the basic rules for the game. It consists of sacred procedures and notions of sacred human rights, and those must remain the central thing, not recognition of the groups constituting society.

3
Communities, Languages, Regions, and the Belgian Constitution, 1831–1985

Jacques Vanderlinden

The Historical Myth

Belgian identity dates back to Julius Caesar (101–44 B.C.) who, in his *Commentaries upon the Wars in Gaul*, divided the inhabitants of Gaul into Aquitanians (inhabiting southwestern France), Belgians (living in the lower countries), and Celts (populating most of present-day France). It is likely that the so-called Belgae (in Latin) were as much Celts as those so-called by the Roman conqueror. That they also included some elements of the Germanic populations also seems certain.

Apart from naming them, Caesar did not provide much detail about the Belgians. He said only, in a terse and famous sentence, that they were the bravest of all the inhabitants of Gaul. From then on the legend grew. And Belgian historians of the nineteenth century, eager to forge a sense of unity in young Belgium, began the process of demonstrating that since the times of Caesar there had always been a Belgian nation. In the forefront of that myth-creating enterprise stood the prominent Belgian historian Henri Pirenne. His views are more and more challenged nowadays, and Belgian regional history is tending to become more fashionable.

"Roman peace" incorporated Belgium into the Roman Empire.[1] After nearly half a millennium of Roman presence, the Celtic elements disappeared almost completely from Belgian culture; and the building of the Roman strategic road from Cologne to Bavai formed the last line of resistance to romanization when the "barbarians" poured into the Empire once the Rhine outposts gave way. As a result, the Cologne–Bavai axis was the first linguistic or cultural border created on what is now Belgian territory, and it corresponds roughly to the present linguistic border.

The invasions and the ensuing fall of the western Roman Empire were followed by the formation of the Merovingian and Carolingian empires. But, in 843, the division of the latter led to the partition of Belgium between two major spheres of influence: France, on the one hand; the Roman-Germanic Holy Empire on the other. At the same time, however, feudalism prevailed throughout Europe, and in Belgium as well. A number of principalities flourished on its territory, among which the most important were (going from the North Sea to the Rhine) the Earldom of Flanders, the Marquisate of Antwerp, the Duchy of Brabant, the Earldom of Hainaut, the Duchy of Limburg, the Principality of Liège, the Earldom of Namur, and the Duchy of Luxembourg. These eight territories were to give their names to the nine provinces of nineteenth-century independent Belgium (Flanders being divided, because of its size, into East and West Flanders). Of these, some came under the French sphere of influence, as the king of France was deemed to be the lord of the local princes (Flanders and Hainaut), while Brabant (and Antwerp, which was at the time incorporated within it), Liège, Limburg, Luxembourg, and Namur paid allegiance to the Emperor. Until the eighteenth century the ruler of Liège was a bishop, conferring on that principality an identity that is still evident today.

Other territorial cleavages were soon imposed on the Belgian provinces. In the fifteenth century, Burgundy acquired Brabant, Luxembourg and some Dutch (in the modern sense of the word) provinces such as Holland, Zeeland, and Friesland. Next to be absorbed, but this time by sheer force, was the principality of Liège. Namur was bought from its bankrupt earl; Antwerp and Limburg were inherited; Luxembourg was bought; and so the center of gravity of the Burgundian "empire," as it could then be styled, moved north toward Brussels, which became its capital in place of Dijon.

The Burgundian territories in the middle of the fifteenth century made up a good deal of Belgium; but the Burgundian heritage was divided after 1487, when Charles the Bold died while trying to add Lorraine to the Burgundian possessions. When Charles V, King of Spain, Emperor of Germany—who had inherited most of contemporary Belgium—organized his empire, he created a new administrative entity known as the Seventeen Provinces, which included Antwerp, Brabant, Flanders, Hainaut, Limburg, Luxembourg, Malines, and Namur, plus a French province, Artois, and eight Dutch provinces: Friesland, Gelderland, Groningen, Holland, Overyssel, Utrecht, Zeeland, and Zutphen. These were the Spanish Netherlands, which never really accepted Spanish rule. They launched a long rebellion, culminating in the independence of the eight Dutch provinces. The present look of Belgium, as differentiated from the Netherlands, began to take shape. But Liège was still out of it and Artois in it. More interesting, perhaps, is the religious cleavage that accompanied the scission of the Seventeen Provinces. Although Catholics and Protestants were united in their opposition to Spanish rule, their resistance was stauncher in the north, where the population was predominantly Protestant.

International politics came to the forefront when the northern provinces (called the United Provinces) entered into an alliance with France against Spain. Spain compromised with both opponents, consenting to a significant transfer of territories to the Netherlands (including the northern parts of Brabant and Flanders) and to France (including Artois, but also including substantial parts of Flanders, Hainaut, and Luxembourg). The northern territorial settlement was to last, but the south was subjected to frequent changes as the European wars began under the reign of Louis XIV. Those wars ended with the transfer of the southern lower countries from Spanish to Austrian rule. In 1789 the combination of the ideas of the French revolution and the unpopularity of Austrian rule led to a short-lived rebellion, mostly in Brussels and Liège; but it was easily suppressed by the Austrians. At that time Belgium was only forty years away from independence and was yet destined to be part of two more countries. First, the Republic armies established French rule beginning in 1792; it was secured by 1794 and lasted until 1814.

The most interesting feature in this period was, perhaps, the loss of autonomy by the Principality of Liège, which was put on the same footing as other parts of the country, although its psychological integration into a Belgian entity was not to be achieved before the 1830 revolution. Second, after the fall of Napoleon, the southern lower countries joined with the former northern part of the region to form the United Kingdom of the Netherlands. This entity, created by the Congress of Vienna, was to last slightly more than fifteen years. In 1830, a revolution led to the creation of Belgium; it started in Brussels but the movement rapidly spread throughout the country. From then on, Belgium existed; but was it, as a famous French historian, Jules Michelet, asked, "an English invention"? Were there signs of a Belgian entity that could disprove the statement of its first King (Leopold I): "Belgium has no nationality and, owing to the character of its inhabitants, shall never have one"?

One thing seems certain: Since the 1789 revolution against the Austrians, the terms Belgian nation and Belgians were regularly invoked to define the region and its inhabitants who lived in the southern lower countries. Thus, the formation of Belgium in 1830 was not an artificial creation of some diplomats around a conference table; its origins can justifiably be traced back at least forty or fifty years earlier, even if, during parts of those years, it was successively incorporated into Austria, France, and the Netherlands.

From 1830 onward, the unitary Belgian state existed, and all efforts were directed toward forging a nation of two communities with no common sociocultural features, no common history, and no "natural" frontiers—all of which are considered the "normal" characteristics of a nation. After 150 years of that nation-building effort, many wonder if it has ever achieved its goal. Four fundamental factors have been involved in the unity-building process: language, ideology, economy, and politics. The latter two have provided a structure, the role of which constitutionalists cannot neglect.

Language and Ideology. Three cultures coexist within Belgium: the Dutch, the French, and the German. Each has its own community and language. The smallest community is that of the German-speaking Belgians living in the province of Luxembourg, to which some 65,000 German speakers were added in 1919 by the Treaty of Versailles. Some twenty years later, they were brought back into Germany for four years, and more than one-third of the males were inducted into the German army. Before the Second World War, however, the position of this population was, to say the least, ambiguous—almost as ambiguous as the policy of the Belgian government. On the one hand, the integrity of most of the local heritage, including the German language, was respected, and no attempt was made to impose the French language. One might wonder, however, whether Belgium had a genuine interest in these marginal populations. One should not forget that the Belgian government considered selling these territories back to Germany in the 1920s, and the idea was apparently dropped only because of the opposition of all those who feared any alteration in the provisions of the Versailles Treaty. A similar ambiguity appeared in the political attitude of the German population: election results, even if they were favorable to the pro-Belgian parties, clearly indicated the vigor of germanophile feelings in the region.

That ambiguity disappeared during the Second World War. When it ended, investigations into unpatriotic behavior were opened, directed against slightly more than one-quarter of the inhabitants of the German-speaking region. But of these, only 10 percent resulted in criminal sentences. This is by far the lowest percentage of such condemnations when compared with other regions of the country. Since then, the German-speaking community, which makes up less than 1 percent of the total population of the country, has consistently demanded the same recognition of its cultural identity as the other communities.

The second community is that of the French speakers. This term must be explained, since there is often confusion between French speakers and Walloons. The latter word originated in ancient germanic languages, which used it to refer to the northern populations of Gaul that had been subjected to Roman influence. One of the resulting local dialects is the Walloon language. The term Walloonia, designating the territory occupied by the Walloons, dates back to the second half of the nineteenth century, when it was used to refer to the romanized part of Belgium. Although many Belgian French speakers have no knowledge of the Walloon language and do not consider themselves part of the Walloon culture, they do share the French language with the Walloons. French has indeed had a major political and cultural influence, not only in the romanized part of the country, but also throughout the centuries in Belgium as a whole.

French political influence was originally manifest in the medieval principalities ruled by the vassals to the king of France; this was the case in Flanders. Its population spoke Flemish, but its rulers spoke French. When feudalism passed, urban aristocracies took over as the ruling classes. Like their predecessors, they also used French. This dominance of French in the area did not end with Spanish rule. It was used in official documents of the period; when the customary laws of the southern Netherlands were put in writing in the sixteenth and seventeenth centuries, in many cases it was done in French, even in regions where the vernacular was Flemish. The eighteenth and nineteenth centuries were the age of supremacy of the French language in Europe. In those centuries, the French language penetrated the bourgeoisie during the Austrian regime and even more so during the French regime. The attempts by William of Orange, the first king of the United Kingdom of the Netherlands, from 1815 to 1830, to eradicate the "aristocratic" phenomenon and to establish Dutch as a national language met with strong opposition among the Belgian elites and failed completely.

Accordingly, in 1830 Belgium came into existence officially as a French-speaking state. The National Congress, which exercised power until the constitution became operational, debated in French; the constitution was drafted and promulgated in French, and legislation was published in French. French was used because it was the language of the bourgeoisie in power and, surely, the international language of the time. Nothing was more "natural" to the constituent than the use of French as an official language. What is more, having one language was considered to be a considerable asset for forging Belgian unity. Thus, there were practical reasons to use French, and its use reflected no hostility toward the Flemish-speaking population. But the attitude of the ruling class was also tainted with an innate feeling of cultural superiority, deriving not only from socioeconomic power (resulting essentially from education and wealth), but also from the inclusion of the ruling class in one of the world's dominant cultures. The French language therefore attracted the "elites," whatever their mother tongues might have been. The identification of the Flemish language with the lower strata of economic, political, and social activities began to cause problems as soon as the Flemish speakers realized the nature of their situation. This brings us to the history of the Flemish movement.

Flemish is the adjective used to refer to the languages (some people prefer to use the word dialects, but unfortunately only in a pejorative sense) spoken in the southern lower countries as distinguished from Dutch, which is used in the northern part of the region, that is, in the contemporary Netherlands. The early development of a Dutch identity following the secession of the northern provinces from the Spanish lower countries in the sixteenth century led in the seventeenth and eighteenth centuries to the establishment of a national written language with a strongly structured syntax and grammar. These developments created what is known today as the common polished Dutch *(Algemeen Beschaafd Nederlands)*. Nothing of the sort took place in the southern provinces, where French was predominant in the ruling circles and in a good deal of the country, since Flemish dialects remained the everyday language of a substantial part of the population.

Under the constitutional principle of freedom in the use of languages (Article 23 of the Constitution), which provides for state intervention by law only in administrative and judicial matters, primary-school education was given in Flemish, and citizens were free to use it unless the law was written to the contrary. The first need to appear in that context was that of providing a uniform spelling for the various Flemish dialects. Associations as well as the government took the matter to heart. Furthermore, in 1840, a petition with more than 100,000 signatures aired some fundamental grievances and sought to show how detrimental the "liberal" attitude of the 1830 Constitution proved to Flemish speakers. The essence of the petition was a demand for official recognition of the Flemish language along with French in the Flemish region. For the first time some fundamental

114

points of the program of the Flemish movement were expressly formulated.

The government first acknowledged the existence of a Flemish problem in 1856. It established a commission "entrusted with the task of examining which measures to adopt for the benefit of Flemish language and literature." The conclusions of the commission were quite moderate and very much along the lines of the 1840 petition. Yet they had little support, the prevalent idea seeming still to be that multilingualism was dangerous for a unitary state. Thus, Belgium nearly reached its fiftieth anniversary before a single step was taken by law to satisfy the grievances of the Flemish movement. In 1873 and 1878, the first laws were passed dealing with the use of Dutch in criminal courts and administrative matters. The new laws followed up on cases in which the accused either had refused to use French or did not understand it. Both defendants had received sentences, in one case, the death penalty.

In 1883 a law was passed requiring the study of the Flemish language in secondary schools located in the Flemish-speaking provinces. It established a teachers' school in Ghent that taught in Flemish, created courses in criminal procedure in Flemish in Ghent and Liège (the court of appeal of Liège had jurisdiction over the Flemish-speaking province of Limburg), and required specific magistrates, civil servants, or teachers in the Flemish-speaking provinces to understand Flemish. In 1886 the Royal Flemish Academy for Language and Literature came into being. In 1891 it was decided that if a case that had been decided in Flemish came before the courts of appeal of Brussels and Liège it had to be judged on appeal in the same language. Finally, from 1898 onward, laws were to be published in the Official Gazette in both languages, although in the event of a conflict the French text would prevail.

Meanwhile, the Flemish movement concentrated its efforts on the use of language in the army (it asked that orders be given in both languages) and in the university (it requested the "flemishization" of the University of Ghent). None of these requests were satisfied before World War I. In fact, none of the reforms of the 1880s and 1890s proved satisfactory to the Flemish movement. They were being made much too late. The adoption of each law provoked a new campaign of demands, and by the time the last of them was adopted the movement had begun to think in terms of linguistic homogeneity in each region.

World War I added a new dimension to the problem when a small Flemish minority openly sided with the Germans; these were the so-called activists. Their activities, encouraged by the Germans, discredited the Flemish cause among the rest of the population. The government, however, wanted to avoid developing an inner opposition during the war and was accordingly inclined to promise equality between the communities when the war was over. As soon as it was, the linguistic problem flared up, during the 1919 electoral campaign. Flemish pressure groups outlined a list of minimal demands, among which were: (1) the introduction of Flemish as the sole language used in education, justice, and administration at all levels; (2) the division of the army into French- and Flemish-speaking units; and (3) the reorganization of the central administration so that matters would be treated in the language of the region concerned. Those demands became reality twenty years later, on the eve of the Second World War. By then, a demand for cultural autonomy had arisen. It was originally quite vaguely defined, but it had a precise objective: the division of the Ministry of Education into two distinct administrations, one for the Flemish- and one for the French-speaking region. This was not realized when the war broke out, but the stage was set for the institutional reforms of the 1970s.

Contributing to this growing division was the fact that the Walloons had not remained inactive; their consciousness only grew in response to Flemish dynamism. The first Walloon organization or congress dates back only to 1877 or 1890. Yet in the southern part of the country there had been people who, since independence, had asked for the union of their region with France. But they were a minority. The majority of the Walloon intellectuals who formed the Walloon movement only reacted to Flemish claims, as they began to see the possibility of a country ultimately governed by the Flemish numerical majority.

Ideology and religion comprise other cultural factors of significance. Statistically speaking, Belgium is a Catholic country. Until the Second World War, more than 90 percent of Belgians were baptized. This is probably not true today, although nominal Catholics still make up a majority of the population. Since no precise figures are available, however, the strength of Catholicism in contemporary Belgium is difficult to assess. One is necessarily limited to indirect means, such as, for instance, the strength of political parties. Using this measure, one could conclude that approximately 45 percent of the population is Catholic, although one should add a percentage of the Flemish nationalist parties and a fraction of the Liberals, assuming that neither Communists nor Socialists would be Catholic (though one cannot be sure). This would bring the total number of active Catholics to around 55–60 percent. Another measure is the strength of the press. The figures available for the numbers of readers of the different newspapers clearly reflect the importance of the Catholic way of thinking. The Catholic press constitutes nearly half of the total Belgian press; an important "undeclared" press makes up one quarter of the total, and the rest are those with liberal, socialist, and communist tendencies, in decreasing order.

The Flemish region is, however, the stronghold of Catholicism. For roughly a century, Catholicism was left to prosper in an essentially rural population, while socialism was active in the industrialized populations of Walloonia. Rural Walloonia—that is, the province of Luxembourg—remained predominantly Catholic, but it is also far less populated than the industrial region of the Walloon industrial basin.

Economy and Politics. For more than a century, Belgians were accustomed to thinking of their economy as national. This is no longer true. And on this matter, the claims of being an ignored minority come primarily from the French speakers. Why?

The picture in the nineteenth century was a fairly simple one: On the one hand, there was an agricultural, Flemish-speaking region; on the other, there was an industrial, French-speaking one. In between stood Brussels, the administrative and financial capital of the kingdom; it provided a basis for a third sector of the economy. For the Flemish-speaking region, the nineteenth century was an era of economic underdevelopment. Its agricultural sector had to compete with foreign imports, fight plant disease, and contend with a low level of literacy among the peasants. The rare industries of the region, all centered on textiles, faced serious crises. One-third of the population of Flanders relied on public assistance to survive in the middle of the century.

By contrast, Walloonia was thriving. Along an axis that extended from Liège to Mons, one of the major industrial powers of the century was developing. It was centered on coal, Belgium being at the end of the century the sixth largest producer in the world. Coal provided a basis for industrial development, and iron, glass, and arms industries flourished in Walloonia. This was coupled with an exceptional development in transportation, especially canals and railways; at the turn of the century, Belgium had the highest density of railroads in the world. Exports of Belgian industrial products and know-how spread from Brazil to China, but all these were essentially of benefit to the French-speaking industrial regions, where the average salary was 25 percent higher than in the other half of the country.

Such matters changed in the twentieth century because of the influence of three factors: The first was the continued development of the harbor of Antwerp as an important trading center. Located in the

Flemish-speaking region, Antwerp was the country's outlet to the world, and its development clearly demonstrated the global impact of Belgium's economy in the nineteenth century. Between 1831 and 1913, the tonnage of ships passing through Antwerp grew more than tenfold and made the harbor the second-ranking in the world after London. The Flemish community had found a center for its economic development, and, therefore, the province of Antwerp had the highest increase in population in the country in the nineteenth century, attracting many of the unemployed from neighboring Flanders.

The second factor was the discovery of the coal fields of Limburg. Oddly enough, this was the result of the efforts of a Liège University professor who saw in his discovery an opportunity for glorifying his university. Quite rapidly, but not before the end of the First World War, the Limburg mines became an essential asset for the Flemish region's industrial development.

As for the third factor, it directly involves the Belgian capitalist community. Confronted with the inevitable decline of the Walloon region as its coal reserves neared exhaustion, industrialists were unwilling to reinvest and modernize their traditional nineteenth-century plants. Quite naturally, they were attracted to the new centers of development in the Flemish region where economic conditions were more favorable. (To mention but one example in a recent period, during the 1970s, industrial investments in the Flemish region were constantly double those in the French-speaking region.)

The economic decline of Walloonia was inescapable, and with it came social evils such as unemployment. The same situation prevailed in Flanders in the nineteenth century. Certain similarities marked the two periods: the earlier Flanders crisis was, at the beginning at least, more easily accepted because the Church provided the people with an ideology of resignation; in the Walloon situation, the socialist presence offered quite satisfactory social compensations for the unemployed. But there was a larger difference as well: the latter situation was viewed with the "neutral" eye of the French-speaking ruling bourgeoisie, which saw the problem as a national issue; the crisis in Flanders provided the manpower for the industrial development of the other part of the country, and the region of Antwerp, where the French-speaking elites ruled. But, by the twentieth century, nationalism had given way to regionalism; thus, the change in the economic situation was no longer perceived in terms of complementarity within a unitary state, but as the domination by one region over the other. This can be explained only by political factors as the state came to play a fundamental role in economic development.

In 1831 when Belgium became an independent nation, suffrage

extended to only a small fraction of the male population. Although existing data are not fully comparable, in 1831, 1.10 percent of the population voted; it reached 23.24 percent in 1919, when universal male suffrage was introduced; in 1949 when there was general, universal suffrage, the corresponding figure was 59.01 percent. Linking these numbers with demographic data leads to the conclusion that the community problem could become an electoral issue only when universal suffrage was adopted. During the entire nineteenth century, this matter was never an issue because the ruling, French-speaking bourgeoisie was firmly entrenched in power through the constitutional structure.

That the majority of Belgians were Flemish speakers had no effect whatsoever on Belgian politics. In the middle of the nineteenth century, the Flemish region included 54.1 percent of the population; at the end of the century, 49.5 percent (most likely because of emigration from the crisis areas to the industrial zones); and around 1950, 53.5 percent. Over the same period, the population of the Walloon region declined, moving from 41.0 percent to 41.9 percent to 35.3 percent (the slight increase at the end of the nineteenth century resulting from the inflow of Flemish migrants). That inflow is, in fact, higher than it appears, because the birth rate in Walloonia was steadily declining in the same period. Thus, the past 150 years have been characterized by regional demographic expansion on the one hand, and by a decline on the other. As soon as the Flemish region offered its population jobs, which prevented migrations, the region became more politically influential. During the nineteenth century the combination of economic and political factors had greatly favored Walloonia.

In 1919, for the first time in Belgian history, a Flemish Nationalist party presented candidates to the electorate; it received between four and seventeen seats in all ensuing elections up to 1939. This represented between 3.04 percent and 8.27 percent of the electorate. There was little change after the Second World War. In the 1949 elections Flemish nationalists reappeared, but without much success. In 1954 they received 2.2 percent of the votes and reached the peak of their popularity in 1971 with 18.8 percent. From then on, it steadily declined as other parties, with more powerful political structures and more elaborate policies in matters other than community problems, adopted the essentials of the Nationalists' platform. Although there was also a *Rassemblement wallon,* it never played a comparable role in the French-speaking region.

More important, perhaps, was the splitting of all the so-called national parties along linguistic lines. This split began in 1968 when one of the three major traditional political parties, the Social Christian party (the heir to the old Catholic party), decided that it would have Flemish- and French-speaking wings. In 1972 the Liberal party had its turn, and finally the Socialist party split in 1978.

These reorganizations and the correlative regionalization and communitarization, have led to a redistribution of political zones of influence. The Flemish Christian party now dominates the Flemish region, while the French-speaking Socialist party has a clear majority in the Walloon region. The Flemish Socialist party stands second in the Flemish region, while the French-speaking Christian party plays the same role in its region. In both regions, the Liberals stand third, but in recent years they have gained credibility by refining their positions, and the possibility exists for them to combine with any of the major parties to form a ruling coalition. The Liberal party has the advantage of being a nonconfessional party, equally divided between the Christian and Socialist ideologies that are dominant in the north (the Flemish-speaking region) and the south (the French-speaking part of the country).

To complete this picture, one must mention the "royal question," which caused a cultural, ideological, and political rift among the communities. It is quite likely that for young Belgians today it has no significance whatsoever, since the younger generation has known only the country's present king and the twenty-five years of his reign, which have been characterized by total unity behind the throne. But, for the previous generation, the impact of the crisis was of primary importance.

King Leopold III was a popular figure until the Second World War; nothing during the first six years (1934–1940) of his reign raised any question about the relationship between the country and its monarch. The king's ambiguous position during the occupation, however, his remarriage, and the fact that, though against his will, he was not in the country when it was liberated, caused roughly half the population to disavow him. The conflict lasted until a referendum was held, resulting in 57.68 percent in favor of the king. Regionally, a "yes" vote was cast by 72.2 percent of the electorate in Flanders and by only 42 percent in Walloonia. From then on, the king was to be "the King of the Flemings," supported by the Christian majority of the country and the Social Christian party, while the Socialist party and the Walloons claimed that Leopold III would never again be their king. In July 1950, the king returned amidst demonstrations, strikes, and riots. Three people were killed in the course of these events and, within a few weeks the king abdicated in favor of his heir, the present king, who was officially enthroned a year later. Peace had come at last, but the crisis left the two communities with bitter feelings, since a minority of the nation had imposed its will on the majority by force.

Brussels: A French-Speaking Population on Flemish Territory

The problem of Brussels is certainly the most difficult one for Belgian constitutionalists.

The territory of the capital includes the agglomeration of Brussels and its nineteen communes. It is located entirely in the traditionally Flemish-speaking part of the country, and all the neighboring communes were originally inhabited by Flemish speakers. But the historical evolution of the original Flemish city—especially the fact that it became, in 1830, the capital of the newly created kingdom—rapidly transformed it into a French-speaking area. In the inevitable argument over what constitutes Flemish or French soil, each party has clung to its own criteria. The efforts of the Flemings have reached the point where questions dealing with languages have been eliminated from the national census; there is thus no official way of defining the language of the inhabitants of Brussels. But all indirect evaluations reveal that approximately 75 percent of the people speak French as against 25 percent who speak Dutch. This imbalance has grown since independence, and should be expected in light of the constant sociocultural pressure on Flemish speakers to adopt the dominant language.

As the capital lost inhabitants, many of whom were moving to the periphery of the capital, the French language slowly but steadily strengthened its grip on the peripheral residential communes. That phenomenon, known in Belgium as the "oil patch," was considered by the Flemish community to be a direct menace to their cultural identity. It resulted in a freezing of the limits of the Brussels capital area and in the absorption of the peripheral communes into the Flemish regions. The only concession to French speakers was to allow French to be used to a limited extent in contacts between the administration and the population in some regions.

The importance of French in the capital and in the consciousness of its French-speaking inhabitants led to the creation of a political party, now in decline, the Front de défense des francophones (FDF). This party met with considerable success some years ago, and at one time could have been considered the major party in the capital. Its platform was essentially local and cultural, preventing the spread of its ideas beyond the limits of Brussels.

Economically, Brussels forms an entity by itself. While the capital includes roughly 10 percent of the population of the kingdom, its share of industrial investments is comparatively low (around 5 percent), as is its contribution to national exports (also around 5 percent). In contrast, Brussels has been taking a slowly increasing share of the gross national product of the country (slightly more than 16 percent). Yet there are regular complaints that the capital does not get a share equal to what it contributes to national production, and that the Flemish and Walloon regions benefit unfairly from the government in terms of investments and spending. These feelings are encouraged by the facts that the constitutional structure of the capital has yet to be defined, and that successive governments have usually preferred to put the problem "in the refrigerator," as one says in Belgian political vocabulary, rather than risk a crisis that could prove detrimental to the interests of Belgians and to those of the two major regions and communities.

Constitutional Mechanisms

The adaptation of the 1831 Belgian Constitution to the ideas that had developed over more than a century of independence took place in three major stages: the constitutional revisions of 1970, 1980, and 1983.[2] Yet it must be underscored that the constitutional adaptation is not yet completed, and more revisions will be necessary in the future.

Communities and Regions. Communities and regions appear in the constitutional revision of December 24, 1970, in Articles 3c, 3b, and 107d. The French, the Dutch, and the German-speaking communities reflect the linguistic and, hence, the cultural divisions of Belgium. In 1970 the communities were called cultural communities; the 1980 constitutional revision dropped the adjective and simply calls them communities. This change reflects the move from a narrow cultural identification of regions to a focus on their wider economic and political characteristics. Creating a corresponding linguistic region for each community would have ignored the problem of Brussels, which stands on the borderline of the linguistic frontier, completely surrounded by Dutch-speaking communities. Thus, four linguistic regions were created in 1970, the first three corresponding roughly to the communities and the fourth being styled "the bilingual region of Brussels-Capital."

The phrase "corresponding roughly to the communities" requires some clarification. The three linguistic regions (the Dutch-, the French-, and the German-speaking) do not strictly correspond territorially to communities, since the German speakers do not have a territory as such. One might say that the legal bonds created among the members of a specific community are personal, while those existing among inhabitants of a specific linguistic region are territorial. This is especially clear in Brussels, where there is a linguistic region but no community. The institutions of the capital are governed by either the Council of the French Community or the Council of the Dutch Community, depending on which community and institution the activities involve. We will come back to this problem of the jurisdiction of community councils.

Finally, some institutions are still considered national or "bicommunitarian," meaning that they simultaneously depend on the two ministries. Some museums are good examples of such institutions.

In addition to communities and linguistic regions, the 1970 constitutional revision established the region. To avoid confusion, it was thought to call the new entities economic or socioeconomic regions; but because these qualifications would restrict regional autonomy the term was left without adjectives to qualify it. There are thus in Belgium both linguistic regions and regions. There are four of the former and three of the latter: the Brussels, Flemish, and Walloon regions. The two sets of regions roughly coincide, though the German-speaking linguistic region is incorporated into the Walloon region, and the area of the bilingual linguistic region of Brussels-Capital does not completely coincide with that of the Brussels region.

The boundaries of these areas result from a variety of legislative enactments. Thus the boundaries of the linguistic regions were defined by the laws dealing with the choice of language in administrative matters, of which the latest was that of July 18, 1966; Article 2 of that law provided for the present borders of the four linguistic regions. These limits can be changed under Article 3b of the revised constitution, but only by a very special majority of the national legislature. Not only is a majority of each linguistic group needed in each house, but the majority of the members of each group have to be present, and two-thirds of the votes cast in each linguistic group must be in the affirmative.

The limits of the nonlinguistic regions result, for the Flemish and Walloon regions, from the provisional law of August 8, 1980, and for the Brussels-Capital region from the law of July 20, 1979, which created *provisional* community and regional institutions. Both laws will likely be superseded, under Article 107d of the constitution, by another which will definitively establish the limits of these regions. Since such a law will have to be subject to the same qualifications as that provided for in Article 3b for the modification of the linguistic regions, the present provisional situation is likely to last for a while, and the "provisional" aspect of these laws should not be taken too seriously.

Finally, the creation of communities, linguistic regions, and other regions has not eliminated preexisting territorial entities recognized by either the constitution or the law. Starting from the wider territorial divisions, altogether different regions existed, beginning in 1962, concerning matters of land planning and urbanization, and beginning in 1970, concerning matters of economic planning and decentralization; they still exist, but are purely administrative and do not involve constitutional problems. Beginning in 1831 there were also nine provinces, which still exist, to which reference was made when today's nonlinguistic regions were defined. Finally, there were urban agglomerations, of which the most important was Brussels; the limits of this urban area do not coincide with those of the linguistic region of Brussels-Capital or of the Brussels region.

The principles for defining the regions of Belgium had to allow for possible exceptions, and there was, indeed, one exception that created (and still creates) much trouble in Belgian political life—the communes of the Voer (or les Fourons, as they are called in French). These six communes, which have been part of the Dutch-speaking region and the Flemish region since 1962 when they were transferred from the province of Liège to Limburg ought to have benefited from Article 1, a4 of the Constitution, which provides that "a law may separate out specific territories . . . and put them directly under governmental authority and place them into a particular status." This modification of the Constitution was adopted on December 24, 1970, and, accordingly, in July 1971, a bill was introduced to bring the communes of the Voer together into one autonomous entity under the direct authority of the government. Later, it was maintained that this would not have affected the inclusion of these communes in the Dutch-speaking linguistic region, but the bill met with considerable and well-founded legal objections from the *Conseil d'Etat* and was never adopted. Thus, no law has yet enforced Article 1, a4, an article that could be applied in places other than the Voer. One thinks immediately of the communes located in the neighborhood of Brussels.

Like many other communes located on the "linguistic border" that separates the various linguistic regions, those near Brussels benefit from a special status insofar as language is concerned; they are commonly called "peripheral communes," "communes with facilities," "linguistic border communes," or, in the Malmedy area next to the German-speaking region, "malmedian communes." The law on the use of language in administrative, educational, or judicial matters either compels or makes possible using a language different from that of the region to which these communes are attached.

The use of language in Belgium is still governed by ordinary legislation, since the changes in the constitution on this matter that were once proposed have been abandoned. The constitutional principle, as laid down in Article 23, is still freedom in the use of language: "The usage of languages in Belgium is optional; it can be regulated only by law and then only concerning acts of public authority and judicial matters." In some cases, the concept of public authority has been stretched beyond recognition, but there is no remedy since it is not possible, under Belgian law, to challenge the constitutionality of a law adopted by the legislature. A very good example of this distortion, before the constitutional revision of 1980, was the requirement that private industrial, commercial, or financial enterprises use the language of the region in which they were located in all "the acts and documents emanating" from such enterprises, and in all "acts and documents imposed by laws or regulations, and those intended for its personnel." This means, for instance, that all commercial books, invoices, statements of accounts, and so on, required by the commercial code had to be in the language of the region where the enterprise was located. One can reasonably contend that such a requirement was within the ambit of "public authority" as that term was used by the constitution drafters in 1831.

Since the constitutional revision of 1980, the contents of Article 23 have been altered slightly in an indirect way through the introduction of Article 59b which, among other things, authorizes the French and Dutch community councils to determine the language used in administrative matters (there was no substantial change in Article 23 concerning this); education in schools subsidized by public money; and in social relations between employers and their personnel, as well as business acts and documents required by law (this constitutionalized the pre-1980 legislative practice). The authority of the community councils, however, was denied over other specific institutions or places, such as national or international institutions, designated by law, where the activity is common to more than one community; services that go beyond the limits of the linguistic region in which the services are established; foreign services or institutions; the bilingual linguistic region of Brussels-Capital; the German-speaking linguistic region; and the communes or groups of communes where the law imposes or allows the use of a language different from that of the region in which they are located.

The use of languages in these excepted institutions or places still comes within the exclusive jurisdiction of the national legislature. The same is true for the use of languages concerning all subject matter not within the ambit of the three above-mentioned fields for which legislative power by decree has been granted to the community councils.

Multicameralism. In post-1970 Belgium there should logically have been six councils in addition to Parliament and its two houses (which have existed since 1831). These would have been the councils for the Dutch-, French-, and German-speaking communities and the councils for the Flemish, Walloon, and Brussels regions, with an executive attached to each. Such logic unfortunately does not characterize the Belgian situation; there are, at present, four councils and five executives.

Before turning to the composition of each of these councils, however, one should note that Article 32b, incorporated into the Constitution by the revision of December 24, 1970, provides for the division of the elected members of both houses of Parliament into linguistic groups, a French-speaking and a Dutch-speaking one for each house. There are, therefore, four of these groups, but there is no German-speaking parliamentary linguistic group. Inclusion in a linguistic group was not left to the choice of either deputies or senators. The law of July 3, 1971, specified that deputies or senators elected in the Dutch-speaking linguistic region would be assigned to that group; those elected in the French- and German-speaking linguistic regions would belong to the French-speaking linguistic group; and those elected in Brussels would be divided according to the language in which they took their oath of office (if they took it in both languages, the first one used would govern).

This noted, one is better able to understand the principles governing the composition of community or regional councils, in light of the fact that there are two community councils, one regional council, and one joint council.

The community council for the French community is composed of the directly elected members of the French-speaking linguistic groups in each house. Since there is no official German-speaking group in Parliament, the twenty-five member community council for the German-speaking community is directly elected in the German-speaking linguistic region. The regional council for the Walloon region is made up of the members of the French-speaking linguistic groups elected for each house of Parliament in the four Walloon provinces, plus those belonging to these groups who are elected in the province of Brabant or by the Senate *and* domiciled in the Walloon region on the date of their election. The Flemish council, which brings together the community and the regional councils for the Dutch community and the Flemish region, is made up of the members of the Flemish-speaking linguistic groups in both houses of Parliament.

The Brussels region has no council and is not referred to, because of the wide political differences on the place of Brussels in the Belgium of tomorrow.

Plans to alter the present composition of the Senate have already been made. When this is done, the community or regional councils will be composed exclusively of directly elected senators.

Each council has an executive body elected by the council members, reflecting an equilibrium among political parties represented, the executive body for the German-speaking community, however, may be chosen from outside the community council "in order to employ a wider basis for the selection" of the executive members. It has been suggested that at some point the executives will be elected on a majoritarian rather than a proportional basis. Each executive body elects a president who must be confirmed by the king. Finally, one cannot be at the same time a member of a community council, a regional executive, and an official of the national government.

The executive body of the Brussels region differs considerably from the other four. As there is no council for the region, its membership is selected from among the members of the national government; it numbers three persons (one minister and two secretaries of state, and at least one of the secretaries must be from a linguistic region different from that of the minister); and all of the members are appointed by the king.

The legislative enactments of the councils are called decrees. Decrees have the force of law, which means that within the jurisdiction of a specific council they may be used to interpret, complete, modify, replace, or abrogate an existing law voted by Parliament. A problem might arise in connection with a decree by the Flemish council under its jurisdiction either as a community or regional institution; this is resolved by an explicit reference in the decree to the article in the constitution that serves as its basis (Article 26b or 59b). The decree must fall within the substantive or territorial jurisdiction of the council that issues it. Thus, one cannot avoid conflicts between decrees on one hand, and national laws on the other, or even between decrees themselves.

Article 107c was included in the 1980 constitutional revision essentially to solve conflicts between the law and decrees or among decrees themselves. It provides for the establishment of the Arbitration Court of which the composition, jurisdiction, and procedures are defined by law. Originally, the court was to be called the "conflicts court," but this seemed too provocative. Thus, despite arguments that confusion would result from the meaning of the word "arbitration" and from the implication that the deciding body would be chosen by the parties, the name was kept. Proposals to adopt the name "constitutional court" were also rejected as evoking the possibility of control of the legislature by a judicial body, which the Belgian legislators have refused to allow since 1831. The court was finally established by the law of June 28, 1983, and formally installed in the last days of September 1984. It has thus just begun to work.[3]

The Arbitration Court is composed of twelve members who must have reached the age of forty. The court must have an equal number of French- and Dutch-speaking judges; half of its membership must be qualified lawyers and half former politicians. The reason for the latter requirement is the fear that the lawyers would confine themselves strictly to legal considerations. The lawyers must have at least five years of professional experience in the Court of Cassation, the Conseil d'Etat, or in university teaching. At least one of the six lawyers and one of the politicians must have a satisfactory knowledge of the German language. The Senate is responsible for presenting to the king a list of twenty-four candidates, from which he appoints the twelve members; each candidate must receive two-thirds majority support from the voting members in the upper house.

The court has two chief justices who preside alternately on an annual basis, each from a different linguistic region. If a case has to be discussed in a language different from that of the sitting chief justice, the other chief justice presides. A "full court" consists of seven members, with one of the two chief justices sitting in all cases and the ten other members serving in turn in accordance with the required balance of lawyers and nonlawyers. In each case the bench, except for the chief justices, changes, and in each case there is parity between French and Dutch speakers, discounting the presiding chief justice. In a case where the unity of case law is at stake, a chief justice may require that the court sit with at least ten members; in such a case, the presiding chief justice casts a vote.

In cases within its jurisdiction concerning conflicting legal decisions, the court may be requested to void any law or decree that contravenes legal or constitutional texts respecting the jurisdictions of the national state, the communities, or the regions. Such actions can be requested only by the Council of Ministers or by the executive bodies of the communities or regions. The Arbitration Court also may be asked by another court to settle a conflict between a law and a decree, or between decrees, prior to a decision by that other court. Thus, access to the court is strictly institutional, and is open only to the government or the judiciary.

Pseudo-federalism. Legally, or even constitutionally, defining communities and regions obviously is not an abstract exercise. It serves a dual purpose in Belgium.

One purpose is to ensure a balanced representation of the different communities. This objective generally is reached through bicameralism and, more specifically, through proportional representation in one house and equal representation in the other. The present Belgian Constitution reflects this principle in some of its articles, but in a manner quite different from the traditional federal scheme.

Article 86b of the constitution, for instance, provides that in every council of ministers there must be an equal number of French- and Dutch-speaking ministers, discounting the prime minister. This provision has a double legal origin: one source is the law of August 2, 1963, which concerns the linguistic qualifications of civil servants and especially higher civil servants. Article 43 of that law provides that, beginning with the rank of director (above which there are, in principle, general inspectors, general directors, and a secretary-general for each ministry), each department has an equal number of French- and Dutch-speaking civil servants. Accordingly, it was thought that if this was the rule for these higher-rank officials, the same should apply to the ministers who head their respective departments and together form the Council of Ministers.

The second legal source of this rule is what Belgian lawyers call "constitutional custom," that is, constitutional practice for which there is no text but which comes into being simply through usage. It is quite difficult to trace the origin of this practice and, as with the establishment of any custom, quite difficult to decide precisely when it became custom. Let us say only that the "customary" character of the provision was obvious to many parliamentarians in the late 1960s.

Subjugation of a specific community is avoided, at least in principle, by requiring qualified majorities or by the device called the "alarm-bell" procedure. The former appears at first in Article 1, a5 which creates a new category of legislation: laws that can be adopted only by a very special majority of Parliament. Until 1970 Belgian legislation included two sorts of laws: ordinary laws voted on by both houses of Parliament, with no specific requirement concerning the nature of the majority, and laws leading to a constitutional amendment, subject to an elaborate procedure under Article 131 of the Constitution. The new category of law can be adopted only "with a majority of votes in each linguistic group of each house, on the condition that a majority of the members of each group are present and that the number of affirmative votes in the two linguistic groups is equal to two-thirds of the total votes cast." The possibility of recourse

129

to this very special legislation appears not only in Article 1, a5, but also in Articles 3b, 59b, 107d and 108 a3. Its purpose is to allay the fears a community might have about possible subjugation in matters not addressed by the constitution. This special legislative procedure has been employed only once.

The same objective of protecting minorities lies behind the so-called alarm-bell provision of Article 38b, which provides that for any law (except budgetary laws and laws already requiring a special majority) that appears to "endanger seriously the relations between communities," at least three-quarters of the linguistic group of either house may require a suspension of the legislative procedure. The controversial text is then submitted for governmental scrutiny, and the executive is free either to consider the observations made or to come back with his original text. Such a procedure can be applied only once by the members of a linguistic group concerning a specific bill. It has never been used to date.

Although the equilibrium between communities is protected by these measures, it is essentially because when the constitution was adopted in 1831, the bicameral national legislature, consisting of a House of Representatives and a Senate, was not designed to solve problems resulting from the federal character of the state; Belgium was then, and would remain for at least 125 years, a unitary, centralized state. The Senate was conceived as a conservative (some prefer reflective) assembly. Reforming the Senate along federal lines— that is, trying to ensure a numerical equality of some sort—might result in the elimination of some of the present safeguards for minorities (that is, the super-qualification of majorities for the adoption of some sensitive laws and the "alarm-bell" provision). Changing the Senate is, in fact, contemplated, but not along these lines. Current plans call for a complete correspondence between community and regional councils and the Senate; the latter would be composed of the sum of the former. But nothing more has been defined, and it is clear that the problem of Brussels must be solved first.

The second objective that was pursued when communities and regions were defined was to entrust them with some of the specific powers of the national state in a centralized structure. This was achieved by giving each council a jurisdiction of its own. The community councils have three fields of governmental action within their jurisdiction: cultural matters, linguistic matters, and personal matters.

Cultural matters. Cultural matters may be divided into cultural matters per se, education, and cooperation. The laws of July 21, 1971, and August 8, 1980, defined cultural matters broadly and gave the community councils authority in seventeen areas that had been under the jurisdiction of the national legislature: (1) defense and illustration of language; (2) encouragement of research training; (3) fine arts; (4) cultural heritage, museums, and other cultural scientific institutions; (5) libraries and similar institutions; (6) radio and television, with the exception of publicity; (7) youth; (8) permanent education and cultural activity; (9) physical education, sports, and outdoor activities; (10) leisure and tourism; (11) preschool education; (12) secondary education; (13) artistic education; (14) intellectual, moral, and social education; (15) social promotion; (16) professional follow-up and reconversion; (17) scientific research if applied to any of the former. Exceptions to this list include criminal legislation dealing with the protection of youth; economic legislation concerning the publishing or cinematographic industry; organization of some national museums or research institutions; and regulation of some sporting activities such as boxing or antidoping measures.

Educational matters were not fully defined in the law but, again, specific exceptions were listed, including the control of school attendance, education curricula, degrees, school funding, teacher salaries, and school population. These exceptions leave little authority to the community legislature; its main task seems to be the enforcement of measures adopted at a national level.

As for matters of cooperation, they can be divided into two fields: cooperation between the communities and international cultural cooperation. Of these, the latter is the most important for our purpose since it led to a major issue, the treaty-making power of the community organs. Under Article 68 of the Constitution, the treaty-making power in Belgium rests with the king, but the national legislature must give its assent. Since that article has not, as yet, been revised, the law of August 8, 1980, should not have been able to grant the community councils the power to assent to treaties, nor to confer treaty-making power on the executive body of each community. But that is what it did. The Counseil d'Etat believed this was an unconstitutional measure, though some lawyers who were constitutional experts consulted by the government did not.

Linguistic matters. Under a3 of Article 59b of the Constitution, the community councils have been granted exclusive jurisdiction in a general major area: the regulation of the use of languages for administrative matters, education, and social relations between employers and employees, as well as documents required of enterprises by law. This is a strictly defined jurisdiction and, accordingly, the national legislature retains jurisdiction over all other matters, such as judicial and military matters. In practice, the area defined in Article 59b already had been limited through various laws dealing with either

131

administrative or educational matters. The basic laws did not seem to raise many issues except concerning the legal documents required of enterprises. These normally are commercial documents or documents required by social legislation.

The problem of jurisdiction over linguistic matters was brought to the forefront when the Dutch Cultural Council, on July 19, 1973, adopted a decree stretching many legal notions far beyond their normal meaning. The most blatant example was the inclusion of the phrase "all relations between the employer and private or public institutions which originate in labor relations." More subtle, but just as extensive, was Article 3 of the decree stating that by "social relations" one must understand all "individual and collective contacts, orally or in writing, between employers and employees, provided they have a direct or indirect connection with employment." This means that in the Flemish region no language other than Dutch could be used in any contact between an employer and his employees, even if the employee is a foreigner: this is difficult to enforce, but such proposals to change that provision have not yet been adopted, and the Court of Cassation has confirmed that all documents or acts in contradiction to the decree as it now stands are absolutely void.

Personal matters. Finally, personal (the word is a poor translation from the French "personnalisable," that which may become personal) matters also fall within the jurisdiction of community councils as a result of Article 59b, par 2b of the Constitution. The "special" law of August 8, 1980, has defined these matters as follows: policy concerning the dispensation of medical treatment, health education, and preventive medicine; familial policy, social aid, assistance to and integration of immigrants, assistance to handicapped persons and old people, protection of youth, and social aid to prisoners and former prisoners; and in the field of applied scientific research, all matters specified in their exclusive jurisdiction.

This provision led recently to a conflict between the French community and the national government. A decree issued by the former implies, in a carefully (but perhaps ambiguously) drafted article, that abortion is authorized within the French community, though it is still an offense under the national penal code. There has been much argument as to the precise scope of the decree and whether it conflicts with national legislation. Consideration has been given to submitting the decree to the Arbitration Court.

Finally, the community councils have jurisdiction, in personal matters, over all problems of cooperation between communities and of international cooperation; as far as the latter is concerned, the same problems arise here as in the area of cultural matters where conflicts with the national treaty-making power may be possible.

The regional councils have within their jurisdiction ten fields of governmental action. But their jurisdiction covers only specific aspects of this area: land use and planning; environment; nature preservation and rural renovation; housing; water resources; economic policy; energy; policy toward subordinate institutions; employment; and applied research. The regional councils have no jurisdiction whatsoever concerning international agreements even if their purposes fall within the regional council's jurisdiction.

Conclusion

Where is Belgium headed in the next decade, and how will the 1831 Constitution—once a "model" European constitution—look when the present process of revision ends? At this stage of the venture, it is still quite difficult to say.

First, it is likely that there will be a greater transfer of jurisdiction to the regions from the national government. Among the areas being considered for decentralization are education and cooperation with developing countries. This means a growing federal system in which the powers of the national institutions will decrease. It also could mean greater clarity since at present there are delicate borderlines defining the respective jurisdictions of the state, the communities, and the regions. Any resulting problems in budgetary allocation and the transfer of personnel will not necessarily be easy to solve.

It is even more difficult to predict the direction the institutions of Brussels-Capital will take. Given the present context of antagonism between the communities, the only solution that seems acceptable, because of its apparent neutrality, would be to place some territories under the direct rule of the national government. But doing so would mean the end to any cultural and political autonomy for the capital, leaving strictly administrative and subordinate powers to the agglomeration. The economic region of Brussels could remain as it is now, provided there is a true will among the three communities to let it apply its economic and social development to benefit its inhabitants, whatever their linguistic regime.

The most sensitive point, however, would be the status of the capital's peripheral communes. They have been the permanent arena of linguistic conflicts, which always concern the use of French as the administrative language. The regular increase in the French-speaking population in these suburban communes, where in some instances it is more and more difficult to consider it a "minority," is a constant factor of irritation for the Flemish community, which tends, as in Brussels, to make "the rights of the soil" prevail over those of persons. Linked to this fundamental problem is the problem of "national" institutions, such as Brussels International Airport, the manpower of which tends to be, because of its location in the Flemish region, exclusively Flemish speaking. This is strongly resented by the French-speaking users of these "national" facilities.

The legal (or even the constitutional) remedies to these problems are often far from effective, and much depends on factors over which the citizen has no control. One is even tempted to believe that the government itself does not wish to tackle these issues. In a period of acute economic crisis there is a strong temptation to shelve institutional problems and to concentrate on fighting unemployment and promoting productivity. Belgium, like many other countries in Europe, is currently waging an economic war, and the administrative difficulties of the communities and regions are not among its priorities. A vital role is now entrusted to the Arbitration Court. Because it has delivered only one ruling, it is difficult to know if it will be as ineffective as some predict, or if instead a leader will appear among its members and shape it into the fundamental institution which it is designed to be.

Notes

1. Throughout this section the word Belgium is used to identity the present Belgian territory, although the word itself was probably not then so used; if it was used, it did not represent anything equivalent to what it means today.

2. The first one led to the law of December 24, 1970, modifying Articles 1, 108, and 132 of the constitutional text and introducing into it Articles 3b, 3c, 32b, 38b, 59b, 59c, 86b, 91b, 107d, and 108c. These constitutional changes were completed by two ordinary laws, those of July 3 and 21, 1971. In the three constitutional amendments of July 17, 27, and 29, 1980, Articles 3c, 28, 59b, 108, 110, 111, and 135 were altered, and Articles 26b and 107c were introduced into the constitution. Two ordinary laws of August 8 and 9, 1980, completed the task. Finally, the constitutional revision of June 1, 1983, modified Article 59c, while an ordinary law of December 31, 1983, organized the institutions of the German-speaking community and that of June 28, 1983, organized the Arbitration Court. That legislative activity resulted in changes in other laws, among them the *Conseil d'Etat*, which was modified on January 12, 1973.

3. The Arbitration Court has just delivered its first judgment on a conflict between national laws and regional decrees. For the first time, French-speaking parliamentarians have taken advantage of the "alarm bell" proviso against a law, which in their view was detrimental to their community. Everyone is awaiting the reaction of the government.

Commentary

Jean-Pierre De Bandt

Belgium presents the case of a nation troubled by conflicting relations between its two primary communities, the French-speaking Walloons and the Dutch-speaking Flemish. Although it is a unitary state built on the principle of bilingualism, the diversity of language and culture has divided the country into two increasingly distinct parts, each jealously seeking to preserve and enhance its separate identity. The alienation and antagonism between these two communities have begun to grow so deep that the schism threatens the very existence of the country.

Jacques Vanderlinden has provided an excellent summary of the Belgian constitutional system, its background, and its general framework. For the constitutionalist and the sociologist, Belgium is a particularly interesting case study. Revisions to the Belgian constitution since 1970, and more particularly in 1980, have moved Belgium from a highly centralized and unitary state toward political regionalism (with two component units) based in part on federalist organization.

Essentially, the changes provide for Flemish and Walloon regions and for Dutch-speaking and French-speaking communities. Brussels is made into a bilingual region with its own communities for each language group. Each region and community has been granted its own rule-making bodies, whose decrees have the force of law. Because the constitutional amendments were not self-executing, a law was enacted in 1980 to apply the contemplated changes. By the terms of this law, the Flemish region and the Dutch-speaking community were merged, with rule-making powers conferred to a Flemish council and a Flemish executive. The Walloon region and the French-speaking community remained separate, with each possessing a council and an executive. The status of Brussels was not addressed. To provide for the resolution of conflicts that could arise in the respective jurisdictions of each organization, a subsequent law established the Arbitration Court.

This commentary is a critical assessment of the new structure described by Vanderlinden. It reviews the content of the constitutional reform and examines the causes of the growing discontent with the system hastily adopted by the Belgian Parliament in July 1980. More particularly, it attempts to compare the principles of the existing Belgian system with some of the basic principles and concepts found in the classic European and U.S. federal systems.

Difficulties arise, however, in attempting to determine what, precisely, federalism is. Reference to the constitutions of those countries usually deemed to be genuine federal states (that is, the "classical" federal states: Australia, Austria, Canada, the Federal Republic of Germany, Switzerland, and the United States) shows that an exact definition, if possible, would be difficult. There are as many variations as there are applications. Certain striking characteristics and fundamental principles, however, are common to all. Although federalism should be seen not as a static, fixed, or immutable structure, but rather as a dynamic design that allows for certain variations and gradations according to the individual and changing needs of the states concerned, we will nevertheless highlight some basic characteristics and compare these with the Belgian system.

This analysis starts with a brief reminder of the historical background.

The 1831 Belgian Constitution, widely heralded as the model upon which the constitutions of other newly emerging European states should be based, and itself modeled on French notions of liberalism and constitutional monarchy, gave Belgium a distinctly unitary and majoritarian character. After the split with the Netherlands, almost all political efforts were directed toward creating a single state from the two communities. Because the Walloon community so completely dominated Belgian political life, it was only natural that the new state was from the very beginning unitary in character, with French as the sole official language. Continuing encroachments of the French language in government, business, and academic life occurred, with the result that the ethnic duality of the country became well hidden. During the latter part of the nineteenth century, however, the unitary character of Belgium, which had suited the interests of the French-speaking majority particularly well, began to be attacked by a Flemish community increasingly aware of its distinct identity and resentful of attempts by the French-speaking community (including the French-speaking members of the Flemish community) to suppress the Flemish language. When in 1898 both

French and Flemish were legally recognized as official national languages for parliamentary legislation, some members of the Walloon population, seeing that Flanders (the region inhabited by Dutch-speaking Belgians) would eventually become officially Flemish-speaking and fearing that the Walloon community would lose its hegemony over the whole of Belgium, began to call for administrative separation of the country. Between the two world wars, when Flanders did become officially Flemish speaking, these calls for administrative separation were joined by similar calls from the Flemish community. After World War II, however, the Flemish movement, severely weakened and paralyzed as a result of collaboration with the Germans by an active minority during the occupation, became for several years an almost nonexistent force in Belgian politics. The Walloon movement, taking advantage of this weakness, saw its own political fortunes greatly increase. Because the unitary system provided certain advantages (not the least of which was economic, given the depressed state of the economy in the Walloon region vis-à-vis that in the Flemish region), the Walloon community as a whole lost interest in the idea of administrative separation for Belgium, although a Walloon National Congress in 1945 had declared itself in favor of a federalist Belgium. It was not until the early 1960s, when the Walloons lost their political majority, that the idea of regional autonomy once again began to take hold in both communities.

In a country where sovereignty rests with the central government, nearly all decisions affecting the people's daily lives are made at the national level. Tocqueville noted that a central power, no matter how enlightened or wise it may be, is bound to give its laws a uniform character that does not fit the diversities existing within a nation; the people are obliged to bend to fit the legislation because the legislation is unable to adapt itself to the needs of the people. The perception of having no voice in the determination of policies affecting their living conditions may lead the people to believe that they are being excluded from the political process, causing frustration and dissatisfaction. It is in this context that regionalist sentiment and the pressure for regional autonomy in Belgium must be seen.

Because of mounting dissatisfaction over what is widely perceived to be the unitary system's inability to deal effectively and fairly with the unique desires and needs of each community, some change has been called for. While the belief is widely held that the government can no longer function purely on the national level, there is little agreement as to what form any eventual change should take.

The recent constitutional revisions demonstrate a recognition that problems do exist and that changes are needed. The actions taken, although inadequate, do at least show a willingness to try to solve the problems. Unfortunately, the changes that have been effected are extraordinarily complex and confusing and tend to treat the symptoms rather than the problems. It is likely, in fact, that they have merely set the stage for further divisions between the communities and for an eventual move toward separatism.

Where, as in Belgium, two or more groups share common values or interests, but are not ready for complete integration, a federal system would seem to be the solution. But a federal system can work only where there is a carefully considered balance between the desire for unity and the desire to ensure preservation of each group's separate identity. Where the balance is not maintained, either the federal system becomes unitary, or federalism leads to separatism.

What has emerged from the constitutional revisions appears to some to be a growing federal system, but is in reality a structure only nominally organized along federal lines that neglects to incorporate the principles embodied in federalism. It is a shell that, while possessing certain characteristics of a federal system, lacks the foundation on which federalism is built. The primary faults lie in the manner in which power is now distributed and in the differing status of each of the governments.

If the essence of federalism is power sharing, then the central question to be asked of any federal system is whether it is conducive to cooperation or to conflict. Thus far the new Belgian system lends itself more to conflict than to cooperation.

The Federalization Process

Federalism, as mentioned earlier, possesses a dynamic character that allows the structure to change as the needs of the states change. It is therefore as much a process as it is a structure. This fact has led a number of commentators on constitutional systems to assert that what differences there may be between decentralization and federalism are differences not of nature, but only of degree (that is, that decentralization is diluted federalism and that federalism is overdeveloped decentralization). Hence, these constitutionalists see federalism as both the process by which individual political units enter into arrangements for making joint decisions on common problems and, conversely, the process by which a unitary state becomes decentralized into separate and distinct political units. Social reality tells us, however, that federal structures are usually brought forth by some process of centralization and not by decentralization.

Belgium is trying to do the reverse—to convert a highly centralized system into a federal state. But noncentralization, not decentralization, is essential for federations.

With decentralization—and this is what makes experiments in regionalism so difficult—there is a natural tendency of the central government and bureaucracy to retain ultimate control over what has been decentralized, with the implied power eventually to recentralize what has been decentralized. With a longstanding tradition of central control and authority over the local governments (those of the provinces and municipalities), those in power at the center find it difficult to accept a genuine and appropriate division of powers.

The habits of centralization are so deeply rooted in the political thinking of the existing political establishments that the newly created Flemish and Walloon regional governments and their respective administrations have adopted a new centralized—and in a sense more centralized—system that leaves no room for delegation of competence to the provinces and municipalities.

The classic federalization process (those in the United States, Switzerland, and the Federal Republic of Germany) typically begins as a union of independent states joining together first in confederation and then in federation. The route toward federalization from a highly centralized state is a much more difficult process. In Belgium, the absence of a federal tradition, the lack of experience, the weight of a centralist tradition, and the self-defense instincts of politicians and bureaucrats all combine to make the task of federalization formidable, demanding, and hazardous.

The Territorial Link. An important aspect of federalism is that it is a union of political organizations, usually states, united by one or more common objectives or designs, bound by common values, interests, or beliefs, but conserving the distinctive characters of each organization. The important feature that sets federalism apart from regionalism or other forms of decentralization is its territorial link. Federalism unites without destroying the individuality of those uniting and consists of organized cooperation of territorial units.

All federal states are composed of territorially defined groups. Member states (for example, Länder, cantons, states, or provinces) are geographically defined areas.

Most federal systems are also organized so that territorial units cut across cleavages of language, religion, or class. Switzerland is an excellent example of a federal system based on such cross-cutting cleavages, where four lines of cleavage (language, religion, class, and cantonal affiliation) cut across each other so that separate coalitions come to be formed on different issues. In Canada, by contrast, cleavages tend to be self-reinforcing and were at one point in its history a source of conflict and a danger for separatism.

The Belgian situation is, on the whole, more akin to the Canadian than to the Swiss. The division between the Flemings and the Walloons is reinforced by the boundaries of the regions and their institutions. Cleavages other than language tend to reinforce the division. Flemings are traditionally Catholic, while a majority of Walloons are not. Flanders has traditionally been more conservative with a strong farmers' lobby *(Boerenbond)*, while Walloonia is traditionally more socialist with a greater concentration of such heavy industries as coal and steel. Unfortunately, these three traditional cleavages in Belgium (Catholic–non-Catholic, Flemish–French, and liberal–conservative) do not cross geographic boundaries.

A second feature of the Belgian system is striking. As explained by Vanderlinden, in addition to territorial division into three regions, there is a further division of the country into three communities, the French-, the Dutch-, and the German-speaking communities.

Originally, in 1970, these communities were expressly called cultural communities. Communities do not correspond to a linguistic region. They are political authorities having personal (and not territorial) jurisdiction over citizens in cultural matters. Vanderlinden has explained in detail how these communities are organized and what jurisdiction they have. It is sufficient to point out at this stage that the mere existence of communities, apart from territorial units, is a striking deviation from classic federal principles. Superimposing territorial jurisdiction on personal jurisdiction creates conflicts and problems that are not easily resolved.

The Distribution of Power. Another exclusive characteristic of a constitutional system that purports to be federal is the presence of an explicit division of power in the constitution. Of course, there is no standard formula, and each division of power (some have named it distribution of authority or distribution of competences) varies from country to country in manner, content, and scale. This is so because each division will necessarily depend on what is advisable and relevant in a given political setting at a particular moment in time. But however the division is effected, a division there must be.

The federal constitutions contain catalogs of authority wherein are listed those functions and tasks assigned or transferred to the central government and those that remain with the states. Hence, clauses list what a central government can do, or what state governments can do, or what neither one nor the other can do, or what both can do. If there are no such clauses, then, to the extent decentralist practices animate the political system, there is no federalism.

One generally considers that there are two ways to divide power: vertically (exemplified by the federal constitutions of Australia, Canada, and the United States), in which wide legislative powers over a large area of policy making are shared, with clear-cut divisions of responsibility; and horizontally (the model adopted by Austria, the Federal Republic of Germany and, to a lesser extent, Switzerland), based on a division of functions, with legislative power remaining predominantly with the central government, but executive powers being transferred.[1]

The new Belgian system is conceived according to the vertical model of federalism (with a number of exceptions, including financial investment incentives, operational permits, and public health). The premise behind the Belgian division of power seems to be that a clear-cut division of responsibility for different areas of policy can and should be established. At least this is what some politicians have advocated in order to improve the present failing and unclear system of division of powers.

It is highly doubtful, however, whether it makes much sense to divide powers in this way because modern government has little place for watertight compartments of competences. Modern government, with its emphasis on the welfare state, places a strain on traditional concepts of division of powers. Political life simply cannot be perfectly or permanently compartmentalized. However ingenious constitutionalists may be in describing a division of powers, their words can rarely be more than approximate. They cannot anticipate what meanings will be given (for example, to "interstate commerce" and "general welfare" as found in the U.S. Constitution) or to what uses their words will be put (for example, "power to tax"). They cannot anticipate new political demands (such as quality-of-life issues) or whether these demands will be dressed in a new language (such as ecological and environmental policy).

In Belgium, draftsmen have created new words and concepts that so far have produced extensive literature in an attempt to find clear definitions. "Matters related to the person" (*persoonsgebonden materies* in Dutch and *matières personnalisables* in French— the French translation being far removed from the Dutch), which fall within the exclusive competence of the regions, will never be properly defined. Wars of lawyers and historians will not settle the matter.

It could be argued that, given the political, economic, and cultural complexity of Belgium, the horizontal model of federalism (that is, the transfer of executive powers) would be more suitable than the classical division of legislative powers, for the horizontal model explicitly recognizes the interdependence of different levels of government.

The horizontal approach can also be combined with the constitutional notions of skeletal law *(Rahmengesetz)* or basic law *(Grundsatzgesetz)*. This method has been successfully used in Austria, in the Federal Republic of Germany, and in Switzerland.

Belgium has a similar tradition in its unitary constitutional system whereby basic laws are voted on by Parliament, and implementation is accomplished through the executive. In the federal framework, perhaps this tradition could be suitable if adapted for two or more levels of government.

Adaptation and Cooperation. In a federal system, adaptation is vital. The delimitation of powers to be transferred to the state level is *not* the main problem for the designer of a federal constitution. The main problem is power sharing. Power sharing depends on two factors: first, how the system can be shaped to ensure its continuous adaptation to change; and second, what the likelihood is of agreement between the states and the central government.

Adaptation. No two federal systems have used the same technique to accommodate change. Federal relations by their very nature are fluctuating relations. The federal concept should be placed in the concrete world of facts rather than in that of constitutional theory.

Federalism is a dynamic process, and all federal states have designed techniques to allow for changes and adaptation. This is generally achieved by a flexible system of constitutional changes (Austria, for example, has had more than 300 changes in less than a century; Switzerland more than seventy since the end of World War II). Other federal countries have a constitutional court (such as the United States Supreme Court or the West German Constitutional Court) that adapts through interpretation.

Belgium lacks any technique to adapt its constitutional framework easily. As Vanderlinden explained, any constitutional change is subject to a particularly burdensome procedure involving special majorities, which are unavoidable in a federal state composed of just two regions. Since 1830, the constitution has been modified only four times. Moreover, the Belgian constitutional framework does not provide for a constitutional court that would allow for a smooth adaptation to changing circumstances.

Cooperation. Power sharing must be effected not only through constant adaptations, but also through constant cooperation between the states and the national government.

Federalism requires a cooperative relationship between and among individual states and between individual states and the national government. The result is that most areas of policy—and certainly those involving social welfare—involve national, state, and perhaps even local levels of government simultaneously. One of the characteristic features of modern federalism is the interdependence of participating units combined with the need for cooperation, with solidarity the result. In general, the extent of the powers it is possible to transfer to a state depends on the degree of consensus between that state and the center. The greater the agreement, the greater the powers that can safely be transferred.

The need for interdependence, solidarity, and reciprocity is at the base of various models for the transfer of power. The main purpose of transfers is to reduce financial inequities among the territories. A second purpose is financial adjustment to correct unequal social conditions in individual states.

Interdependence will normally rely on a number of techniques. It is important that states be given considerable influence over primary legislation, including, where constitutionally possible, influence over prelegislative actions. Hence a Senate in which states are represented exhibits the so-called interlocking principle, securing political representation of the states at the center.

Intergovernmental negotiations between ministers and officials have become an accepted feature of most federal governments (except in the United States), playing a particularly important role in Canada and West Germany. Such negotiations often reveal vertical links between levels of government, which cut across horizontal allegiances. A federal minister of education, for example, might find that he has more in common with regional ministers of education than with other federal ministers.

In the Belgian system there are no built-in mechanisms to organize cooperation and solidarity: first, there is no regional representation in the parliamentary system; and second, there are no procedures developed for the conduct of intergovernmental negotiations. Nor is there any mechanism that ensures that transfers of power equalize economic or social conditions. This lack of unifying procedures should probably be expected in a system in which regions must focus on resolving conflicts rather than on establishing common regional policies.

Proper Income Sources. There is an impressive unanimity of views among constitutionalists that in federal states each level of government should finance its own expenditures with its own resources. Taxing power cannot be separated from spending power. The actual distribution of taxing powers shows a wide variety of approaches. Therefore, it is not possible in the framework of this limited analysis to describe the various systems in use in federal states. It will suffice to note that the tendency during recent decades has been to centralize collection without touching the principle of individual resources.

In this respect the Belgian system is different. The resources of the regions are transfers from the national budget. The distribution is based on a complicated formula in which population plays a key role. Curiously, the only tax that is regionalized is the estate tax, which is the result of a complicated compromise involving the steel industry. Though the estate tax is collected by the national government, it belongs exclusively to the regions, including the Brussels region (which technically is not a separate region in the federal system).

The Supremacy Clause. All federal states have adopted implicitly or explicitly the principle of supremacy of federal law over regional law. As regards any given question, it is clear that the law must speak with only one voice.

Federalism is basically a distribution of powers and competences. Because it has not been possible to find convincing general criteria to justify a strict distribution of competences, conflicts inevitably arise between different levels of government regarding the exact delimitation of competences. This is so in all cases and not only, as some have suggested, in cases of concurrent or parallel competences. Hence the need to establish a hierarchy that will allow any conflict of competences to be adjudicated properly.

The United States has solved the potential problem by providing in Article VI of its Constitution a "supremacy clause" under which national laws enacted pursuant to the Constitution shall enjoy legal superiority over any conflicting provision of a state constitution or law. The constitutions of the other classic federal states contain similar provisions.

The Belgian system, neither federal nor unitary, is in this respect different from all other federal systems. Each of the constituent units of a federal state must enjoy absolute equality of legal status within the federation. Accordingly, the two regional governments have been placed on equal juridical footing. But the two regional governments have also been placed on an equal juridical footing with the national government! Thus there is no hierarchy. What results is a system in which regional laws and decrees have the same juridical force and value as national laws and decrees. The problems inherent in this sort of arrangement are obvious and will surface every time a law or decree of one government conflicts with a law or decree of another.

This striking difference from any other established federal system can easily be explained—but not necessarily approved—in view of the special relationship between the two regions. Flanders carries a majority vote in Parliament (both chambers), and the francophone minority saw a danger in having a national norm overrule a Walloon regional decree.

Representation of Member States' Interests. Another essential feature of federalism is the use of the interlocking principle, which secures political representation of the member states at the center. In a well-organized federal state, national politics has to be seen not as a self-contained sphere of competence and action, but as a forum for the resolution of territorial matters and conflicts.

The most common way of securing representation of member states' interests at the center is through a senate or second house. The senate represents the interests of member states in almost all federal systems, with Canada being the most notable exception (though the Canadian Senate was originally conceived as a chamber representing provincial interests). The member states may be represented in the senate either on the basis of parity (as in the United States and Switzerland) or population (as in the Federal Republic of Germany and Austria). The representatives of the member states can be chosen by popular election (the United States and Switzerland, except for the canton of Berne), by the provincial parliament (Spain), or by the government of the state (the Federal Republic of Germany).

In Belgium, there is no state representation whatsoever in the Senate. The composition of the Belgian Senate has not been modified by the constitutional reform of 1980, and the Senate functions as before: all acts of Parliament are reviewed and approved by the two houses. Senators are elected—as are members of the House of Representatives—during general elections.

It has been claimed that a senate representing the two member states would present no advantages. The risk is indeed great that equal representation of two linguistic groups would enhance confrontation and conflicts. The proper representation of Brussels, with its status of being bilingual and a region in its own right, would also be a problem.

The Court Organization. Federal court systems fall into one of the following three categories: (1) exclusive federal jurisdiction; (2) parallel jurisdiction; or (3) a combination of member-state jurisdiction with central superior courts. Exclusive federal jurisdiction is by and large the case in Argentina, Austria, Malaysia, Pakistan, and Venezuela, whereas parallel jurisdiction is typical for the United States. In all other federal states, the administration of justice is a member-state concern. Federal superior and supreme courts guarantee a uniformity of the application of the law throughout the country. This is in essence the situation in Australia, Brazil, Canada, Czechoslovakia, West Germany, India, Nigeria, the Soviet Union, Switzerland, Tanzania, and Yugoslavia.

In Belgium, the new constitutional system has brought no change in the existing pattern and organization of the courts. The judiciary remains a classic unitary system. The one change that has been effected—but only recently, in 1984—is the establishment of an Arbitration Court (consisting half of judges and half of former politicians). The Arbitration Court is competent to adjudicate any conflict between national law and regional and community decrees and between decrees of regions and communities. It does not act as a constitutional court empowered to review the constitutionality of laws and decrees, nor is it competent for "conflicts of interest" between the state, regions, and communities. Conflicts of interest are not—unlike in the traditional federal state—reviewed by the judiciary, but by a group of national ministers meeting in a claims commission.

Conclusion

Belgium is an interesting case study of the problems and difficulties encountered when a highly centralized and unitary state seeks to become a federal system composed of two units. The federalization process has thus far been very difficult and is far from finished. More and more, citizens are voicing serious concerns about the problems of the present structure based on two regions with different languages and ideologies and at different stages of economic development.

Note

1. There is no pure example of the horizontal model in any federal state in which all legislative power remains with the center, with only executive powers being transferred, although the 1978 Wales Act that never took effect would have been such an example. In Austria, the Federal Republic of Germany, and Switzerland, however, the regional levels of government do enjoy some legislative authority.

Discussion

ROBERT GOLDWIN: According to Mr. Vanderlinden's paper, it has been said that Belgium has no nationality and that the Belgians are a people with no common sociocultural features, no common history, and no natural frontiers. Reading the paper, one gets the impression that all the present constitutional arrangements are designed to intensify the divisions among the Belgians. It becomes unclear, for example, whether national law and the Constitution are supreme or whether council decrees are; it is extraordinary that it is unclear what the supreme law is. One gets the impression that everything is being done as if there were, in Belgium, two hostile and incompatible communities.

My question is this: is there any conceivable constitution that could give Belgium the requisite unity, that could build a nation capable of dealing with its national problems on a national basis? If we had a completely free hand to employ the greatest constitution-writing geniuses and we did not have to consult anyone in Belgium—thereby avoiding political parties, language groups, and the existing communities—could we devise a constitution that would enable Belgium as a nation to deal with its great national problems on a national basis?

JACQUES VANDERLINDEN: That question is surprising, because the way it is phrased suggests that we should ignore all the real problems and work in the abstract to find a solution. We simply cannot, at the same time, ignore the problems and find a solution to them.

I do not believe at this stage that there is a solution to our problems. We could, of course, clarify the respective jurisdictions of the different existing councils. At present children in school are governed by at least two different ministers and councils, with one deciding on the curriculum and the other deciding on the time devoted to classes. That is unimaginable.

The treaty-making power should also be clarified. As things stand now, agreements are concluded every day by regions or communities, which in principle have no constitutional value, because only the king may legitimately negotiate them.

Another point to settle is the Brussels problem. We have an executive for the Brussels region but no legislature in a system where we believe executives must depend on a legislature. Central government ministers are detailed to take care of the Brussels region, and they are not always the best ministers because Brussels is not considered a pleasant portfolio. Furthermore, the Flemish-speaking people consider Brussels to be Flemish territory—and according to the territorial basis for power, they are undoubtedly right. If one does not rely on that basis but rather on social practices like language, then one has to consider that 75 percent of the population in Brussels are French speakers. This, then, is another major issue.

JEAN-PIERRE DE BANDT: I will be somewhat more optimistic about the future of Belgium, which is the core of Europe, where three major cultures meet, the French, the Dutch, and the German. If that little country fell apart, it would be a disaster for the European Community and European federalism. So I think this would not happen and cannot happen.

Perhaps as a solution we could just do what the occupation forces did in Germany after the war. They asked the distinguished Harvard professor Karl Friedrich to take six months and draft a new constitution. It has worked beautifully ever since and is considered one of the best working federal constitutions in the world today.

Perhaps we need to seek advice from people with federalist traditions in their own country. Our system today is only a transition system, and as such it will not work. But it is not finished—a number of things still have to be settled, among them the status of Brussels, the reform of the Senate, and the like. A number of people believe that the only solution is to go back to the pre-French period: that is, we should reestablish a federalism, not one with two units only as we have under the 1970 and 1980 reforms, but a true federalism of nine provincial units, Brussels perhaps being the central territory.

Although there are potential solutions, they are not to be found in a pseudo-federal system with only two units. There are no precedents in history where this has worked. Czechoslovakia is not a good example, nor are Tanzania, Cyprus, or Lebanon. A federal state built around two units, two peoples with different languages, will experience confrontation over every issue, especially when not much has been delegated to the units.

JOHN SORZANO: One theme from our earlier discussions was that the unity that was forged from diversity in both the United States and India had more to do with cultural factors such as tolerance and assimilation than with the constitutions of the respective countries. One underlying assumption of this conference is that constitutions can forge unity out of diversity. But from Mr. Vanderlinden's paper, it would appear that sometimes, rather than forging unity, a constitution may actually freeze and preserve diversity and cleavages in the society.

As Professor Glazer observed, whenever distinctions reflecting ethnic, cultural, or language groups in the society are recognized in the constitution and resources and power are allocated based on those distinctions, then the differences become self-perpetuating. Interests form behind the distinctions. Then, rather than serving to bring together the diverse groups in the society, the constitution only perpetuates divisions and sometimes may actually bring about confrontation.

Where major groups in the society lack mutual trust—Cyprus, Lebanon, and other places come to mind—no amount of constitutional ingenuity can solve the problem of diversity, because the basic problem is social trust. The constitution, and the skill of the constitution makers, cannot solve those problems.

In Belgian society do sociological conditions allow the groups to work toward a common objective? On the basis of these papers, it seems that repeated efforts at constitution making have only created and sustained a situation in which each group has, and would cling to, its own representatives and hierarchies of power. The past several presidential elections in the United States demonstrated that as long as groups believe that the only legitimate form of representation is representation by one of their own kind—that is, Hispanics must represent Hispanics, blacks must represent blacks, women must represent women—then, to use the terminology of Jesse Jackson, no "rainbow coalition" is possible. That is obviously a distorted view of representation, and as long as a constitution is based on that kind of thinking, the problem is magnified rather than ameliorated.

JACOB LANDAU: The language issue in Belgium is apparently no nearer a solution in recent years than before, so would it not be correct to predict a further worsening of intercommunal relations, despite constitutional attempts to moderate the issue? And federalization does not seem to be a solution for the language problem in Belgium, since linguistic frontiers do not fit those of the communities. At any rate, increasing mobility would make federalism even more problematic in the future, possibly rendering it of little use in the language controversy.

Instead, I suggest one or all of the following options. First, follow the example of the authorities in Finland who granted the Swedish minority very generous conditions concerning their language and culture. They could have universities, museums, theaters, and other cultural institutions in their own language, regardless of the heavy expense and difficult administrative measures. Second, create opportunities for countrywide organizations to serve as a meeting ground for fruitful social and cultural exchange between the opposing groups. Third, offer inducements to everyone to study both Flemish and French, despite the expense and trouble, so that although everyone would be truly fluent only in one's mother tongue, one would know enough of the other's language to communicate freely. Finally, try all of these options together.

I have one last point. Since constitutional change is intentionally difficult, the Belgian Constitution is essentially perpetuating language divisions, rather than moderating them. In such a case the Belgian Constitution does not serve society but, rather, undermines it; hence, I have a rather extreme suggestion. The Belgian Constitution is too long anyway, especially compared to the U.S. Constitution, one of whose greatest assets is its brevity. So why not scrap all the provisions regarding language and start again from the beginning? The point would be to try to foster a spirit of moderation, which seems lacking now, and only then to seek an accommodation between the linguistic communities—perhaps along the lines I suggested above or some better ones that our Belgian colleagues can devise themselves.

MR. GOLDWIN: That is what this conference needed—in the spirit of Jonathan Swift, a "modest proposal." [Laughter]

TERENCE MARSHALL: These papers point out that earlier Belgians commonly spoke of themselves and thought of themselves as Belgians. Now, perhaps the common saying is true, that the only Belgian is the king. When we talked earlier about the American Constitution, we recognized the problem that constitutions can freeze diversity instead of using diversity for constructive purposes—purposes that might assist broader constitutional aims. I want to examine some of the diverse elements of Belgium to see to what extent Belgian unity is possible.

If we compare Belgium with other countries, we notice, among other things, that Belgium is moving toward some form of federal system. When we compare federalism in Belgium with federalism in other countries, some possibilities for solutions are evident. Unlike the situation in the United States, Belgian federalism would take place in the context of linguistic diversity. In that sense, federalism in such countries as Switzerland, Canada, or India might be applicable.

Belgium, of course, was traditionally composed of nine provinces. Mr. De Bandt suggested it might be possible to establish a Belgian federal system using the nine provinces as opposed to the two communities. With the nine provinces, it would make possible Senate representation that, because of the unequal number of provinces, might produce majorities not necessarily based on community distinctions. Brussels, for example, is economically distinct from Walloonia. Walloonia is the industrial sector of the Belgian economy, Flanders is traditionally agricultural, and Brussels is the tertiary sector. As a result, the linguistic identification with Walloonia in Brussels is somewhat modified by the economic situation in Brussels, which ties it more closely with Flanders. In that case, if a senate were to be established in Belgium according to federal criteria, would it not be possible for majorities in the different provinces to maneuver among themselves based on these other elements of diversity, thereby attenuating the sharp distinction between the Flemish and the Walloonian communities?

JUAN LINZ: Several positive factors make me optimistic. First, the Belgians agree basically on being Belgians. That is, they do not want to be Dutch, they do not want to be German, and they do not want to be French. The movements advocating splitting Belgium have never been successful. The identity of Belgians, therefore, is a dual one. A national identity does not necessarily have to be exclusive—it can be dual. One can be both Catalan and Spanish, for instance. And so most Belgians would be both Flemish and Belgian or both Dutch and Belgian.

Another element of unity not yet mentioned is the common identification with the crown. Furthermore, within the political parties, in spite of their division for representation of the linguistic communities, there is still something that unites Socialists or voters of the Christian party across the linguistic boundary—certain ideological outlooks and organizational links. There is not a regional nationalist party system; parties are still at least symbolically ideological, producing cross-cutting loyalties.

Finally, maybe some problems in society just cannot be solved. Nations may be like a person with a chronic illness that, nonetheless, does not impede normal functioning. Once the patient accepts that necessity, as some patients must, he can go on.

Perhaps our problem with Belgium or Spain is that we have been reared with the idea that a nation-state must resemble the French model. That is, our standard is a centralized, national state, with a rational, Napoleonic legal system. This expectation renders us incapable of understanding premodern forms or forms with inconsistencies and overlapping jurisdictions that for a man of the sixteenth or seventeenth century would have been perfectly understandable and acceptable.

In some ways the countries that never evolved into a modern state, like Switzerland or even to some degree the United Kingdom, are societies that have accepted incongruities and irrationalities in a way that we as Spaniards or Belgians have not. Particularly our intellectual elites cannot accept the fact that something as irrational as what is developing in Belgium or Spain in many respects can still work. Once we accept that it can work, however, it does work.

My plea, then, is that we consider, first, that nationalism is not necessarily exclusive, but that there may be dual national identities and, second, that certain nonrational systems can work.

MR. LANDAU: Mr. Vanderlinden's main point that the difficulties in Belgium are immense and are very difficult to reconcile is true. But precisely because the difficulties are so great maybe new ways of thinking, even heroic measures, are necessary.

These difficulties are reflected, for example, in Brussels. The linguistic situation in Brussels is not what the 1971 Constitution would have us think: it is a bewildering collection of speech varieties, which range from a language with the syntactic structure of French and elements of Dutch vocabulary, to a language with the syntactic structure of Dutch and elements of French vocabulary, and languages that include all the possible intermediary stages between these two poles. Given this sort of confusion, perhaps one should think of less orthodox or more radical ways of tackling the problems, along the lines of my earlier so-called "modest approach."

MR. GOLDWIN: Mr. Landau, I didn't say that what you offered was a modest approach; I said it was a modest proposal. "A Modest Proposal" is the title of an essay by Jonathan Swift, who proposed to solve the problem of hunger in Ireland by killing the children and using them for food. That "modest proposal" would have simultaneously reduced the population and increased the food supply. [Laughter]

So there is a difference between a modest approach and a modest proposal.

NATHAN GLAZER: I suggest a different radical approach, knowing how unlikely it is. The complexity in Belgium is such as to boggle my mind. I have never yet quite figured out, despite the brilliance of Mr. Vanderlinden's paper, just what the various communities and regions are. It was just too much, and for that reason I thought of something very different.

Suppose the emphasis in the Constitution were on rights, rather than on structures—rights as absolutely defined as possible, rights to schooling in a language, rights to courts, rights to everything. Who would not be satisfied with that? The only people who would not be satisfied are those who believe that the assimilative power of one or the other language is greater, and I assume that means French rather than Flemish.

RUTH BADER GINSBURG: Apart from their potential as an inspiration and model, have the European Community and other European alliances had any tangible impact in lessening tension or promoting accommodation between the Flemish and the Walloon camps in Belgium?

MR. DE BANDT: Thus far there has been no interference from any other country or any international organization in our internal problems. The development of the European Community is of course a slow process, and I think it will be a matter of a few generations before we see a federation of Europe. So there will be no short-term solution for Belgium there.

In answer to Professor Glazer's remarks, I think we have insisted a bit too much on the linguistic aspects of the Belgian problem. Linguistics has been the main objective of the Flemish movement for about a century, but we can say that today, certainly since 1963, all linguistic issues are practically resolved. We now have basically two linguistic regions, and we have defined the rights for these regions. The only problem that remains as part of the linguistic issue is Brussels, and even there most matters have been resolved.

The problem has now shifted from a purely linguistic issue to a much broader economic one. The two major communities believe they are subsidizing each other. The Flemish economy, for instance, is made up of very dynamic small enterprises. The Flemish nationalist movement believes that the Flemish are subsidizing the others, so they want to move to a confederation of two independent states, which would delegate to a central government certain limited powers such as treaties, national defense, foreign affairs, and the like.

Mr. Vanderlinden: It is true that the Flemish-speaking community believes it is subsidizing the French-speaking, nonetheless the French speakers can point to various things that they believe they have been financing exclusively for the advantage of the Flemish-speaking community. In such a context, to emphasize rights rather than structures would ignore precisely the collective identity that has been building up so strongly.

Mr. De Bandt: To understand some of the nonlinguistic problems Belgium faces, consider the first important decision by the Arbitration Court: it pertained to the structure of the court itself. As Mr. Vanderlinden's paper pointed out, the so-called Arbitration Court—which is not a constitutional court—consists of an equal number of Flemish judges and French judges but is presided over on an alternating annual basis by either a Flemish or a French judge. The obvious tactic of the lawyers, then, is to have a French president for a case involving the French community and vice versa.

The first case addressed that very subject. The lawyer of the French community felt that the judges should simply resign on the anniversary date of their appointment, even if the case had been pleaded before the end of their term. The court finally ruled that the judges who heard the case should decide the case, which only makes sense. But this shows how dangerous it is to think that this court, which many politicians considered to be the crown jewel in the structure of federalism, can resolve all the issues we face.

Thomas Fleiner: Switzerland has been mentioned quite a few times, and I would be interested to know why the example of the French Revolution did not succeed in Switzerland, whereas it succeeded in Belgium, with regard to centralism. Napoleon tried to implement a very centralized constitution in Switzerland, which did not succeed, because, I think, the Swiss are too rebellious. They already had a certain kind of democratic tradition and did not accept centralism. Somehow they succeeded in being the first federal state in Europe to implement the American example.

With regard to the language problem, if a country has a diversity of languages, I think it can cope with the diversity only if it accepts it as an asset. That is, if a country has different languages, it is open to the richness of different cultures. If this concept is accepted, the educational system must ensure that the children learn at least two or even three different languages.

With regard to rights versus institutions as a way to handle the problem in a nation like Belgium, the state cannot simply refrain from establishing any language or any religion, because the state has to publish rules in a certain language and it has to support facilities in languages, especially in education. If the notion prevails that persons have individual rights to use their own language, the state must then expend money for such facilities for education, for courts, and for administration. The concept of individual rights, therefore, does not fit with regard to language.

MR. VANDERLINDEN: I contend that Switzerland resisted the French model because it had developed a stronger identity before French rule than Belgium had. I reject the psychological argument that the Belgians are just weak dogs and the Swiss are courageous Alpine oaks, who will never submit. We were the bravest long before you. [Laughter]

I would not have wanted to be the one responsible in 1798 or 1800 for imposing a centralized administration on Switzerland; for one thing, communication is extraordinarily difficult. Belgium, however, is a flat country, and it is easier to establish a centralized administration under such circumstances.

ENOCH DUMBUTSHENA: Is the problem in Belgium not one of a conflict between a superior culture or a superior national identity in the case of the French, on the one hand, and, on the other hand, an ordinary nation with an ordinary language? In such circumstances, the natural course of things would be for the superior nation, for the superior language, to assimilate the inferior culture. This point is interesting because the same language issue is present in Canada. In Canada, the French language is winning, even though the French in that country are a minority.

MR. VANDERLINDEN: As far as I am concerned, there are no superior cultures or civilizations. All people have their own cultures and to claim a superiority of culture is wrong.

MR. DUMBUTSHENA: But the point is that the French were at one time the dominant nation in Europe, and French was an international language. Other nations do not have to accept that the French have a superior culture or language. It is what is in the mind of the French that is important.

MR. VANDERLINDEN. I fully agree with that. Even before the French Revolution, in the Flemish-speaking region the elite were speaking French, because French was, in their mind, the language of the superior culture. The Flemish were considered peasants, who spoke only dialects. The French community used the word "dialects" to describe what the Flemish were speaking, while the French had a "language."

MR. GOLDWIN: This last point by Mr. Vanderlinden, I think, tells us a great deal, as we conclude this discussion, about the profundity and persistence of the divisions among Belgians.

4
The Canadian Constitution
and Diversity

Barry L. Strayer

By virtue of its geographic size and a population drawn from all over the world, Canada is truly a land of diversity. In this paper I attempt to depict some of this diversity and show how it has been modified and nurtured by our institutions. I focus particularly on diversity in language and the constitutional or legal means that affect that dimension of diversity in Canada. In doing so, I discuss, among other things, the protection of diversity through legal recognition of both collective and individual rights; the role played by the federal system in the preservation of diversity; and the roles of courts, legislatures, and government administration. In this field, however, there is not, and has never been, total agreement among Canadians on either ends or means.

Canada Today

Canada is the second largest country in the world, its area exceeded only by that of the Soviet Union. In contrast, in mid-1983 its population of approximately 25 million ranked thirty-first among the nations of the world. Canada's comparatively short collective experience, beginning essentially with the political union of British North American colonies in 1867, combined with the scattering of its relatively small population over such a vast area, has helped to preserve and promote diversity and has left an abiding challenge to the cohesion of the state. As one of our former prime ministers once said, Canada has too much geography and too little history.

Canada is an independent state with a democratic form of government. Because of our origins the head of state is Queen Elizabeth II, who is queen of Canada as well as queen of the United Kingdom and head of the Commonwealth. Canada remains a member of the Commonwealth of Nations. Virtually all functions of the head of state

157

are performed by the governor general, who is a Canadian appointed by the queen on the recommendation of the prime minister of Canada.

We have a parliamentary form of responsible government and a federal system with a central government and legislature and governments and legislatures in each of the ten provinces and two territories. The provinces have constitutionally entrenched powers making them autonomous with respect to a very wide range of matters, going well beyond the powers of constituent units in many other federal states. The two territories do not have constitutionally entrenched autonomy comparable to that of the provinces, although in practice they are evolving an increasing measure of self-government less subject to control by federal authorities in Ottawa.

Canada has no established religion. The Constitution does, however, refer in passing to "the supremacy of God" and contains guarantees of tax-supported schools for Roman Catholics or Protestants in certain provinces where either of those groups is in a minority.

Canadians are diverse in their racial or national origins. Approximately 45 percent of them can trace their origins to the British Isles and another 28 percent to France; about half a million, or some 2 percent of the population, are descended from the aboriginal inhabitants, the Indians and Inuit, whose ancestors inhabited large parts of what is now Canada for many centuries before the Europeans first came to this continent. The rest of the population is predominantly of other European origins, the most numerous being German, Italian, and Ukrainian, but also includes many people of African, Caribbean, and Asian (particularly Chinese and Japanese) origin.[1]

Notwithstanding this wealth of linguistic backgrounds, only two languages have official status in Canada: English and French.[2] In the institutions of the federal government and in the regulation of matters within federal control, English and French have equal status, as they have in the provincial government of New Brunswick and, to a limited extent, in the provincial governments of Quebec and Manitoba and the government of the Northwest Territories.[3] An array of laws and practices exists with respect to the use of one or both of these languages in provincial affairs.

A brief profile of knowledge of the official languages is also important. Although mother tongue is not a completely reliable test of current language use, in 1981 English was the mother tongue of 61 percent of the population and French of 25 percent. Of those whose mother tongue was French, some 85 percent lived in the province of Quebec, where they made up 82.4 percent of the population. They made up 5.3 percent of the population outside Quebec, but they were considerably concentrated in New Brunswick, where they constituted 33.6 percent of the population.

To understand the dynamics of this situation further, however, we must consider the degree to which Canadians know the official language that is not their mother tongue. In 1981 some 92 percent of those whose mother tongue was English spoke only English, and 63 percent of those whose mother tongue was French spoke only French. Thus 8 percent of those whose mother tongue was English and 37 percent of those whose mother tongue was French were bilingual. In New Brunswick 91 percent of those whose mother tongue was English but only 39 percent of those whose mother tongue was French spoke only one language. In Quebec the picture was strikingly different: 71 percent of those whose mother tongue was French and only 45 percent of those whose mother tongue was English spoke only one language, the rest being bilingual.[4] These figures demonstrate the importance of a critical mass in the daily use and maintenance of language.

Little more than one-fifth of the aboriginal population, about 108,000 people, use aboriginal languages at home; the vast majority (72 percent) use English, and 4 percent use French.[5] A variety of other languages are spoken in Canadian homes, the most common being Italian, which was, according to 1971 census statistics, spoken at home by some 425,000 people.[6]

Thus Canada today is a democratic federal state with a heterogeneous society. To understand its present one must look at its past, which I now propose to do.

Canada at the Commencement of European Settlement

Canada appears to have been visited by Norsemen perhaps 1,000 years ago. We know that the explorer John Cabot, sponsored by English merchants, came at the end of the fifteenth century. Exploration, mainly by Frenchmen, continued throughout the sixteenth century, but it was not until 1605 that the first permanent French settlement was established at Port Royal in what is now Nova Scotia. Further French settlements followed soon thereafter in the valley of the St. Lawrence, and the occupation of Canada by a predominantly European population continued steadily thereafter.

Of course, an indigenous population was already in Canada before the Europeans came. This population, whose origins are still somewhat obscure, is thought to have numbered no more than 220,000 people at that time. Most of them were described by the Europeans as "Indians" (as a result of Columbus's error in thinking that he had landed in India in 1492) and still are today. Those aborigines inhabiting the far north were commonly referred to by Europeans as Eskimos or Esquimaux, but they themselves prefer their own term, the Inuit. Such governmental institutions as the aboriginal peoples had at that time were generally weak and geographically limited. The great majority of the Indians spoke some form of Algonkian, a family of languages used from the Atlantic almost to the Rocky Mountains. There were a variety of local Indian languages, particularly in what is now British Columbia. The Inuit spoke a distinct language, Inuktitut.[7]

Contemporaneously with the beginning of colonization by France in Canada, England established its first North American colony at Jamestown. The development of Canadian institutions and Canadian society was dominated during the next two centuries by the colonial policies of England and France and the rivalries between those two European imperial powers.

Colonial Canada, 1600–1867

The earliest colonization efforts by France came to be centered on the St. Lawrence River in what was soon to be called La Nouvelle France, or New France. France had had an extensive and growing fur trade with this region during the latter part of the sixteenth century. The establishment of a colony was to a large extent a natural outgrowth of this trade and was initially put in the hands of a succession of private companies authorized by the king of France. An important driving force for colonization also came from the Roman Catholic church in France, as various orders vigorously pursued opportunities to convert the indigenous peoples of New France to Christianity or, more precisely, to Catholicism.

In the 1660s the king of France assumed direct control of New France. He established a system of government that was essentially nonrepresentative and over whose decisions he had final authority. There was no pretense of separation of church and state: the Roman Catholic bishop was by right a member of the governing body of the colony, the Sovereign Council. Education, such as it was, was in the hands of the church. By royal decree the legal system to be applied in the colony was that of the Custom of Paris, one of the many bodies of customary or common law then operating in different regions of pre-Napoleonic France. A feudal system of landholding based on that of the homeland was also introduced, although it operated on a somewhat more egalitarian basis in the colony. Of course, French was the official language of the colony. Generally speaking, then, the institutions of government and the status of religion and language were similar to their counterparts in prerevolutionary France. This situation continued until the fall of Quebec in 1759 and its aftermath, the Treaty of Paris of 1763, by which France surrendered the colony to Britain.

In the meantime continuing rivalry between the two major European powers had other repercussions in Canada. In the late seventeenth century the English had successfully established a presence in the areas surrounding Hudson's Bay to the north and west of New France, although this did not go unchallenged by the French. The small French colony in Acadia—what is now Nova Scotia and part of New Brunswick on Canada's east coast—changed hands between the French and the British, as had territory in Newfoundland. By the Treaty of Utrecht of 1713 France surrendered its claims in those three areas, leaving a small French population in Acadia of some 1,800 people. Although the surrender caused few immediate problems for these inhabitants, their descendants of the 1750s and 1760s, who had grown to a sizable population, were expelled in large numbers by the British administration, not for reasons of language or religion but because of doubts about their loyalty to the British Crown. Yet many Acadians of French ancestry remained in the region, and many of those expelled later returned, leaving today a substantial French-speaking population in that area of Canada.

It is necessary to return in this narrative to the valley of the St. Lawrence and the colony of New France, the antecedent of the modern province of Quebec, to survey briefly the salient constitutional, legal, and political developments that shaped in important ways the Canada of today. It was with the Treaty of Paris in 1763 that France surrendered almost all its possessions in North America and British hegemony was established. With the commencement of British rule a pattern emerged that has continued to modern times: the natural tendency to assimilate the French-speaking population was tempered at crucial points by the need to preserve the existence of the Canadian colony and later the Canadian nation.

The Royal Proclamation of 1763, issued by George III, established governments for Quebec and the newly acquired territories. The measures were not very generous, in form at least, to the inhabitants of Quebec. Although the king guaranteed them the freedom to practice the Roman Catholic religion, as he had committed himself to do by the Treaty of Paris, and directed the governor to summon a general assembly similar to those found in the American colonies, anyone participating in the executive council or general assembly would have to take the same oath as then required in England in similar circumstances. That oath in effect required those who took it to renounce the Roman Catholic religion. As a result no general assembly was called during the first thirty years of British rule. The Royal Proclamation of 1763 also imposed on the colony English law to be administered by courts conducted in English. Again, the institutions of the new motherland had been transplanted to the North American colony.

This situation might have endured for some time had not the wider needs of British colonial policy dictated a more liberal regime for Quebec. In this period the American colonies were becoming more and more restless under British rule. Considering the growing menace of revolution in its American colonies to the south, the British government wished to secure if possible the loyalty of Quebec. Given the differences in religion and language, governmental traditions, and attitude toward authority, most Quebeckers of that period were not naturally sympathetic to the aspirations of the American colonists.

The loyalty of Quebeckers was largely secured by the Quebec Act of 1774, adopted by the British Parliament, which superseded the Royal Proclamation of 1763. It secured the support of the clergy by guaranteeing their "accustomed Dues and Rights." It abolished for Roman Catholics the oath that would previously have excluded them from government. While preserving English criminal law for the colony, it restored with respect to other matters the French civil law that had existed in the colony before the conquest. The restoration of French law concerning matters of property and civil rights particularly engaged the loyalty of the seigneurs, or feudal landowners. It also meant that much of the law could be administered in French. The act also extended the boundaries of Quebec as far south as the Ohio River and as far west as the Mississippi, covering parts of what are now the American states of Pennsylvania, Indiana, Illinois, Michigan, and Wisconsin.

The adoption of the Quebec Act of 1774 contributed significantly to the commencement of the American Revolution, because in the view of Americans it constituted interference by the British Parliament (rather than the sovereign) in colonial affairs, laid claim to territory coveted by the American colonies, gave a privileged status to the Roman Catholic religion, and preserved the French language and law. These institutional guarantees were repugnant to the more revolutionary-minded in the American colonies.

Although Quebec did not join in the American Revolution and withstood minor attacks by the revolutionaries, it ultimately felt very heavily the effects of that war. After the war Americans who had remained loyal to the British Crown were widely persecuted, and some 35,000 of them moved to Quebec and the areas that are now

Nova Scotia and New Brunswick. These people were predominantly Protestant and were used to English common law and a representative form of government. Those who settled in Quebec did so mostly in the western part of the province. Tensions soon developed over the lack of a representative assembly and over established Quebec institutions that were important to the French inhabitants but alien or repugnant to the so-called United Empire Loyalists.

In 1791 the British Parliament adopted the Constitution Act, which allowed for the division of Quebec as it then was into two parts: Upper Canada, consisting of the southern part of what is now Ontario; and Lower Canada, consisting of the southern part of what is now Quebec. Each province was to have an elected assembly, and each could establish its own system of laws. In retrospect this can be seen as an early venture in federalism as a means of accommodating diversity of religion, language, and culture. Lower Canada, though containing a minority of English speakers and non-Catholics, was able through its local autonomy to preserve the French language in its institutions and to continue to enjoy the system of law to which it was accustomed. Upper Canada was able to adopt English law and to use the English language. Ultimate legal authority over the two provinces rested, of course, with the British government and Parliament.

The two provinces of Upper and Lower Canada continued thus for some fifty years. As a result of armed uprisings in both provinces in 1837–1838, their constitutions were replaced by another British statute, the Union Act of 1840. This act was antifederalist, combining the two former provinces into a single province of Canada with one government and legislature. It was frankly assimilationist in design: it prescribed English as the only official language to be used in the records of the legislature; and it provided equal representation from each of the areas previously constituting Upper Canada and Lower Canada. This provision gave an advantage to the predominantly English-speaking population of Upper Canada, which was smaller than the French-speaking population of Lower Canada. In practice the act did not have an assimilating effect. Each region retained its distinctive laws and institutions. As a matter of political practice it became widely accepted that important measures could be passed in the legislature only with a majority from each of the two regions. French also continued to be used as a language of debate in the legislature, and by 1848 the constitutional provisions restricting its use as an official language were repealed.

In the meantime the colonies of Nova Scotia, New Brunswick, Prince Edward Island, and Newfoundland had been established, each with its own government and legislature. The constitutional development of these colonies was more like that of the prerevolutionary American colonies.

Confederation to 1982

Constitutional Protection of Diversity. Canadians generally regard July 1, 1867, as the date their country was born. On that day occurred what is generally referred to as confederation, the coming into force of what was then called the British North America Act, 1867 (now known as the Constitution Act, 1867), which federally united the provinces of Canada, Nova Scotia, and New Brunswick.[8] The new entity thus created was entitled the Dominion of Canada; it had a central government in Ottawa and four provinces—Quebec, Ontario, Nova Scotia, and New Brunswick—each with its own provincial government. The act distributed powers between the provincial and federal governments and established a number of other institutions.

Although the Constitution Act did not complete the process of nation building, it provided a vehicle by which this has been accomplished. It included means by which other British territories in North America could be added to the nucleus, and this has been done, the process being completed in 1949 with the union of Newfoundland as the tenth province of Canada. Although the act confirmed and enlarged the area of self-government enjoyed by British North Americans, it did not make the Dominion of Canada fully independent. Control over Canada's external relations and initially much of its defense policy was retained by British authorities. Full independence came about as an evolutionary process that was not completed until after the First World War, in which Canada played an important role. For some sixty years Canada has been, for all practical purposes, an independent nation.

It is not within the scope of this paper to discuss the reasons for confederation in 1867, but it is of interest to note that once again Canadian events were strongly influenced by those in the United States: there was fear that after the American Civil War, in which Britain had antagonized the United States, the successful Union armies might be turned northward. The union of separate British colonies became important to preserve their distinct identity. Not only did the Civil War provide an incentive for Canadian union, but the exaggerated states' rights doctrine that had brought on that war influenced Canadian and British statesmen to try (not entirely successfully, as it turned out) to ensure a strong central government for the Canadian federation.

The Constitution was shaped in other ways by reaction to external events. The tendency to accept authority, which was part of the Quebec tradition going back to the days of New France, had some counterpart among the Loyalist settlements established by those who had fled the United States because they rejected the premises on which the American Revolution was based. Nineteenth-century Britain, partly as the aftermath of reaction to the French Revolution, was not much interested in theories of fundamental rights. Positivism as represented by the doctrine of parliamentary supremacy pervaded English and Canadian legal and political thought.

As a result the Constitution Act, 1867, which we have long regarded as our basic Constitution, contained nothing by way of a comprehensive declaration or guarantee of individual rights. Its preamble, in expressing the desire of the provinces concerned to be federally united "with a constitution similar in principle to that of the United Kingdom," was generally understood to adopt by reference the principles of parliamentary supremacy. Nevertheless, confederation, with its benefits of maintaining a separate British North American identity, was possible only on terms that would preserve the diversity of its two main languages and religions.

The adoption of a federal system was itself a means of preserving the diversity existing among the previously separate colonies. In no respect was this more important than in gaining the adherence of Quebec to the scheme: federation, with its distribution of powers, detached the governance of the new province of Quebec from the old province of Canada and put it in the hands of a new provincial government elected by a majority of French-speaking Roman Catholics. Given the wide scope of provincial powers, including education and "property and civil rights," this was thought to put in the hands of Quebeckers the power to preserve and shape their own culture.

Apart from the federal system itself, the Constitution provided two specific forms of protection for diversity: one with respect to language and the other with respect to religion. French speakers would be in the majority in one province, Quebec, although that province would continue to have a substantial English-speaking minority. In the dominion as a whole, however, the French would be in a minority. Section 133 of the Constitution Act, 1867, guaranteed the right of individuals to use either English or French in the federal parliament, the legislature of Quebec, federally created courts, and the courts of Quebec.[9] An additional requirement was that the bills and statutes and other records of the two legislative bodies be published in both languages, which has been interpreted to mean that laws must be enacted in both languages, not merely translated later from one language to the other. In 1870, when the province of Manitoba was established, a similar guarantee was provided with respect to its legislature and courts. These guarantees created individual rights—freedom to choose either English or French as a means of expressing oneself in the courts or legislatures concerned, as well as the right to use the records of those legislatures in either language and to be governed by laws enacted in both languages.

The religious guarantees are found in section 93 of the Constitution Act, 1867,[10] and counterparts adopted in respect of provinces later joining the confederation. Although the Constitution did not establish a religion, it tried to protect the established rights of certain religious minorities to public funding of their denominational schools. Section 93 assumed that the population could be divided into two categories—Protestants and Roman Catholics—and provided that where at the time of confederation a system of publicly funded denominational schools existed in any province for either of those religious minorities, the province was obliged to continue that system. Apart from opening an avenue to judicial review when any province denied such rights, the section provided that when a province denied such rights as existed at union or as may have been granted since union, an appeal would lie to the federal cabinet, which could require the province to take remedial action. If the province failed to comply with such a directive, Parliament could enact the necessary remedial laws.

Because these guarantees were designed to protect the status quo at the time of union, they are generally thought to apply in only six of the ten provinces. Certain modifications of section 93 have been adopted with respect to provinces that came in after 1867. One of these provinces, Newfoundland, has in effect no system of public schools, and therefore a comparable guarantee protects the funding of a variety of denominational schools in that province.

For present purposes there are a few salient points to note. First, section 93 appears to be a protection of collective rights since it refers to rights or privileges "with respect to denominational schools which any class of persons have by law in the province at the Union." Obviously, the assertion of the right to establish a school requires a collective effort by a large number of like-minded people, and this is not a right that attaches to an individual.

Second, and as a corollary of the preceding point, these guarantees have occasionally worked to the detriment of the individual right of choice. They have sometimes, for example, been held to preclude children not of the minority faith from attending its schools, and vice versa.

Third, in spite of several efforts through the courts to do so, it has not been possible to use these guarantees to protect the use of a minority language as the medium of instruction in denominational schools run by religious minorities. Over the years both the French-speaking Roman Catholics of Ontario and the English-speaking Protestants of Quebec have unsuccessfully sought to invoke section 93 for this purpose.

Fourth, this is the only clear assignment by the Canadian Constitution of authority to the federal government and Parliament to protect individual or collective rights, through appeal to the federal cabinet and, if necessary, remedial federal legislation. In this respect it is somewhat analogous to the provisions in the Thirteenth, Fourteenth, and Fifteenth amendments to the United States Constitution, which authorize Congress to enforce by legislation the guarantees in those amendments. It must be noted, however, that these powers have never been successfully used, because of the political difficulties, and at least one federal government has been defeated largely as a result of trying to adopt remedial legislation. It seems unlikely that we will see direct federal intervention under section 93.

The only other provisions of the 1867 Constitution that have come to be seen as devices for protecting individual and collective rights in the face of provincial legislative majorities are the power given to the federal cabinet to "reserve assent" to provincial bills (that is, through the lieutenant governor of the province, to have a bill referred to the federal cabinet for a decision whether royal assent, normally a matter for the lieutenant governor, should be given to the bill) and the federal cabinet's power to disallow provincial laws already enacted and assented to. These federal powers were extensively used in the earlier days of the dominion, but their use came to be thought appropriate only in limited circumstances, one of which would be a flagrant denial of collective or individual rights. The political feasibility of using these powers now appears much in doubt: the power of reservation has not been used since 1960 and the power of disallowance not since 1943.

The guarantees of specific forms of diversity provided by the original Constitution of 1867, then, were limited in many respects. The language guarantees, while giving some protection to the individual at the federal level and in the provinces of Quebec and Manitoba, did nothing in the provinces of New Brunswick and Ontario, where there were, and still are, large French-speaking minorities. In jurisdictions where the guarantees did apply, they gave protection to the use of the minority language only in the legislative and judicial branches of government. They did not address the use of the minority language in the executive branch, the branch with which the average citizen would most frequently come into contact. Nor did they in any way recognize or protect the use of indigenous languages employed by native peoples long before either the English or the French came to Canada.

The religious guarantees protected collective, not individual, rights. They did not protect freedom of religion and tended to be a negation of freedom of conscience insofar as that embraces freedom from religion.

Position in Law and Fact. *1867–1960.* I have chosen somewhat arbitrarily here to look first at the period from confederation to 1960. There is a certain pattern with respect to the use of language during this period, however. While the French language enjoyed a fairly stable position in Quebec during this period, perhaps not expanding in use but at least holding its own, the rest of the country experienced strong trends toward assimilation, trends that have not been completely halted in recent years but have encountered countervailing institutional changes. Up to 1960 legal and administrative developments more often reinforced assimilation. During that time, it is estimated, some 10 percent of Canadians of French ethnic origin adopted English as their mother tongue. By far the largest portion of them would have lived outside Quebec, the only province where French speakers have always formed a majority.

French speakers have been in the minority in each of the other provinces since confederation. In certain provinces, such as Ontario and New Brunswick, persons whose mother tongue is French have formed a substantial minority: today they make up approximately 33.6 percent (234,000) of the population of New Brunswick and some 5.5 percent (over 475,000) of the population of Ontario.[11] In these provinces of greater concentration, the critical mass was sufficient to sustain the popular use of the French language, although it had no official status in government and a limited use in business and education.

Legal developments during this period outside Quebec did little to preserve or enhance the French language. In the English-speaking provinces to which the denominational-schools guarantees of section 93 or its equivalent applied, the protection of minority denominational education did not embrace the use of the minority language as a medium of instruction. In both Manitoba and Ontario schools the use of French as a medium of instruction was almost eliminated at one point, and the Constitution was held to be no bar.

In 1870 Manitoba had a non-native population almost equally divided between French and English speakers. It was for this reason that the language guarantees concerning the use of French and English in the legislature and courts were included in its constitution. In the next two decades the province experienced a wave of English-speaking immigration, and by 1890 its legislature abolished the use of French in those institutions. Not until the 1970s was that abolition successfully attacked in the higher courts, and not until 1985 did the Supreme Court of Canada finally rule that the use of both languages in the legislation of that province was mandatory, with the consequence that all laws passed in the English language only are invalid.[12]

These direct measures to curtail the use of French outside Quebec are salient examples of a general assimilative trend. Most provinces had from the outset an overwhelmingly English-speaking population that paid scant regard to the use of French in government, schools, business, or social affairs. The federal government, while recognizing its obligations under section 133 to use both languages in its laws and to permit the use of both languages in debates and in its courts, did little to enhance the role of French in government institutions. Even in the federally created courts of that period the use of French was not always practicable for a litigant.[13] The executive branch of the federal government was operated predominantly in English, and outside certain parts of Quebec a French speaker could not assume that he would be able to deal with that government in his own language. Certainly the executive branch had no constitutional or legal obligation to provide such service.

This situation may be contrasted to that in the province of Quebec, where members of the English-speaking minority, at least in the areas where they were concentrated, were able to live their lives in English with little pressure for assimilation. Schools using English as a medium of instruction were readily available, federal and provincial government services were available in English, and Quebec courts were able and willing to conduct cases in either language. This practical recognition of the needs of the English-speaking minority, which in 1971 amounted to no more than 15 percent of the population of Quebec, largely reflected the fact that English was and is the language of the majority of Canadians and of North Americans and that all manner of governmental, commercial, professional, and social communications in North America will inevitably occur in English. The negative side of this situation was that the use of French tended to be diluted in Quebec, even for the French-speaking majority, particularly in commercial affairs. The position of French in Quebec was somewhat static, the language being preserved and used within the family, the church, and the school but having practical limits in the world of government and business, limits that were generally accepted in fact and not challenged by law.

1960–1982. I next turn to the period from 1960 to 1982, both dates again being chosen somewhat arbitrarily. The year 1960 was the approximate point in our political development when a resurgence of French Canadian nationalism focused on the use of government, particularly the government of the province of Quebec, as a vehicle for enhancing the French language and French Canadian social and cultural values. This was the beginning of what has come to be called the quiet revolution in Quebec. It included a revamping of the provincial government and an expansion of its role into both traditional and nontraditional areas. One faction of nationalist opinion has taken the position that only the independence of Quebec would suffice to preserve and enhance the French culture and language in North America: the party in power in Quebec when this paper was written still has sovereignty for the province as its stated ultimate goal.[14] In a referendum held in Quebec in 1980 seeking approval for the provincial government to negotiate some different form of association between Quebec and the rest of Canada, some 60 percent of the voters voted against such an initiative.

This is not the appropriate place to detail such developments, but they reflect a change from a defensive preservation of the status quo for French Canadians, particularly in Quebec, to a dynamic and expansive view of their role. The date with which I close my discussion of this period, 1982, marks the coming into force of the Canadian Charter of Rights and Freedoms, which was a significant event in relation to the subject of diversity and constitutionalism.

Two broad and often conflicting approaches to the development of French Canadian society must be seen as running through the latter half of the twentieth century. One view, held in varying degrees by successive governments of the province of Quebec and their supporters, is a form of what might be called Quebec nationalism, that is, the identification of the welfare of French Canadians with that of Quebec and the government of the province of Quebec. Notwithstanding that (in 1981) some 11 percent of the Quebec population claimed English as their mother tongue and that outside Quebec some 5.3 percent of the population claimed French as theirs, Quebec is viewed in this school of thought as more or less coterminous with French Canadian society. It follows that Quebec should, to the greatest extent possible, be unilingually French, and it is a matter of no great consequence whether the rest of the country is unilingually

English. The government of Quebec is seen as the representative of French Canadian society dealing with "Ottawa," which is largely seen as the representative of English-speaking Canada. This approach emphasizes the rights of the French Canadian collectivity in Quebec and the importance of provincial powers to protect that collectivity. It logically leads to a form of territorial linguistic rights, in which the right to use French would be essentially confined to Quebec and the right to use English to the other provinces and territories.

The other polar view might be called pan-Canadianism. This view has been embraced in varying degrees, explicitly or implicitly, by the government of Canada and many of its supporters. In this view both French Canadian and Anglo-Canadian society exist throughout the country, and neither is identified with a particular government. Consequently, Canadians of either group should be able to move freely about the country and wherever at all practicable have access to essential services and education in their own language. This approach emphasizes the mobility of individuals and thus more readily finds legal expression in the form of individual rights. A corollary of pan-Canadianism is that each government, whether federal, provincial, or territorial, should so regulate matters within its jurisdiction as to protect the interests of official language minorities, be they the English-speaking minority in Quebec, the French-speaking minority of the Canadian population as a whole, or the French-speaking minorities in the nine provinces other than Quebec and in the two territories.

This dichotomy of approach has had serious implications for the federal system in Canada. Quebec nationalists, in identifying the position of French Canadians with that of the government of Quebec, have naturally pressed for more powers for that government to achieve the flowering of French language and culture. Taken to its logical conclusion, this approach leads at the least to special status for Quebec, with powers greater than those of other provinces, and at most to independence for Quebec. Pan-Canadianism suggests that each government in Canada, federal or provincial, has a role in protecting linguistic minorities in respect of those matters otherwise coming within its jurisdiction. Since the French-speaking minorities outside Quebec have no vote in Quebec, they must be protected by their federal and provincial governments. And since our history has demonstrated that electoral majorities have too often ignored or curtailed the interests of minorities, it is also important that basic linguistic rights be constitutionally protected.

Much of the constitutional turmoil in Canada in the past two and a half decades has flowed from the tension between the adherents of these views. This controversy has been reflected in legal and administrative measures taken by various governments.

One of the first major responses of the federal government to the revival of Quebec nationalism and growing support for separation was the establishment in 1963 of the Royal Commission on Bilingualism and Biculturalism. In 1967 the commission recommended a number of reforms to establish an equal status for English and French in Canada. It recommended that at the federal level of government the two languages be declared official, with equal status in all matters, executive, legislative, and judicial, rather than the somewhat limited status that French then enjoyed in the legislative and judicial areas. The commission also called for equality of the two languages for legislative and judicial purposes in Ontario and New Brunswick comparable to that already constitutionally established in Quebec. Further, it called for a kind of territorial bilingualism in provinces or areas with a substantial linguistic minority. In this it appears to have borrowed from the Finnish model. Part of this report was implemented in the Official Languages Act adopted by the Parliament of Canada in 1969,[15] such reforms being spurred by growing nationalist pressures in Quebec.

The Official Languages Act was of dramatic importance, both for its symbolism and for its content. Symbolically it was important because it declared English and French equal in status as the official languages of the government and Parliament of Canada. This went well beyond the rather limited 1867 constitutional provision for the use of both languages in Parliament and federally created courts.

Its practical requirements included the publication in both languages not only of the statutes but also of regulations and other delegated legislation, public notices and information provided by the executive branch of government to the public, and judgments or orders of federal courts and tribunals. It required that federal departments and agencies be equipped to provide services in both languages in the National Capital Region, at their head offices wherever they might be, and at other offices where there was a sufficient demand to warrant it. Corporations owned and directly controlled by the federal government were made subject to the requirements of the act. Services to the traveling public provided by the federal government or its agencies, directly or indirectly, were required to be available in both languages. The office of commissioner of official languages was established as a language ombudsman to receive complaints and oversee the observance of the spirit as well as the letter of the act.

The impact of the act has been dramatic since its adoption. French, which had had no legal status in the operations of the executive branch of the federal government, now enjoys equal status. This is not to say that old habits have died easily or that the legal requirements of the act are always met, but the effects have been very visible. Signs on federal institutions from one end of the country to the other are now in both languages, and most government forms and publications are bilingual or are readily available in either language.

In the federal public service all positions have been categorized as requiring knowledge of English, knowledge of French, or knowledge of both languages. In 1974 some 40,000 bilingual positions were identified, but by 1984 there were 63,000, or 28 percent of all positions in the public service.[16] A massive language training program has been used to enable public servants to meet linguistic requirements: 80,000 have been provided with language training in the past twenty years.[17]

Three objectives have been identified by Parliament for official language policy in the public service: first, and most important, providing service to members of the public in the official language chosen by them; second, enabling public servants to work to the greatest degree possible in their own language; and third, ensuring "full participation" by persons of both language groups (meaning that the composition of the public service should more or less reflect the linguistic composition of the Canadian population). Before the Official Languages Act French speakers were underrepresented in the federal public service and very substantially underrepresented in its senior levels. Although this situation has not been completely eliminated, it has much improved. Those whose mother tongue was French constituted approximately 26 percent of the population in 1981; in 1984 they made up 27.8 percent of federal public servants, an increase of three and one-half percentage points in a decade, and 19.9 percent in the management category, an increase of approximately one and one-half percentage points in a decade.[18]

Outside the public service the direct and indirect effects of the Official Languages Act have also been important. Two decades ago broadcasting services in the French language were very limited outside central Canada, but today services of the state-owned Canadian Broadcasting Corporation (Radio-Canada) are available in both languages coast to coast. Services are available in the minority official language wherever there are communities of 500 or more members of that language minority. Federally owned transportation systems and facilities such as airports strive, not always with complete success, to provide service in both languages throughout the country. These measures are all typical of the thrust of the languages policy of

173

successive federal governments: to maximize the mobility and equalize the opportunities of individual Canadians of both official language groups.

Consistent with these measures respecting the apparatus of the federal government, the legislature of the Northwest Territories has recently adopted an ordinance making English and French the official languages of the territorial government and legislature.[19] Also consistent with this approach are legislative and administrative measures in the province of New Brunswick. Although New Brunswick has a large French-speaking population, now some 33 percent, with its origins going back to the French colony of Acadia, no provision was made in the 1867 Constitution for the protection of the French language in that province. Nevertheless, in 1969 the legislature of New Brunswick adopted the Official Languages of New Brunswick Act, which has subsequently been amended and enlarged upon.[20] The act generally parallels the federal law in declaring both languages official for all provincial purposes and specifically provides for their use in the legislature and in the enactment and publication of legislation. It requires that services of the executive branch of government be available in the official language of choice, and it makes certain provisions guaranteeing education in both languages and the use of both languages in provincial courts.

Also consistent with the concept of bilingualism, though without establishing formal legal equality, are the legislative and administrative measures taken by Ontario and to a lesser extent by other English-speaking provinces to enhance the use of French. Ontario has no doubt gone the furthest in assuring the availability of trials in both languages and rapidly expanding governmental services available in French. The publicly funded school system has been extensively adjusted to provide education using French as the medium of instruction for children whose parents wish them to be so educated. While this development has been more dramatic in Ontario, with its large French-speaking minority (some 475,000), parallel developments have occurred in most English-speaking provinces, where public funding is provided by one means or another for a growing number of schools or school programs using French as the medium of instruction. The federal government shares in the costs of minority language education in all provinces, transferring over $200 million to the provinces for this purpose in fiscal year 1984–1985.[21]

These developments in the predominantly English-speaking provinces have largely been a response to Quebec nationalism. At the very least that movement has made English-speaking Canadians far more conscious of the legitimate concerns of French Canadians about the preservation of their culture and language. At another level the implicit threat of the separation of Quebec to achieve this goal has induced other provinces to recognize and encourage the use of the French language within their borders in the interests of national unity. Bilingualism has obtained ever wider acceptance in these provinces as a condition of our nationhood, although there is still far from a general consensus on the matter.

The legislative and administrative trends in Quebec have been, in form at least, in somewhat the opposite direction. The percentage of the Quebec population whose mother tongue was English was 13.3 percent in 1961 but only 11 percent in 1981. During this time successive governments in Quebec have consistently moved to give legal and practical priority to the French language. The Charter of the French Language, adopted by the National Assembly (legislature) of Quebec in 1977, though by no means the first such law, is now the most notable.[22]

The charter declares that "French is the official language of Quebec." It guarantees, as far as is within provincial powers, that every person in Quebec has the right to communicate with both public and private institutions and agencies in the province in French. It seeks to limit in various ways the use of English in the courts, although this has been held to be unconstitutional as contrary to section 133 of the Constitution Act, 1867. It attempts to ensure that French will become the predominant language of business. It requires a knowledge of French for those seeking a career in public administration or the professions. It seeks to prevent the use of English in commercial signs, although this prohibition has also been successfully attacked in the courts.

One of the most controversial provisions of the charter essentially restricts entrance to schools using English as the medium of instruction to children of parents who have themselves been educated in English in Quebec. Apart from certain exceptions, this prevented recent immigrants to Quebec, whether from non-English-speaking countries or from the United States, the United Kingdom, Australia, New Zealand, or other parts of the English-speaking world (including the nine other provinces of Canada), from having their children educated in English in Quebec. This provision has been held invalid because it conflicts with the Canadian Charter of Rights and Freedoms, adopted in 1982.[23]

Although the Quebec law and the administration by which it has been implemented have been attacked as Draconian and destructive of support for French minority language rights in other provinces, the situation in which the Quebec National Assembly thought it necessary to legislate priority for French in its own territory was very different from that obtaining in the English-speaking provinces, where the priority of the majority language had never been in doubt. French as the language of some 5 million persons in Quebec is under very great pressure in a country of some 20 million English speakers and in a continent with over 250 million English speakers. It is only fair to remember that the English-speaking minority in Quebec, which once numbered some 1 million, traditionally enjoyed services and education in its own language comparable to those available in other parts of the country. In business English tended to dominate as the language of management, and it was widely acceptable in government. The consequence was that, rightly or wrongly, many of the majority language in Quebec felt threatened by English, the language of a group that was provincially a minority but nationally a majority. Nevertheless, the effect of Quebec measures on language and associated matters has been a net emigration of English speakers from Quebec in the past twenty years, sometimes estimated to number in the hundreds of thousands. This has contributed to a trend toward unilingualism in Quebec that is consistent with Quebec nationalism.

I would be remiss in leaving this critical period of our national life without observing that in all the attention and controversy concerning the role of English and French, the languages of what are often referred to as our "two founding peoples," little has been said or done about the preservation of aboriginal languages. They have no legal protection except in the Northwest Territories, where seven of them have been declared the "official aboriginal languages" of the territory. The trends have mostly been in the direction of assimilation of our native peoples insofar as language is concerned, and that assimilation has been predominantly in favor of the English language, even in Quebec. Presumably, on the arrival of Europeans, all of the 220,000 aboriginal peoples spoke their own language. Of the half-million descendants of those people, according to a study made in 1981, only 22.1 percent spoke an aboriginal language at home; 71.7 percent spoke English, and 3.9 percent spoke French. Many governments have been giving more attention to education in aboriginal languages: in 1981–1982 some 34,000 students were enrolled in schools where an aboriginal language was used as a medium of instruction or taught as a language.[24]

Canadian Charter of Rights and Freedoms, 1982. The adoption of the charter was the culmination of a long and contentious constitutional debate in Canada.[25] Apart from some of its more formal aspects (such as the termination of the authority of the British Parliament, exercisable with our consent, to amend our Constitution), basic issues going to the preservation of our nation were involved. Underlying the debate for many years were the conflicting themes that I have discussed: Quebec nationalism, with its emphasis on collective rights preserved by the French Canadian collectivity in Quebec through the government of that province; and pan-Canadianism, to be fostered by the legal recognition of both official languages and the guarantee of individual rights of Canadians to live to the greatest extent practicable in their own language anywhere in Canada. While this debate is by no means off our national agenda and the legitimacy of the charter is not universally recognized, it embodies in a constitutional instrument the elements of pan-Canadian bilingualism and individual rights. In this sense it reflects priorities asserted by the federal government and ultimately accepted by the nine English-speaking provinces.

Most of the charter came into operation as part of a constitutional package on April 17, 1982. It constitutes an amendment to the Canadian Constitution of pervasive importance. Our basic Constitution of 1867 was a positivist document that unquestioningly recognized the supremacy of Parliament and paid little heed to declaring the rights of individuals, which were thought to be best secured through the wisdom of duly elected legislators. In contrast, the charter guarantees a variety of individual rights and perhaps at least one that is collective. It thus limits in important ways the powers of legislators and leaves many decisions to the courts by recognizing their power of judicial review over governmental activities and laws thought to contravene those rights.

I will not deal with general aspects of the charter, much of which is not germane to the subject under consideration, except to refer to section 1, which states: "The Canadian Charter of Rights and Freedoms guarantees the rights and freedoms set out in it subject only to such reasonable limits prescribed by law as can be demonstrably justified in a free and democratic society." This provision reflects a compromise between the interests of the individual on the one hand and those of the public as represented by elected governments on the other. It means that the rights set out in the charter cannot be abrogated without a law purporting to have that effect, and even then the onus is on those who rely on such a law to show that it is "justified in a free and democratic society."

The charter guarantees a number of individual rights typical of democratic pluralistic societies. These include freedom of conscience and religion, protection from arbitrary use of the legal system, the right to vote and to hold public office, the right to enter and leave Canada and to move about in it, freedom from arbitrary state action, and the right to be treated equally under the law without discrimination. Such rights protect diversity in whatever form it may be found.

Other provisions in the charter, however, give priority to certain forms of diversity individually or collectively. The charter makes it clear that the guarantees of equal rights for all are not to be taken to interfere with the rights to publicly supported schools of certain denominations or to abridge treaty or aboriginal rights of our native people (particularly aboriginal claims to the traditional use and enjoyment of land). The charter must be interpreted "in a manner consistent with the preservation and enhancement of the multicultural heritage of Canadians." So, while the charter endorses the freedom of choice of the individual, it tempers that freedom with respect for certain collective interests.

In this same vein—and more germane to the focus of this paper—the charter gives clear constitutional priority to only two languages, English and French.[26] It continues, in effect, the existing constitutional guarantees with respect to English and French in the Parliament of Canada, the legislature of Quebec, and the federal and Quebec courts. But it provides important new constitutional language guarantees. For the first time the Constitution guarantees the use of both languages in the legislature, the laws, and the courts of New Brunswick. It also guarantees the right of any member of the public to receive services in either English or French from the executive branch of the federal government and from the executive branch of the New Brunswick government. For the first time English and French are constitutionally the official languages of Canada in all federal institutions and the official languages of New Brunswick in all its institutions of government. These language provisions essentially give rise to individual rights.

The other kind of linguistic right provided for in the charter, though framed as an individual right, is more a collective right. That is the right given to members of English- or French-speaking minorities, wherever they may be found in the country, to have their children educated at public expense in their language. This right applies when they belong to the minority language group in the province in which they reside or when, although the children's mother tongue is that of the majority of the province, the parents were educated somewhere in Canada in the other official language. For example, if a person whose mother tongue is English was nevertheless educated in French in Quebec, he could insist, in moving to Ontario, that his children be educated in French. This provision has been held by the courts to override the "Quebec clause" in the Quebec Charter of the French Language, which purported to limit the right to an education in English in Quebec to children of parents who had been educated in English in Quebec.[27]

There is an important qualification to the minority language educational rights: such rights cannot be asserted except where the number of children entitled to benefit "is sufficient to warrant the provision to them out of public funds of minority language instruction." In effect, then, an individual cannot assert these rights unless there are enough persons in similar circumstances to warrant the provision of minority language education in that area. In this sense minority language educational rights are collective.

The thrust of these language guarantees in the charter is that to the greatest extent possible every Canadian should be able to move about his or her country and use his or her own language, provided it is one of the two official languages. Of course, most of the language guarantees apply to the federal and New Brunswick governments, while other limited constitutional guarantees apply to the use of either language in respect to the governments of Quebec and Manitoba. The extent to which a French speaker may find provincial governmental services available in other provinces will vary greatly and will depend on legal and administrative measures other than constitutional guarantees.

Nevertheless, the uniform provision in section 23 of the charter concerning minority language education is of fundamental importance. Applying in every province, it means that Canadians with school-age children moving to a province of a different majority language need not accept as inevitable the abandonment by their children of their mother tongue. That all the provinces with an English-speaking majority were able to agree to this constitutional amendment in 1982 reflects the fact that, with federal financial aid, much progress has been made outside Quebec in strengthening the facilities for offering primary and secondary education using French as the medium of instruction.

One important effect of the constitutionalization of language guarantees in the charter is that language disputes are moving more and more from the legislatures to the courts. Since the adoption of the charter, important decisions have been handed down in Quebec and Ontario concerning the validity of provincial minority language education laws in relation to the charter. The "Quebec clause" was held invalid in the face of the "Canada clause" of the charter, by which persons educated in English anywhere in Canada had the right to have their children educated in English in Quebec.[28] And section 23 of the charter was held to require that the French linguistic minority in Ontario be entitled to manage and control the facilities for the provision of education in French.[29] Other cases will no doubt follow as it becomes necessary to interpret the charter.

Conclusion

If maximizing diversity for its own sake were the only valid social goal, probably the best policy for any state would, in principle, be to put all persons on the same legal basis, regardless of race, language, or religion. Canadian experience suggests that, in matters of language at least, the long-term effect of such a purely neutral policy would be the assimilation of minorities by majorities. Outside Quebec the result would have been and still may be the assimilation of French-speaking minorities. In Quebec, without any governmental intervention, the long-term result might arguably have been the assimilation of the French speakers, though a majority in Quebec, into the Canadian English-speaking majority. Apprehension of this prospect has long fueled Quebec nationalism, which has found its expression in demands for greater autonomy within the Canadian federation or for complete independence.

The Constitution as it has developed, to establish and preserve the federation, has thus provided special protection for certain minorities. At the time of confederation in 1867, while there was some recognition of linguistic rights, constitutional guarantees for Protestant or Roman Catholic minorities concerning education were regarded as an important condition for federation. The national understanding was revised and updated by the adoption of the Canadian Charter of Rights and Freedoms in 1982, in which mutual respect for, and preservation of, the two official languages were seen by the governments endorsing the charter as more relevant for the continuation of our nation. The government of Quebec did not subscribe to that view or to the charter, although the charter nevertheless applies in Quebec.

In looking at the ways in which assimilation has been countered and the two languages have been protected, one sees many devices at work in Canada. In part, diversity as between English and French has been fostered by the federal system, in which each government responds to its particular constituency, with the English-speaking majorities in nine provinces giving priority in their institutions to the English language and the French-speaking majority in Quebec giving priority to French in its institutions. In this sense we have an element of territorial language rights. The federal government has sought to be responsive to both language groups, both of them being electorally important within the political structures of the national government.

In exercising its responsibility to preserve the Canadian nation, the rights of Canadian citizenship, and the political and economic integration of the country, it has sought to enhance the use of both languages throughout Canada.

Diversity has also been maintained in Canada through constitutional guarantees of collective rights. These were found in section 93 of the original Constitution Act, 1867, with respect to denominational schools. More recently new collective rights have been established with respect to minority language education by means of section 23 of the Canadian Charter of Rights and Freedoms.

Most recently Canada has entrenched in its Constitution a series of individual rights. These, apart from basic equality and freedom of choice, include rights to the use of the language of choice as long as that choice is either English or French.

We thus see no consistent pattern or logic in the means adopted in the governance of Canada during the past two centuries to accommodate linguistic or other forms of diversity. Any consistency that exists is with respect to ends rather than means: the desire to accommodate such diversity within one political unit on the principle that Canadians still believe they have more in common with one another than they have with the outside world, even their closest neighbor.

Appendix A
Excerpts from Constitution Act, 1867, 30–31 Vict. c.3
(Sections 93 and 133)

93. In and for each Province the Legislature may exclusively make Laws in relation to Education, subject and according to the following Provisions:

(1) Nothing in any such Law shall prejudicially affect any Right or Privilege with respect to Denominational Schools which any Class of Persons have by Law in the Province at the Union:

(2) All the Powers, Privileges, and Duties at the Union by Law conferred and imposed in Upper Canada on the Separate Schools and School Trustees of the Queen's Roman Catholic Subjects shall be and the same are hereby extended to the Dissentient Schools of the Queen's Protestant and Roman Catholic Subjects in Quebec:

(3) Where in any Province a System of Separate or Dissentient Schools exists by Law at the Union or is thereafter established by the Legislature of the Province, an Appeal shall lie to the Gover-

nor General in Council from any Act or Decision of any Provincial Authority affecting any Right or Privilege of the Protestant or Roman Catholic Minority of the Queen's Subjects in relation to Education:

(4) In case any such Provincial Law as from Time to Time seems to the Governor General in Council requisite for the due Execution of the Provisions of this Section is not made, or in case any Decision of the Governor General in Council on any Appeal under this Section is not duly executed by the proper Provincial Authority in that Behalf, then and in every such Case, and as far only as the Circumstances of each Case require, the Parliament of Canada may make remedial Laws for the due Execution of the Provisions of this Section and of any Decision of the Governor General in Council under this Section.

133. Either the English or the French Language may be used by any Person in the Debates of the Houses of the Parliament of Canada and of the Houses of the Legislature of Quebec; and both those Languages shall be used in the respective Records and Journals of those Houses; and either of those Languages may be used by any Person or in any Pleading or Process in or issuing from any Court of Canada established under this Act, and in or from all or any of the Courts of Quebec.

The Acts of the Parliament of Canada and of the Legislature of Quebec shall be printed and published in both those languages.

Appendix B
Excerpt from Canadian Charter of Rights and Freedoms, enacted by the Canada Act, 1982 (U.K.) 1982 c.11

Official Languages of Canada

16. (1) English and French are the official languages of Canada and have equality of status and equal rights and privileges as to their use in all institutions of the Parliament and government of Canada.

(2) English and French are the official languages of New Brunswick and have equality of status and equal rights and privileges as to their use in all institutions of the legislature and government of New Brunswick.

(3) Nothing in this Charter limits the authority of Parliament or a legislature to advance the equality of status or use of English and French.

17. (1) Everyone has the right to use English or French in any debates and other proceedings of Parliament.

(2) Everyone has the right to use English or French in any debates and other proceedings of the legislature of New Brunswick.

18. (1) The statutes, records and journals of Parliament shall be printed and published in English and French and both language versions are equally authoritative.

(2) The statutes, records and journals of the legislature of New Brunswick shall be printed and published in English and French and both language versions are equally authoritative.

19. (1) Either English or French may be used by any person in, or in any pleading in or process issuing from, any court established by Parliament.

(2) Either English or French may be used by any person in, or in any pleading in or process issuing from, any court of New Brunswick.

20. (1) Any member of the public in Canada has the right to communicate with, and to receive available services from, any head or central office of an institution of the Parliament or government of Canada in English or French, and has the same right with respect to any other office of any such institution where

(a) there is a significant demand for communications with and services from that office in such language; or

(b) due to the nature of the office, it is reasonable that communications with and services from that office be available in both English and French.

(2) Any member of the public in New Brunswick has the right to communicate with, and to receive available services from, any office of an institution of the legislature or government of New Brunswick in English or French.

21. Nothing in sections 16 to 20 abrogates or derogates from any right, privilege or obligation with respect to the English and French languages, or either of them, that exists or is continued by virtue of any other provision of the Constitution of Canada.

22.   Nothing in sections 16 to 20 abrogates or derogates from any legal or customary right or privilege acquired or enjoyed either before or after the coming into force of this Charter with respect to any language that is not English or French.

Minority Language Educational Rights

23. (1) Citizens of Canada

   (a)   whose first language learned and still understood is that of the English or French linguistic minority population of the province in which they reside, or

   (b)   who have received their primary school instruction of Canada in English or French and reside in a province where the language in which they received that instruction is the language of the English or French linguistic minority population of the province,

have the right to have their children receive primary and secondary school instruction in that language in that province.

(2) Citizens of Canada of whom any child has received or is receiving primary or secondary school instruction in English or French in Canada, have the right to have all their children receive primary and secondary school instruction in the same language.

(3) The right of citizens of Canada under subsections (1) and (2) to have their children receive primary and secondary school instruction in the language of the English or French linguistic minority population of a province

   (a)   applies wherever in the province the number of children of citizens who have such a right is sufficient to warrant the provision to them out of public funds of minority language instruction; and

   (b)   includes, where the number of those children so warrants, the right to have them receive that instruction in minority language educational facilities provided out of public funds.

Notes

1. Statistics Canada, *Canada Year Book, 1980–81* (Ottawa, 1981), p. 137.
2. The Official Languages Ordinance of the Northwest Territories, adopted in 1984, while naming English and French as the "official lan-

guages," lists seven native languages as "official aboriginal languages." No specific rights are conferred with respect to the latter; the ordinance only enables special provisions to be made with respect to them. Numerous rights are established by the ordinance with respect to English and French.

3. Ibid. The legal position of the French language in Alberta and Saskatchewan is still uncertain and still before the courts.

4. *La langue française au Canada hors Quebec*, Centre de Recherche et de Consultation (Quebec: CERECO, 1985), pp. 6–9. Most of the statistics are drawn from the 1981 census; sources noted in this study.

5. Statistics Canada, *Aboriginal Languages in Canada* (Ottawa, 1984), passim.

6. Statistics Canada, *Canada Year Book*, p. 136.

7. Statistics Canada, *Aboriginal Languages;* and Statistics Canada, *Canada's Native People* (Ottawa, 1984), passim.

8. 30–31 Vict., c.3 (U.K.).

9. See appendix A.

10. Ibid.

11. CERECO, *La langue française*, pp. 6–7.

12. In re Manitoba Act, 1870, s.23 (1985), 19 D.L.R. (4th) 1.

13. See, for example, Russell, "Constitutional Reform of the Canadian Judiciary," *Alberta Law Review,* vol. 7, no. 103 (1969), pp. 114–15.

14. Since this paper was written, the party referred to, the Parti Québecois, was defeated in a provincial election on December 2, 1985.

15. Revised Statutes of Canada, 1970, c. 0-2. For a brief review of the recommendations of the royal commission and their implementation, see Commissioner of Official Languages, *Annual Report, 1984* (Ottawa, 1985), pp. 3–8.

16. Public Service Commission, *Brief to Standing Joint Committee of Senate and House of Commons on Official Languages Policy and Programs* (Ottawa, March 5, 1985), pp. 4–6.

17. Ibid., p. 8.

18. Ibid., pp. 5, 6.

19. Northwest Territories, Official Languages Ordinance, 1984.

20. Statutes of New Brunswick, 1969, c. 14.

21. For a summary of developments in the various provinces see Commissioner of Official Languages, *Annual Report, 1984,* pp. 180–200.

22. Revised Statutes of Quebec, 1977, c. C-11.

23. A.G. of Quebec v. Quebec Association of Protestant School Boards et al. [1984] 2 S.C.R. 66.

24. Statistics Canada, *Aboriginal Languages.*

25. Part I of the Constitution Act, 1982, which was enacted as Schedule B to the Canada Act, 1982 (U.K.), 1982, c-11.

26. For the text of charter linguistic rights, see appendix B.

27. A.G. of Quebec v. Quebec Association of Protestant School Boards.

28. Ibid.

29. Reference re Education Act of Ontario and Minority Language Education Rights (1984), 10 D.L.R. (4th) 491 (Ont. C.A.).

Bibliography

Coleman. "From Bill 22 to Bill 101—the Politics of Language Rights under the Parti Québecois." *Canadian Journal of Political Science* 14 (1981): 459.

Finlay and Sprague. *The Structure of Canadian History.* Prentice-Hall of Canada, 1979.

Friedenberg. *Deference to Authority: The Case of Canada.* White Plains, N.Y.: M. E. Sharpe, 1980.

Jenness. *Indians of Canada,* 7th ed. Toronto: University of Toronto Press, 1977.

McInnis. *Canada: A Political and Social History,* 4th ed.: Holt, Rinehart and Winston of Canada, 1982.

Ollivier. *British North America Acts and Selected Statutes, 1867–1962.* Ottawa: Queen's Printer, 1962.

Scott. "Language Rights and Language Policy in Canada." *Manitoba Law Journal* 5 (1971): 243.

Strayer. *The Canadian Constitution and the Courts.* Toronto: Butterworth, 1983.

Tremblay. "The Language Rights." In *The Canadian Charter of Rights and Freedoms: A Commentary,* edited by Tarnopolsky and Beaudoin. Toronto: Carswell, 1982, pp. 443–66.

Commentary

Robert C. Vipond

Canada is a land of diversity, and its history is shot through with attempts to meet the challenges that diversity brings with it. Justice Strayer presents an extremely rich and varied account of some of the most important forms of diversity in Canada, emphasizing the legal and constitutional means by which the Canadian nation has throughout its history attempted to accommodate this diversity. He concludes that the Canadian experience with diversity, even when limited to constitutional matters, is itself so diverse that it confounds any attempt to generalize. There is, he says, "no consistent pattern or logic in the means adopted in the governance of Canada during the past two centuries to accommodate linguistic or other forms of diversity."[1]

I will be less cautious. I will argue that, at least from the conception of the Canadian confederation in 1867, a pattern and logic have developed in Canada that have tended to protect diversity principally through the constitutional establishment of federalism. The Constitution of 1867 established provincial sovereignty as a fundamental constitutional principle. It put federalism first, if necessary at the expense both of the religious and linguistic rights of minority populations in the provinces and of the federal government's attempts to intervene politically to protect those rights. Moreover, I will argue that the Constitution Act, 1982, constitutes a challenge to this logic by providing a more secure legal foundation for the protection of rights that is independent of and higher than any governmental body.

When the fathers of the Canadian confederation gathered in 1864 to design the constitutional underpinnings for what is now called Canada, they were forced to confront the stubborn sociological fact that Canada is composed of two sets of overlapping and clearly identifiable majorities and minorities. French Canadians, who form a minority in the country as a whole, nevertheless form a majority in the province of Quebec; English Canadians, who constitute the majority in the country as a whole, nevertheless constitute a minority in

Quebec. The dilemma for the fathers of confederation was to find some way to accommodate the interests of both sets of majorities and minorities.

The creation of a federation that allowed local populations to control local affairs offered a partial solution to the problem. Politicians from Quebec clearly insisted on some such protection for the province's "individuality," especially for its distinctive legal, educational, and religious institutions.[2] But federalism was an attractive alternative outside Quebec as well. The Maritime provinces were no less proud of their local institutions and no less insistent that their distinctiveness be protected. Even in Ontario, where the powerful Reform party somewhat perversely feared the "domination" of French Canadians, the demand for "local control over local affairs" became a cliché of preconfederation political discourse.[3] While there was disagreement about whether the proposed federal scheme *would* protect local diversity, there was consensus that it *should*. From the start, then, the protection of diversity in Canada has been associated with federalism.

Yet the fathers of confederation understood that federalism created almost as many problems as it solved. While federalism might protect provincial majorities, it might actually threaten the equally legitimate rights and interests of those identifiable groups that make up provincial minorities and are therefore vulnerable to unsympathetic or downright intolerant provincial legislatures. Apart from the justice of the case, they understood that their proposed union would not succeed if they ignored the claims of their supporters among these minorities, especially the English Protestant community in Quebec. For this reason they considered it important to provide protection for the most numerous, identifiable, and influential provincial minorities as well, to achieve some sort of workable balance between the requirements of federalism on the one hand and the protection of provincial minorities on the other. When the chief architect of the confederation plan, Sir John A. Macdonald, praised the confederation scheme as a "happy medium" between two conflicting alternatives, he was referring in part to the creation of some such balance.[4]

The course of Canadian political history since 1867, however, suggests that no such balance between federal and subfederal diversity has actually been achieved. While the provincial governments have become far stronger and more assertive than Macdonald would have wanted, the most identifiable provincial minorities have been progressively assimilated, threatened with assimilation, or, at the very least, placed on the defensive.

The reasons for the imbalance go back to the design of the

Constitution of 1867. First, legally enforceable constitutional protection for provincial minorities was really rather limited. Section 133 of the Constitution guaranteed the right of individuals to use either French or English in the federal Parliament, the legislature of Quebec, federally created courts, and the courts of Quebec. Yet as Justice Strayer points out, this provision excluded far more than it included. It did not apply to executive actions of either of the governments mentioned, even though the executive branch is "the branch with which the ordinary citizen would most frequently come into contact."[5] Nor did it apply to any of the provinces beyond Quebec (and ultimately Manitoba), even though several other provinces had and have sizable French-speaking minorities.

Section 93, which guarantees public support for religious education, is similarly limited. It protects the existence of "denominational schools" but not "the use of a minority language as the medium of instruction in denominational schools run by religious minorities."[6] It is limited to Catholic and Protestant schools, apparently excluding other denominational schools from its coverage. Most contentiously, it protects only those denominational school systems established in law at the time of union. Over the years this has excluded both separate school systems that developed haphazardly without a secure foundation in law and those whose legal foundation was established after the province entered the confederation. The former condition excluded the de facto separate school system in New Brunswick.[7] The latter affected Manitoba, where a separate school system was established the year after the province joined the confederation.[8]

The parsimony of the constitutional protection for provincial minorities has often been interpreted to mean that the architects of confederation were halfhearted in their commitment to the rights of provincial minorities. That is not the only reading, however. It may equally mean that they placed their hopes in the political rather than the legal protection of those rights. Considerable evidence suggests, in fact, that many of the most prominent fathers of confederation expected the federal government to take an active part in supervising the provincial governments to ensure that they treated the minority groups under their jurisdiction fairly. Section 93 of the Constitution Act, for instance, provides an appeal to the federal cabinet and empowers the federal government to pass remedial legislation to redress the denial of educational rights. More important, the federal government was given the unconditional, potentially limitless power to veto or strike down any provincial legislation, either by having a provincial lieutenant governor reserve his assent from a provincial bill or simply by "disallowing" an act of the provincial legislature.

Justice Strayer is no doubt right in his assertion that the Constitu-

189

tion Act does not clearly assign the use of either of these veto powers to cases in which the rights of provincial minorities have been violated.[9] But it appears evident from the debates that preceded the adoption of the act that its most important supporters believed that the veto powers would indeed be used to protect provincial minorities. During the legislative debates called in 1865 to discuss the confederation proposal, several of the delegates argued that a veto power was crucial to protect the interests, especially, of English Protestants in Quebec.

One such delegate, John Rose, noted the apprehension of his constituents, who feared that a legislature dominated by those of another "race and religion" might attempt to manipulate the electoral laws so as to reduce the influence of the English Protestant minority in Quebec. Rose entertained no such apprehension, however. "If the Local Legislature exercised power in any such unjust manner, it would be competent for the General Government to veto its action— even although the power be one which is declared to be absolutely vested in the Local Government." As if on cue, George Etienne Cartier, the leading French Canadian proponent of confederation, rose to reinforce the point. If ever the Quebec legislature should attempt to disenfranchise English Canadians in Quebec, "the General Government will have the right to veto any law it might pass to this effect and set it at nought."[10] Macdonald had put it even more bluntly to the delegates to the Quebec conference the year before. Under the confederation scheme, he said, "we shall . . . be able to protect the minority by having a powerful central government."[11]

Whether or not these sentiments were shared by all the fathers of confederation, at the very least the veto powers gave the federal government the means to protect the rights of provincial minorities.[12] The potential inherent in the veto powers was probably best understood by the provincial minorities themselves. Once the ink was dry on the Constitution Act, the federal government was indeed urged in several key cases—in New Brunswick, Quebec, Ontario, and Manitoba—to exercise its veto powers to redress such grievances.[13]

Yet in the early years after confederation the hopes vested in the federal government's power to check provincial legislation were consistently dashed. As Justice Strayer notes, the provision for remedial legislation contained in section 93 of the Constitution Act has never been used.[14] Indeed, the threat of its use in the 1890s against the Manitoba legislature led directly to one of the most important electoral defeats in Canadian history. Moreover, the veto powers of reservation and disallowance were never used to protect minority linguistic, educational, or cultural rights, and both have long since passed into virtual disuse, unloaded pistols held at provincial heads.

Why did the federal government abandon its use of the veto powers? The answer in part is that as the first governments after confederation began to sort out the implications of the Constitution, they were forced to confront the fact that the veto powers could not easily be reconciled with the Constitution's underlying principles. Macdonald, who was prime minister for most of the first generation after confederation, came slowly but surely to appreciate the extent to which the Constitution had altered the terms of Canadian politics by recasting the longstanding demand for local control in the form of a constitutional principle. The Constitution Act had entrenched the principle that within their sphere of jurisdiction the provincial legislatures have the exclusive right to legislate.[15] Certain strictly defined exceptions to this "fixed principle"[16] might exist; the remedial provision of section 93 was one such exception. But the principle itself remained fixed, firm, and authoritative.

Thus, despite his clear preference for a highly centralized federation, Macdonald was forced to admit that the principle of provincial sovereignty and the integrity of the provincial legislatures could not be placed at the mercy of an unlimited veto power lodged in a political body like the federal cabinet. Whatever promises he and his colleagues may have made before confederation to provincial minorities, he soon came to realize that regular federal intervention in provincial affairs would be inappropriate, not only because it would threaten the place of French Canadians in Quebec but because it would violate the first rules of liberal constitutionalism. Reservation and disallowance are veto powers; provincial autonomy is a constitutional principle. Macdonald was a sufficiently skilled constitutionalist to know that principle prevails over and limits power.[17]

Macdonald's own actions as prime minister were by no means completely consistent with the principle of noninterference in provincial affairs. On several occasions his Conservative government struck down provincial legislation that was clearly within provincial jurisdiction to gain partisan advantage or to enforce some shadowy notion of the national interest.[18] Nevertheless, the principle of provincial sovereignty, once loosed, was difficult to cabin.[19] Any time a federal administration threatened to veto provincial legislation on the pretext of protecting provincial minorities, the provincial governments were able to argue persuasively that such intervention would violate one of the fundamental principles of the Constitution, the principle of provincial sovereignty. By the turn of the century this argument had become unassailable, and it served the useful purpose of focusing political opposition to federal supervision.[20]

In sum, the authors of the Constitution of 1867 believed that they had created a fine balance between the protection of federal diversity (through the constitutional entrenchment of provincial autonomy) and the protection of subfederal diversity (through the largely political protection of provincial minorities). In fact, however, they created a constitutional system in which the balance soon tilted to the protection of provincial majorities at the expense of their minorities.

This is not to say that the federal government has been helpless over the years to affect the position of those provincial minorities. It may exhort the provincial governments to deal fairly with their minorities (as the Macdonald government did in the case of the New Brunswick schools). It may use its spending power to encourage the provincial governments to provide educational services to its minority populations (as the government of Canada now does). It may even act within its own sphere of jurisdiction to protect the rights of minorities (this is the object of the Official Languages Act). But it is now accepted that the federal government may not act to protect individuals or groups against otherwise valid provincial legislation. If the course of Canadian constitutional history has accomplished nothing else, it has established the principle of autonomy, of noninterference.

Yet once the principle of provincial sovereignty was accepted, the assimilation of subfederal groups became easier. Indeed, the rise of provincial sovereignty did correspond to a "general assimilative trend" outside Quebec, where those provinces that have always been overwhelmingly English-speaking have "paid scant regard to the use of French in government, schools, business, or social affairs." The situation was rather different for the English-speaking minority in Quebec, most of whom "were able to live their lives in English with little pressure for assimilation," but this difference reflected the peculiar social, economic, and political conditions of Quebec more than any constitutional restraint.[21]

One can understand in this context why the claims of Quebec nationalism took hold as they did in the 1960s and 1970s. Quebec nationalism appealed to all those Quebeckers who wanted at least the same control over their affairs that other provinces enjoyed, if not more; it appealed to those who wanted educational, linguistic, and cultural policy in Quebec to respond to provincial priorities without fear of federal interference. The goal, in other words, was autonomy, if not within the Canadian federation, then outside it.

As Justice Strayer points out, the response to the ferment of Quebec nationalism in the 1960s and 1970s was spearheaded by Prime Minister Pierre Trudeau and involved the development of an alternative, pan-Canadian view of Canadian society. This pan-Canadianism rests on the view that "both French Canadian and Anglo-Canadian society exist throughout the country, and neither is identified with a particular government."[22] From this it follows, Strayer argues, that each government in Canada should protect the sub-federal linguistic minorities within its jurisdiction.[23] Pan-Canadi-anism rests, in other words, on a view of Canadian society sharply different from that espoused by Quebec nationalists, and it has given rise, predictably, to two decades of conflict among Quebec, Ottawa, and, to some extent, the other provinces.

The most recent salvo in this continuing constitutional conflict is the passage of the Constitution Act, 1982. In one sense the context of this most recent constitutional debate appears utterly familiar; it is but the latest attempt to balance federal and subfederal diversity in Can-ada. In a deeper sense, however, the Constitution Act, especially its Charter of Rights and Freedoms, is a bold attempt to recast the constitutional question of diversity. Justice Strayer argues that the charter has "revised and updated" the "national understanding" that has existed since confederation regarding the linguistic and educa-tional rights of subfederal minorities.[24] My view is that the charter signifies not merely the revision and updating of this national under-standing but the uncertain transformation of the Constitution as a whole.

This transformation has two elements. It consists, first, in what might be called the legalization of constitutional questions in Canada. As Justice Strayer notes, the charter has dealt the courts into many questions of Canadian political life from which they were previously excluded or in which their part was less significant, questions of language and educational rights included. The charter provides im-portant new language guarantees, especially in education and other public services; it guarantees "a number of individual rights typical of democratic pluralistic societies,"[25] and it provides for the "equal pro-tection and equal benefit" of the law. The task of interpreting these broad, even open-ended, provisions has already given the courts a higher profile in the Canadian political system.

It is not as if the courts played no part in such disputes before 1982. Of course they did, and Justice Strayer has referred to several of the most important cases. But if I am right that pan-Canadianism originally manifested itself in the institutional form of a strong, even domineering, central government that would act as a political coun-terpoise to illiberal provincial policy, the charter is an important departure from our political and constitutional tradition. Indeed, the charter reflects the historical judgment that such political checks have largely failed to prevent the provincial governments from acting as they wished toward the minorities in their midst. It reflects the recognition that, in light of the entrenchment of provincial autonomy, the federal government was in important respects powerless to protect those minorities. The charter creates a constitutional standard independent of and higher than any governmental body.[26] It creates a constitutional rather than a political counterpoise to provincial power and thus attempts to establish the balance between federal and sub-federal diversity that the Constitution of 1867 failed to establish.

The charter of rights is, or at least is likely to be, transformative in a second way that goes beyond its effects on the courts and the legal profession. For a Constitution of this sort cannot be understood merely as a legal code that designates the limits of governmental power. It must be understood more broadly as a statement of fundamental political principles that anchors and guides political discourse; a statement of political purpose that directs the way in which political questions are discussed in public, opening certain possibilities while foreclosing others.

The Constitution of 1867 performed precisely this function in relation to the principle of provincial sovereignty. In giving the long-standing call for local control constitutional status in the form of provincial sovereignty, the framers of the original Constitution gave that political goal an authority and weight that it had hitherto lacked. Once established, the principle of provincial autonomy became an immensely powerful and public standard that parliamentarians, electioneering politicians, and publicists constantly referred to and that lent an unmistakable tone to the continuing debate about federalism in Canada.[27]

If it has not already done so, the establishment of a constitutional Charter of Rights and Freedoms seems almost sure to affect Canadian political discourse equally fundamentally. The charter, after all, mandates not merely that some value be placed on free expression, freedom of conscience and religion, freedom of the press, and the like but that these freedoms be considered fundamental. It enjoins Canadians to put rights first and to reflect on the "reasonable limitations" to which these rights are subject. It thus creates a way to think about and discuss political questions. It establishes a framework for political deliberation that entails intellectual and political choices rather different from the ones Canadians have traditionally had to make. The courts may approach the Constitution gingerly, and the government of Quebec may continue to deny its legitimacy. But for a country in which the political alternatives have often seemed limited to the choice between provincial autonomy on the one hand and "peace, order and good government"[28] on the other, the enactment of a constitutional Charter of Rights and Freedoms is a significant event indeed.

Notes

1. Barry L. Strayer, "The Canadian Constitution and Diversity."
2. See A. I. Silver, *The French-Canadian Idea of Confederation* (Toronto: University of Toronto Press, 1982).
3. See W. L. Morton, *The Critical Years, 1857–1873* (Toronto: McClelland and Stewart, 1964).
4. Canada, Legislative Assembly, *Parliamentary Debates on the Subject of the Confederation of the British North American Provinces* (Quebec: Hunter, Rose, and Co., 1865), p. 32 (hereafter cited as *Confederation Debates*).
5. Strayer, "Canadian Constitution and Diversity."
6. Ibid.
7. For background to the New Brunswick schools question, see Peter M. Toner, "New Brunswick Schools and Provincial Rights," in Bruce Hodgins, Don Wright, and W. H. Heick, eds., *Federalism in Canada and Australia: The Early Years* (Waterloo: Wilfrid Laurier University Press, 1978).
8. For background on the Manitoba schools question, see P. B. Waite, *Canada: Arduous Destiny, 1874–1896* (Toronto: McClelland and Stewart, 1971), chaps. 11–13.
9. Strayer, "Canadian Constitution and Diversity"; see also Constitution Act, 1867, secs. 56, 90.
10. *Confederation Debates*, p. 407.
11. G. P. Browne, ed., *Documents on the Confederation of British North America* (Toronto: McClelland and Stewart, 1969), p. 95. See also the statement by the third member of the Great Coalition triumvirate, George Brown: "By vesting the appointment of the lieutenant governors in the General Government, and giving a veto for all local measures, we have secured that no injustice shall be done without appeal in local legislation." *Confederation Debates*, p. 108.
12. The federal veto power was in fact a highly controversial part of the confederation proposal. For instance, while Cartier thought the veto a useful means by which to protect provincial minorities, many of the French Canadians involved in the confederation negotiations—both pro and con—were more concerned to ensure Quebec's complete legislative control over its own affairs. They opposed the regular use of the federal veto power on the grounds that this would undermine provincial autonomy, even if that meant being indifferent to the fate of the French Canadian minority outside Quebec. See Silver, *French-Canadian Idea*, chaps. 2, 3.
13. I am referring here to the New Brunswick schools question, the Jesuit estates affair (involving the disposition of assets belonging to the Jesuits in Quebec), the Orange Lodge controversy (involving the controversial reservation of an Ontario bill that incorporated the anti-Catholic Orange Lodge) and the Manitoba schools question.
14. Strayer, "Canadian Constitution and Diversity."
15. Constitution Act, 1867, sec. 92.
16. Canada, Parliament, *House of Commons Debates* (May 14, 1873), col. 177.
17. Macdonald elaborated on this argument in the course of the debates on the New Brunswick schools question. See, especially, his speech of May 14,

1873 (cited in note 16). The same argument, playing on the difference between constitutional principle and political power, was subsequently incorporated into Liberal party doctrine and used against Macdonald.

18. See Gerard La Forest, *Disallowance and Reservation of Provincial Legislation* (Ottawa: Queen's Printer, 1955).

19. I have borrowed the phrase from Archibald Cox's assessment of the U.S. Supreme Court's interpretation of the equal protection clause of the Fourteenth Amendment. See Archibald Cox, *The Role of the Supreme Court in American Government* (London: Oxford University Press, 1976), chaps. 3, 4.

20. Thus Ernest Lapointe, Mackenzie King's minister of justice, noted before Parliament in 1937 that "for many years the power of disallowance ha[d] not been resorted to by the Government of Canada." He explained that as long as "the provincial legislatures feel that they are still supreme and sovereign within the sphere of their jurisdiction," it would be difficult for the central government to exercise the power of disallowance. Canada, Parliament, *House of Commons Debates*, 1937, vol. 3, p. 2294.

21. Strayer, "Canadian Constitution and Diversity."

22. Ibid.

23. Ibid.

24. Ibid.

25. Ibid.

26. The one apparently large exception to this characterization is the "notwithstanding" clause. By section 33 of the charter of rights, either Parliament or the legislature of a province may explicitly declare that one (or more) of its acts shall operate "notwithstanding a provision included in section 2 or sections 7 to 15 of this Charter." Parliament or a provincial legislature may, in other words, exempt itself from the charter's coverage. It is to be noted, however, that this provision does not apply to the sections of the charter dealing with official languages (secs. 16–22) or minority language educational rights (sec. 23).

27. For an elaboration of this argument, see Robert C. Vipond, "Constitutional Politics and the Legacy of the Provincial Movement in Canada," *Canadian Journal of Political Science*, vol. 18, no. 2 (June 1985), pp. 267–94.

28. Constitution Act, 1867, sec. 91.

Discussion

ROBERT GOLDWIN: Canada has a written constitution that includes many important concessions to the French-speaking population. It makes French speaking acceptable and constitutional anywhere and everywhere in Canada. The government of Quebec does not accept its principles, however, and does not accept pan-Canadianism. That government has not approved the Constitution, and there is doubt whether it will accept the supremacy of that document. What does this tell us about Canada and its Constitution? What does it tell us about the efficacy of written constitutions? Is the problem in the Constitution of Canada or in the way the Canadian nation is constituted?

BARRY STRAYER: This tells us that Canada is a diverse country and that there is no unanimous agreement on these matters and probably never will be. Let me speak to the idea of "concession" to French-speaking Canadians. Most French-Canadians would resist the term concession, insisting that at last a fuller measure of justice is being provided and that their proper place in the Canadian scheme of things is finally being recognized.

The question refers to the position of the government of Quebec and to the fact that it does not accept the new Constitution. The new Constitution is really a sizable amendment to our old Constitution, which we have had in place for 120 years or so. It changes our constitutional scheme of things by putting in place guarantees of individual rights and an amendment process. But the old Constitution is still there; it has a lot in it of importance to Quebec as well as to other provinces, as it provides for the distribution of powers, giving very substantial authority to the provinces with respect to language and cultural matters—particularly in education—but also in business, commerce, and civil law.

The government of Quebec may in fact oppose the new or amended Constitution, but there are obviously conflicting views among the people of the province of Quebec and within the French-Canadian community, which does not end at the border of Quebec. At least until something dramatically different happens, I am per-

197

suaded that the new Constitution or amended Constitution has full legal application in Quebec.

In a more general sense, the whole issue of independence for Quebec, for the moment, seems to be quiescent and not to be affecting politics. The province of Quebec is represented fully in the federal institutions of the government. The present government has many ministers from that province, and federalist politics goes on as usual there, notwithstanding the rather dramatic events of three or four years ago. It should also be kept in mind that—apart from the obvious dichotomy of view within Quebec between the Parti Québecois, the provincialist party, and the two major national or federalist parties— there are about a million Francophones outside Quebec, who obviously have a somewhat different perspective. They are, on the whole, much more enthusiastic about the pan-Canadian approach, because the individual rights in the new Constitution tend to give them the most in respect of minority language education. All this suggests that French Canadians have by no means rejected pan-Canadianism or the individual rights approach.

All that aside, I don't think what I called the pan-Canadian approach in my paper will ever be the complete answer to the problems of diversity of language in Canada. As much as we may espouse the principles of pan-Canadianism, it will always be tempered by the special place of Quebec and the partial identification of Francophone interests with the interests of the province of Quebec.

This whole debate became very acerbic during the time of our former prime minister, Pierre Trudeau, himself a French-Canadian. He insisted that the aspirations of the Quebec nationalists were in the nature of tribalism and that French-Canadians, to realize themselves, had to break out of the "fortress Quebec" mentality and make their presence known throughout the country. That approach led to a number of the developments described in my paper. But there will always be a certain "fortress Quebec" mentality in the minds of many people in that province.

ROBERT VIPOND: For at least twenty years, the question of constitutional renewal has been one of the most important questions on the political agenda in Canada, culminating in the passage of the Constitution Act of 1982, including the Charter of Rights and Freedoms. I was caught up in most of the academic reaction to that charter and to the Constitution. During that period, I used in my introductory Canadian politics course at the University of Toronto the book *And No One Cheered*. It was fully of gloomy predictions about the Constitution and dark analyses of how badly the constitutional process had been managed. Many believed that the new founding fathers had missed an opportunity to solve Canada's problems and instead had merely deepened them.

One of the entries in this anthology, "The Great Misdeed," described the referendum in Quebec in 1980, which at least indirectly posed the question of separation. The electorate responded that they did not want to authorize the government of Quebec to begin negotiations for autonomy. The essay suggested that the Quebec population was convinced that they ought to give Canada one more chance to restructure Canadian federalism in such a way as to recognize the important interests and rights of Quebec. According to this argument, the new Constitution, which actually excluded Quebec, was therefore a misdeed.

Thus we are surprised that the movement for autonomy for Quebec is so quiet today. How could the citizens of Quebec have interpreted the new Constitution in a way so radically different from the predictions of Canada's best political scientists? One might answer that this shows how successful and how relevant constitutionalism has been for Canadian politics. As is frequently argued in the political science literature, one simply cannot understand constitutions as formal, descriptive, or prescriptive documents; one must also understand the political, social, and economic contexts in which they are developed. Indeed, one must perhaps understand constitutions as vehicles through which various groups try to see that their interests are solidified, deepened, and strengthened.

The obverse, however, is equally important: constitutions themselves may affect social and political behavior as well. A constitution can be a list of priorities or a set of political principles that puts certain things first. In the case of 1867, clearly the fathers of confederation put federalism first. Initially, they may not have understood the full implications of that, but within twenty or thirty years of the Confederation Settlement of 1867, they began to appreciate what it meant to enshrine as a legal constitutional principle something called federalism.

Notwithstanding Mr. De Bandt's point in his paper that it is now difficult to think of the units of federal societies as water-tight compartments, one might interpret the Canadian experience as the triumph of the constitutionalization of diversity through the principle of provincial autonomy. This has informed the way Canadians think of their politics and the value they place on the provinces. In that context, it might not be too much to argue that the ascendency of

Quebec nationalism over the past twenty or twenty-five years has had something to do in fact with federalism. Indeed, it essentially takes provincial autonomy to its logical conclusion.

The Canadian case offers a very interesting example of the precise interrelation between social, political, and economic factors on the one hand and constitutions on the other. The case suggests a triumph of constitutionalism—especially of the constitutionalization of diversity—not simply the triumph of a formal document but a triumph of the way people actually think about politics and the way political principles are then strengthened in conventions, in legislative acts, and indeed in social behavior.

WALTER BERNS: It was argued earlier that a major unifying force in both Zimbabwe and India was the colonial power of Britain. Britain was also the colonial power involved in Canada, but, of course, I think no one would say that it has been a force for unity there. The reason for that is quite clear: the British constituted one of the two major peoples of Canada. One might therefore conclude that there is a greater degree of disunity in Canada than in other places. Yet, compared with Belgium, and probably with other countries represented in this conference, there is much more unity in Canada than in Belgium and other nations.

Why is this so? I would suggest that the past few years have shown that Canada was *not* a country divided into two cultures—a French-Canadian culture and an English-Canadian culture—it was rather a country divided linguistically. And solving the linguistic problem would go a long way toward solving the problem of disunity in Canada. Today, the people of Quebec seem to be satisfied with the fact that the French language is now constitutionally enshrined, and so the problem is less serious. And there is indeed one culture in Canada. What the French wanted, and what they have, is the right to tune in to "Dynasty" and "Dallas" in French, just as the people of so-called upper Canada, the English speaking, may tune in to those programs in English. One major reason for the lack of disunity in Canada, then, is its presence in a larger bourgeois society in North America.

THOMAS PANGLE: Professor Vipond argues that the past few years have seen a fundamental transformation in the basic political regime of Canada, the consequences of which are not yet clear, any more than the consequences of 1867 were altogether clear immediately. This transformation involves a shift from an essentially federal system—and, we could add from Professor Strayer's paper, a positivistic conception of the law—to a much more rights-oriented conception of the law, bringing with it an antagonism not between provinces so much as between groups. Isn't this to say that Canada is being Americanized in a rather radical way?

MR. VIPOND: There is some truth to that. In the British North America Act, there is no ringing declaration of inalienable rights to life, liberty, or the pursuit of happiness. We are simply told that the government of Canada has the power to make laws for the peace, order, and good government of Canada. It is striking that that is in a way the only "normative" sentiment included in the old 1867 act. It does seem that there will be a tremendous difference when we start thinking about rights. Now, this is not to say that Canadians have not placed any value upon liberty, upon individual freedom. Obviously it has been a liberal democratic regime, but there are important nuances of differences. It does make a difference to say that one has a *right* to a certain thing, say, to free speech, on the one hand, and, on the other, to say that there is a certain importance in protecting free speech, which, however, has to be balanced against some other aspect of the public interest. The latter formulation would require one to think about the purposes for which speech might be used as opposed to the purposes for which the state might be asked to act. That would involve one in rather different reflections and perhaps have political consequences different from those occurring if one simply says there is a right and rights always trump governmental action.

JACOB LANDAU: Previous speakers are a bit too optimistic in their appraisal of the general situation in Canada. Some progress has been made, of course, but to say that cultural differences are nonexistent exaggerates. I get the impression from my conversations with the Canadian political and literary elite that the French read very little English literature, books, or newspapers and that the English read even fewer French publications. There is a cultural cleavage that is far from being bridged. Territorial unilingualism seems no better than overall bilingualism in securing political and economic accommodation.

MR. BERNS: I doubt very much that there is something that might be called real French culture in Quebec. The typical resident of Quebec does not spend his time reading Molière, Racine, and the like. And, while there may have been a time in the past when the typical well-educated citizen of English Canada read Dickens and Shakespeare, I suspect that what has happened in the United States has happened in

201

English-speaking Canada, too: so not much time is spent reading those classics now.

What is it to which the souls of the French-Canadians and the English-Canadians are attracted? More or less the same things to which the souls of Americans are attracted. We are all bourgeois together. There is not really much that divides Canadians otherwise except language.

MR. STRAYER: On the cultural question, starting in the 1950s and 1960s, a real development and enrichment of a Quebec-French culture have occurred, which should not be underrated. This has been true in literature, dance, music, and film. It is in many ways quite different from English-Canadian culture.

People live side-by-side who do not talk to each other and who do not understand each other, and that is unfortunate. Things are changing a little, and I think the culture gap may be narrowing a bit. There are more efforts being made to translate English-Canadian literature into French and French-Canadian literature into English. The government funds this activity, and commercial publishers are more interested in it these days. So I have again permitted myself a bit of optimism there.

MR. GOLDWIN: I have another "modest proposal": perhaps we should move Belgium to North America so that the influence of North American bourgeois culture could help Belgium achieve the success Canada has enjoyed.

JACQUES VANDERLINDEN: We are already all bourgeois in Western Europe. Yet look at Switzerland compared with France, Belgium compared with France, or the French-speaking community of Belgium compared with the Dutch-speaking community. That argument would never hold. I wonder if Canada's increasing unity is not just a reflection of the tremendous power of the United States and the reaction against that power.

MR. BERNS: To respond to Mr. Vanderlinden's point, I refer him to the argument of a gentleman I would describe as "Mr. Canada," George Grant. His family left New Jersey in 1776 and has since become what might be called an establishment family in Canada, from which has come a long line of distinguished Canadians in public service and in educational circles. He wrote a lovely book, *Lament for a Nation*, and the nation he was lamenting was, of course, Canada. George Grant would have been willing to accept a much lower standard of living if

that were required—and he understood it would have been required—to erect some sort of barrier between the country that he
loved and the United States, this monster to the south. He was
concerned that Canada would join the universal homogeneous state. I
think there is really reason to fear the existence of something that
might fairly be called the universal homogeneous state.

So when Mr. Vanderlinden suggested I am oversimplifying when
I talk about bourgeois culture, I wonder whether I am. I think of the
influence of American rock music around the world, including Canada, of course. I am all in favor of cultural exchange with the Soviet
Union, for example. They send us world-famous cellists, who become
directors of our symphony orchestras, and world-class dancers, many
of whom defect. What do we send them? We send them rock music,
which has the salutary effect of corrupting their younger generation,
just as it has corrupted ours. One cannot overestimate the extent to
which this bourgeois culture, which finds its natural home in the
United States, is spreading throughout the world.

DANIEL ELAZAR: This returns us to some of the points that were made
yesterday about the relationship between political culture and constitutionalism that might be worth exploring for a minute. I have always
been much more optimistic about the future of Canadian federalism
than the Canadians seem to have been. The new constitutional framework does seem to have helped firm up that part of Canada, which I
think has been less eroded by what some call bourgeois culture. There
seems to be much more of a common Canadian political culture—at
least for certain purposes and allowing for the existence of sub-
cultures—than maybe Canadians themselves had perceived. And this
has been embodied in the constitutional settlement. This constitutional settlement has taken on a life of its own, bringing forward those
common elements in the political culture.

MR. VIPOND: It is hard to explain some of the very deeply felt and
deeply entrenched diversity that exists, especially in Europe, without
considering history and the social fabric that has developed over time.
The same is true in Canada. It is extremely significant that to this day
are inscribed the words, "The Conquest, 1763," on license plates in
the province of Quebec. This is not an unimportant symbol of Quebec
nationalism and a reflection of the extent to which that phenomenon
has persisted. Québecois historians tell us that at any given time in
Quebec's history at least 25 percent of the population have wanted
out. That has risen in some years and came close to 50 percent in the
late 1970s, but there has always been that common thread.

203

On the other hand, it is important to remember one thing that does differentiate Europe—and that part of North America that might seem most European, namely Quebec—from North America: as Louis Hartz always used to say, America did not experience feudalism. That makes a difference in the sorts of disputes that will occur on the ideological spectrum. One sees the supremacy of political and economic issues of management in the past three, four, or five years, over the question of separation in Quebec. That is a very North American way to frame political questions.

MICHEL TROPER: Our discussion indicates that diversity is mainly a psychological phenomenon and that it transcends linguistic differences and any other religious or ethnic differences. Similarly, constitutionalism seems to be a psychological phenomenon—a general belief that a constitution can have a certain political effect on the structure of a country and on the exercise of power. In Canada, for instance, it has operated precisely on the psychological beliefs of the two groups. Have we come to a dead end: constitutionalism is a belief that the Constitution works, and it only works if people believe in the Constitution?

MR. VIPOND: One usually understands constitutions as devices to channel and limit power, in a way that reacts to or is informed by social, political, and economic conditions. My hypothesis is that constitutionalism may also inform behavior of these various sorts. I don't think it is a tautology. The empirical evidence of Canadian history illustrates my point.

In that sense it is psychological: a constitution affects the way people think and the way they weigh different purposes to which power may be put or the different ways in which power may be limited. A constitution creates a hierarchy of sorts; it ranks political ends to resolve conflicts and dilemmas as they appear.

P. K. TRIPATHI: Now that Canadians have the Charter of Rights and Liberties, will the courts be asked to enforce the rights of French-speaking citizens against the Quebec government and of the English-speaking citizens against governments with an English-speaking majority? Would the focus not therefore change from language differences to issues of citizens versus government? This would surely lead to a greater understanding between the communities and would deemphasize whatever divisive opinions there might be.

MR. STRAYER: Although supporters of the Constitution did believe it was important to protect individual rights, nonetheless, it was clear that there was also a government strategy to move the constitutional debate off the question of the distribution of powers. Controversy had mostly centered there, and the conflict over what powers might be transferred to the provinces seemed insoluble. The adoption of a charter of rights was seen as very important to national unity as it extended the area of shared values and eventually shared experience to all Canadians. The centrifugal forces in Canada are always quite strong, and so there have been many efforts over the years to try to establish and reinforce national institutions of one sort or another to give Canadians a sense of commonality. We did not have even proper Canadian citizenship until after the Second World War. We did not have a proper Canadian flag until 1965. It was only about three or four years ago that Parliament adopted a national anthem, and even there, a careful reading shows that the English words are quite different from the French words. In any event, I think the Charter of Rights and Liberties was seen as another common institution that Canadians could share.

5
Swiss Federalism
Otto K. Kaufmann

The Swiss confederation has often been admired for its stability and its ability to promote the general welfare of its inhabitants. But Swiss federal democracy is no product for exportation. It is a skilled form of government that has grown up through seven centuries, a flower that may flourish only on the ground of its birth. It is very difficult to govern within the Swiss governmental system. This paper attempts to show the difficult functioning of this system.

Swiss democracy is a very slow-working form of democracy. But no Swiss group believes that it would be better to join Germany, France, Italy, or Austria. So the Swiss stay together, quarreling among themselves and criticizing the activity and inactivity of the federal and the twenty-six cantonal governments. They are bound together; there is no escape. The Swiss federal democracy may be a political miracle, but it is worthwhile to study this unique democracy of 6.3 million people in the middle of Europe. Most Swiss people are convinced that a decentralized, democratic state power is nearer to the people than a centralized, uniform system such as exists in France.

A Bit of Swiss History

Swiss people celebrate the first of August 1291 as the birthday of the Swiss confederation. That is the date of the oldest document (written in Latin) proving the existence of a sworn treaty among the people of the valleys, of Uri, Schwyz, and Unterwalden (Nidwalden and Ob-walden), around the lake that is now called the Vierwaldstättersee. The "men of the valleys" promised each other, "forever," help and assistance whenever "anybody" (that is, the House of Habsburg) should try to impose on them "a foreign judge" and declared that they accepted no authority other than the emperor of the Reich. In fact, Uri and Schwyz had received "freedom letters" from the emperors similar to those given to many "free cities" *(Reichsstädte)* with a guarantee of not depending on a prince or a king. We call the unity of these three old independent local communities the *Urschweiz*, or *la Suisse primitive*. The treaty was reaffirmed in 1315 after an unsuccessful attempt by the duke of Habsburg to conquer the valleys.[1]

In the years 1332 to 1353 the three valleys made similar defense treaties with three cities—Lucerne, Zurich, and Berne—and with two other rural communities, Glarus and Zug; these five new members were "free under the emperor" *(reichsunmittelbar)* or declared to be so. There was, therefore, a confederation of eight members—five rural members and three cities. It was consolidated after a victorious battle at Sempach in 1386 against the nobility residing in the German-speaking part of present-day Switzerland.

A century later, in 1476, the eight members entered into a war with Charles the Bold after having settled their old conflicts with the House of Habsburg. The Swiss had numerous allies, the closest being the cities of Fribourg and Soleure. Lucerne, Zurich, and Berne asked for the admission of these two cities as new members; the rural members opposed this but finally admitted the two cities in the Treaty of Stans in 1481.

After the next war, against the German Emperor Maximilian, they admitted the cities of Basel and Schaffhausen on the Rhine in 1501 and the rural community of Appenzell in 1513. This brought to thirteen the number of governing members, and this so-called old confederation lasted for more than two and a half centuries until the French Revolution, when Napoleon conquered Switzerland. All thirteen members were German-speaking, and only Fribourg was on the border of a French-speaking population; they met regularly as the Diet *(Tagsatzung,* convention). Each of those thirteen members had the treaty power, and after the Reformation the Protestant members signed defense treaties with Protestant cities or areas (Berne with Geneva and Neuchatel, Zurich with the city of St. Gall). The Valais and the three Grisons federations were other allies of the confederation.

The governing members also administered some conquered territories *(gemeine Vogteien)* in common, for instance, the Thurgau and the Ticino. In the middle of the sixteenth century, the thirteen governing members, the allies, and the conquered territories covered most of present Swiss territory.

The confederation of the thirteen members with its allies and conquered territories survived the Reformation, but the confessional split between the Catholic and the Protestant members was very deep. At least, they all agreed to remain neutral during the Thirty Years' War (1618–1648), and at the end of that war it was finally admitted that the members of the Swiss confederation, with all their territories, no longer belonged to the German Reich; Swiss neutrality, therefore, dates from that time.

When Napoleon conquered Switzerland, he first tried to create a centralized state like France, but this form of government did not work. So in 1803 he created, by the Mediation Act, the Swiss confederation of nineteen cantons, the new cantons being St. Gall, Grisons, Aargau, Thurgau, Ticino, and Vaud, formed out of ancient allies or conquered or dependent territories.

After the defeat of Napoleon, the European powers agreed in the Treaty of Vienna in 1815 that the Valais, the principality of Neuchatel, and the city of Geneva join the confederation, making twenty-two cantons. At that time the confederation's present frontiers were defined. Also at the Congress of Vienna the European powers recognized Swiss neutrality as a stabilizing factor in European politics.

In 1830 the liberal movement conquered most of the Protestant cantons. Liberal cantonal constitutions were accepted with bills of rights and guarantees of equality between the urban and the rural populations. A first federal constitution was drafted, but it did not pass in the Diet because of the opposition of the conservative Catholic cantons.

After eighteen years of tensions the liberal cantons defeated the conservative Catholic cantons in a short civil war and finally created a federal government, on the basis of a federal constitution accepted by the majority of the people and the cantons in 1848. The form of this federal government is discussed below. Since 1848 there have been Swiss citizens, who are at the same time citizens of Zurich, Berne, or another canton. All toll duties inside Switzerland were abolished at that time, and federal customs collected at the Swiss frontier were the main income of the new federal government. The powers of the new government were very limited, but twenty years later the necessity of enlarging the federal power became obvious; a first attempt in 1872 failed, but in 1874 "the majority of the people and the states" accepted the new Constitution, which is still in force today, although 105 amendments have greatly changed its contents.

The main rule, however, has been preserved (Article 3): "The cantons are sovereign insofar as their sovereignty is not limited by the Federal Constitution and . . . exercise all rights not entrusted to the federal power."

The so-called cantons are qualified as member states (Gliedstaaten) of the confederation; their executive is called, in French, Conseil d'Etat. In German the central power is called Bund, and the whole concern of the Bund and the cantons is called *Eidgenossenschaft.*

In French and Italian the words *confederation* and *confederazione* convey both meanings: *Bund* and *Eidgenossenschaft*.

Most of the 105 amendments since 1874 have served to enlarge the jurisdiction of the central power, the Bund, primarily so that it might issue uniform federal laws. Switzerland established federal laws of contracts and torts and a uniform commercial code *(code des obligations)* in 1881, a uniform civil code in 1907–1912, a uniform penal code in 1942, a general federal labor law in 1966, and a national bank issuing Swiss banknotes in 1907, by which time it had also passed several federal social security acts.

Since the present Constitution went into effect, the Swiss population has participated in the tremendous development of Western civilization. Two world wars have been fought all around its frontiers. Switzerland has become a highly industrialized nation, and today it stands very well in the competitive world economy. As in the United States, there is no movement to change the fundamental rules of its government.

The number of cantons and their frontiers remained unchanged for more than 150 years. But since 1952 the French-speaking northern part of the canton of Berne had wanted to become an independent canton; the majority of the people and the states accepted the division in 1978, and the new canton of Jura was formed. So the present Federal Constitution mentions "twenty-three sovereign cantons."

Three cantons, however—Unterwalden, Appenzell, and Basel— are split into half-cantons. Half-cantons are as independent as full cantons, so that—in spite of the text of the Constitution—there are in fact twenty-six member states. For historical reasons half-cantons have fewer rights than full cantons in two respects: they elect only *one* member of the Council of States (Conseil des Etats) in the Federal Assembly, whereas full cantons elect two; and in counting the votes of the cantons for the purpose of passing constitutional amendments, the half-cantons have only a half-vote. So an amendment of the Federal Constitution will be accepted, for instance, by 12½ to 10½ votes of "the states" (cantons).

The reasons for the divisions of the cantons are quite different in each case: in Unterwalden, two separate local communities (above and below the wood of Kerns) already existed in 1291; Appenzell was split by the reformation into Protestant and Catholic half-states; in Basel the citizens of the city refused in 1832 to give equal rights to the citizens of the countryside, who built their own half-state, Basel-Land. All endeavors to bring the two parts of Basel together again have failed. The theory is clear: the Unterwaldner, the Basler, and the

Appenzeller each form one people, but each is organized into two cantons.

Therefore, Article 1 of the Federal Constitution now reads as follows:

Together the peoples of the twenty-three sovereign cantons united by the present alliance, Zurich, Berne, Lucerne, Uri, Schwyz, Unterwalden (Upper and Lower), Glarus, Zug, Fribourg, Soleure, Basel (city and rural), Schaffhausen, Appenzell (both Rhodes), St. Gall, Grisons, Aargau, Thurgau, Ticino, Vaud, Valais, Neuchatel, Geneva, and Jura form the Swiss confederation.

This Swiss history in a nutshell shows at least one thing: *the federal structure of the Swiss confederation is very old, and the desire of the people to belong to their particular cantons is very much alive today.*

No other European state has a similar history. Although this history is not present in all Swiss minds, there is at least a feeling that Swiss democracy is not a construction but a living organism. The frontiers have been settled for centuries, but within these frontiers the Swiss know that from decade to decade they have to solve new problems with great patience.

The Present Cantons and Half-Cantons

The twenty-six cantons and half-cantons may be grouped according to their size as shown in table 1.[2] The two largest cantons include one-third of the population, the five largest cantons more than half the population, and the ten smallest member states (six cantons and four half-cantons) only 8 percent of the population. Twelve cantons form a majority of the states, and this majority can prevent any change in the Constitution; the twelve smallest states, with one-fifth of the population, can stop a change in the Constitution that is accepted by both houses of the Federal Assembly and by a huge majority of the population, so strong is the federal structure.

In eleven cantons and six half-cantons German is the official language; in four cantons (Vaud, Geneva, Neuchatel, Jura) French is the official language; in three cantons German and French are the official languages, two predominantly French (Valais, Fribourg) and one predominantly German (Berne); in one canton (Ticino) Italian is the official language; and in one canton (Grisons) German, Romansch, and Italian are official languages.[3]

The Swiss population in 1980 included 5.4 million Swiss and 945,000 foreigners (15 percent). This high percentage of foreigners is

TABLE 1
Cantons and Half-Cantons, by Population, 1980

	Population (thousands)	Language	Percentage of Total Population (6.3 million)
About 1 million inhabitants			32
Zurich	1,123	main language German	
Berne	912	85% German-, 8% French- speaking	
390,000–520,000 inhabitants			21
Vaud	512	French-speaking	
Aargau	453	German-speaking	
St. Gall	392	German-speaking	
200,000–350,000 inhabitants			28
Geneva	349	French-speaking	
Lucerne	296	German-speaking	
Ticino	261	Italian-speaking	
Basel-Land[a]	220	German-speaking	
Valais	219	60% French-, 32% German- speaking	
Soleure	218	German-speaking	
Basel-City[a]	204	German-speaking	
100,000–200,000 inhabitants			11
Fribourg	185	61% French-, 32% German- speaking	
Thurgau	184	German-speaking	
Grisons	165	60% German-, 22% Romansch-, 13.5% Italian- speaking	
Neuchatel	158	French-speaking	
Under 100,000 inhabitants			8
Schwyz	97	German-speaking	
Zug	76	German-speaking	
Schaffhausen	69	German-speaking	

(Table continues)

211

TABLE 1 (continued)

	Population (thousands)	Language	Percentage of Total Population (6.3 million)
Jura	65	French-speaking	
Appenzell[a]	48	German-speaking	
Glarus	37	German-speaking	
Uri	34	German-speaking	
Nidwalden[a]	29	German-speaking	
Obwalden[a]	26	German-speaking	
Appenzell[a]	13	German-speaking	

a. Half-canton.

unique in Europe, and it deeply influences the linguistic distribution in Switzerland. That distribution is shown in table 2.

The French-, Italian-, and Romansch-speaking parts of Switzerland are minority groups (French-speaking one-fifth, Italian-speaking one-twentieth, Romansch-speaking one-hundredth of the Swiss citizens), and Swiss federalism is the main tool with which these minorities fight for their rights. The western, French-speaking part of Switzerland is called the Romandie, and *les cantons romands*—Vaud, Geneva, Valais, Fribourg, Neuchatel, and Jura—collaborate in many fields to safeguard French culture in Switzerland.

Above all, however, each of the twenty-six member states tries to safeguard its own identity, and to this day most Swiss men and women see themselves as members at the same time of a cantonal people—Zurcher, Berner, Vaudois, Genevois—and of the Swiss people. As stated in Article 43 of the Federal Constitution: "Every citizen of a canton is a Swiss citizen."

In fact, sociological patterns change from one canton to the next. Swiss German—a medieval form of German—varies from canton to canton. In Zurich they say *immer* (always); in Berne, *gäng*. The mentality in Geneva is quite different from the mentality in Vaud. Zurich became "the big city," and the whole canton is characterized by it. Berne is completely different: the expansive countryside is characteristic, while the city of Berne is just the capital of Switzerland (although it is not an industrial or business center). Even today life in a mountain canton is quite different from life in a canton of the *Mittelland* (plateau).

Present Tensions in Switzerland:
Is Federalism a Calming or an Aggravating Factor?

Switzerland is a peaceful country, and internal tensions have not become dramatic in the past fifty years. The Swiss population was relatively well united against nazism during the Second World War. The peace agreement between the trade unions and the employers' associations in the metal and watch industries has been renewed several times. Swiss farmers receive better prices than farmers in other European countries. Although everyone criticizes the government, the critics finally cancel one another out. Therefore, one should not dramatize the tensions to be discussed next. They exist; they are in the center of political disputes; but they are not perilous to Swiss democracy. To this day, there has been no polarization either in the linguistic and cultural areas, as in Belgium, or between right and left, as in France. The opposing groups vary according to the subject in dispute.

There is no guarantee of eternal blue skies. But at least Switzerland has had forty years of progressive prosperity, and even the most recent economic crisis, with the breakdown of the watch industry, did not disrupt the basic mutual understanding of all groups inside Switzerland. The firebrands—fortunately—have not had much success.

Nevertheless, tensions do exist

- between industrial, urban areas and rural areas
- between the French-speaking and the German-speaking parts of Switzerland
- between the working class and the so-called bourgeois groups in the population

TABLE 2

LINGUISTIC DISTRIBUTION OF SWISS POPULATION, 1980
(percent)

	Total Population	Swiss Citizens	Foreigners
German-speaking	65.0	73.5	16.3
French-speaking	18.4	20.1	8.9
Italian-speaking	9.8	4.5	40.3
Romansch-speaking	0.8	0.9	0.1
Other languages (mainly Spanish, Turkish, Yugoslav)	6.0	1.0	34.4

213

- between Swiss citizens and foreigners
- among the political parties

Tensions between Cities and Rural Areas. There are typical urban cantons, like Basel-City, Geneva, and (more and more) Zurich, and typical rural cantons, like the small cantons of central Switzerland and Appenzell. But most of the cantons do not fit in either group because industry, handicrafts, and small businesses are widespread throughout the country. Tourism has created many places of work in nonindustrialized areas. Persons working in the primary sector (agriculture and forestry) make up only 191,000 of the 3.1 million members of the working population. Some 1.65 million people work in the third sector (services) and 1.2 million in the second sector (industry, construction, handicrafts).

Nevertheless, the old tension between rural states and cities that for centuries troubled the old Swiss confederation, persists; it is a problem of mentality, a feeling that the cities may acquire too much influence and democratic power. The rural population feels a permanent threat that the "too modern" moral and cultural views of the cities may conquer the whole country. They especially fear that Zurich will become too big and have too much weight. Certainly social ideas and new life styles do not stop at cantonal frontiers, but strong cantonal autonomy is a safeguard against the imposition by federal law of views not yet generally accepted. The big cities may have very liberal nightclubs that are tolerated by their own cantonal regulations of restaurants, but the cantons of central Switzerland dislike this kind of "progress"; they want their own rules for restaurants and dancing, their own school systems, and so on. These examples show why rural cantons are strong federalists and why they try to fight many proposals to broaden the federal power.

Tensions between French- and German-speaking Areas. Some tensions between the French- and German-speaking parts of Switzerland have existed since the admission of French-speaking cantons. In recent years this tension has grown because the Romands (the French-speaking Swiss) think that economic development is faster in some parts of German-speaking Switzerland than in the Romandie. The Romands maintain careful watch over the federal administration to protect their share, and they want at all costs to safeguard their cultural identity, asking for federal financial help in this effort. Four French-speaking cantons have their own universities (Fribourg, Vaud, Neuchatel, Geneva); these universities depend to a large extent on federal subsidies, but they are centers of cultural life in their cantons.

The Romands fight more often than their German-speaking compatriots against new federal laws. A few years ago the legal requirement to wear safety belts while driving in a car became a political issue; the majority of the German-speaking Swiss emphasized security, the Romands, liberty: liberty not to use a safety belt. The Romands lost the battle in the voting, but this was not a national catastrophe. A linguistic limitation is a frontier of culture, but the differences between German and French culture in our time cannot be easily defined. To moderate tensions, the cantons have very broad authority to establish and organize schools. The Swiss people prefer variety to uniformity and accordingly walk slowly but safely through history.

After the Second World War the English language was increasingly taught in Switzerland. The second language of many Swiss is not another national language but English. The consequence is that people read more English publications and fewer books or periodicals of other cultural areas of Switzerland.

The Italian- and the Romansch-speaking parts of Switzerland have also had to fight to maintain their cultural identity. They have the sympathy of the rest of the Swiss, but the people of Ticino in Lugano, Locarno, and Ascona especially feel submerged by German-speaking immigrants from the north. Nevertheless, all residents of Switzerland are free to maintain their cultural heritage.

Legally, German, French, Italian, and Romansch are the national languages of Switzerland; the first three are official languages (Article 116), which means that all laws are published in those three languages. When there is a difference in meaning, the Federal Court finds a solution most appropriate to the aims of the law. In the Federal Assembly, in federal commissions, in the Federal Council, and in the Federal Court, everyone speaks his own language. The Tessinois often prefer to speak German or French. Judges in the Federal Court must be able to read papers in all three official languages. Federalism is the key enabling peoples of different languages and cultures to live together.

Tensions between the Working Class and the Bourgeoisie. Social tensions are not as strong in Switzerland as in other European countries. The Socialist party has always been a minority party; in many areas federal social security laws came later than in other European countries. But there is some truth to the saying that the Socialists point out the social aims to be realized and the so-called bourgeois parties find the ways and means to solve the problems. Trade unions know that Swiss industry must be competitive in the world market, and employers know best how to deal with their personnel. Swiss Socialists are very pragmatic. Some democratic feeling is not only a political but a social fact. Many managers participate in the general cultural and sporting activities of the people. They "hear how the mind is turning." Extensive strikes, therefore, have been infrequent, and inflation is kept down fairly well. Wage agreements are common. In the metal and watch industry, a so-called peace agreement has survived all difficulties; it provides that all collective labor disputes must be resolved by arbiters without strikes or lockouts. The federal pattern may have influence even in this field: the cantonal sections of professional groups want to keep their autonomy; in this way they are influenced by the federal pattern of the state.

Tensions among Political Parties. Tensions among political parties are normal and necessary in a democracy; everything depends on fair fighting. In Switzerland this fairness is widely respected. It is even said that the programs of some parties are so similar to one another that elections for the Federal Assembly are no great national event. The main parties' percentages of votes in the latest election for the National Council (the lower house) were as follows:

Radical Democratic party	23
Christian Democratic party	21
Socialists	23
People's party	11
Independents party	4
Liberal party	3
Evangelical party	2
National Action party	3
Workers party (Communists)	1
Others	9

The first four parties together have formed the government for some forty years; they have more than three-fourths of all the votes, and their strength does not vary much from one election to the next. The opposition, therefore, is left to small groups with limited weight. But there is no 5 percent minimum quota for small groups as in West Germany. Since the Socialists (even with the Communist party) do not get even one-fourth of the votes, the right is well established. Within the cantons, however, the strengths of the parties may be quite different, and the political battles are often more vigorous there than in federal elections. The parties are organized on a cantonal basis. Once an election is over, the winners and losers of all parties begin to work together again.

Tensions between Citizens and Foreigners. The strongest tensions in Switzerland exist between Swiss citizens and some groups of foreigners. The very fact that one-seventh of the population is foreign creates a strong feeling that Switzerland may be overwhelmed by aliens. Application of the alien policy is to a large extent left to the cantons. Since Switzerland does not belong to the European Economic Community, it is free to regulate immigration, and for more than ten years the dispute over the regulation of foreigners in Switzerland has been heated. Some alarming signs of xenophobia exist, but even in this area the situation varies from one canton to the next.

Differences of Religion. For centuries the tensions caused by the division of Christianity into Catholics and Protestants were of primary importance. There were and are Catholic cantons, Protestant cantons, and mixed cantons. In the census (taken every ten years) most people declare the denomination to which they belong, and most also pay public church taxes. The statistics, therefore, still reveal Protestant cantons (for instance, Berne, which is 77 percent Protestant) and Catholic cantons (for instance, the cantons of central Switzerland, which are 86–91 percent Catholic); but religion does not have the same weight as in the past, and fortunately religious tensions have diminished significantly. Nevertheless, religion has its political impact; the Christian Democratic party, composed mostly of Catholics (90 percent), is a very federalist party.

The Influence of Federalism. Swiss federalism is at the same time an aggravating and a calming factor. On the one hand, the cantons are places of experiment where new ideas may be put into practice before they are given a chance on the federal level. For instance, voting rights for women were introduced in some French-speaking cantons twelve years before the victory in the confederation as a whole. On the other hand, new ideas will not inundate the whole country because it is hard to take over a confederation of twenty-six member states—even though they are very small. Nothing is eaten when it is too hot—that is Swiss wisdom. An efficient state organization has to work in spite of the existing tensions in the society. The following sections discuss the working of the Swiss political system—a system that, in spite of its creaking, is more or less satisfying.

The Federal Constitution in Its Substantive and Formal Aspects

To understand the Swiss system of democracy, one must distinguish between two senses of the word "constitution." The constitution in its *substantive sense* is formed by the basic rules of the organization of the state. These rules may be written or simply accepted as unwritten. There is no clear line between them and other organizational rules of the state.

The constitution in its *formal sense* is a written law accepted by a "constitutional body" and declared to be the fundamental law of the state. Amending the constitution is normally more difficult than making changes in statutory law, because the constitution expresses the fundamental agreement of a people about its organization, that is, the "social contract."

It might be considered normal that all the basic rules of organization of a state be set out in a written constitution and that a written constitution include only such basic rules: in this way the constitution in the material sense and in the formal sense would be more or less the same. But the contrary is true for the Swiss Federal Constitution. The written Federal Constitution of 1874 is full of gaps on the one hand and of secondary rules on the other. This ought to be explained.

The authors of the Constitutions of 1848 and 1874 were practical politicians, not professors of constitutional law. They were solving problems of their own day. Afterward, each of the more than 100 amendments to the Federal Constitution addressed one specific item, and each new rule was introduced between any two already existing paragraphs; for instance, after the paragraph about freedom of commerce (Article 31) there are now seven articles (Article 31b, 31c, . . . 31g) about federal regulation of the economy. Many articles are the result of long-discussed compromises and therefore are sometimes very detailed. There are, for instance, three long articles on distilled spirits (Articles 32b, 32c, 32d), but there is not one line about the separation of powers.

Therefore, the problem of unwritten, but generally accepted, constitutional law is very important for the Swiss confederation. The Swiss Federal Court has "deduced" from the provision in Article 4 "All Swiss citizens are equal before the law" a great number of specific constitutional rights, such as the right to due process of law, the right not to be harmed by "arbitrary decisions" *(Willkürverbot)*, the protection of good faith in the relations between administration and citizens, and so on. Furthermore, the Federal Court has admitted the existence of "fundamental unwritten rights" that are generally recognized in Western democracies, such as freedom of opinion, personal liberty, and guarantee of property. Some of these unwritten freedoms are now guaranteed by the European Convention on Human Rights. These guarantees of civil liberty are binding on the central power and on the cantons; every law must respect the Federal Constitution as interpreted by the Federal Court. Further, the limitations on cantonal autonomy mean that all federal statutory law prevails over cantonal law (Article 2). The effect of these limitations is discussed below.

A large number of constitutional amendments have been added to the first chapter, "General Provisions." This part has become, so to speak, a bramble bush (Articles 1–70). The second chapter, "Federal Authorities" (Articles 71–117), has not been much changed. It is well drafted and a good introduction to the organization of Swiss government.

Many articles in the first part of the Constitution go into greater detail than, for instance, the U.S. Constitution. There are no broad articles like the interstate commerce clause of the U.S. Constitution. Therefore, the jurisdiction of the federal power cannot be broadened by a new interpretation by the Federal Court; the Constitution must be adapted to new needs practically every year.

The Organization of the Federal Power *(Bund)*

The main constitutional organs of the federal power are the people, (the Federal Assembly with two houses), the Federal Council (the head of the executive), and the Federal Court. The function of the people is discussed in the next section; what follows is a short outline of the other organs.

The Federal Assembly. In 1848 the Swiss confederation copied the American idea of a bicameral legislature. The National Council is analogous to the U.S. House of Representatives and the Council of States to the U.S. Senate.

The 200 seats in the National Council are distributed among the cantons and half-cantons in proportion to their resident populations (Article 72). Zurich has thirty-five seats; the smallest cantons and half-cantons have one seat each. Each canton or half-canton forms an electoral district, and elections are based on a sophisticated system of proportional representation.

The Council of States is composed of forty-six representatives of the cantons, two for every canton and one for every half-canton. The Council of States is more to the right than the National Council because it includes only six Socialists among forty-six representatives whereas the National Council includes forty-seven Socialists among its 200 representatives.

Each council deliberates separately (Article 92), and a law is passed only if both councils agree on all points. Both have exactly the same rights; half the legislative items are first treated by the National

Council, half by the Council of States. A bill may go back and forth until a compromise is found. The two councils assemble for a joint meeting for the election of the members of the Federal Council and the Federal Court.

Because members in both houses have previously been active in cantonal politics, both houses have a strong tendency to safeguard cantonal autonomy. The Socialists are most in favor of strengthening the federal power.

The Federal Council. The supreme executive and governing authority is called the Federal Council. It is composed of seven members, elected by the Federal Assembly for a four-year term (Articles 95 and 96). The chairman of the Federal Council is called president of the confederation (Bundespräsident), but he has no more power than the six other members; each of the seven becomes president for one year in rotation. Most Swiss citizens do not know who is president in any given year.

This system is unique. For about forty years the political composition of the Federal Council has been based on the so-called magic formula: two Radical Democrats, two Christian Democrats, two Socialists, one member of the People's party. The election of the Federal Council takes place after the election of the National Council every four years; a federal councilor who has been "satisfying" will be reelected. His higher officers will help him do the job. There are four or five German-speaking councilors and two or three French- or Italian-speaking councilors. The first woman was elected in 1984.

The members of the Federal Council become independent of their own party when they are elected. In choosing them, the Federal Assembly is not even bound by the proportions of the party factions. The minority candidate in a party faction may better please the representatives of the other parties because he seems to be collaborating more with the "team of the seven fathers of the country." Therefore, they elect him.

Every federal councilor is the head of a department, but all important decisions are made by the Federal Council as a body (Article 103). Every federal councilor must therefore look into the work of the others. They are all overburdened, but they have secretaries to develop their positions on issues. This shared responsibility is essential to the Swiss system.

The Federal Court. Justice is a matter for the cantons. There are no lower federal courts, just the Federal Court at Lausanne and its autonomous branch, the Federal Court for social insurance at Lucerne. The

Federal Court is composed of thirty judges from all parts of the country and is a multifaceted court: a court of appeals for civil law matters, a court of cassation for criminal cases, a penal court for some very important criminal cases, an administrative court, and a constitutional court. Only its constitutional functions are addressed here.

The means to bring a case on a constitutional matter before the Federal Court is called *staatsrechtliche Beschwerde,* or *recours de droit public.* It can be directed only against cantonal laws and cantonal decisions. The Federal Court is bound by federal laws (Article 113), and it cannot review decisions of the Federal Council.

The plaintiff before the court must show that the cantonal law or the cantonal decision violates one of his constitutional rights or a right guaranteed by an international treaty. This remedy is the most efficient protection of the citizens against arbitrary behavior by cantonal authorities.

The Organization of the Cantons

The organization of all the cantons is very similar. All have unicameral parliaments, most of which are elected on a proportional basis.

The executive is elected by the people on the day they elect the parliament. In all cantons every change in a cantonal constitution and almost every new law is submitted to a referendum. In five cantons and half-cantons (Nidwalden, Obwalden, Glarus, Appenzell-Outer Rhodes, Appenzell-Inner Rhodes), new laws must be passed once every year in the Landsgemeinde (country assembly) by visible hand raising. In Appenzell women are not yet allowed to vote.

Referendums on financial matters are either required or optional in most cantons. When expenses of more than a certain amount are concerned, as for the construction of streets or public buildings, approval of the people is needed.

In all cantons the local communities (*Gemeinden,* or communes) are very important, and in most cantons voting rights are well established in the local communities. Even the schoolteachers or the parish priest may be elected by popular vote. Local officers very often execute federal and cantonal law. The local communities insist on autonomy. If their autonomy is restricted illegally through cantonal decisions, they may accuse the canton before the Federal Court.

The judiciary varies widely from one canton to another. In cities the judges are mostly lawyers trained in the law faculty of a university; in the countryside laymen-judges elected by the people are common, and they work well in a large majority of cases.

The Specific Tools of Swiss Democracy:
Referendums and Popular Initiatives

Swiss federalism is deeply entwined with the specific form of Swiss democracy; the special tools of this form of direct or semidirect democracy used by the central power and the cantons are the referendum and the popular initiative. The referendum is an instrument used to overturn laws and (in the cantons) large expenses already accepted by parliament but opposed by a group of citizens. The popular initiative is a "prodding instrument." A sufficiently large group of citizens, by collecting signatures, may force the government and the parliament to discuss acts with which they disagree. They have the right to a popular vote on their proposition, even if the government and the parliament recommend that the citizens reject it.

The Referendum. In the second half of the nineteenth century, the so-called democratic movement, inspired by the Landsgemeinden in some small cantons, marshaled public opinion behind the idea that all new laws should be ratified by the people. The assent of the people may take two forms: (1) every law must be submitted to a popular vote (required referendum), as in the majority of the cantons; or (2) a popular vote takes place if a specified number of citizens, by their signatures on referendum forms, request it (an optional referendum), as in the Bund and in some cantons. In the Bund 50,000 signatures are needed, and they must be submitted within ninety days after publication of the act of the Federal Assembly. In the cantons and in the local communities, required or optional referendums are even more important for large expenses.

The optional referendum is used for only a minority of federal statutes, but it is used whenever there is clear-cut opposition. In Switzerland it is said, "The people are the opposition." To reduce the opposition, all groups of the population (and in federal matters all the cantons) are asked to submit their views about a bill before it is introduced in the parliament. Switzerland has thus become a "democracy of compromise." The threat of a referendum strongly influences discussion in the Federal Assembly. If the opposition collects its 50,000 signatures in time (and for some large organizations that is easy), a debate about the strong and weak points of the new law begins; the government sends more or less neutral information to all voters. The political parties recommend acceptance or rejection of the law. In this way some important laws, such as the penal code and the Agricultural Act, have been accepted; others, such as the Alien Act, have been rejected.

For the acceptance of normal laws, a simple majority of votes is sufficient. But a broader majority is needed for a change in the Federal Constitution. *Every change in the Constitution must be approved through a required referendum and must be accepted by a majority of both the people and the cantons;* without this double majority no change in the Constitution, especially no broadening of the central power, is possible. Since the Swiss people vote every year on one or more amendments to the Constitution, this double majority is the principal stronghold of the cantons.

In Switzerland, therefore, the parliament and the people together constitute the legislature, and the people and the states (cantons) together constitute the constitutional power. This rule gives to all laws a higher authority than in countries where the majority of the parliament is sufficient to create new laws.

Even important parts of international treaties are submitted to the optional referendum. Parliamentary decisions to enter "an organization of collective security" (such as the United Nations) or "a supranational community" (such as the European Economic Community) are submitted to the obligatory referendum; they must be approved by a majority of the people and a majority of the cantons. In 1985 the Federal Assembly decided to join the United Nations; but in the vote of March 1986 the people (by a majority of 3:1) and all twenty-six cantons and half-cantons voted against joining—a very rare unanimous opposition to the federal government and the Federal Assembly.

The Popular Initiative. The popular initiative in the cantons is a tool for requesting a popular vote for a change in the constitution, for a new law, or for a change in a law despite opposition from the government and the parliament. In the Bund the only aim of a popular initiative is to change the Constitution; it therefore needs a double majority of both the people and the cantons. On the federal level a group of citizens must collect, within six months, at least 100,000 signatures for a "formulated" or an "unformulated" initiative. The formulated initiative contains a fixed text for a new article (or a changed article) of the Federal Constitution; the unformulated initiative contains only an order for the Federal Assembly to change a portion of the constitutional text on a certain topic (Article 121). The text of the unformulated popular initiative is completely open, provided that it deals with just one topic.

The Federal Assembly has a strong weapon against popular initiatives: the *counterproposition* (Article 121, paragraph 6), which normally has less reach than the initiative. The people must vote on both the popular initiative and the counterproposition the same day. A citizen may reject both, accept one and reject the other, or vote primarily for the popular initiative and eventually (if the initiative does not gain the required double majority) for the counterproposition. This is a very recent solution in order to favor the acceptance of the counterproposition and to avoid a completely negative result. The popular initiative is a very original weapon for minorities to introduce new ideas in the political debate, to force the government and the parliament to enter in the discussion, and eventually to win the majority of the people and the cantons in spite of the opposition of the government and the parliament.

Popular initiatives must be voted on within four years after submission. During this time the government and the Federal Assembly must decide what recommendation and eventually what counterproposition they will issue for the popular vote. The counterproposition may include a change in an article of the Federal Constitution and a law based on the new article (as was the case with the counterproposition for the protection of tenants against excessive rents and other abuses in rental housing in 1985).

Most popular initiatives are rejected, but there have been exceptions. The most spectacular acceptance was in 1949. After the years of war a popular initiative requested a quick restoration of the constitutional order and elimination of all "war laws." The government, the Federal Assembly, and all the political parties recommended rejection of the proposal, but the majority of the people and the states accepted it and in this way restored the traditional constitutional order in a very short time.

Between January 1, 1979, and July 1, 1985, the Swiss people voted on forty matters. They

- accepted fourteen changes in the Constitution proposed by the Federal Assembly
- rejected six changes in the Constitution proposed by the Federal Assembly
- accepted one popular initiative (against abusive prices)
- rejected twelve popular initiatives[4]
- accepted three counterpropositions of the Federal Assembly to popular initiatives
- accepted three federal laws on which referendums were requested
- rejected one federal law on which a referendum was requested (Alien Act)

Between 1875 and 1983, 103 amendments to the Constitution were accepted, and 102 were rejected.

Referendums and popular initiatives are means of inquiring what the voters really think about a problem, and their opinion is independent of the recommendation of the government and of the parties. At least some of the people think that politics cannot go over the people's heads, and they like the Swiss form of government. Others, however, especially many youngsters, are not interested in politics; they do not believe in "people's rights," and they think that the main weight of power lies with the executive, which does what it wants to do. The political maturity of the Swiss nation, therefore, is not beyond doubt, and there is no proof that the majority of voters have a better view of problems than members of the Federal Assembly. But at least the voters are the supreme authority. In recent years 30 to 53 percent of the people with voting rights have voted, but the voters speak, one may say, for the whole people.

The Swiss system of semidirect democracy increases the power of pressure groups of all kinds. With the threat to use the optional referendum or the popular initiative, they influence members of the government and the Federal Assembly. There is widespread debate, for instance, about whether it is necessary to limit speed on the national highways to 100 kilometers per hour (60 miles per hour) to reduce air pollution and to protect the woods. The automobile clubs are planning to launch a popular initiative to set the limit at 130 km/h (80 mph) if the Federal Council proposes that it fall below 120 km/h (75 mph). Social progress has often been pushed forward by popular initiatives, and sometimes it has been good when laws that have not been thought through have been rejected by the people.

The price paid for the Swiss form of democracy is *slowness*. It is much easier to pass a bill through a parliament by a clear majority of its members, as in other countries, than to win the majority of the people, as is necessary in Switzerland. "A truth needs a generation to enter into the mind and the heart of the population." Sometimes two battles must be won: first, to create a federal power in the Federal Constitution; and second, to establish a federal law based on this power. The constitutional basis for a uniform penal code was laid in 1898, for example, but the penal code itself was not accepted until 1937 (after a referendum). The constitutional basis for old age and survivors' insurance and disability insurance was created in 1925, but the Old Age Insurance Act dates only from 1947 and the Disability Insurance Act from 1959. Voting rights for women were rejected in 1959 and accepted in 1971. Swiss family law was made uniform in 1907, but its modernization, based on the equality of husband and wife, was only recently accepted (after referendum). The Swiss confederation goes on, however, even with old laws.

The voting rights of the people—the so-called people's rights—

are individual rights of every citizen, protected by the Federal Court (where there are no fees, even if an appeal is dismissed). These political rights strengthen the political personality of every citizen. A Swiss citizen has both his assault rifle (with ammunition) and his voting card in his home. His voting right has some weight—together with the voting rights of fellow-citizens of his same mind—at least if he uses it. It has greatest weight in the local community, less in the canton, and even less in the confederation, but it always has more weight than in a mere parliamentary democracy where citizens elect only members of parliament. In Switzerland federalism and direct democracy are closely bound together.

The Division of Powers between the Central Power and the Cantons

Article 3 states: "The cantons are sovereign insofar as their sovereignty is not limited by the Federal Constitution and, as such, exercise all rights not entrusted to the federal power." The idea is clear: sovereignty may be divided into federal and cantonal sectors. Some areas are exclusively under federal jurisdiction and others under cantonal jurisdiction. For instance, the federal railroads and the federal postal and telecommunications systems are exclusively under the jurisdiction of the federal power. All personnel are federal officers or federal employees; profits and losses concern the federal treasury. The relationship between church and state, however (subject to the constitutional protection of freedom of religion), is left entirely to the cantons and varies widely from one canton to another. Geneva has a separation of church and state; in neighboring Vaud the ministers of the Protestant and Catholic churches are paid by the canton out of taxpayers' money. In other cantons the members of the recognized churches pay a special public church tax.

In most fields, however, no clear division exists between the powers of the federal government and those of the cantons. Sometimes a confusing collaboration prevails between them. On the one hand, most federal laws must be executed by the cantonal authority; on the other hand, the cantons may receive federal subsidies in the area of their own exclusive tasks (for example, the federal government partly finances the cantonal universities).

It is very difficult to illustrate briefly the system of autonomy and collaboration in Swiss federalism. It has become a bramble bush, and attempts to simplify its relations are very tiresome.[5]

The expert Committee for a Total Revision of the Present Federal Constitution tried to classify the powers in the system by introducing new terms, "responsibility" and "principal responsibility," relative to the central power on the one hand and the cantons on the other. I have included in an appendix to this paper the chapters that best illustrate this classification of powers, "Relations among Cantons and between Cantons and the Confederation" and "Responsibilities of the Confederation and the Cantons" (Articles 43 to 53 of the draft constitution, which is more progressive than the Constitution now in force.) Although these chapters have been strongly criticized for not defining the jurisdictions of the federal power and the cantons more clearly, they illustrate, at least in a simple way, the actual pattern of those relations. The cantons watch closely to see that their autonomy is not restricted and that they remain free to organize as they choose, but they gratefully accept financial help from the federal power.

The cantons insist most strongly on their autonomy in the area of schools and education. Every canton has its own school system; each freely chooses its schoolbooks, and in many cantons, local communities select their own schoolteachers. A long-fought change in the Federal Constitution was needed to impose on all cantons a common beginning of the school year in all "obligatory schools" (Article 27). But the confederation regulates access to the study of human and veterinary medicine, pharmacology, and all studies in the two federal technical universities of Zurich and Lausanne. The confederation therefore regulates access to the universities in general. Examinations are prepared by cantonal professors under the control of federal experts. Unlike the primary and secondary schools, the vocational schools are under the control of the federal Department of Economics, but they are still cantonal schools.

In the German-speaking part of Switzerland only the cantons of Zurich, Berne, and Basel have complete universities, and St. Gall has a university for business and public administration. In the French-speaking part of Switzerland, four cantons—Geneva, Vaud, Neuchatel, and Fribourg—have their own universities. The confederation has only the two technical universities.

In the field of economics the Federal Constitution (Article 31) emphasizes that "freedom of trade and industry is guaranteed throughout the territory of the confederation subject to such limitations as contained in the Federal Constitution and legislation enacted under its authority" (Article 31, paragraph 1). The limitations must be regulated by federal laws and federal decrees on which a popular vote can be requested (Article 32), and they must have constitutional bases. Federal laws restricting economic freedom have been enacted to maintain good agriculture (Article 31b, paragraph 3b), but the general approach is not to reduce free enterprise; it is to promote economic activity. The cantons have no right to limit economic freedom, except insofar as necessary for the protection of health or good faith in business (police power, Article 31, paragraph 2). There is one exception: the canton may restrict the number of establishments serving food or drink so that there are no more than needed.

Today the confederation and the cantons must work together to stabilize economic development. Therefore, in 1978 the people and the states accepted Article 31e of the Federal Constitution, with the following text:

1. The confederation shall take measures to ensure balanced economic development and, in particular, to prevent and combat unemployment and price inflation. It shall collaborate with the cantons and private enterprises.

2. In the case of measures taken in the monetary and banking spheres, public finances, and foreign trade, the confederation may depart, if necessary, from the principle of freedom of trade and industry. It may require firms to form tax-privileged employment creation reserves. After their release, the firms shall decide freely how to use them within the purposes laid down by law.

3. When drawing up their budgets, the confederation, the cantons, and the communes shall take into consideration the requirements of the economic situation. The confederation may temporarily levy surcharges or grant rebates on federal taxes to stabilize the economy. The money withdrawn from circulation is to be frozen for as long as the economic situation requires. Direct taxes shall then be refunded individually, and indirect ones shall be used for the granting of rebates or for work creation.

4. The confederation shall take into consideration the varying economic development of the individual regions of the country.

5. The confederation shall conduct the necessary economic policy surveys.

This article shows the meshing of the confederation and the cantons in the area of economic policy.

There are no federal police in Switzerland. The attorney general of the confederation looks to cooperation among the cantonal police troops.

Because of the rule that the federal laws must be executed by the cantons, there are no lower federal courts, and the number of officers and employees in the federal administration (except the federal post, telephone, and telegraph services, the railroads, and other establishments) is fairly small (8,849 persons in 1983). In 1982 the confederation spent SFr 2.25 million, the cantons SFr 9.95 million, and the local communities SFr 6.94 million for salaries. The uniform application of federal civil, penal, and administrative law is safeguarded by the right of the citizens and of the appropriate federal authorities to bring any case before the Federal Court if federal law has been violated. The parties to the right, especially the Christian Democrats, generally favor the maintenance of cantonal powers, whereas the Socialists think that progress has to be achieved mainly through the central power.

The Financial Order

In Switzerland, as elsewhere, expenses and revenues of the public sector have increased enormously since the Second World War, but the burdens of the three branches of the public sector—the central power, the cantons, and the local communities—have grown in proportion (in the cantons even more than in the confederation).

PUBLIC SECTOR EXPENSES 1950–1983 (MILLIONS OF SWISS FRANCS)

	1950	1960	1983
Confederation	1,650	2,620	20,283
Cantons	1,490	2,800	26,762
Local communities	1,240	2,040	20,334

Even though the Swiss franc has lost two-thirds of its value since 1950, the progressive increase of the expenses of the public sector is very impressive.

In 1982 none of the three branches of the public sector could completely cover its expenses (the deficit of the confederation was SFr 424 million; of the cantons, SFr 630 million; and of the local communities, SFr 388 million). But the sources of revenue of the three branches are very different.

The confederation gets nearly two-thirds of its revenue from taxes on consumption (the turnover tax, taxes on tobacco, and the like) and only one-third from the federal income tax, including the anticipatory tax. The cantons get half their revenues from the cantonal income tax and a good part of the rest from participation in the federal income tax and from federal subsidies. The situation of the local communities is similar. The cantons are free to set cantonal income taxes for persons and for corporations. They also collect the

229

federal income tax for the confederation. The local communities set the income tax, as a percentage of the cantonal tax, according to their needs. Therefore, the tax burden differs from canton to canton and from one local community to another.

The financial strength of the cantons and of the local communities varies widely. Laws on fiscal equalization look to better distribution of revenues among financially strong and financially weak cantons and communities. But important differences in the amounts of income taxes cannot be avoided. A married man without children and a salary income of SFr 100,000 in 1983 paid SFr 10,500 in cantonal and communal income tax in Zug; SFr 18,800 in Berne; and SFr 21,100 in Sion (a ratio between Zug and Sion of 1:2). This inequality of the tax burden (in spite of fiscal equalization) is the price paid for the fiscal autonomy of the cantons and local communities. The same taxes for all citizens in the country cannot coexist with wide autonomy of the cantons and the local communities.

Although most people do not realize the great differences, they generally accept the fiscal autonomy of the cantons and local communities and the inequality of the tax burden. It is obvious, however, that rich people choose their homes in tax havens. Tax counselors are well informed about these problems. Financially, most cantons cannot live off their income taxes; federal subsidies are therefore a great part of their revenues—in Uri, for instance, more than 50 percent.

Obviously the confederation has expenses different from those of the cantons and local communities. It has the main burden of providing military defense, financing of social insurance, protecting agriculture, and covering the deficit of the federal railroads. The cantons and local communities need funds primarily for schools, health expenses, roads, protection of the natural environment (water and air), and the administration of justice. New, larger expenses of the cantons and local communities must be accepted by popular vote. This financial order, with all its problems, is a keystone of Swiss federalism.

Civil Liberties and Cantonal Autonomy

The federal legislature and the federal government as well as the cantonal legislatures and governments, have to respect the civil liberties defined in the Federal Constitution and the European Convention on Human Rights. The Federal Court, however, cannot decide whether federal laws (submitted to a referendum) are in conformity with the Constitution (Article 113, paragraph 3); it does decide the constitutionality of cantonal laws and all kinds of cantonal decisions. This power to decide is very important because the Federal Court may annul laws and decisions as violating equality under law or as being "arbitrary." An act is arbitrary if it has no legal basis or cannot be sustained by reasonable means (Article 4). In 1984, 1,663 citizens attacked cantonal laws or cantonal decisions by a *recours de droit public* for violating the Constitution; 209 appeals were allowed. A citizen can go to the Federal Court only if he has tried in vain to invoke the protections provided by cantonal law. This control over the protection of civil liberties by the cantons is an important wheel in the "gearing" of Swiss democracy.

A Test Case for Swiss Federalism:
The Birth of the Canton of Jura, 1978

The most critical situation of the Swiss confederation in recent years was the tension surrounding the separatist movement in the northern, French-speaking part of the canton of Berne; it was finally solved in a democratic way through the creation of a new Swiss canton (by amendment of Article 1). The procedure, not foreseen in the Constitution, reveals in an interesting way the persistence, and also the difficulties, of decision making in Swiss federal democracy.

Berne, a mostly German-speaking canton, was reorganized at the Congress of Vienna in 1815 and at the "Long Diet" thereafter. It received "in compensation for lost territories, the Cantons Aargau and Vaud," the French-speaking territories of the prince-bishop of Basel in the Jura, in the northwestern part of the canton. The people became Bernese citizens, and the French-speaking parts of the new canton held equal rights with the German-speaking majority of "the old canton." The French-speaking minority was itself split into two parts. The Protestant, industrialized southern part wanted to be closer to the Protestant German-speaking part of the canton of Berne rather than the northern Catholic part "behind the mountains." This northern, French-speaking part of the canton was always somewhat isolated, and some tensions always existed.

In 1943 they requested some degree of autonomy, and in 1951 they created a political movement, the Jurassian Rally (Rassemblement Jurassien), which held that the whole French-speaking part (north *and* south) should leave the canton of Berne and form a separate new canton, Jura. They wanted to be free from Berne, as Vaud had been "liberated" from Berne by Napoleon. In 1957 the so-called separatists first chose the democratic procedure of a cantonal popular initiative for the creation of this canton. But they lost the battle by 87,000 no votes to 23,130 yes votes because the old German-speaking Bernese saw no reason for dividing their canton. The north of the Jura voted for separation; the French-speaking south voted against it. But the determined minority in the north did not accept the decision of the Bernese people. In 1963–1964 the Front for the Liberation of Jura (Front de Liberation Jurassien) began acts of terrorism, and rejected every idea of limited autonomy for Jura inside the canton and Berne. Dialogue between the Bernese government and the leaders of the separatists became impossible. The fighting group of the separatists were the *beliers* (the books), the fighting group of the antiseparatists the *sangliers* (wild boars); many families were deeply divided by this political fight.

Finally the Federal Council intervened; in 1970 a constitutional complement was accepted by the old Bernese voters and the Jura voters, and they settled on a democratic procedure. The people of north and south Jura had to decide together first whether a canton of Jura should be created and then what French-speaking districts of Jura should belong to the new canton.

This procedure allowed some southerners to vote yes the first time and no the second time; on June 23, 1974, therefore, 52 percent of the Jura voters voted for a new canton, 48 percent against it; in the second vote, of March 16, 1975, only the three northern districts chose to become part of the new canton. A third vote provided the local communities on the borderline an opportunity to choose. The tension during the vote was very high, but the votes were free and secret, and they were accepted—though with anger—by the population.

After the third vote the voters of the northern district elected a constitutional council; within one year this council drafted a constitution for the new canton, which had to be ratified by the Federal Assembly. Once the new cantonal constitution was established, the Federal Constitution had to be changed to include the new canton in the confederation. On September 24, 1978, this change was accepted by more than 80 percent of the Swiss voters and by all the cantons, and on January 1, 1979, the new canton was born—twenty-eight years after the beginning of the Jurassian Rally. The governments of the old and the new cantons agreed on the details of the separation. The extremists among the separatists still do not want peace; they think that sooner or later the south must be "conquered." But peace has returned, and the story shows that ways and means can be found to overcome even very serious tensions by a prudent use of democratic means.

A New Federal Constitution?

The present Federal Constitution dates from 1874; it has been changed to adapt to the times by more than 100 amendments, in recent times by several amendments a year. For more than twenty years some groups, especially professors of public law, have believed that a new Federal Constitution should be adopted.

The father of the idea was the late professor Max Imboden. He wrote a first draft, *Die Bundesverfassung wie sie sein könnte* [The present constitutional system in new modern words] in 1959. In 1965 both houses of the Federal Assembly accepted a motion inviting the government to collect materials for a new constitution and to nominate an expert group to make proposals. A first working group, under the direction of the old Federal Councilor F. T. Wahlen, invited the cantons, the political parties, and all other interested private organizations to make suggestions. The responses were published in five volumes with a final report of the working group in 1972. The group thought a new constitution desirable and formulated guiding principles for the development of a draft. On May 8, 1974, the Federal Council nominated a committee of forty-six experts, with the Federal Councilor Kurt Furgler, chief of the Department of Justice and Police, as chairman. This committee issued a draft constitution including a report in 1977. It was published in the three official languages, and an English translation was also issued.

The draft constitution and the report of the expert committee were submitted to the cantons, to the political parties, and to all other interested private organizations for critical remarks, and responses were published. The parts of the draft about human rights, on one hand, and the organization of the federal authorities, on the other were more or less accepted. People on the right thought that freedom of enterprise was not sufficiently protected, and people on the left wanted a clearer definition of basic social rights.

But the center of criticism was the chapter about the relations among the cantons and between the cantons and the confederation, quoted in the appendix. Although this chapter shows in a comprehensive way the actual sharing of responsibilities between cantons and central power, it was said that the limits of the central federal power were not sharply drawn. The draft was said to be too open and did not give enough guarantees of cantonal autonomy. Officers of the Department of Justice and police, therefore, were ordered to amend the experts' draft to satisfy at least the most critical voices among the cantons.

The Federal Council published the two drafts in its report of November 6, 1985 (Bundesblatt/feuille fédérale 1985 III 1) and asked the Federal Assembly for an order to elaborate a definitive proposal for a new Federal Constitution. But the Parliament was reluctant: it ordered only a draft that shows the actual written and unwritten constitutional law in a comprehensive way and in a systematic order.

For any material change a separate partial revision of the Constitution is needed. This resolution of June 3, 1987 is again a victory for the conservative forces in the country. A new draft will be published only in the next decade. There is a predominant feeling that the balance between unity and diversity is still appropriate and that in the next decade Switzerland with its existing structure and problems may enter into a closer contact to the European Common Market.

Appendix: Excerpts from the 1977 Draft for a New Federal Constitution

Chapter 2: Relations among Cantons and between Cantons and the Confederation

Article 43: Confederate allegiance and cooperation

1. The confederation and the cantons, as well as the cantons among themselves, owe one another mutual consideration and assistance.
2. They aid one another in the fulfillment of their tasks. They cooperate, in particular, through common planning.
3. The confederation may regulate by law the cooperation among neighboring cantons.

Article 44: Agreements and common institutions

1. The cantons may enter into agreements with one another.
2. The confederation and the cantons may enter into administrative agreements with one another.
3. The cantons may create, among themselves or with the confederation, common institutions and organs.

Article 45: Relations between legal systems

1. Federal law prevails over cantonal law.
2. The confederation may delineate the realm of application of cantonal legal systems.
3. Intercantonal double taxation is prohibited.

Article 46: Federal supervision

1. The confederation supervises the canton(s)' conformity with federal law.
2. If necessary, it takes appropriate measures for the enforcement of federal law.

Article 47: Protection of the constitutional order of the cantons

1. The confederation safeguards the constitutional order of the cantons.
2. It intervenes to ensure or restore the internal order of the cantons if this order is gravely threatened or disturbed and if the cantons cannot maintain it on their own.
3. It may, to this effect, use cantonal police forces.

Chapter 3: Responsibilities of the Confederation and the Cantons

Article 48: Concept of responsibility

1. The tasks of government are the responsibility of the confederation or the cantons.
2. Responsibility implies the right and the obligation to take the proper measures for fulfilling these tasks.

Article 49: Foreign affairs

1. The confederation is responsible for relations with foreign countries.
2. The cantons may, within their realms of responsibility, enter into international agreements on matters of neighborly relations. They act under the supervision of the confederation and, if it deems necessary, through its mediation.

Article 50: Principal responsibilities of the confederation

1. The confederation has the principal responsibility in the following realms:
   a. the defense of the country;
   b. the law of nationality, the status of aliens, and the granting of asylum;
   c. the civil and criminal law, the collection of debts, and the law of bankruptcy;
   d. social security and the protection of workers;
   e. the system and policies of property;
   f. the economic system and economic policy;
   g. money and currency;
   h. energy policy;
   i. railroad traffic, navigation, and air traffic;
   j. road traffic and national highways;
   k. national land use planning;
   l. the postal system and telecommunications;

m. radio and television;
n. weights and measures.
2. The cantons may take action in these domains if federal laws do not exclude it.

Article 51: Principal responsibilities of the cantons

1. The cantons have the principal responsibility in the following domains:
   a. the maintenance of public order;
   b. public welfare;
   c. hospitals and other establishments of health care;
   d. schools and education;
   e. relations between state and church;
   f. regional and local land use planning;
   g. highways;
   h. use of public waters and of subsoil resources.

2. In these domains the confederation may:
   a. enact outline laws to establish minimum requirements or to ensure coordination among the cantons;
   b. in certain cases, create institutions of its own.

3. The confederation may, for its security, use cantonal police forces.

Article 52: Responsibility in other domains

1. In the domains in which neither the confederation nor the cantons have the principal responsibility, the cantons remain responsible unless federal laws assign it otherwise.
2. These domains are, in particular:
   a. the protection of health;
   b. the protection of the environment, the landscape, and residential areas;
   c. the encouragement of cultural activities;
   d. the encouragement of research, science, and the arts;
   e. the universities;
   f. vocational education and training.

Article 53: Guarantee of cantonal autonomy

1. Whenever the confederation legislates, or acts in other ways, it guarantees to the cantons all the autonomy compatible with the accomplishment of the tasks of government.
2. The cantons put federal law into effect if it is not necessary for the confederation to do so.

Notes

1. For details, see Andrey et al., *Nouvelle histoire de la Suisse et des suisses,* published in German, French, and Italian (Lausanne-Basel-Bellinzona, 1982), vol. 3.

2. The characteristics of the twenty-six member-states are well described in Fritz Rene Allemann, *25 mal die Schweiz* (Piper-Munchen, 1965) (the canton of Jura was not yet born).

3. A good introduction to Swiss *multilinguiseme* is Jean Pierre Vouga, *Romands, Alemaniques, Tessinois* (Neuchatel, 1978), pp. 144ff.

4. These were as follows: February 18, 1979, concerning publicity for alcohol and tobacco; February 18, 1979, for limitation of nuclear power plants; March 2, 1980, for separation of church and state (rejected in all cantons); May 4, 1981, for better collaboration between immigrants and the Swiss (in favor of the immigrants); February 24, 1984, for a free choice of civil service; May 20, 1984, for better control of banking and limitation of the banks' secrecy; May 20, 1984, for a stronger limitation on sales of land to foreigners (beyond the existing restrictions); September 23, 1984, for a future without new atomic power plants; September 23, 1984, for a safe economic energy supply protecting the environment (also for limitation of atomic energy plants); February 12, 1985, for effective protection of motherhood (for the delay solution in abortion legislation); March 10, 1985, for more vacations; and June 6, 1985, for the right to life (against liberal legislation about abortion).

5. At the Swiss Lawyers' Conference of 1984, Peter Saladin and Blaise Knapp tried to explain this system in all its complexity; *Revue du droit Suisse,* vol. 103, no. 2 (1984), pp. 275ff., 431ff.

Bibliography

History: Andrey et al. *Geschichte der Schweiz und der Schweizer; Nouvelle histoire de la Suisse et des suisses; Nuova storia della Svizzera e degli svizzeri,* vol. 3. Basel, Lausanne, Bellinzona, 1982.

Politics: *Handbuch politisches System der Schweiz; Manuel système politique de la Suisse,* vols. 1, 2 (1983); vol. 3 (1986).

Constitutional law: Jean-Francois Aubert. *Traite de droit constitutionel suisse,* two vols. Neuchatel, 1967, with annex, 1982.

Aubert, Eichenberger, Müller, et al. *Kommentar zur Bundesverfassung der schweizerischen Eidgenossenschaft/Commentaire de la Constitution fédérale.* Three files: Basel, Zürich, Berne, 1987–1989.

Ulrich Haefelin and Walter Haller. *Schweizerisches Bundesstraatsrecht.* Zurich, 2d ed., 1988.

Rene Rhinow and Andreas Auer. "Grundprobleme der schweizerischen Demokratie." *Zeitschrift fur Schweizerisches Recht/Revue de Droit Suisse,* vol. 103, no. 2 (1984); 1ff., 111ff.

Peter Saladin and Blaise Knapp. "Bund und Kantone"/"Le federalisme." *Zeitschrift fur Schweizerisches Recht/Revue de Droit Suisse,* vol. 103, no. 2 (1984): 275ff., 431ff.

"Bericht über die Totalrevision der Bundesverfassung"/"Message concernant la revision totale de la Constitution fédérale." *Bundesplatt/Feuille Fédérale,* vol. 3, no. 1 (1985).

Jura conflict: "Botschaft des Bundesrates für die Gründung des Kantons Jura"/"Message du Conseil Federal sur la fondation du Canton du Jura." *Bundesblatt/Feuille Fédérale,* 1977–767.

Commentary

Thomas Fleiner

Governments have developed different ways of coping with diversity. The United States—always considered a melting pot—has tried to deal with the problem of diversity by emphasizing individual rights. Through them everyone can develop and safeguard his or her own identity in society. The American Constitution's clauses mandating no establishment of religion and equal protection of the laws—and especially affirmative action programs for American blacks—are examples of how the Supreme Court prohibits discrimination and guarantees the integrity of racial diversity.

Governments may also cope with problems of diversity through a constitution that gives rights not only to individuals but to linguistic, religious, or cultural groups. Giving rights to *groups,* however, may diminish the rights of *individuals.* Rights may be given to such groups in several ways. The first is on a territorial basis. That is how Switzerland has tried in most cases to cope with diversity; the autonomy of the cantons and the local authorities has developed mainly on the basis of rights given to minority groups.

Second, group rights may be provided on the basis of religion or creed; that is how traditional Islamic countries and Israel have tried to deal with the diversity of religious groups. In Switzerland this way has been followed in a few cases; for instance, the canton of St. Gall tried in the past century to give certain autonomous rights to the two most important religious groups, Catholics and Protestants. This example, which should have been followed by other cantons (such as Aargau), failed because the majority of the canton did not want to accept division into two or three parts. This, of course, is the problem of giving autonomy to different groups in one territory.

States and governments can also cope with diversity by allowing certain groups and autonomous units to take part in decision making. Democracy and the rights of minorities, such as veto powers or other privileges in the decision-making process, are part of this way of coping with diversity. Today the United States tries to cope with diversity through affirmative action programs, giving privileges to minority groups with respect to access to schools or government jobs.

The ways to cope with diversity vary because the problems and their historical backgrounds differ from one country to another. It is essential, however, that solutions to the problems of minorities be found through democratic procedures. Only through democracy can flexible solutions be found and adapted to varying situations. In addressing diversity in Switzerland, I first focus on facts about minorities and then show how Switzerland tries to cope with diversity on a territorial basis and how its governmental system permits important participation by groups in the decision-making process. Finally I discuss the autonomy of cantons, not only in decision making but also in implementing federal law within their territories.

Minorities in Switzerland

Switzerland is a very small country. The United States, for instance, is 223 times the size of Switzerland. Switzerland has only 7 million inhabitants. The country is divided into twenty-six cantons, which differ greatly from one another in size and number of inhabitants. The canton of Zurich has about 1 million inhabitants while the canton of Appenzell-Innerrhoden has only 14,000. Several cantons are much smaller than some of the municipalities of our mountain cantons. So diversity exists not only in the people but also in the structure of the cantons.

Switzerland is a confederation, which emerged amid the former German empire, the French absolutist state, and the Italian principalities. Cultural, linguistic, and religious territories belonging to the cultures of the neighboring states joined together to enjoy the democratic freedom granted by the treaty of the Swiss cantons. Although in the twentieth century Switzerland has remained a confederation with practically no consistent majority, it is composed of varied cultural, linguistic, religious, historical, and political minority groups.

Unlike Belgium, which is composed of two linguistic groups of almost equal size, and Canada, with a French-speaking minority and a large English-speaking majority, Switzerland has no clear-cut minority of, for example, French-speaking people with an identity distinguished from a majority of German-speaking people. The French-speaking part of the population is composed of different religious groups that find their counterparts in the German- or the Italian-speaking population of Switzerland. Thus every Swiss belongs to a political, linguistic, or religious minority and at the same time to another majority. A French-speaking Protestant living in the canton of Fribourg and belonging to the Radical party belongs both to a linguistic minority and to a minority party of Fribourg.

Unlike many countries faced with diversity throughout their lands, such as Lebanon and in a way the United States with regard to black people, Switzerland experiences diversity among its territorial areas. Minorities identify themselves either with their local municipality or with their canton. The Swiss Constitution has developed procedures and institutions to cope with territorial minorities but not with discrimination against social minorities, such as aliens or political groups opposed to the views of the social or political majority.

A common historical heritage permits people to identify with their immediate territory much more than with the confederation. A citizen of the canton of Geneva, for example, sees himself first as a citizen of Geneva and only second as a citizen of Switzerland.

These facts about diversity in Switzerland must be kept in mind as we look at the solutions the Swiss Constitution provides. What institutions in Switzerland deal with diversity? First, the federal structure of the state, which provides autonomy to cantons and local authorities; second, the governmental system, which permits participation in the decision-making process by territorial units and political and economic groups; and third, implementation of federal laws with respect for the differences among territorial units.

Federalism and Autonomy

Taxing Power. The Swiss Constitution allows the cantons much greater autonomy than other federal systems allow their provinces or states. The cantons retain greater political power because cantonal policy depends not only on the cantonal parliament but also on the decisions of the citizens by popular vote. In Switzerland every citizen must pay income tax to the local authority, to the cantonal authority, and to the confederation. All three are autonomous in determining the amount of taxes that must be paid to them.

Police Authority. The responsibility for public order lies with the cantons. They have their own police forces, and sometimes police power is divided between the cantonal and local governments. The cantons protect public order and the life and health of the citizens and ensure good faith in commercial affairs. They also execute federal laws through their own police in matters over which the Constitution gives authority to the federal legislature. They regulate food and drug quality according to federal law through their own chemists, who are responsible to cantonal government.

Culture, Economy, and Health. Cantons are also autonomous with regard to education and cultural development. The Federal Constitution obliges them to provide an opportunity for every child to be educated in a public school. It is up to the cantons, however, to organize the public schools and to decide on their curriculums.

Residual Power. Autonomy is granted not only to the cantons but also to the local authorities. The democratically organized public assemblies of the municipal units in many cantons are the very basis of state power. In fact, since Switzerland has never had a monarch or a head of state, the residual power is to be found in the canton, and in most cantons it is to be found in the municipalities. For this reason municipalities are granted autonomy by the Federal Court.

Organization. Cantons and to some extent municipalities are autonomous with regard to their own organization. Each canton has developed its own democratic institutions, horizontal structure, vertical separation of powers among municipalities, districts, and cantons, and relationship between church and state. The church-state relationship is determined to a great extent by the historical identity of the cantons; greatly diverse relationships have developed according to the religious majorities in the cantons and still affect the organizational structure of the cantons.

Federal Grants. While in the United States federal grants can be given to the states without a specific constitutional power, federal grants can be given to cantons in Switzerland only if they are voted on by the legislature and if the power to do so is conveyed to the federal government by the Constitution. It is thus not possible to limit cantonal authority through federal grants since the confederation has no unlimited power to subsidize cantonal activities.

The Governmental System of Switzerland

A number of aspects of the governmental system affect questions of diversity in Switzerland. These include the separation of powers, the function and structure of the executive (the Federal Council), and the participation of the cantons and of political and economic groups in the decision-making process.

Separation of Powers. Switzerland has not adopted the Westminster model of parliamentary sovereignty. Neither has it followed the American Founding Fathers in adopting full separation of powers as well as federalism (dual sovereignty).

In Switzerland the Federal Assembly, or parliament (consisting of two chambers), the Federal Council as the executive power, and the judiciary are separate from one another. The imposition by the Constitution of 1874 and the Amendment of 1891 of direct democracy over the three separate powers of the government has had some consequences for that separation. Theoretically, the parliament is the most important power, according to the model of the French Revolution. In practice, however, the parliament has always respected a certain degree of independence of the executive.

The separation of powers can also be extended to the federal structure. Switzerland has accepted the idea of dual sovereignty, conveying some sovereign powers to the cantons and some to the confederation. The federal power issues and has been developed from cantonal sovereignty. This historical fact is very important for dual sovereignty in Switzerland.

Structure and Function of the Executive Power. The great difference between Switzerland and almost all other states is to be found not so much in direct democracy—in respect to which Switzerland is often considered a model—but in the structure of the executive power. The Federal Council, the Swiss executive, is composed of seven members with equal powers. All seven are elected individually by the parliament, and none can be removed during a period of four years. In this century all members of the Federal Council have been reelected after four years by the parliament unless they have resigned.

This governmental structure has been influenced by two concepts: the old "town government," always seen to some extent as a collegial government, and the Directory of the French Revolution from 1795 to 1799 in Paris. The Directory was the first government in France without a monarch, serving at the same time as head of state and head of the cabinet of ministers.

The collegial structure of the Federal Council, independent of the majority of the parliament, is the main reason why a parliamentary system with a cabinet directed by a prime minister, such as that of Great Britain, could not be established in Switzerland. For this reason also the members of the government are not at the same time the leaders of their political parties. Thus the Swiss government is by no means a coalition government but is a government composed of seven members with seven independent opinions. Of course, they are influenced by the views of their parties.

The Federal Constitution provides that no two members of the Federal Council may be citizens of the same canton; the several linguistic and religious groups of Switzerland must therefore be represented in the government. As Kaufmann points out, however, since 1955 the members of the government have belonged to the four leading parties; this shows that the parliament, in electing the Federal Council, recognizes that the council must represent different political groups as well as different cantons.

The government's independence from the parliament has had an effect on the independence of parties. The majority party does not directly influence governmental policy, and thus the executive need not seek its support for every decision. As a consequence the executive enjoys great independence from political parties, from the parliamentary groups of the parties, and from the individual members of the parliament. At the same time the members of parliament see themselves as independent of their government and of the majority party. The parliament can include not only two or three large parties representing the government and the opposition but several large and small parties. For this reason by 1918 the Constitution provided for proportional representation of the parties in the parliament. The parliament does not depend on one large majority; it must reflect different opinions and the diverse political, religious, and economic interests of the people. The governmental system has directly influenced the system of proportional representation, allowing for better representation of diversity.

Cantonal Influence in the Decision-making Process. The governmental system also permits cantons to influence the decision making of the parliament more directly than is possible in a system of parliamentary democracy. Such direct influence is possible only in a system that establishes an independent executive power and allows equal powers to the two chambers of parliament—the chamber representing the people and the chamber representing the cantons. For this reason influencing parliament is much easier for Swiss cantons than, for example, for the federal units in Canada, Germany, or Australia.

Electoral districts in Switzerland are identical with cantonal territories. If someone wants to be elected even to the lower chamber and to be a candidate of the party in his canton, he must find majority support there. Thus the cantonal political parties are much more important than the federal parties because the cantonal parties choose the candidates for the federal parliament. In many cantons, before a session of the federal parliament, the members of both chambers of the parliament from a canton meet with their cantonal government to prepare their cantonal policy.

The government must submit all constitutional amendments to a vote of the people and the cantons. Every law adopted by the parliament may be submitted to a referendum. Consequently it is never possible for a small majority of a party or an interest group in the parliament to get a law adopted against the wishes of an important minority. The socialists, for instance, are always able to prevent the adoption of a law if important social interests are neglected. For much of the past century conservative Catholics used direct democracy to prevent laws that discriminated against their interests. Direct democracy gives significant minorities an effective veto power.

This veto power can also be used by the cantons. Important cantonal interests can never be neglected by federal constitutional amendments or by federal statutes. The Constitution obliges the executive to consult the cantons and important interest groups before adopting a law or proposing a draft of it to the parliament. This obligation gives the cantons and interest groups a great influence on decision making and on the executive's preparation of a law.

Federal Government by Compromise. The independence of the executive from the parliament, proportional representation in the parliament, the power of the cantons in the decision-making process, and the obligation to consult various interest groups have had a great effect on the political culture of Switzerland. Important decisions are based on compromise since every authority must seek such a compromise between groups. It thus takes a long time to prepare statutes and make governmental decisions, but once adopted they are usually implemented and adhered to by the citizens. The system of proportional influence of interest groups has also had the consequence that not only the government but every cantonal, federal, or judicial authority is composed of officials representing different political parties or groups. Even the administration reflects differing political ideas and groups, and this "proportionalism" gives rise to a stability of the government and a due respect for diverse political interests.

Implementation of Federal Law in the Cantons

We have already seen that many laws are made by the cantons autonomously. The federal government issues federal laws, but most of them are implemented by the cantons—in most cantons by the local authorities. Thus a federal law usually requires a cantonal law or

245

at least an ordinance. The consequence is that federal laws are not always implemented in the same way in all the cantons.

Civil law or penal law (implemented by cantonal courts under the control of the Federal Court) can be interpreted differently by cantonal authorities. Abortion and divorce decisions are not made in the same way in a Catholic canton as in a Protestant canton. This aspect of diversity appears even more important if we take into account the implementation of other federal laws that need additional cantonal statutes to be implemented in the cantonal territories. The cantonal executive and especially the cantonal administration must execute federal laws, and the way they fulfill this obligation depends on the political opinions and structures of the cantons.

For the same reason, even individual liberties and rights can be implemented in different ways. For a long time religious liberty has been interpreted in Catholic and Protestant cantons according to their different political histories. In some cantons schools have long been integrated into the religious culture, although the Constitution clearly provides that freedom of religion cannot be infringed by cantonal schools.

An amendment of Article 4 of the Constitution provides "equal rights for men and women," but the canton of Appenzell still does not allow women to vote. Even though a large majority of the Swiss people and the cantons adopted the equal rights amendment, the parliament is not willing to impose on two small cantons women's right to vote.

For a long time the Federal Court has allowed constitutional rights to be interpreted in different ways in the various cantons. The political culture of Switzerland, the political institutions, and the Constitution have developed over a long period, and it is certainly only this long historical development that enables political institutions to cope with the great diversity in Switzerland. It has never been possible to impose the will of a majority on a minority through democracy because no clear-cut line exists between a majority and a minority.

For this reason some advantages of democracy, of strong majority rule, have not emerged. But the democratic decision-making process has permitted minorities to develop sufficient power to force the authorities to take their interests into account and to institute proportional representation.

We must be aware, however, that fundamental human rights, such as equality, cannot be subject to democratic procedures. They cannot be understood differently in different cantons according to the will of their legislatures, as the right of women to vote is. Switzerland has always given priority to democratic rights; it will have to find ways to permit implementation of fundamental rights on an equal basis for all citizens.

Problems of Diversity and Federalism in Switzerland

Switzerland can certainly be considered a country that strongly respects the interests of minorities. But it has many problems concerning diversity.

Liberty of Commerce. That the state does not intervene in economic affairs has had the consequence that the country's economic structure has become more and more centralized. Most important economic decisions are made at the headquarters of banks and industries in Zurich, Basel, or Berne. All those towns are German-speaking, and none of the headquarters of large economic enterprises has been located in Geneva or Lausanne, both French-speaking. Thus, as Switzerland has become more and more economically centralized, the French-speaking part has felt more and more marginal in commerce and industry. That is because most citizens living in French-speaking Switzerland are not willing to give up a lower position and move to join a headquarters in Zurich or Basel. They prefer to stay in the lower position and remain integrated within their social group. Of course, some leading industries have realized these problems and strive to consider the interests of minorities.

Linguistic Minorities within the Cantons. Four of the Swiss cantons have to cope with two to four languages. In those cantons the problems of diversity can be solved only by giving more autonomy—especially in cultural and educational affairs—to the local communities. Minority problems still exist in those cantons, however. A strict territorial concept cannot be the solution, because people do not choose their homes only according to linguistic borderlines; they also consider economic and other reasons. For instance, one problem in bilingual or multilingual cantons is that parents may want to send their children not to schools in their local community but to neighboring schools that speak their language.

Social Justice. The centralization of power in the federal state was largely promoted for social reasons. It was possible to implement social justice only through federal laws because poorer cantons were unable or unwilling to grant financial help to elderly, sick, or handicapped people. For this reason the people wanted social justice to be a federal concern, not only with regard to social security but also with regard to schools, health, and other public matters. Now that the federal government seems to be facing financial difficulties, it wants to hand some responsibilities over social security and justice to the cantons, but the parties promoting social justice strongly oppose such a move. To them social justice is better guaranteed by the federal government and should not depend on cantonal democracy, which may have priorities higher than taking care of underprivileged social groups.

Conclusion

Direct democracy in the cantons was the important factor in countering the tendency to centralize power. Parliaments would have agreed much more easily to give up a part of their autonomy to the federal authority, but they could not decide on their own; they had to decide with the people. The people of the cantons do not easily acquiesce when asked to give up some of their power. This may be why Switzerland is facing a "renaissance of federalism" and realizing the importance of respecting diversity, especially of language and culture.

Discussion

ROBERT GOLDWIN: The papers on Switzerland seem to argue that the significant factors of Swiss federal democracy—as they apply to the problems of differences of language, nationality, and the like—are in the ways the Swiss people have constituted themselves over the centuries and not in any special character of the Swiss people that distinguishes them from other peoples with similar problems. Why, then, should we agree with what Professor Kaufmann says at the beginning of his paper that Swiss federal democracy is not exportable? If the decisive factor were some special characteristic of the Swiss, we could agree. But if the decisive factors are in the Constitution, why can others not imitate the Swiss? Are there not lessons to be learned by, and practices and institutions that can be adapted to, other nations? Even if these two authors ascribe Swiss institutions to accidents of history or force, are these institutions not, nevertheless, sustained by reason and choice? If so, what are the principles and practices of the Swiss that others could adopt by choice?

OTTO KAUFMANN: In Switzerland the protection of linguistic minorities is not in itself the primary function of the Constitution. The main function of this federalist Constitution is to protect territorial diversity. For instance, two cantons—Geneva and Vaud, both French-speaking, both with a Calvinist background—are nevertheless two quite different cantons. And they want to maintain their diversity. The question is, therefore, To what extent can protection of such territorial diversity be exported?

Once the minister of justice of New Guinea came to me at the Supreme Court to ask for advice about how to organize his country. He wanted to know if I thought New Guinea should adopt something like the Swiss Constitution. I said to him, "Do not do that. You may preserve diversity, but completely lose unity." That is one of the dangers with such a system as ours. Another experience came after the Second World War, when a lot of German professors and politicians came into Switzerland and asked, "To what extent should we copy Swiss institutions to rebuild democracy after Nazi Germany?" And in the end, they did not use much from us, either.

The question of exporting our variety of democracy is very troubling. We have democracy not only at the local community level but at the canton level and at the federal level. Direct democracy is a great danger nowadays, with possible mass psychological reactions, a danger much increased by modern mass media. Perhaps we have avoided such dangers because we have a reasonable political education among the whole population.

THOMAS FLEINER: This is a very difficult question because, to paraphrase Ronald Dworkin, the Swiss take diversity seriously. That being so, the Swiss cannot go to another country and tell its citizens that they should adopt only one or two of their constitutional provisions. That is the reason we Swiss are very hesitant to recommend that Swiss institutions be exported. We should recall that the Founding Fathers of the American Constitution had one principle that animated their discussions: "Let us be guided by experience, because reason might mislead us." I think that is what the Swiss Constitution is, something developed by experience. It is certainly not something that would have been developed by reason.

For instance, in his writings Montesquieu considers the kinds of taxation systems different countries have. He notes that countries with great liberty have high taxes and countries with less liberty have low taxes. But then he asks, What about the Swiss? They have a lot of liberty and yet have low taxes. He finds the explanation in the fact that the Swiss have to pay as much to geography and climate as the Turkish have to pay to the sultan.

Adam Smith also tried to find out why the Swiss had such a curious tax system that it could not be exported either to England or to any other country. He found the explanation in the fact that the Swiss declare their taxes themselves. That was already the case in 1800. He says, therefore, that the Swiss are convinced that the taxes they pay are used wisely by their government, because they themselves decide for what those taxes will be used. In Great Britain, meanwhile, citizens are not convinced that their government will use taxes as they should and therefore are not prepared to pay their taxes freely.

Both Montesquieu and Adam Smith therefore examined Swiss institutions and found that the differences arose because of different conditions—different conditions prevent the easy export of an institution to another nation.

Certainly some constitutional institutions may be applied in other countries. This is much more the case with regard to the principles of our constitution than to the institutions themselves, however. First, the concept of dual sovereignty might help countries that are trying to come together to create a new union. Although this device would not help Spain, which is a federation from a centralized state, it might help where unions like that of the American states are to be created.

The second principle that might be exported is that of our collegial government. International organizations especially have to devise ways to create an executive that somehow represents the different units merging into one new state. Our Swiss Federal Council, is, of course, a governmental system of seven colleagues with equal powers and equal rights.

Direct democracy of a certain sort could also be implemented in other states. The Swiss democracy, however, is not at all similar to, for instance, the plebiscite of the French democracy. That plebiscite is an instrument for the president to implement Rousseau's "general will," and to prove to the Parliament that he, finally, is the man who effects the will of the people. Direct democracy in Switzerland depends on the will of the people. In accordance with direct democracy, the people should be able to influence the Parliament directly through initiatives, new motions, and new ideas. In Switzerland the executive is always the most progressive; Parliament is less progressive; and the people are always most conservative. They have decided in many cases against the Parliament and even against the political parties.

These Swiss institutions might be exportable, especially to federal countries. Those countries that are really willing to take diversity seriously must somehow implement direct democracy locally, because I think only local, direct democracy will be able to prevent the tendency toward centralization, which always occurs in the executive branches of federal units.

DANIEL ELAZAR: The democracies have found three principal ways to protect diversity while maintaining unity: the protection of local liberties, federalism, and the protection of individual rights.

Some political systems might combine these approaches, as they are not mutually exclusive by any means. In fact, some combination is probably the best way. If we contrast, for example, Switzerland with the United States, the burden in Switzerland is on a local liberties *cum* federalist approach; and in the United States, the burden would be on the federalist *cum* individual rights approach. And this might help us analyze what kinds of diversity are protected and how well in different systems, as well as what methods and procedures should be used for protecting diversity in different systems.

With regard to the issue of reflection and choice, I think that, in fact, the Swiss system *has* developed out of reflection and choice in

251

bits and pieces. There is very little that is accidental in the Swiss system. A lot of reflection and choice, based upon experience, has led to certain decisions that may seem at times to be contradictory or incompatible. In general, we probably have not paid enough attention to "reflection and choice in bits and pieces" as a constitutional process, because we have emphasized the American model of "one fell swoop," one great act of reflection and choice, as if that were the only way to achieve the constitutional qualities we seek. We might do well to consider the Swiss model as an alternative. It can be done and has been done in some other cases, as well. Israel, for example, built a network of institutions from the 1870s to 1948 that later became the state of Israel through "reflection and choice in bits and pieces."

Finally, we see in the Swiss situation that relationships and procedures are even more important than structures. Structures may be inconsistent, but relationships and procedures, or what we Americans call due process, have been developed to their fullest extent in the Swiss experience. That is why the emphasis on local liberties and federalism, with less emphasis on individual rights, has still probably protected rights better than in many other parts of the world.

The issue of exportability is usually phrased as, Can we export structures? And there the answer has to be no. But we may be able to export relationships and procedures.

HERMAN BELZ: The problem of diversity seems to be a recent one in modern history. In the medieval period and the early modern period, diversity was simply understood to be the condition of things in the world. People were different, conditions were different all over the world, and the problem was to overcome the diversity and create some degree of unity. The purpose in creating unity in Switzerland, for example, was to achieve some degree of freedom that was not possible as long as there was constant pressure from outside forces jeopardizing the Swiss situation.

In the modern world, the problem of diversity seems to be part of the problem of overcoming inequality. Today there is a great emphasis on equality, unity, and uniformity. The very term modernization seems to include the concept of uniformity.

Localism implies diversity and inequality. The Swiss seem to have been successful in dealing with the problem of diversity because they undertook to do so before it was really a problem, in the modern sense, of overcoming inequality. The emphasis now is to have enough unity and uniformity to create some kind of equality while recognizing diversity. When recognizing diversity, however, we do not want people or groups to be unequal.

Switzerland is exceptional in many ways. In the heart of Europe, it is the most up-to-date, progressive country in the region. It has been depoliticized, in effect, for a long time, so the exceptionalism stands out. Surely, though, Switzerland has some things to export, and one of the lessons from Switzerland is to keep things simple and not be too doctrinaire. That can be taught, that can be learned, and that can be insisted upon. The constitutional structures involved are really very simple treaties, promises, and covenants, to protect each other in certain situations when danger is imminent.

JACQUES VANDERLINDEN: Are there no problems in Switzerland with violations of minority rights? How do we address the possibility that a minority might decide it wants to become autonomous? This question came to my mind as I read these papers on Switzerland.

MR. KAUFMANN: As Mr. Elazar indicated, local autonomy is very important in our country, and every local municipality may come before the Supreme Court and claim violation of its autonomy, exactly as individual citizens may claim violation of civil rights. That, then, is a very strong protection of local autonomy.

As for the problem of minority rights inside cantons, in most cantons minorities get quite good protection, although it is somewhat different with the Italians. Italian is an official language of the confederation, but it is not an official language in any of the cantons. (Most of the Italian-speaking people are in Zurich.) In my opinion, we do not sufficiently protect the mother tongue of all these Italians or of the Spanish people now living inside Switzerland. I think we do not do enough for bilingual education. I moved with four German-speaking children to the French-speaking part of Switzerland, and the school officials just told me to put my children in the normal school; it did not work well. Generally speaking, I think, approaching the Supreme Court with grievances is a simple procedure, and in that respect rights are adequately protected, although within the cantons not every right receives perfect protection.

MR. FLEINER: One of the tenets of Swiss political ethics is that the majority generally does not want to implement its will at the expense of the minority. As we take diversity seriously, so we take the minorities seriously. A second principle of our political ethics is to try to find a consensus—not unanimity—but a way to avoid war between the majority and the minority. A third is conciliation. If there are struggles or if there are problems, we try to conciliate them. The fourth, certainly, is federalism. Every new political issue that has to be solved people usually think we first have to try to solve at the local level, not on the federal level. The fifth, of course, is neutrality, which has a great impact on Swiss politics.

NATHAN GLAZER: Switzerland is fortunate in not having a coincidence between economic deprivation and language. Or perhaps the Swiss are simply frightfully enlightened and insist on spending vast sums to make sure that no area is deprived, as they spend great sums on the maintenance of the very small Romansch language.

One important element mentioned in the papers, which might also be exportable, is the Supreme Court's remarkably loose enforcement of nationwide principles or rules. It occurred to me that this willingness to accept local differences might help us a great deal in the United States. I find it hard to believe, for example, that Switzerland would ever have had, as we had, a Prohibition Amendment forbidding the production or sale of alcoholic beverages throughout the entire country. Fortunately, now each state, and in may states each community, has its own rules. This situation no longer troubles anyone. An enormous area of conflict therefore has simply been eliminated by repealing a constitutional amendment that applied a national rule with too great a rigor. That is a general tendency in this country, where conceivably the U.S. Supreme Court could learn from the Swiss courts.

For example—and I know this will be controversial—when the Supreme Court decides that a moment of silence prescribed by a state transgresses the establishment of religion, the Court may have resorted too rigorously to a single rule for a country of 240 million people and probably 150 religions.

RUTH BADER GINSBURG: Switzerland's wonderful direct democracy could perhaps be imported to some states of the United States, but Switzerland has 7 million people. In countries that have hundreds of millions, the Swiss way would not work, it would not be a salable export.

The Swiss idea of cantons as laboratories for experiment is similar to what Brandeis said was one of the great strengths of the federal system in the United States. The example he offered appears strange in modern times—trying out, state by state, the wisdom of allowing women to vote before foisting that suffrage on the nation. But the notion is sound: try novel proposals out at a state or local level; then, if the proposal does not work, it can be abandoned. If it does work, it can be adopted more widely.

I was also intrigued by the notion of constitutional review for cantonal laws but not for Swiss federal law. We have both review of state laws and review of federal legislation, but many have suggested that we could get along well enough without constitutional review of federal legislation. I suspect we would not do so well as a nation if the courts could not review state legislation for consistency with the fundamental charter.

Finally, I find interesting the comment in Mr. Kaufmann's paper on the expansive interpretation of the constitutional clause stating that all Swiss citizens are equal before the law. That is similar to the expansive interpretation of the fifth amendment due process clause (and the equal protection component read into it) that we have witnessed in the United States. Expansive interpretation of due process and equal protection principles by courts in the United States has been strongly criticized by some commentators and jurists as veering far from anything the Founding Fathers ever dreamed of. In this regard, Switzerland faces a dilemma over the treatment of the one-seventh of the Swiss population who are aliens and who are on renewable work permits or resident permits, with no right to remain or to become citizens. That is a difficult situation.

JUAN LINZ: Several elements underlying the Swiss example make export difficult. One is the desire, noted before, of the Swiss to be Swiss and not Germans, French, or Italians. Survey data show that the two identities that are most powerful in Switzerland are the cantonal identity and the Swiss identity. The linguistic identity is chosen by few people. There is, in a strange way, a lack of Swiss nationalism. One can be in Switzerland without hearing the word Switzerland mentioned in a speech or in any kind of situation—all references are to the canton. In contrast, there is a strong feeling of being Swiss. We have to understand things within that framework.

Moreover, Swiss society may be very liberal politically, with many guaranteed freedoms, but it is a very constrictive society in the sense of social control by the community or neighborhood. A Spaniard once remarked to me that in Franco's Spain there was no political freedom but that he wished Switzerland was as free as Spain: in Spain, he could throw a piece of paper on the street without being chastised by passing citizens. In some ways, then, the society exercises a control not exercised by the political system. Are there not many societies in which the individual has a lot of social freedom, because the society does not bother to control his behavior in the way that it does in Switzerland?

We must also recall that Switzerland is a country of less than 7 million, compared with major metropolitan areas like Barcelona and

Madrid, with close to 4 million inhabitants each. That is a totally different social setting—the small, communal milieu of even the large cantons, to say nothing of the many smaller cantons. And that, I think, has to be retained.

As for exportability, one experiment has been attempted: the collective executive was exported to Uruguay. It certainly did not seem to be a success. The founders of the Czech republic, with Switzerland as the model, thought they could make Czechoslovakia a multinational society like Switzerland; they failed very seriously in that endeavor.

Finally, the Swiss case is clearly one of cross-cutting cleavages, a society in which alignments on values, party alignments, religious alignments, linguistic alignments, and territorial alignments of the cantons all cross-cut each other. Therefore, everybody is in the minority position in one situation and in the majority position in another. That pattern facilitates the maintenance of a certain kind of majority principle, because the majority is never constant and permanent and nobody is in the permanent minority. That cross-cutting alignment results from the peculiar historical division of the territory, which was not based on nationality, language, or other criteria. The boundaries are the result of other historical factors.

MR. VANDERLINDEN: As a Belgian, I am tempted to seek a parallel between our two small countries. We have in Belgium, perhaps, a few more inhabitants, 10 million versus 6½ million, but what we have in common is that the two major European cultures—the German and the Latin—meet in our countries. So why has Switzerland become such a success story and Belgium had such difficulties?

Mr. Fleiner earlier commented that at the Congress of Vienna in 1815 after the Napoleonic War, Switzerland went back to its original federal system. Belgium, very much influenced by French thinking, went to the unitary, very centralized state. In general in continental Europe there have been those two approaches: the very centralized approach, which appeared in most of the countries while Napoleon ruled—from Spain to Denmark, Norway and Sweden—and the Swiss, federal approach. I believe this Swiss federal system is exportable. Progress has been made with that federal principle in continental Europe since the end of the war. Progress has been remarkable: in Germany, in Spain, but also in the European federalist movement, which should not be underestimated.

KEITH KYLE: The news that the Swiss system is not a product for export, while possibly true, would be very bad news to many people who have looked to the Swiss system as a last hope of resolving their problems. There is a good deal of admiration for Switzerland in the intensive care unit of national constitutions. Cases are arising in which people will desperately try to apply Swiss rules. Lebanon represents one attempt to re-create a political society. In the medium term, there will be the opportunity to provide the proper institutions for South Africa, a major challenge to constitutionalists.

The Swiss example was often cited in the great period of decolonization; I know of two occasions when Swiss constitutional advisers were used, and a serious attempt was made to apply something from the Swiss experience. The first was in the case of Kenya, when the assumption was made that the differences between tribes were analogous to national differences and required accommodation accordingly; the idea of a cantonal system seemed to provide a model. The constitution derived from this effort did not command sufficient consensus to survive. It was criticized from the outset by the KANU (Kenya African National Union) party, of which Jomo Kenyatta was the leader, although it was accepted as an instrument for achieving independence. Its detractors objected to it on the ground that it would entrench and reinforce the ethnic differences, which many national leaders hoped to diminish. This is a major problem that arises whenever the consociational approach is suggested in a situation; some group divisions that the constitution ought to diminish are thereby defined and reinforced.

Many also objected that the Swiss system as adopted in Kenya in the first instance was too slow moving. There appears to be ample reinforcement for that view in the two papers before us.

The other example where a Swiss constitution adviser was used was for the Constitution of Cyprus, whose initial principles were in fact drawn up in Zurich. There the problem stemmed from the division of society into two elements only. The proposed constitution was reminiscent of the new Belgian Constitution because of the problem of two units, the Greeks and the Turks. The two-unit federation is always difficult to contemplate and scarcely ever successful. Furthermore, the Greeks and Turks lived among each other, not separated territorially.

Although a constitution was drawn up with the aid of a Swiss constitution adviser, the objection was that it was far too complex for a small country without political experience and that it tended to lead to deadlock and inhibited rapid decision. It broke down in under four years.

The attempt is now being made to reconstruct the unity of Cyprus, and people are talking again of a two-part federation. The distinction is made between a system with minority rights—a group of rights that a consensus holds to be appropriate for a linguistic, religious, or other well-defined minority within the country—and a federation in which two partners have joint and equal rights within the country. In Cyprus, federation would mean that the Turks, who are 18 percent of the population, and the Greeks, who are 80 percent, would be equal founders of the country. Elements of both approaches appear in the initial constitution, and each side, of course, refers to those elements in the Constitution that seem to support its own plan for the future.

Similarly, in Sri Lanka, when for the first time the Ceylonese started approaching the problem of a constitution, the Tamils claimed that they should be a separate founder of the new state and should be treated as coequal with the Sinhalese majority. Again, a two-state federation would result. Nations often thus turn to the Swiss example out of a misunderstanding. They think that the cantonal element of the Swiss Constitution will make a federation possible despite the fact that the constituents of the federation are mixed up among each other. A suggestion has been made, for example, that Switzerland suggests a possible solution to the problem of Northern Ireland. The problem in Northern Ireland, apart from everything else, arises from the fact that Catholics and Protestants live close to each other: to produce the Swiss effect would require cantons too small to be really practicable in a modern state.

MR. KAUFMANN: One thing now seems clear: some elements simply cannot be exported from one constitution to another. Different constitutions may be inspiring to countries that are looking for models, however. From that standpoint, we have to emphasize the fact that the American Constitution was very inspiring for the Swiss Constitution. We took over the idea of the two houses, the Senate and the Congress, as we call them. We did not borrow the idea of the president, but we were inspired by the American idea. I think Switzerland was the first federal republic in Europe, and to some extent the American example became known all over Europe through Switzerland when America still seemed far away.

MR. FLEINER: Some final observations: from the point of view of individual rights, one must seek unity; from the point of view of democracy, one must seek diversity. And then we face the question, To what extent may individual rights or fundamental rights be submitted to democratic vote? That is, of course, a question that can be answered only according to our history. Thus, for instance, as Mr.

Glazer noted, in one canton we have no voting rights for women, although we have equal protection in the Constitution. The Court has allowed the cantonal democracy to decide this issue. This is an example of certain individual rights that are not observed in all cantons; diversity in some instances is stronger than unity with regard to fundamental rights.

With regard to democratic institutions in Switzerland, all important political issues—for instance, abortion, energy conservation, atomic power, environmental issues, and alcohol—are all decided locally through direct democracy. That is the way we try to solve important political problems.

MR. GOLDWIN: I am surprised at most of the answers to my question, because in my personal opinion, Swiss national character is very much an element of Swiss success, and I think it explains why so little of the Swiss constitutional experience is exportable. An incredible self-restraint is evident throughout their political behavior and political institutions: there is a governing coalition of the major parties that never varies, and the federal counselors, once elected, are always reelected. In light of the politics of almost any other country, these things are incredible. Swiss direct democracy furthermore may have started out resembling the U.S. constitutional arrangement for the legislature, but it is no longer accurately described as a representative government. The Swiss have turned the Madisonian provision for auxiliary precautions upside down. In the United States, the two houses of Congress and other provisions are designed to put a check on popular enthusiasms. In Switzerland the general population is a check on the legislature.

The Swiss system can work only with a population with a tremendous tolerance for delay, for lack of uniformity, and for lack of neatness in political procedures. It seems to me that those characteristics, in a circular way, are constantly forming the Constitution and that the Constitution is constantly forming the political character of the people. And my guess is that the only way to export the Swiss Constitution is to export the Swiss people. [Laughter.]

MR. KAUFMANN: We would not want that.

6
Spanish Democracy and
the Estado de las Autonomías

Juan J. Linz

The Spanish constitution of 1978 represents an effort—and a largely successful one—to provide a framework for a new democracy and a new type of state in Spain. Although often interrupted, Spain's long liberal tradition dates to the early nineteenth century, when the battle cry was *Constitución o muerte*—"constitution or death." Its first efforts at writing a modern constitution had considerable influence in Europe, as the term liberal spread from Spain across the continent. Like other European countries, Spain moved slowly from constitutional monarchy to more democratic forms of government. The political stability under the constitution of the Monarchy, enacted in 1876, might have led to a development like that of other European monarchies had it not been cut short by the military coup of Primo de Rivera in 1923. The republic that was proclaimed in 1931 enacted a technically complex and innovative constitution, which did not survive the crisis of democracy that gripped all of Europe in the 1930s. The Civil War in Spain in 1936–1939 led to the installation of the Franco regime.[1]

Peripheral nationalisms appeared at the turn of the century in Catalonia and the Basque Country.[2] They were reinforced by the repressive policies of the Franco regime, by the social, economic, and cultural changes that had taken place in those regions, and by a new leftist ideology in much of Western Europe that incorporated the new nationalisms. Spain therefore faced the difficult task of transforming a centralized unitary state into a new kind of state, the Estado de las Autonomías, abandoning the deep-seated idea of only one Spanish nation and recognizing the multinational and multilingual character of Spanish society. The process of transformation, which in many Western countries has taken place very slowly, had to occur quickly in Spain and, in the case of the Basque Country, under the threat of popular mobilization and terrorism. Although democratization achieved wide support in the whole society from the beginning, a consensus on restructuring the state was more difficult to reach. On the one hand, minorities intensely voiced their demands, and on the other, many citizens showed little concern with the issue.

The human, political, and social rights now enshrined in Spain's liberal democratic constitution constitute a break with the authoritarian and corporatist patterns of the Franco regime. The way the transition to democracy took place, however, eliminated from the constitution-making agenda any fundamental changes in the economic and social system. Unlike the Portuguese constitution, the Spanish constitution includes no reference to a particular model of society. It contains no commitment either to capitalism or to socialism, and its provisions are sufficiently ambiguous to allow both a democratic transition to socialism and guarantees of the right to private property. When the constitution was written, the equilibrium of political forces imposed an open framework and excluded the more pronounced structural reforms discussed by the opposition to Franco.

The Catholic Church recognized that Spanish society had become more secular, that the church had been favored under Franco and might be identified with the fallen regime, and that it would now encounter increased hostility. The hierarchy therefore accepted separation of church and state and withdrew from an active political role during the transition in the 1970s. The Left, particularly the Communists, realizing the deep distrust that antireligious policies had generated among Catholics, emphasized the need for understanding and a policy of the outstretched hand. In this area too, negotiations on the constitution and subsequent laws were based on a search for consensus, though they did not prevent the conflicts encountered on religious and moral issues in other Western democracies.

Thus the 1978 constitution was based on consensus—in contrast to that of 1931, which was consciously partisan—and gained the support of all parties, from the Communists to the conservative Alianza Popular (although some of its deputies did not vote for it). It was opposed only by the Basque nationalists. Unlike the constitutions of Germany, Italy, Portugal, and other Western democracies, the Spanish constitution of 1978 was approved in a free popular referendum, thereby attaining a degree of democractic legitimacy matched by few other constitutions.

Although the autonomy statutes (the Estatutos) of the regions are not technically part of the constitution, they are derived from it and therefore occupy an important position in the Spanish political system. Because they were negotiated by the central government and the representatives of the regions—particularly of the Basque Country—

they are part of the real constitution of Spain. In fact, one could say that the transition after Franco was not completed and the constitution of the future remained uncertain until final approval was given by referendum to the Catalan and the Basque Estatutos in the fall of 1979.

The transition from authoritarianism to democracy, the institutionalization of that democracy, and the consolidation of it in the past decade have been remarkable achievements of Spanish political leadership.[3] No less an achievement—and more controversial in its details—was the transformation of the previously unitary, centralized state into a new kind of polity whose ultimate character and function is still open. Many of the decisions of the Constitutional Court have therefore dealt with this aspect of the development of new institutions; Spain today is, after all, the largest and most complex multilingual and, some would say, multinational society in Western Europe.

The Growth of Peripheral Nationalism and Anticentralism

The period before the June 1977 election is central to an understanding of the development of the Estado de las Autonomías, although the first formal and legal steps toward it were not taken until the constitution-making period in the fall of 1977 and early 1978.

In the earlier period, a variety of collective bodies of the opposition emerged. At the national level, the Junta Democrática, which was created before the death of Franco and in which the Communists played a major role, and the Plataforma Democrática, constituted by a number of parties of the opposition, combined to become the counterpart to the government during the transition. At the regional level, bodies of various composition emerged to represent the parties and organizations of the opposition. In these bodies, nationalist and regional parties of the opposition, though they had only limited support, played an important role. They articulated demands ranging from independence and self-government to autonomy of minorities and mobilized their supporters in the streets. That mobilization was particularly important in the Basque Country and Navarra, where proamnesty committees held massive demonstrations, organized successful strikes, and constantly confronted the authorities. In Catalonia these organizations, already born under Franco, carried on the struggle under the banner of the restoration of the Estatuto that Catalonia had obtained under the republic and organized a massive celebration of the Catalan national holiday, the Diada. The appeal of these regional parties was unclear before and even after the election.

The idea that the regional problem was not limited to the regions that historically had enjoyed autonomy under the republic became widely accepted. In addition, the forming of larger parties—including the government party, the Union of the Democratic Center (UCD)—by the fusion of parties and the federation of regional parties contributed decisively to the climate of opinion in which the constitution was drafted.

Violence in the Background

Although Spain had suffered a terrible civil war from 1936 to 1939, revolutionary and counterrevolutionary violence, bloody repression by the victors, and years of political repression, the change from an authoritarian regime to democracy was basically peaceful and orderly, without the vengeance expected by those who feared a reenactment of the Civil War. This was one of the great achievements of the political elites, from the Communists to the heirs of the Franco regime.

Unfortunately, this was not the case in the Basque Country and Navarra. Late in the Franco regime, a nationalist extremist organization, Euzkadi ta Azcatasuna (Basque Homeland and Liberty), or ETA, turned to terrorist actions against the regime, culminating in the assassination of Prime Minister Carrero Blanco in December 1973. During the trial of some of its members at Burgos ETA gained international attention and sympathy. It won widespread support in the Basque Country as a result of the indiscriminate repressive actions of the police and the government. State terror delegitimizes a government as nothing else does and was ineffective against the communal society of the Basques. The terrorists learned the political efficacy of the spiral of terror—which leads to repression, leading to more terror—and thus used it adroitly for their purposes.

That pattern of struggle against the Franco regime did not spread to the rest of Spain except among some isolated groups, and the major political forces, even of the extreme Left, refused to engage in it. But wide segments of the population admired the ETA because it struggled with arms against the regime. They ignored the ideology and aims of the ETA and believed that, with amnesty for everyone who had struggled against the regime by word or deed and with free elections, terrorism would end. Later they hoped that, with a constitution granting autonomy to minorities and with approval of the Basque Estatuto, ETA would lose its support.[4]

Free elections with the participation of Basque parties (including the nationalists of the Left, advocating independence and rejecting the constitution and the Estatuto) and the election of their representa-

263

tives to both the Madrid and the Basque regional parliaments and to municipal councils in Euskadi and Navarra again created the hope that terrorism would end. In the urgency of establishing pre-autonomy status and, later, enacting the Estatuto, the pattern of negotiation and many political decisions were conditioned by the hope that ETA would cease its activities or lose its support. That, however, has not happened. Although an increasingly large segment of the Basque population considers ETA extremists criminal, mad, or manipulated, a significant minority still consider them idealists or patriots. Many casualties have resulted over the years from the activities of ETA and from efforts to control terrorism in Spain. In most revolutionary situations, more victims suffer from the actions of the state, the police, and the armed forces than from its opponents, but not in the Basque Country.

The events of this period show that, contrary to hopes, democratic freedom does not necessarily end violence. A period of real change often contributes to conflict, as Tocqueville noted long ago. A democratic government must live with terrorism and not respond in kind and thereby generate the spiral of terrorism and repression on which terrorist actions are based.

Spanish leaders have responded politically to revolutionary nationalism in the Basque Country and Navarra, a fact that should not be ignored as the changes that have taken place with autonomy are analyzed.

The Estado de las Autonomías

No aspect of the political change in Spain and of the Constitution of 1978 is more complex and difficult to describe than the territorial restructuring of the Spanish state. The consequences of this process are still very much in doubt. This aspect of the constitution may be the only one about which serious reforms have been suggested. Reforms could not take place, however, without a serious crisis. Some articles of the constitution and of the autonomy statutes do have difficulties that, in the absence of mechanisms to decide legislative jurisdiction and other matters, lead to conflicts that must be brought before the Constitutional Court.

The following major themes are involved in this aspect of the constitution:

1. The historical analysis of the building of the Spanish state, including the efforts at centralization, the search for uniformity, and the rise of peripheral nationalism, which involves different con-

ceptions of the Spanish state and of the national future, particularly in Catalonia and the Basque Country.

2. The constitutional solutions and conflicts of the Second Republic, which have served as a point of departure for the changes introduced after 1975.

3. The historical context in which these complex issues were debated, solutions formulated, and policies and legislation negotiated, and the subsequent changes in the political climate, resulting in part from those enactments, and in the positions subsequently taken by different political parties. The process of establishing autonomous communities has undergone significant change during the past decade.

4. The model of the Spanish state underlying the present constitution and subsequent laws, and the divergent interpretations of that model.

5. The dynamics of the question of nationalism and its reflection in the constitution and in legislation, as well as in political practice. An understanding requires an analysis of the regional party systems in Catalonia and particularly the Basque Country, where four nationalist parties compete with one another as well as with the nationwide parties.

Spain, with its present borders, is one of the oldest European states dating from 1516 under Emperor Charles V. The union of different medieval monarchies allowed different institutions to persist, and efforts to introduce greater uniformity encountered resistance, such as the rebellion of the Catalans in 1640. Only with the Bourbon dynasty in the eighteenth century did the confederal character of the Habsburg monarchy begin to be destroyed. Early in the nineteenth century, the Napoleonic invasion—the last foreign threat of significance to the Spanish homeland—aroused a new sense of national identity. Combined with the revolutionary ideas of national sovereignty, it led to the constitutional efforts of the liberals (beginning in 1812) to create a unitary state based on a national consciousness.

During the civil wars that resulted from dynastic conflicts and other circumstances, parts of the periphery, particularly the countryside in the Basque Country and Navarra, resisted the liberals and defended a traditional conception of society. This conception was based first on strong religious sentiments, but then increasingly on the legal distinctiveness of regional institutions. When the liberal state could not achieve a clear victory, the exhausted opponents concluded a compromise peace and a promise to recognize some of those institutions within the constitutional unity of the nation. This accounts for what has been called the *ley paccionada*—the negotiated law—regulating relationships between the central government and Navarra in 1841. This law has remained in force.

Since the Navarrese Carlists provided the Franco regime with some of its most enthusiastic supporters, Navarra never lost its privileged status. After considerable conflict and negotiations, the three Basque provinces received special tax treatment through the Conciertos económicos (1876), which have remained in force for Alava. Guipúzcoa and Vizcaya were deprived of it after the Basque nationalists sided with the Madrid republican government against the nationalist military insurrection.

Catalonia did not retain its own institutions in modern times, although its distinctive sense of identity was affirmed from time to time. The rise of a cultural and, later, political nationalism was linked to both the conflicting economic interests of this early industrialized region and the cultural revival of the Catalan language.

These developments in the periphery contrast with the very early building of a modern unified state in the Kingdom of Castile, which was facilitated by the relative weakness of feudalism, the importance of bourgeois cities, the conquest of the lands dominated by the Moors, and the internal colonialization by Christians of the Castilian domains. This long historical process began in the Middle Ages, was reinforced in the course of modern state-building under the Habsburgs and the Bourbons, and was completed by the nineteenth-century governments. As a result, Castile achieved linguistic and cultural hegemony over other parts of Spain, which lost their distinctive institutional traditions and sense of identity (with the partial exception of Galicia, which has its own language). In fact, no such distinctiveness existed in insular Spain or the Canaries or in the Balearic Islands though dialects of Catalan are spoken in the latter and used in all spheres of society to this day. The same is largely true of the territories of the old Kingdom of Valencia that had been part of the Aragonese Crown in the Middle Ages, another area with a distinctive language, which some consider a variant of Catalan and others a separate language.

Spain, therefore, has been united under a single king, but not always with the same institutions and political traditions. It is a multilingual country with four languages: Castilian, Catalan, Basque, and Galician, as well as variants of Catalan and other local languages. Economic development also varies from the wealth of Catalonia and the Basque Country, which were industrialized early, to the relative underdevelopment of the Castilian interior, of the overpopulated Andalusian South, and of the more peripheral and largely peasant-populated Galicia. Much of the conflict between Catalonia and the central government around the turn of the century can be characterized as a conflict between a modern commercial and industrial bourgeoisie, on the one hand, and centralist, bureaucratic, professional, military, and intellectual elites, not always sympathetic to the bourgeois values of Catalonia, on the other.

Historical patterns account for the different ways autonomy developed in the peripheries and in Castilian-speaking Spain. These differences made the introduction of the uniformity of a truly federal state difficult. Autonomy has very different meanings in different parts of Spain. In some cases, autonomy resulted from history and cultural and linguistic identity, sometimes reinforced even by a national identity more or less compatible with a Spanish national identity. In other cases, it was a political or administrative innovation with limited popular support. The historical, cultural, linguistic, and national identity of some of the Comunidades Autónomas obviously is not comparable to that of states or *Länder* in other federal countries. Two regions with the most distinctive identities are not small and marginal but have large populations, high per capita incomes, important metropolitan areas, high industrialization (which attracts Castilian-speaking immigrants as workers), and complex class divisions.

The historical process in the nineteenth century generated a sense of national identity among most Spaniards, whatever their emotional attachment to their region, province, or community. That process did not, however, reduce the sense of separate identity for significant segments of the population as much as among the ethnic minorities of France. In Catalonia, a minority feel totally Catalan; the majority among the native population and even a significant number of the sons of immigrants feel as much Catalan as Spanish; others feel more Catalan than Spanish, but still Spanish. In the Basque Country a significant proportion identify themselves as just Basque, and appreciably fewer feel a dual national identity than in Catalonia. Bilingualism does not indicate a sense of national identity in the Balearic Islands, for instance, or in Valencia or even in Galicia, where there is some sense of separate identity.

The crisis of the Franco regime was accompanied by a crisis of the Spanish state and of Spanish nationalism, by an explosion of nationalist sentiment in the periphery, and by an emerging anti-centralism among political elites elsewhere. Difficult political and constitutional decisions had to be made in this crisis, in which the terrorism of the Basque nationalist revolutionary organization, ETA, played a central role. This atmosphere made the enactment of the new constitution different in Spain from that, say, in the Federal Republic of Germany or even from the long process of political and institutional innovation in Belgium or Canada.

It is idle to discuss whether those decisions could have been made differently, because they are enshrined in the constitution and the Estatutos. The building of regional polities, including the autonomous communities that were to some extent artificial creations, has created vested interests that make any attempt at reversal difficult, if not impossible.

To realize how central a place the Basque problem occupied in this crisis, one has only to look at press coverage of it in comparison with other issues and at the time politicians gave to issues connected with it. It prevented a serious debate about the kind of state to be created and about the implications of the decisions that were being made. The suppression of the peripheral nationalism issue during the Franco regime left most Spaniards—including the new political elite emerging from the opposition in the universities, the labor movement, and the illegal parties—with little understanding of the problem and limited knowledge of comparable experiences in other societies. Some experts, particularly legal experts, had limited sensitivity to the meaning of nationalism for politicians on the periphery.

On language policy, only the sociolinguists of the bilingual regions knew of scholarship on this subject and had done research on bilingualism in Spain. Other Spanish intellectuals either were committed to the idea of Castilian Spanish as the common language or felt sympathy for those whose language and culture had been repressed by Franco.[5] These intellectuals ignored those committed to language policies in the periphery that would eliminate bilingualism in order to achieve the hegemony of the autochthonous language. The linguistic rights of the large minorities of Castilian speakers who immigrated into these regions tended to be neglected. The lack of intellectual preparation for these complex issues together with pressures generated by the crisis atmosphere—and by the hope of undermining the support for terrorism by agreeing to some sort of autonomy—contributed to the difficulties with the model of the emerging Spanish state.

Another difficulty was that the traditions of Spanish democracy were shaped by French and English democratic thought based on majority rule. During the transition, Prime Minister Suárez and other Spanish leaders discovered that the issues of a multiethnic, multilingual, and segmented society could not be handled within that type of democratic conception. That is why so much of this process took place in the framework of what was called the *consenso* and by negotiation, often behind closed doors, with many political leaders of Parliament excluded and with no public debate.

The actions of the Spanish leaders fitted both the style and the outcomes of consociational democracy, though they did not know it and had not read the extensive literature on the model (such as the writings of Arend Lijphart). Without a tradition of such a style of politics, except perhaps in Catalonia, their actions were misinterpreted as sheer manipulation, opportunism, and a lack of principle and not in conformity with democratic procedures. The context of consociational politics afforded no room for a great national debate. Many important decisions were never really discussed, and the great achievements in reaching compromises, under far from easy conditions, could not be explained to the country in the way that other crucial decisions, such as the model of transition by the Law of Political Reform or the legalization of the Communist Party, had been. In fact, some hoped that the leadership in the periphery, particularly the Partido Nacionalista Vasco (PNV) in the Basque Country, could legitimize itself by claiming to have succeeded in imposing its views. The consociational strategy was partly the result of a constellation of forces in Parliament and the pressure of time.

On the Way from the Regionalized State to a Federalized State

Spanish constitutionalists have found the Spanish state that emerged from the process of political decentralization difficult to characterize. Many different concepts have been suggested for the political and institutional structure created by the 1978 constitution.[6] In some respects it fits the model of the Italian regionalized state, which was in turn influenced by the Spanish Constitution of 1931. Politically, however, Euskadi or Catalonia cannot be compared to Italian regions, even to a region like Sicily. Some similarities can be found in Article 1.2 of the Spanish Constitution, which states "national sovereignty is vested in the Spanish people from whom emanate the powers of the State" and in the fact that the Estatutos of the regions are approved by the Cortes as Organic Laws, according to Article 81. In addition autonomous regions can be established by the Cortes, according to Article 144, provided that the territorial area does not exceed that of the province or, in the case of territories, does not form part of the provincial organization. This provision was intended for Ceuta and Melilla (two Spanish enclaves in North Africa) and for the possible future incorporation of Gibraltar into Spain. The establishment of a number of autonomous communities similar to those of Italy, however, is unlikely.

The basic constitutional formulation in Article 2 states: "The Constitution is based on the indissoluble unity of the Spanish nation, the common and indivisible country of all Spaniards, and recognizes and guarantees the right of self-government of the nationalities and regions of which it is composed and solidarity among them all." The use of the term "nationalities" rather than either "nations" or "regions" was the object of bitter debate in the Cortes and resulted from a compromise. The formulation implied a distinction between nationalities and regions that was never pursued in the constitutional text. In fact, the term nationalities appears only in Article 2 as quoted. By using that term rather than nations, the constitution makers were clearly unwilling to recognize the multinational character of the new state as the nationalists of the periphery wanted. Yet the constitutional text could not ignore the sense of nation and speak only of regions, as in the case of Italy, or of *Länder*, or even of states, as in other federal constitutions. Much of the conflict with the Basque nationalists, including the moderate Partido Nacionalista Vasco (PNV), about the recognition of historical rights turned on the issue of the right of self-determination and whether any choice would exist between secession and voluntary integration into the Spanish state. The affirmation of national sovereignty, of the indissoluble unity of all Spaniards, implied the rejection of such claims.

The process by which the Estatutos of the nationalities were enacted makes the Spanish way of dealing with different national identities fundamentally different from the Italian and other cases of political decentralization. According to Transitory Provision 2, the territories that, under the Second Republic, had approved draft statutes of autonomy by plebiscite (in Catalonia, the Basque Country, and Galicia) could initiate a transition to self-government by a simplified procedure different from the normal one of Article 143. Article 151 provides that the government shall summon all the deputies and senators who have been elected in districts within the territory seeking self-government to constitute an assembly to draw up an Estatuto to be sent to the Constitutional Committee of the Congress. Within two months, this committee shall examine it, with the assistance of the delegation of the assembly that has proposed it, to determine by common agreement its final formulation. This article, therefore, provides for negotiation between delegates of the Drafting Assembly and the Constitutional Committee of the lower house. In this, the Constitution links with the precedent of the negotiated law regulating the status of Navarra after the end of the civil war between Carlists and Isabelinos—the *ley paccionada* of 1841. In the context of nationalist movements, such a negotiation differs basically from an effort to iron out differences between draft proposals of two bodies, as is done in a conference committee of the U.S. House and Senate.

270

In the atmosphere of 1979, the process of negotiating draft statutes was highly political and tense. In the Basque case the negotiation ultimately could not be handled by the parliamentarians in committee, but had to be resolved by difficult and seemingly endless meetings between Prime Minister Suárez and the Basque leader Garaikoetxea.[7]

The cases of Catalonia, the Basque Country, and Galicia differ from a regionalization enacted by a national legislature with the cooperation of local representatives not only because of the negotiated character of the autonomy statutes. In addition, after an agreement is reached according to Article 151.3, the resulting text must be submitted to a referendum in the provinces within the territory to be covered by the proposed Estatuto. The text must be approved in each province by a majority of validly cast votes.

The referendum in Euskadi approved the text after a difficult campaign in which the pro-Estatuto parties won narrowly against those advocating no-votes and abstentions. To understand the political significance one should look at the results of the constitutional referendum in which the PNV had advocated abstention. In Alava, of the 59.3 percent of the voters who went to the polls, 71.4 percent approved the constitution (or 42.3 percent of the electorate); in Guipúzcoa the percentages were 43.4 and 63.9 (27.7); and in Vizcaya, 43.9 and 70.9 (31.1) respectively.[8]

This lack of support for the constitution contrasts with the participation in the referendum of the Estatuto and the support it gained. In Alava the participation was 63.2 percent with 83.7 percent voting yes (52.9 percent of the electorate); in Guipúzcoa, participation was 59.9 percent with 91.9 percent voting yes (55.0 percent of the electorate); and in Vizcaya participation was 59.0 percent with 90.8 percent voting yes (53.6 percent of the electorate). The lack of support for the constitution and the approval of the Estatuto gives to the latter a particular legitimacy. The approval of the Estatuto, derived from the constitution and approved by the Spanish legislature, could be considered an indirect approval of the constitution, and the initial lack of support for the constitution may be due to its approval being conditioned on the acceptance of the Estatuto. Politically, although not juridically, one could say that in Euskadi the Estatuto legitimized the constitution, while in all other regions the legitimacy of the constitution was the basis for the legitimization of the autonomous communities.[9]

The Spanish regionalized state differs from the Italian not only in introducing the notion of nationality, but in the process of negotiating and then submitting an Estatuto to a referendum. They also differ in the kind of institutions and jurisdictions that are created. Spain is not a federal state in the traditional nineteenth-century sense; in spite of the claims of the nationalists, independent, sovereign political entities did not join together into a larger federal state. The Spanish legislature was reluctant in 1931 and 1978 to define the Spanish state as federal, although the political system resulting from the 1978 constitution and subsequent developments, through the distribution of powers and the character of its institutions, resembles a federal regime. Spanish jurists speak of quasifederalism. Many Catalan and Basque politicians were reluctant to favor a federal state because members of a federation have a basically equal and uniform status. These politicians emphasized that their status within the Spanish political system would be distinct, if not privileged and that the other autonomous communities could not be considered their equal in capacity for self-government, at least at the time. Many of these politicians would have been happier if regionalization had stopped with the so-called historical regions and if the rest of Spain had been limited thereby to an administrative decentralization.

Between September 1977 and October 1978, the government decided to establish the so-called *preautonomías*, accelerating political regionalization. This process undermined the idea of the territorial structure of the Spanish state implicit in the constitution, particularly in the contrast between regionalization according to Article 143 and Article 151. An initiative from the grass roots up, by a decision of two-thirds of the municipalities (representing at least the majority of the electorate in each province or island) became less important than the desires of the political elite represented in the preautonomy institutions. According to Transitory Provision 1, by means of an agreement adopted by an absolute majority of the members of the pre-autonomous institutions, these institutions could assume for themselves the initiative for self-government conferred in clause 2 of Article 143 to the provincial councils or interisland bodies. The organs of the *preautonomías* had three years to exercise the initiative or be dissolved and naturally this meant that the regionalization process would be extended to the whole of Spain.[10]

The preautonomy laws resulted from the pressing need to satisfy the demands of Catalonia and the Basque Country before the approval of a constitution and to reach an agreement with an outstanding Catalan leader, Josep Tarradellas, thereby defusing the Catalan problem. Tarradellas had been the head of the Catalan Generalitat under the Estatuto of 1932, living in exile, and his negotiation with Suárez led to the recognition of Catalan autonomy on September 29, 1977 "without prejudice toward the future constitution." He represented the only legal continuity with the institutions before the civil war. The process initiated by that decision and the decision creating the Consejo General Vasco in January 1978 were soon followed by similar institutions in Galicia, Aragón, Canarias, and the País Valenciano (March 1978) and later in seven other regions. This process, called in the Spanish political language of the time "coffee for all," was intended to defuse the image of privileged autonomy for the historical nationalities. This process was also a response to emerging nationalist groups, agitation during the transition period, and minor terrorist centers in the Canaries. The preautonomy bodies inevitably created a vested interest of the political class of all parties, including the government party, in the regionalization process. The preautonomy decrees, with some exceptions, determined the regional division of Spain without testing the popular support for autonomy in different parts of Spain, though such testing had been intended by the constitutional provisions.

The preautonomy stage illuminates the difference between the legal, constitutional, and technical aspects of a devolution process, on the one hand, and the mixture of nationalist, social, and political considerations in determining the actual process of regionalization, on the other. It also illustrates something that those studying transitions from authoritarian regimes to democracy should never forget: decisions made during the transition period by a government that is either weak or not fully institutionalized become irreversible at a later stage.

The Suárez government from 1977 to 1979 was not a provisional government like those of Portugal before the first election following the approval of its constitution. Those Portuguese governments did not need parliamentary support, in contrast to the Suárez government. Although it had such support, the Suárez government was still a weak government, particularly when faced with the opposition of nationalities, the pressure of terrorist activity (which reached its high point during this period in the Basque Country), and the blame for tensions in the regions, particularly in Euskadi, attributed by the Socialist Workers Party of Spain (PSOE) to the slowness in granting autonomy. In a transition period, a provisional government often has uncertain legitimacy and is subject to the pressure of activist minorities and violence in the streets. It can be forced to respond to emergencies by making decisions that a normal legislature would make only after more deliberation over long-term consequences. Without stretching the analogy too far, the Spanish government until the approval of the constitution, and even until approval of the Estatutos of Catalonia and the Basque Country, found itself in such a situation.

This should be remembered by those who criticize the Estado de las Autonomías and the existence of seventeen autonomous regions, some of which are of dubious viability from a purely rational or technocratic point of view and probably have limited popular support.

Much of the regionalization process cannot be understood without taking into account the partisan interests of the main opposition party. Those interests became clear in the process leading to the extended autonomy of Andalusia, which in turn accelerated the extension of autonomy to all the other regions of Spain. Rapid and unplanned regionalization and devolution could not be slowed down, and the distinctions between types of autonomy foreseen in the constitution became blurred. The leaders of the governing UCD and the leader of the PSOE, Felipe González, all wished to slow down the process. An understanding that led the UCD national leadership to advocate abstention in the Andalusian autonomy referendum was probably broken, leading to an increase in feelings of relative deprivation in Andalusia and a defeat of the UCD position. That defeat contributed decisively to the crisis of the Suárez leadership and of the party in subsequent years.

Scholars have suggested that different phases of the process of regionalization should be distinguished, including the attempts to rationalize that process through the Organic Law of the Constitutional Court, the Commission of Experts on Autonomies, the Acuerdos Autonómicos, and the Organic Law of Harmonization of the Autonomy Process (LOAPA). Some of the ambiguities in the constitution's distribution of powers between the central government and the autonomous communities have thereby been clarified. Spain differs from the many countries where the process is greatly debated and takes place slowly over a long period in partial measures that lead to increased powers of the different units of the state. The circumstances of the Spanish transition led to a rapid and, at least at the legal level (though not in practice), extended transfer of power to the territorial components and, later, to a largely failed effort to control that process by enacting new legislation, some of whose constitutionality was contested.

Efforts at Harmonizing the Autonomy Process

The year 1981 was a turning point in the development of the Estado de las Autonomías, reflected more in a different attitude of the policy makers and an emphasis on specific problems than in new legislative developments. Until then the process was based on the *principio dispositivo,* that is, the use by the political forces in the periphery of the opportunities provided by the constitution to achieve autonomy and to obtain maximum powers. During this time, the central government made little effort to use the constitutional provisions to create a national organization of the state and to adapt its administration to the new political structure. The report of the Commission of Experts on the Autonomies and the Acuerdos Autonómicos—signed by the Spanish government of the nation and the PSOE—represented respectively by the president of the government and the general secretary of the Socialist party on July 31, 1981—reflected a desire to bring some order to the process of devolution.[11]

Despite the shift in policy, there was continuity as well as change in political style from the previous stage. The continuity is found in the policy of consensus on constitutional matters negotiated at the highest level, with some exclusion of broader participation in decision making. Such continuity was inaugurated in the constitution-making process itself (rejecting, by implication, decision making by a minimum winning coalition or majority). The discontinuity is found in the way the agreements on autonomy were worked out between the two national majority parties, the UCD and the PSOE, without participation of the minor parties and without initial participation of the regional nationalist parties. This step departed from the pattern of consociationalism between center and periphery. It, perhaps more than the substantive content of the law, accounts for the rejection by the regional governments of Catalonia and Euskadi of the LOAPA and the mobilization of opinion by the nationalist parties of the periphery against it.

How such a shift in policy came about, and what the intent of the policy makers was at that time are unclear. A period of uncertainty followed the approval of the Estatutos of Catalonia, Euskadi, Galicia, and Andalusia. The potential development of autonomy in other regions—where identity was dubious and where local elites found it difficult to agree on the geographic limits, institutional structure, division of powers, and procedures to follow to attain autonomy— created doubts about the structure of the state and the prospects for coexistence of the remnants of a highly centralized state and the newly federalized system. The unsystematic application of the *principio dispositivo* would have left the administration in a state of uncertainty and paralysis for a prolonged period. As a result of the events surrounding the Andalusian autonomy, reflecting a lack of agreement between the major parties, regionalization ultimately had to be extended to all of Spain—not as under the 1931–1936 republic, when autonomy was gained only by regions with a strong sentiment in favor of it. The prospect of having to deal with some twelve new autonomous regions and to negotiate arrangements with each of them separately, was perceived as politically too costly. The shift in policy and in style of decision making was more a response to the new, rather than the historical, autonomous communities, but indirectly, by establishing general principles and making specific provisions about finances and the transfer of state bureaucratic apparatus, it also affected the autonomies already approved.

The new proposals raised the question of the compatibility of the new autonomous communities with the Estatutos previously negotiated, approved, and legitimated by plebiscite. The political leaders and the legislature were undoubtedly aware of the impossibility of modifying the approved Estatutos by new laws and reiterated constantly that this was not the purpose. They wanted to clarify the meaning of some constitutional provisions, in line with the relationship in other countries, particularly the German Federal Republic, between the federal state and its component parts. Their purpose was to limit the ambiguities left in the constitutional text without waiting for interpretations by the Constitutional Court.

A less benevolent interpretation of the shift attributes it to a change in the climate of opinion resulting from the failed coup of February 23, 1981. This attempted coup was correctly perceived as an expression of discontent among the armed forces with what they saw as disintegrative tendencies and disrespect for, if not a direct threat to, the idea of one Spanish nation. Recent years have seen a reassertion of Spanish national identity, as symbolized by conflicts over display of the Spanish flag on public buildings and by ceremonies involving the flag. The PSOE has changed its position on this matter since the transition.

In early 1981 Adolfo Suárez was replaced as prime minister by Leopoldo Calvo Sotelo, who probably had a different conception of politics and the state. In addition, with a growing crisis in the UCD, Felipe González, the secretary general of the PSOE, saw himself more as a prime minister having to govern the country than as a leader of the opposition.

The initial constitution-making process was in the hands of politicians facing a crisis. Once the constitution was enacted and the most controversial Estatutos were approved, however, there was room for scholarly elaboration of the legal principles, academic debate about the meaning of the constitutional provisions, and stipulation of technical criteria—particularly in financial matters—by the experts. Technical, legal, and administrative criteria were developed. These new policies were first articulated by a commission of experts in which a

leading professor of public administration, Eduardo García de Enterría, played an important role.

It could be argued that 1981 does not represent such a shift. By
November–December 1979 the UCD leadership had begun to search
for an upper limit in the autonomies, the so-called *techo autonómico*, a
homogeneity in the process, and a uniformity of the model by using
sectoral laws and Article 143—abandoning Article 151 except for the
historical nationalities of Transitory Norm 2. Even if this interpretation
were correct, however, in the case of both the Galician Estatuto and
especially the Andalusian, such a policy had not been successful, so
1981 would still represent a turning point.

The Acuerdos Autonómicos of 1981 included an agreement on a
map defining the boundaries of seventeen autonomous regions. With
the exception of the four that were granted autonomy earlier and
Navarra, all would follow the procedures of Article 143. This agreement also set a deadline, February 1, 1983, for the approval of all the
Estatutos, thereby completing the process of transforming the territorial structure of the state and abandoning in that respect the
principio dispositivo. In addition the agreement provided for a number
of principles of homogeneity: all elections to the assemblies of the
communities would take place the same day; legislative terms would
be limited; regional governments would be subject to the constructive
no-confidence vote (by an absolute majority with the presentation of
an alternative candidate) upon the petition of 15 percent of the members of each assembly; and, in the event a lack of agreement leads to
dissolution, the newly elected assembly could not function beyond
the date on which regional elections would have to take place in the
remaining communities. The agreement limited the governments of
the autonomous communities to ten members and provided that the
Diputaciones Provinciales would assume administration under the
direction of the regional government. It also provided for uniform
principles in the electoral legislation, making the province the single
district for both multiple- and single-province regions. The 1981 Acuerdos Autonómicos were not a legal, binding text, but, given the
hegemony of the two parties signing them in all the regions outside of
Catalonia, Euskadi, Navarra, and Galicia, they could be considered
so. In some cases (as in Segovia), however, initial refusal to join
Castile-León forced the legislature to apply Article 144c of the constitution in March 1983 in order to incorporate that province under it.
The agreements also developed economic and financial matters in
great detail, including a proposed bill for harmonizing the autonomy
process, with provisions on the transfer of civil servants, and a bill
regulating the fund for interterritorial compensation.

The Acuerdos are a definitive step away from the possibility implicit in the constitution of coexistence of (1) the autonomous communities in the historic regions, (2) a more or less decentralized state in other parts of Spain (to be regionalized slowly on the basis of local initiatives), and (3) the persistence of rule by the central administration in parts of the territory. The agreements shifted toward a model based on greater homogeneity among most of the autonomous communities. They also provided for the establishment of the province of Madrid as an autonomous region, including the national capital. Significantly, the constitution-making process lacked any serious discussion about creating a federal district, in spite of the declaration in Article 5 that Madrid is the capital of the state. Perhaps this omission was due to the constant rejection of the idea of federalism and the implicit reference to the Italian and German constitutional models.

The map with seventeen autonomic regions is one of the obstacles to coordination between the regional governments. The disparity in the historical, political, economic, and demographic importance among the new regions, in addition to the high number of them, makes it difficult to conceive of them as equal to the historic regions. The agreements of 1981 and the subsequent approval of all the Estatutos have to some extent frozen that territorial structure, although political leaders were aware of the desirability, on historical and other grounds, of a future reduction in the number of regions. The Acuerdos have special provisions for the possibility that Cantabria and La Rioja would join Castile-León; therefore, the agreements recommended that the Estatutos of those regions include provisions to make such an integration possible. Article 22 of the 1931 constitution allowed the provinces of an autonomous region to renounce that status and return to that of a province directly dependent on the central power, so that a large part of the old Castilian-Leonese domain could remain under the government of Madrid. That provision finds no parallel, however, in the 1978 constitution. The present territorial map of Spain is therefore the result both of the history and economic interests of some provinces and of the desires of local politicians. It is neither the result of a rational plan imposed from above nor, as originally intended, of strong autonomous sentiments at the grass roots; at the same time, however, its institutionalization has gone so far that it seems unlikely it will experience major changes in the near future.

Conflicting Principles in the Definition of a Region

On the basis of Article 2 and 143.1, the Spanish Constitution allows the right to autonomy of bordering provinces with common historic, cultural, and economic characteristics and to island territories and provinces with historical regional status. Thus it links autonomy to democratic decision making, particularly approval by referendum. This combination of conditions has led to the problems well known from the literature on self-determination and on secession in the international context. Within the Spanish state, such principles of territorial reorganization have encountered the same difficulties as the peacemakers at Versailles encountered after World War I in applying the principle of national self-determination. The remark of Sir Ivor Jennings is applicable here: "On the surface it seemed reasonable: Let the people decide. It was in fact ridiculous because the people cannot decide until somebody decides who are the people."[12] Constitutional principles include many criteria to define which people may make decisions, but the makers of the Spanish Constitution made the province the basic unit for democratic decision making.

Regional boundaries defined by language, for example, would have been very different from those defined by history. Historical boundaries change over the centuries; those created by the provincial division in the nineteenth century differ from those of the old medieval kingdoms. In any process of recognizing nationalist aspirations, very different criteria may be used simultaneously to expand the new political unit. In framing the conditions for self-determination and defining the people who have the right to decide, any criterion chosen by the legislature will be unacceptable on the basis of other criteria and will be challenged on that ground. The use of objective criteria cannot be easily combined with popular democratic decision making. Once Spanish political leaders established the *principio dispositivo* and the use of the referendum to legitimize the new regional structure of the state, they inevitably had to face such problems.

These problems have been particularly acute in the case of the Basque Country, where different criteria for defining the people lead to different boundaries of an autonomous Basque community. History cannot define the Basque Country as clearly as it defines Catalonia because, except for less than a century in the earliest Middle Ages, the territories claimed by the Basque nationalists today never constituted a political or administrative unit; they were divided among the Kingdoms of Navarra, which covered territories on both sides of the Spanish-French border, the Duchy of Aquitania, which was incorporated under the French Crown, and the Kingdom of Castile. The provinces of Alava, Guipúzcoa, and Vizcaya had been part of the crown of Castile and had different institutions of medieval origin. All three, however, had a consciousness of their unity as the Basque Country.

Parts of those three provinces, particularly Alava and Vizcaya, were not Basque-speaking for long periods of time, in some cases for centuries.[13] Today, the Basque language boundaries would include only parts of those three provinces and of Navarra, ignoring the loss of the language in the cities and the presence of a large immigrant population (around 30 percent) that does not know it. For the Basque nationalists, the boundaries include the three provinces, Navarra, and three territories in France, disregarding the linguistic and historical boundaries. Unfortunately for the nationalists, a large part of the population of Navarra identify themselves not as Basque but as Navarrese, and they reject Basque nationalism to the extent that it has as its ultimate goal a Basque nation-state separate from Spain. If autonomy is attained by the choice of the people, the will of the majority would be imposed on a large minority, often simply as a result of the definition of the unit in which the vote is taken. This would be the case among the Basques in the northern tier bordering on Alava and Guipúzcoa of the Province of Navarra. The historical criterion is felt so strongly, however, by both the majority and the minority that both reject the idea of a division of the historic Kingdom of Navarra.[14]

The integration of Navarra into a Basque region (Euskadi to the nationalists) has long been a central issue in the politics of the region, a constant source of major and minor conflicts, and an argument used by the left *abertzales* against the acceptance not only of the constitution but of the Estatuto. The issue still has not come to a final vote. Transitory Rule 4 of the constitution states that:

> In the case of Navarra, and for the purposes of its incorporation into the General Basque Council or the Basque self-governing regime replacing it, instead of the procedure established by the provisions of Article 143 of the Constitution, the initiative shall be with the competent forum which shall adopt its decision by a majority vote of the members comprising it. In order for the initiative to be valid the decision of the competent forum must also be ratified by a referendum expressly held for this purpose, passed by a majority of the valid votes cast.

If the initiative does not succeed, it may be repeated during a different term of office of the competent forum after the minimum period stated in Article 143.

This provision has never been used because a majority in the forum never initiated such a process of incorporation. In fact, after a period of indecision, they opted instead for the process of updating its distinctive institutions of the Fuero (the *amejoramiento,* or improvement). Theoretically, that process should have taken place according to Articles 143 or 151. Actually, it took place on the basis of additional provision 1 of the constitution, which says that "it [the Constitution] protects and respects the historic rights of territories with Fueros," ignoring the second part of that rule: "the general updating of the Fuero system shall be carried out when appropriate within the framework of the Constitution and of the statutes of self-government." Navarra was finally recognized by the Acuerdos Autonómicos and the Ley Orgánica de Reintegracíon y Amejoramiento de la Región Foral Navarra as an autonomous region on August 10, 1982. The complex process that would have been initiated by a decision to join with Euskadi never came into play. It would have involved (1) a referendum to approve that decision, (2) a renegotiation, (3) probably a redrafting of the Estatuto of Euskadi that would have had to be approved by the Spanish Cortes, and (4) a referendum on the new draft in the four provinces.

The difficulties of combining historical or other criteria with popular democratic decision making played a major role in the process leading to Andalusian autonomy under Article 151. Andalusia, the most populous region of Spain (with 17.1 percent of the population) and the largest in area, had historically been unified, although it never had separate political institutions. It had been a part of the Kingdom of Castile since it was captured from the Moors, and it was later part of the Spanish crown without any distinctive institutions of representation. More recently, a regional consciousness had been developing, along with a sense of distinctiveness and relative deprivation reflected in a small nationalist movement. This sentiment found expression in a regional party, the Partido Socialista de Andalusia-Partido Andaluz, although the national parties were dominant in the region.

The Andalusian political elite decided to pursue autonomy through the drafting of an Estatuto, according to Article 151. After some delays and indecision of the central government, a referendum took place on February 28, 1980, according to the procedure of a hastily passed Ley Orgánica de las Diversas Modalidades del Referendum (LODMR) of January 18, 1980, which established that "once the referendum has taken place, if approval by affirmative vote of an absolute majority of the voters in each province has not been obtained, the initiative cannot be repeated for five years." According to this requirement—which was different from Article 151.3 of the constitution—the defeat of the proposal in one province meant rejection of autonomy under Article 151. The government party in this referendum, having decided to slow down the process of extending autonomy (according to Article 151 rather than 143) to regions that had not obtained it, advocated abstention in order to defeat the proposal and was joined by the conservative party, Alianza Popular. Since many municipal counselors of the government party and other leaders had supported the drafting of the Estatuto according to Article 151, this position led to considerable discontent among the voters, the resignation of an Andalusian UCD cabinet member, and an active campaign of the Junta de Andalusia (the preautonomy regional body controlled by the Left) in favor of the proposed Estatuto. It drew an unexpectedly high participation because of the sense of relative deprivation in comparison with the recognition of other nationalities, such as the Basque Country and Catalonia, together with the loyalty to the parties of the Left, which was from the beginning strong in the region. Seven provinces showed favorable outcomes (although in Jaén not until the reported vote had been challenged). Only in Almería—a province bordering on Murcia, far from the demographic and political center of Andalusia and tied economically to the Mediterranean area, where UCD was relatively strong—was the required vote not obtained, thereby frustrating immediate full Andalusian autonomy.[15]

After attempts to resolve the impasse through political maneuvering and a search for solutions within the constitutional text, the LODMR was reformed by another Organic Law of December 16, 1980. This one stated that the initiative must be approved in the provinces by an absolute majority and that those affirmative votes constitute an absolute majority of the electorate in the whole territory aspiring to autonomy. In addition, after a request of the majority of deputies and senators of the province or provinces in which the initiative otherwise would not have been ratified, the Cortes Generales, by an organic law, could substitute the autonomy initiative of Article 151. By an organic law of the same date, at the request of the deputies and senators from Almería, that province was incorporated into the region. Many scholars have questioned the constitutionality of this process.

A referendum is ultimately determined by the definition of the territorial units making the decision and by the rules regulating the decision-making process. Political and historical arguments tend to prevail over those formal rules and the will of the people expressed according to them. After the muddle of the Andalusian autonomy process, the remaining twelve autonomous communities were decided by the Acuerdos Autonómicos and organic laws ratifying their Estatutos, ignoring the complex procedures of Article 151 and the direct participation of the people.

Democratic decision making requires agreement on the preexisting political and territorial units that will be bound by the decision. Such decisions cannot be made effectively or legitimately without this prior agreement and an institutional framework. In Spain the democratic conception of the *principio dispositivo*, of the initiative of the representative leaders and through the participation of the electorate was conditioned by the traditional provincial boundaries. When that framework led to decisions contradicting other valid criteria, such as history, geography, and even rationality, the latter took precedence. The Spanish experience should certainly be a warning to those who rest their hope for solving the problems of multinational, multilingual, and multiethnic societies on strictly democratic criteria—on letting "the people decide."

The Legal System of the Estatutos de Autonomía

Central to the process of institutionalizing the new Spanish state are the Estatutos de Autonomía of each community within the framework established by the constitution to grant access to self-government, Articles 143.1 and 147.1. The nationalities and regions, therefore, can exercise the right to gain autonomy through the Estatutos. To what extent are the Estatutos rules of the autonomous region, or rules of the state? The answer is that they are both; they are elaborated through the initiatives of the regions (Articles 143 and 151), by the representatives of the territories (Article 146), but also, in the cases of the higher thresholds for autonomy, by approval of the Cortes Generales, the Spanish legislature, normally after a process of negotiation and agreement (Article 151.2). Once approved, the Estatutos acquire special status since they cannot be modified except by consent of the representatives of the autonomous region.

The Estatutos are rules of the state because, according to Article 147.1, "within the terms of the present constitution the Estatutos shall constitute the basic institutional rules of each self-governing community and the state shall recognize and protect them as integral parts of its legal order." They are organic laws as defined by Articles 81.1, 146, 147.3, and 151. Within the framework of the constitution, they are the highest rules within each autonomous region. They are not, however, equal to the constitution since their content is limited, particularly by Articles 137, 139, 148, 149, 150 and 155 and, ultimately, by Article 2. To avoid any ambiguity, the Organic Law of the Constitutional Court, in Article 27.2, states that the court is competent to declare the unconstitutionality of the Estatutos. The Constitutional Court, in a decision of May 4, 1982, rejected the idea that only the text of an Estatuto should be taken into account in arriving at an interpretation to define powers. The Court said explicitly: "If one were to proceed in that way, one would ignore the principle of supremacy of the constitution over the remainder of the legal order, of which the Estatutos of Autonomy are part as the basic institutional norm of the autonomous community that the state recognizes and protects. . . ." A number of other decisions restated this principle and it was also applied to the Organic Law of Reintegration and Improvement of the Navarrese Region.

Within their territories of application, however, the Estatutos have a higher rank than any other law, including even organic laws. They are endowed with a special rigidity derived from the fact that according to Article 147.3, "Amendment of the Estatutos shall conform to the procedure established therein and shall, in any case, require the approval of the Cortes through an organic law," and 152.2, "Once the respective Estatutos have been sanctioned and promulgated they may only be amended by means of the procedures established therein and through a referendum of the electorate. . . ." This normally implies a vote of three-fifths or two-thirds or an absolute majority of the legislatures of the autonomous communities, depending on the cases or, in the case of the Estatutos of maximum autonomy, on a referendum. It is clear that the Cortes Generales do not have the sole power to reform, modify, or abrogate an Estatuto as they have to modify or abrogate an organic law on any other matter. Because the affected populations must agree, the Estatutos are immune to the legislative power of the national legislature. The requirement of their final approval by an organic law means, however, that the regional legislatures alone also cannot modify the Estatutos.

Aside from the possibilities of reform foreseen in each Estatuto, in the approval by the national legislature of such reform, and, where applicable, in a referendum, the only way the national legislature could modify the Estatutos would be by constitutional reform. Such reform has to be done according to Articles 166 and following of the constitution, which provide for a complex process of amendment, with special obstacles to changing some parts of the constitution, including Article 2, which serves as the basis for the state of the autonomies.

From the preceding, one can conclude that the Estatutos occupy a special position above other laws, including the organic laws, and that in practice any modification requires agreement among the state and the representatives of the regions and, in some cases, the approval by the electorate within the autonomous community. Only a fundamental constitutional change—involving qualified majorities and probably an election of a new legislature afterward so that it could approve it, as well as, in all likelihood, a constitutional referendum—could modify the Estatutos without the participation of the representatives and the electorate of the autonomous communities. Such change in the constitution, however, and such modification of the Estatutos by constitutional change would create a most serious political crisis and represent a change in the regime. As the system has developed, the Estatutos are unlikely to be modified in the near future, at least not in the direction of reducing the autonomy acquired. Initiatives at the level of nationalities and regions to improve and extend the autonomy by reform are unlikely to be easily accepted under normal circumstances by the national legislature. Therefore, although the Estatutos seem to be derived from the constitution and subject in their interpretation to the test of conformity with the constitution and its framework, they are politically, although not juridically, part of the present Spanish Constitution. For this reason, some commentators have spoken of a quasi-constitutional character of the Estatutos.

The Institutions and Powers of the Autonomous Communities

The communities that have attained autonomy by Article 151 or Transitory Rule 2 according to Article 152 elect a legislature every four years by some method of proportional representation that reflects the internal heterogeneity. That legislature can dictate rules within its jurisdiction and may propose laws to the Spanish Cortes. It elects the president of the autonomous community—who depends on its confidence and is subject, as is his government, to its control—and a number of senators. It also takes claims of unconstitutionality to the Constitutional Court. The head of the regional government, elected by the legislature and appointed by the king, represents the community and is normally the representative of the state in the community. Article 152 also recognizes in those communities the possibility of establishing a Tribunal Superior de Justicia, a superior court of justice, the actions of which "should be exercised with respect to the judicial unity of the nation" as found in Title 6 of the constitution. The application of this provision has created many problems.

The most complex issue is the distribution of powers and jurisdictions between the state and the autonomous communities, a topic that more than any other has attracted the attention of scholars. Extremely technical and complex issues stem from the ambiguity in the way the Spanish Constitution addresses this problem, the lack of principles as clear as those found in some federal states, and the effort to develop outside the constitution and the Estatutos after their enactment more general principles to interpret the specific provisions of the constitution and the Estatutos, by now practically unchangeable. Since there is no agreement on how to interpret the relevant constitutional and legal texts, we would have to look to the jurisprudence of the Constitutional Court and to the different interpretations of the jurists, something that cannot be done here. Only the bare outlines of the legal texts and the basic issues raised by scholars interpreting them will be discussed.

The problem stems from the failure of the Spanish constitution makers to define three basic areas of power and jurisdiction: that in which the state has exclusive jurisdiction; that in which the autonomous community has exclusive jurisdiction; and that in which both the state and the autonomous community have jurisdiction. Spanish legislation has been based on the *principio dispositivo*, by which each community assumes different powers within the limits established by the constitution. In addition, there is the gradual assumption of powers based on the different ways regions gain autonomy. Therefore both legally and in practice situations differ greatly in different places.

Apparently, the constitution, in Articles 148 and 149, adopts a system with two areas of jurisdiction: the first contains the powers of the autonomous communities, and the second the exclusive powers of the state. The two areas are not, however, simply mutually exclusive, as Article 149 includes matters that can be shared by both. Furthermore Article 150 allows the state, under certain conditions and by its own volition, to modify the distribution of powers either by extending or by limiting the powers of the autonomous communities in accordance with the general interest. Besides those constitutional rules, one must look to the specific formulations found in the Estatutos. They contain their own lists of powers (which presumably cannot be in conflict with those the state has reserved to itself) and express the will of the autonomous communities to assume those powers, or the readiness to do so; but this requires the transfer of them by the state. The state sometimes reserves to itself the formulation of general principles while leaving other matters and implementation to the autonomous communities.

The body of rules in the constitution distinguishes, in principle, the following types of powers:

- matters of exclusive jurisdiction of the state
- matters of jurisdiction of the state, but over which the autonomous community may have concurrent jurisdiction
- matters of exclusive jurisdiction of the state, but which can be delegated to the autonomous communities
- matters not attributed by the constitution to the state nor to the autonomous communities

- matters of exclusive jurisdiction of the autonomous communities according to Article 148
- matters that can be shared between the state and the autonomous communities
- matters over which the state and the communities share legislative and executive power
- matters in the communities that have achieved autonomy by the rapid process, consisting of those in which legislation falls under the jurisdiction of the state, but the execution of the laws might be within the powers of the communities, and of those in which the state sets the basic framework while the communities can develop and execute laws

This list could be organized differently by changing the combinations of exclusivity and concurrency, basic legislation and other types of legislation, and legislation and execution or implementation; this shows the complexity of the problem. Because of the *principio dispositivo*, different communities at different times can claim different powers, given the possibilities provided by the constitution. The past few years have seen efforts to rationalize the process by obtaining homogeneity in the autonomous communities established after those of Catalonia, Euskadi, Galicia, and Andalusia and by providing general principles to resolve conflicts between the autonomous communities and the state and to prevent those conflicts from blocking government action until the Constitutional Court can decide them. The Acuerdos Autonómicos were reached in this context, and the LOAPA was enacted with the support of the two major parties.

When Articles 143 and 151 were drafted, the constitution makers tried to differentiate the autonomous communities on the basis of the strength of the nationalist or the regionalist sentiment—the intensity of the demands, on the one side, and on the other, the preexisting political, administrative, and economic structures that would make autonomy effective in the short run. This attempt would also seem logical to any scholarly observer of the social, cultural, economic, and political realities of Spanish society.

Both the constitution makers and the intellectual observers neglected, however, two other factors: first, the sense of relative deprivation, the permanent desire for equality characteristic of our age (at least formal legal equality); and, second, the interests of politicians and political parties in power—their status, prestige, and economic rewards. Political elites and parties with dominant positions in a region were unlikely to be satisfied with a design that frustrated their ambitions. The relative deprivation and the particular historical circumstances of underdevelopment, the hostility to centralism associated with the Franco regime, and the crisis of the state all made the elites, the activists, and the voters susceptible to politicians who demanded maximum autonomy and thereby frustrated that differentiation of types of autonomy explicit in the constitutional text. Because the constitution did allow for all regions to obtain the same level of autonomy in time, those demands could not be stopped.

The Spanish experience suggests, therefore, that once a state and its representatives embark on a process of devolution or decentralization, particularly in a period of political transition or instability, they will not be able to deal with different situations in different ways. The principle of equality and the sentiments associated with it will inevitably push toward uniformity, as so many social theorists have noted.

A New Centralism?

An interesting question, still not debated much except in the Basque Country, concerns the relationships between the regions and their governments and the provinces and their administration. Article 137 of the constitution mentions both the autonomous communities and the provinces, and Article 141 states that the province is a local entity "with its own legal personality" and that "any alteration of the provincial boundaries must be approved by the Cortes Generales by means of an organic law." The same rule applies to the Cabildos of the Canary Islands. The provinces, as they have evolved since they were created in 1833 (in some cases on the basis of historical divisions of the Ancien Regime), have become powerful social and political realities with capitals that, with few exceptions, have become the centers of communication, administrative life, economic activities, and culture. The Committee of Experts clearly opposed a regional centralism. Instead, they suggested that the Diputaciones become the basic administrative echelon within the region, to administer the services of the state transferred to the regions and the regional services normally attributed to them. The Diputaciones Provinciales are also representative bodies elected by the municipalities thereby ensuring representation by population and territory.

It would be interesting to compare both the legal and the actual status of the Spanish provinces with the status of the Italian provinces and the German Regierungsbezirke, as well as with the counties in the Anglo-American tradition. The Spanish provinces are certainly larger than those in most countries and have a much more clearly defined historical, social, and political character. They are also the basic electoral districts for national and regional elections, and, though the products of a centralized unitary state, they have existed for 150 years and served as seats of the whole administrative structure. Citizens are unlikely to prefer going to a regional capital (sometimes afflicted with bad communications because of the nationwide, centralized grid of communications created in the nineteenth century) rather than to the familiar provincial capital. In some regions the provinces represent the rural and small-town sentiments in the face of hegemonic, metropolitan areas where the regional capital is located, as in the cases of Catalonia, Valencia, and Andalusia. In some cases, as in the regions constituted by two provinces, the location of the regional capital has been an issue. If, however, the main functions of the region are to plan and coordinate and only exceptionally to administer, some of the regions cover too small a geographic and economic area for those functions. Their boundaries were based on criteria of history and politics more than of planning, in contrast to the French process of regionalization. Following criteria like those used in France, some provinces would have been attached to a different region, as in the case of Soria with respect to Aragón and of Almería with respect to Murcia. This fact may have contributed to the outcome of the Andalusian referendum in Almería mentioned above.

The regional powers would probably like to build centralized regional structures, but they would encounter resistance in the provinces, particularly in those on the peripheries of the regions. Fear of such resistance explains why, in the process of devolution, regions like Cantabria and La Rioja emerged as single-province regions. It also explains the opposition of Segovia to joining Castile-León.

In formulating the Basque Estatuto consideration had to be given to the special status that the three historical provinces in the Basque Country have enjoyed, their distinctive financial agreements with the central government (the *conciertos económicos*, which in the case of Alava survived even during the Franco period), their identity as the so-called Territorios Históricos, and the absence of a fully Basque hegemonic center (given the dominance of the Castilian language in the metropolitan area of Bilbao). Article 3 of that Estatuto states: "Each of the Territorios Históricos that integrate the Basque Country will be able to retain or reestablish and actualize their organization and distinctive institutions of self-government." The Basque Parliament was seriously divided over the law regulating the autonomy of each of the provinces with respect to the central regional government. The debate within the governing party, the PNV, on this issue led to a crisis of leadership and the removal of Garaikoetxea as prime minister, and later contributed to the split of the party. The powers transferred to the regional government probably will have to be passed on to the

Diputaciones Forales, leaving the government in Vitoria an empty shell unable to coordinate the policies and administration of the Basque Country.

Equality in a Multilingual State

The constitution is explicit concerning equality. Article 14 states: "Spaniards are equal before the law and may not in any way be discriminated against on account of birth, race, sex, religion, or opinion, or on account of any other condition or personal or social circumstance." Article 19 states: "Spaniards have the right to choose their place of residence freely and to move about freely in the national territory." Article 139.1 says that all Spaniards have the same rights and obligations in any part of the state territory, and 139.2 states: "No authority may adopt measures which directly or indirectly obstruct freedom of movement and settlement of persons, and free movement of goods, throughout the Spanish territory." Political rights, both active and passive, in the whole territory and for all bodies, whether national, regional, or local, are linked to Spanish citizenship.

The Spanish polity, therefore, does not make any distinction between nationalities in regard to citizenship rights. In regard to language, Article 3.1 states: "Castilian is the official Spanish language of the state. All Spaniards have the duty to know it and the right to use it." In Article 3.2, the constitution states: "The other languages of Spain shall also be official in the respective self-governing communities in accordance with their statutes." Article 3.3 states: "The wealth of language variations in Spain is a cultural heritage which shall be the object of special respect and protection."

The problem is how linguistic diversity and the recognition of Castilian and the languages of the bilingual regions, including their co-officiality, will be made compatible in practice with those principles of equality, free movement, and nondiscrimination. Some of the Estatutos—like the Basque Estatuto in Article 6.3, and the Galician Estatuto in Article 5.4—explicitly say that no one can be discriminated against by reason of language; such a provision is not found in the Catalan Estatuto, although it probably can be inferred from the basic antidiscrimination principle of Article 14 of the constitution.

In practice, however, the officiality of several languages and the efforts to strengthen the position of the regional languages through educational policies and administrative practices inevitably will lead to the necessity of knowing the language of the region in which one lives. Even with the best intentions and the most prudent and moderate language policy, some linguistic conflict is unavoidable. In bilingual regions, those who can speak and, above all, write the regional language will have different opportunities from those who speak only Castilian. A segmentation of occupational opportunities, at least in the public sector, will be almost unavoidable.

Not everyone living in a bilingual region is bilingual. In large parts of the Basque Country, Castilian has been spoken exclusively for centuries. Moreover, in all regions, particularly the highly industrialized Basque Country and Catalonia, large proportions of the population have emigrated from Castilian-speaking parts of Spain in the twentieth century, especially since the rapid economic expansion of the 1960s. Immigrants constitute approximately 30 percent of the population in the Basque Country and Catalonia. The metropolitan areas of Barcelona and Bilbao and their industrial suburbs have an even larger proportion. Despite efforts at assimilation through the educational process such as those in Catalonia, immigrants concentrated in fairly homogeneous communities are unlikely to learn Catalan or Basque (a nonromance language) well enough to compete for many positions with natives. Social mobility in those regions will be linked to full bilingualism, which is less accessible to the generations educated before official recognition of the local languages or to children growing up in a largely homogeneous Castilian milieu.[16]

Recognition of linguistic diversity in the constitution and the Estatutos probably constitutes the greatest social change in Spain in recent years. It is a change with far-reaching implications for geographic and social mobility within Spanish society.

The Financial Restructuring of the State and the Principle of Solidarity

The crisis of the unitary state reflects not only cultural and linguistic heterogeneity but also the imbalances of economic development of the regions of Spain. The nationalism in the Catalan and Basque peripheries does not fit the theories of Michael Hechter and others about internal colonialism because these two regions are economically the most developed.[17] And in spite of strong feelings of relative deprivation in less-developed regions such as Andalusia, efforts to create a nationalist sentiment were unsuccessful given their historical integration into the Spanish nation. In creating the new territorial structure of the Spanish state, the legislature had to take into account the resentment against the centralized state based on these two divergent socioeconomic factors. Recognizing nationalities and regions, therefore, Article 2 of the constitution says that it is "based on the solidarity among them all."

The financial restructuring of the state was the object of Articles 156 to 158, which restate the principle of autonomy but add the principle of solidarity among all Spaniards. These provisions classify the different sources of financing of the autonomous communities, ranging from their own taxes to those transferred to them by the state derived from surcharges on state taxes as well as from transfers from the Fondo de Compensación (Fund for Compensation) and other allocations to be charged to the general state budget. Article 158.1 provides for central budget allocations in proportion to the services and activities for which the communities assume responsibility, to guarantee that they provide a minimum level of basic public services throughout the Spanish territory (later specified as being equivalent to the national mean in those services, a confusing standard). To correct economic imbalances and to implement the principle of solidarity, Article 158.2 provides for the Fondo de Compensación to be set up for investment and for the resources to be distributed by the Cortes Generales among the self-governing communities and provinces.

The development of these principles was the object of the Ley Orgánica de Financiación de las Comunidades Autónomas (LOFCA). The many technical, legal, and economic problems posed by the law begin with the question of how the two principles of Article 158, 1 and 2, would be defined and whether they should be considered complementary. The Fondo de Compensación Interterritorial (FCI), according to Article 16 of the LOFCA, must be granted at least 30 percent of public investment of the general budget of the state annually for investment expenditures in the less-developed regions.[18]

The criteria specified for investment in less-developed regions were these: an inverse relationship to the per capita income; the rate of out-migration in the past ten years; the percentage of unemployment among the active population; and area, insularity, and "other criteria that might be relevant." The weighting of these indexes must be revised by law every five years, and investments must be made to help diminish the differences in income and wealth among inhabitants of the regions.

The transfer of functions to the autonomous communities, together with the financial resources of the state to cover them, reduces the state income and implies a reduction in the general budget of the state. Its investment budget, therefore, is also reduced, decreasing the financial significance of the FCI. This reduction diminishes its capacity to compensate for unequal development. As one commentator has noted, only by including the finances of the regions in a consolidated national budget could this danger to the FCI and to the future efficacy of the solidarity principle be circumvented.

The particular financial arrangements between the central state and Euskadi and Navarra in the *conciertos económicos,* which provide for a negotiated contribution to the national treasury, pose additional problems for the implementation of the principle of equality stated in Article 138.2. According to that article, "the differences between the Estatutos of the different communities may in no case imply economic and social privileges."

Spain faces the great question of whether federalization and decentralization, on the one hand, or centralization, on the other, is the better instrument to achieve social equality within the modern state and whether a federalized state provides the best instruments for economic and social planning. These are central questions, which have attracted the attention of legislators and of scholars, although developments since autonomy was introduced in each region have yet to be analyzed definitively. Government policies, both at the central and the regional level, appear unable, however, to overcome some of the structural problems of the economy in the different regions. The crises gripping entire industrial sectors, the presence or absence of entrepreneurial spirit, the impact of demographic changes—such as population growth in the Canary Islands—and, in the near future, the differential impact on the regional economies of the entry of Spain into the Common Market will all be at least as important as those policies.[19]

The economic inequalities within Spain will continue as a source of frustration expressed by the regional governments in their relations with the central government. Those inequalities may even affect foreign policy. Inevitably efforts to find solutions to regional problems will not always be compatible with the principle of a unified internal market. Given the ambiguity of the articles of the constitution regulating the powers of the regional and central governments, these efforts will require complex negotiations or will lead to constitutional conflicts to be decided by the Constitutional Court. They might also lead to a reassessment of the value of autonomy.

The Constitutional Court and the Autonomous Communities

The Tribunal Constitucional, or Constitutional Court, regulated by Articles 159 and 165 and the Organic Law of October 1979, is a central institution in the new Spanish state. It is particularly important given the ambiguity and the potential for conflict surrounding the powers of the state and the autonomous communities. Since its establishment, its jurisprudence has gained considerable authority, and its decisions on many controversial issues—particularly in relationship to the autonomous communities—have been respected. The Second Republic's Tribunal de Garantías Constitucionales in a famous conflict between the central government and the Generalitat failed to achieve such authority.[20]

The Constitutional Court has general power in matters of the constitutionality of laws and rules having the force of law, as well as in those matters attributed to it by the constitution or the organic laws. Article 161c also assigns to it "the conflicts of jurisdiction between the state and the autonomous communities and between autonomous communities." Article 161.2 states that the government can contest before the Constitutional Court the provisions and the resolutions adopted by the agencies of the autonomous communities. Such impugnation leads to the suspension of a rule or a decision, but the tribunal must either ratify or lift the suspension within a period of no more than five months.

Actions on constitutionality can be taken before the court not only by the president of the government, the defender of the people, fifty deputies, and fifty senators, but also by the executive corporate bodies of the autonomous communities and, where applicable, by their assemblies. The Organic Law of the Constitutional Court (LOTC) developed this principle in a number of its articles. Article 27.2 states explicitly that the Estatutos de Autonomía and the Organic Laws are subject to declarations of unconstitutionality; Article 27f makes such declarations possible with regard to the Reglamentos of the legislative assemblies of the communities.

The Coordination of Seventeen Autonomous Communities

Because of extensive powers assumed by the autonomous communities, the desire of some of them to assert their independence from the central government, the ambiguity concerning the powers granted to them by the constitution and the Estatutos, the transfer agreements, and the conflicting economic interests between the regions, some coordination and homogeneity of policies must be achieved. The report of the Commission of Experts, the Acuerdos Autonómicos, and the LOAPA attempted to deal with this problem, but neither the constitution nor political practice has yet created formal or informal institutions to deal with it. Once the *transferencias* (the devolution of powers and administrative services from the central administration) have been completed and the new autonomous governments and legislatures start acting, the problem will become more salient. Entry into the European Community and its impact on the Spanish economy (and legislation) will probably make such coordination even more imperative.

Bilateral negotiations between the autonomous communities and the central government are likely to be too time-consuming and conflictive. The central government will have to act as spokesman for the interests of some autonomous communities that are in conflict with others, rather than acting only as an arbitrator during their confrontations. In bilateral relations, the onus of opposing particularistic aspirations in the periphery falls on the central government, which has limited legitimacy in confrontations with some of the autonomous communities.

The absence of a body like the German Bundesrat, in which the governments of the autonomous communities would be represented and would be responsible for nationwide policy making and participation in the legislative process, is a weakness of the system. Although the Senate has been called a "chamber of territorial representation" and theoretically should serve such a function, its size, its composition by direct election (although some members are indirectly elected by the parliaments of the autonomous communities), and the predominance of the national party alignments within it tend to make it unsuitable for coordinating the policies of the regional governments. Without a formal law and institutionalization, functional alternatives could emerge in practice, such as periodic meetings of the heads of the autonomous governments. Article 9 of the Acuerdos Autonómicos suggested sectoral conferences of the cabinet members of the different communities and the minister or ministers in charge of each particular sector on a regular basis, at least twice a year. Significantly, this proposal was made at a lower level than the heads of regional governments, more along the lines of the Länderminister Konferenzen in Germany. Such a pattern of conferences should prove an interesting development.

Some structural difficulties probably derive from the number of autonomous communities—seventeen—more than the eleven German *Länder* (counting Berlin) and the ten provinces of Canada, although fewer than the twenty Italian regions. Because of the very different character and "self-consciousness" of those regions, representatives of large and wealthy regions with their own historical identity, like Catalonia, are unlikely to consider the smaller, single-provincial regions like La Rioja their equal. Catalonia has 6,319,000 inhabitants, 17.3 percent of the total Spanish population, and accounts for 20.1 percent of the Spanish Gross National Product (GNP); La Rioja has 249,000 inhabitants, or .68 percent of the population and accounts for 1.9 percent of the Spanish GNP.[21]

To this variety at least four language groups (five if Valencian is distinguished from Catalan) have to be added. Furthermore, the regional leaders represent widely differing elements. Some speak for regional parties, appealing to nationalist sentiment; others are elected more as representatives of nationwide parties within their regions, reflecting national rather than regional electoral trends and depend on national leadership (which forced one leader of a regional government to resign under pressure). Any body of this type must show an imbalance between the nationalist periphery and the nonnationalist remaining regions in which, for the immediate future, one of the parties is likely to be hegemonic. Since the party (PSOE, 1981–1988) with the absolute majority in the national parliament (and therefore in control of the government) also controls the majority of the regions, the minority would seem unlikely to favor a more collective decision-making process.

The future role of the Ministry for Territorial Administration in the relationship between the central government and the autonomous communities is unclear. Its incumbents have had a very unstable position and are sometimes excluded from policy making on autonomy, which has been assumed by parliamentary leaders of the parties or by the prime minister himself. The role of the Delegado del Gobierno in each region is also unclear. Significantly, there was a serious conflict over whether to give him the title of Gobernador General; certainly, those holding that position have not always played an important role in the relationship between the central government and the heads of the regional governments, the president of the Generalitat, and the Lendhakari. The Delegado del Gobierno, an office created by Article 154, is defined as the head of the administration of the state in the territory of the autonomous community. He coordinates with the administration of the community when required, but the constitution does not seem to attribute to him any function of control in the relationship to the communities.

Since the provincial structure is anchored in the constitution, the formerly powerful provincial governor—the equivalent of the French prefect—has not disappeared. How his relationships with the regional government, the Delegado del Gobierno, and the central government will be structured and developed, however, remain unclear. The implementation of the constitution and the Estatutos and, ultimately, the smooth functioning of the new system of government will be worked out in actual, rather than legal and theoretical, interaction between the different levels of government and the officeholders.

New Leadership or a New Political Class?

In some federal states national leaders have emerged from party leadership at the regional level, as has been the case with state governors in the United States and with *Länder* prime ministers in the Federal Republic of Germany. Will regionalization facilitate the emergence of a new leadership from the periphery rather than from the central arena of politics, the national leadership of the parties and the Madrid Parliament? Although that question cannot yet be answered a number of reasons make this outcome less likely in Spain than in other countries.

In at least two regions—Catalonia and the Basque Country—nationalist parties have produced the head of the regional government since the autonomous communities were institutionalized. Because those leaders represent a nationalist sentiment and appeal to their constituencies on the basis of that sentiment, they would find it difficult to gain acceptance outside of their own communities. Basque nationalist leaders seem unlikely to exchange their regional arena for a national Spanish one, since they would lose authority and prestige in the Basque community by accepting integration into Spain, which a significant minority of their constituents reject. Apart from nationalism, factors such as the emphasis on distinctive languages and cultures and the tensions generated by efforts at linguistic normalization would detract from the popularity of such leaders in the rest of Spain, just as the Bavarian identity of Franz Joseph Strauss contributed to the failure of his bid for the chancellorship of West Germany. Catalonia and the Basque Country are, however, the most economically developed and industrialized regions of the country, and Barcelona is the second largest metropolitan area; they should logically produce national leaders. Obviously, such a possibility would be greater if the head of the regional government came from a nationwide party.

Single-province and sparsely populated regions seem unlikely to provide a sufficient power base within the parties or in national public opinion to support a bid for nationwide leadership. And since quite a few of the regions are economically underdeveloped, their governments have little chance to prove successful and innovative. In addition, cleavages within the parties have not been along regional lines except in the Catalan wing of those parties. In conflicts between the central leadership and that of the regional party (at least in the PSOE), the outcomes have been decided by and favorable to the center.

Interim Conclusion

It is still premature to analyze the political, social, and economic implications of the new quasi-federal structure of the Spanish state. The autonomous regions of Catalonia, Euskadi, Navarra, and Galicia were constituted in 1980–1981, and the parliament of Andalusia was elected in May 1982. The first regional elections in the other twelve autonomous communities took place only in May 1983. Because of the complexity of the process of transferring powers and administrative structures from the central government, the performance of the regional parliaments and governments cannot yet be judged.

Any analysis of the new structure of the state would have to distinguish Catalonia and the Basque Country, the two regions with nationalist parties, strong representation, and the ability to assume power. From the perspective of the Spanish state as a whole, the most important consequence in the short run has been the creation of a new political elite. Seventeen regional governments have been formed, each with a prime minister who has recruited a staff in addition to the civil servants transferred from the old administration, and 1,154 parliamentarians have been elected. The traditional Provincial representative bodies, the Diputaciones Provinciales, have survived in most of Spain. Therefore, the Spanish political class now consists of the municipal leadership, mayors and town counselors, the provincial representatives in the Diputaciones or equivalent bodies, the members of the parliaments and governments of the regions, and the national political elite. Thus the number of officeholders has greatly expanded, and a totally new level of government has been introduced in most of Spain.

At the regional level this new elite is recruited almost exclusively through the political parties, overwhelmingly through the nationwide parties except in Catalonia, Euskadi, and Navarra. Since 1982, the PSOE and AP have provided most of these officeholders, and the Communists, minor center parties, and a few local parties have supplied a few. The PSOE and other parties have a very weak membership basis, however, and their internal life and party democracy are not proportionate to the role they play in the recruitment of the new elite.

Unfortunately, little is known about the internal processes within the political parties, the mechanisms by which candidates are selected, the decision making within the party parliamentary caucuses, and the degree of independence of local leaders and provincial and local organizations from the regional and national leadership. Whether the new autonomous communities will provide for political participation of those closer to the people, and whether they will be responsive, representative, and accountable to regional and local interests cannot yet be said. The nationwide parties, however, with some exceptions still seem to be highly centralized organizations. This centralization would undermine some of the expectations generated by the autonomy process, but would also provide a check on ill-conceived actions by an inexperienced regional leadership.

Notes

1. For the constitutional history of Spain, see: Luis Sánchez Agesta, *Historia del Constitucionalismo español* (Madrid: 1955); Miguel Artola, *El modelo constitucional español del siglo XIX* (Madrid: Fundación Juan March, 1979), Serie Universitaria no. 75, Nicolás Pérez Serrano, *La Constitución española (9 diciembre 1931) Antecedentes, texto, comentarios* (Madrid: Revista de Derecho Privado, 1932).

2. On the peripheral nationalisms: Juan J. Linz, "Early state-building and late peripheral nationalism against the state," in *Building States and Nations: Models, Analyses, and Data across Three Worlds*, vol. II, eds. S. N. Eisenstadt and S. Rokkan (Beverly Hills, Sage, 1973), pp. 32–112; Juan J. Linz, "La crisis de un estado unitario, nacionalismos periféricos y regionalismo," in *La España de las autonomías, (Pasado, presente y futuro)*, vol. II, ed. R. Acosta (Madrid: Espasa Calpe, 1981), pp. 651–751; Rafael Acosta España et al., *La España de las autonomías. (Pasado, presente y futuro)*, Madrid: Espasa Calpe, 1981. 2 vols.; Francesc Mercadé, Francesc Hernàndez and Benjamín Oltra, *Once tesis sobre la cuestión nacional en España* (Barcelona: Anthropos, 1983), a useful brief synthesis of nationalist thought; Stanley G. Payne, *Basque Nationalism* (Reno, Nevada: University of Nevada Press, 1975).; Robert P. Clark, *The Basques. The Franco Years and Beyond* (Reno, Nevada: University of Nevada Press, 1979); José Miguel de Azaola, "El hecho vasco," in *España: un presente para el futuro*, Juan J. Linz, ed. (Madrid: Instituto de Estudios Económicos, 1984), pp. 213–283; Juan Pablo Fusi Aizpurua, *El problema vasco en la II República* (Madrid: Turner, 1979); Juan Pablo Fusi, *El País Vasco. Pluralismo y nacionalidad* (Madrid: Alianza, 1984); Juan J. Linz, *Conflicto en Euskadi* (Madrid: Espasa-Calpe, 1985); Juan J. Linz et al. *Atlas electoral del País Vasco y Navarra* (Madrid: Centro de Investigaciones Sociológicas), 1981; Juan J. Linz, "From Primordialism to Nationalism," in *New Nationalisms in the Developed West*, E. A. Tyriakian and R. Rogowski eds. (Winchester, Ma.: Allen Unwin, 1985); Andrés Barrera, *La dialéctica de la identidad en Cataluña. Un estudio de antropología social* (Madrid: Centro de Investigaciones Sociológicas, 1985), see chapter 4; Richard

Gunther, Giacomo Sani and Goldie Shabad, *Spain after Franco. The Making of a Competitive Party System* (Berkeley: University of California Press, 1985).
    3. An excellent source for the Spanish transition is the special issue of *Sistema*, November 1985, pp. 68–69, which includes a bibliographical essay and a complete bibliography, as well as several outstanding essays and the responses to a questionnaire by politicians and intellectuals on their views on the transition process; José María Maravall and Julián Santamaría, "Political Change in Spain and the Prospects for Democracy," in Guillermo O'Donnell, Philippe Schmitter and Laurence Whitehead, eds. *Transitions from Authoritarian Rule: Southern Europe* (Baltimore: Johns Hopkins, 1986), pp. 70–108; José María Maravall, *La política de la transición 1975–1980* (Madrid: Taurus, 1981); in English *The Transition to Democracy in Spain* (London: Croom Helm, 1982); Carlos Huneeus, *La Unión de Centro Democrático y la transición a la democracia en España* (Madrid: Centro de Investigaciones Sociológicas-Siglo XXI de España, 1985); Donald Share, *The Making of Spanish Democracy* (Westport, Conn.: Praeger, 1986).
    For a history of the period see Raymond Carr and Juan Pablo Fusi, *Spain from Dictatorship to Democracy* (London: George Allen & Unwin, 1979).
    On public opinion in the transition see Juan J. Linz, Manuel Gómez-Reino, Francisco A. Orizo and Darío Vila, *Informe sociológico sobre el cambio político en España, 1975–1981*, vol. I, Fundación FOESSA, IV Informe FOESSA (Madrid: Euramérica, 1981).
    On the Law for political reform see Pablo Lucas Verdú, *La octava Ley Fundamental*, with a foreword by Enrique Tierno (Madrid: Tecnos, 1976); Antonio Hernández Gil, *El cambio político español y la Constitución* (Barcelona: Planeta, 1981); Richard Gunther and Roger A. Blough, "Conflicto religioso y consenso en España: Historia de dos constituciones," *Revista de Estudios Políticos*, 14, March–April 1980.
    4. On terrorism in this period see Alejando Muñoz Alonso, *El terrorismo en España* (Barcelona: Planeta-Instituto de Estudios Económicos, 1984); Robert P. Clark, *The Basque Insurgents. ETA, 1952–1980* (Madison: University of Wisconsin Press, 1984); Ricardo García Damborenea, *La encrucijada vasca* (Barcelona: Argos Vergara, 1985), pp. 51–57; Gerhard Brunn, "Nationalist Violence and Terror in the Spanish Border Provinces: ETA," in Wolfgang J. Mommsen and Gerhard Hirschfeld, *Social Protest. Violence and Terror in Nineteenth- and Twentieth-century Europe* (New York: St. Martin's Press, 1982), pp. 112–136.
    For a view of the conflict from a pro ETA perspective see Miguel Castells Arteche, *Radiografía de un modelo represivo* (San Sebastián: Ediciones Vascas Argitaletxea, 1982).
    5. On multilingualism in Spain and its political implications: Rafael Niyoles, *Cuatro idiomas para un Estado* (Madrid: Cambio 16, 1977); Luis C. Núñez, *Opresión y defensa del euskera* (San Sebastian: Txertoa, 1977); Goldie Shabad and Richard Gunther, "Language, nationalism and political conflict in Spain," *Comparative Politics*, vol. 14, no. 4, July 1982, pp. 443–477; Robert P. Clark, "Language and Politics in Spain's Basque Provinces," *West European Studies*, vol. 4, no. 1, 1981.
    6. The scholarly literature on the Spanish 1978 Constitution, the auton-

omy statutes, the Constitutional Court and its decisions, and so on, is extensive. Basic references on the constitution making process include: Andrea Bonime-Blanc, *Spain's Transition to Democracy. The Politics of Constitution-making* (Boulder, Colo.: Westview, 1984); Antonio Hernández Gil, *El cambio político español y la Constitución* (Barcelona: Planeta, 1982); Emilio Attard, *La Constitución por dentro. Evocaciones del proceso constituyente. Valores, derechos y libertades* (Barcelona: Argos Vergara, 1983).

On the legitimacy gained by the constitution and the political institutions, see the surveys by the Centro de Estudios Sociológicos, *Actitudes y opiniones de los españoles ante la constitución y las instituciones democráticas* (Madrid: CIS, n.d.) (1986), and *Revista Española de Investigaciones Sociológicas*, 39, July–September, 1987, pp. 267–317. On the different response to the Basque Estatuto see my *Conflicto en Euskadi*.

Among the commentaries on the constitution See: Gregorio Peces Barba et al., *La izquierda y la Constitución* (Barcelona: Edicions Taula de Canvi, 1978); Alberto Predieri and Eduardo García de Enterría, eds., *La Constitución española de 1978* (Madrid: Civitas, 1980); Jorge de Estaban and Luis López Guerra, *El régimen constitucional español* (Barcelona: Labor, 1982), 2 vols; Manuel Ramírez, ed., *Estudios sobre la Constitución española de 1978* (Zaragoza: Pórtico, 1979); Miguel Martínez Cuadrado, *La Constitución de 1978 en la historia del Constitucionalismo español* (Madrid: Mezquita, 1982); Oscar Alzaga, *La Constitución española de 1978 (comentario sistemático)* (Madrid: Foro, 1978).

A useful reference work is José J. González Encinar, ed., *Diccionario del sistema político español* (Torrejón de Ardoz: Akal, 1984).

On the legal status of the autonomies see Santiago Muñoz Machado, *Las potestades legislativas de las Comunidades Autónomas* (Madrid: Civitas, 1981); Gaspar Ariño Ortiz, "El Estado de las Autonomías: una interpretación jurídica," in *La España de las Autonomías*, Fernando Fernández Rodríguez, ed. (Madrid: Instituto de Estudios de Administración Local, 1985), pp. 279–344; in the same volume, Ramón Martín Retortillo, "Los Estados de las Autonomías," pp. 345–446.

On the autonomy statutes see Eduardo García de Enterría, *Estudios sobre autonomías territoriales* (Madrid: Civitas, 1985); Cruz Martínez Esteruelas et al., *Estudios jurídicos sobre el Estatuto Vasco* (Madrid: n.p., 1980).

On the 1932 Catalan Estatuto see Manuel Gerpe Landin, *L'Estatut d'autonomia de Catalunya i l'Estat Integral* (Barcelona: Edicions 62, 1977); on the reestablishment of Catalan autonomy, Servei Central de Publicacions de la Generalitat de Catalunya, Department de la Presidència, *La Generalitat de Catalunya. Origins i restabliment* (Barcelona, 1979).

7. Kepa Bordegarai and Robert Pastor, *Estatuto Vasco* (San Sebastián: Ediciones Vascas, 1979); Ortzi (pseud. Francisco Letamendía), *El No vasco a la reforma. 1: La consolidación de la reforma, 2: La ofensiva de la reforma* (San Sebastián: Txertoa, 1979).

8. For the returns on the two referenda by province and municipalities, showing the internal heterogeneity of the Basque country, see Juan J. Linz et al., *Atlas electoral*, and for an analysis of public opinion on the Constitution and the Estatuto, Juan J. Linz, *Conflicto en Euskadi*.

9. The nationalist newspaper *Deia* remarked on this "inverse legitimation"

of the constitution in this way: "While the majority of Spaniards win access to the autonomy statutes on the basis of the constitution, the majority of the Basques can win access to the constitution on the basis of the Estatuto of Gernika."

10. On the preautonomies, Instituto de Estudios de Administración Local, *Legislación preautonómica* (Madrid: IEAL, 1980); Juan Ferrando Badía, *El Estado unitario, el federal y el Estado autonómico* (Madrid: Tecnos, 1986).

11. The two basic documents discussed in the text are:

Informe de la Comisión de Expertos sobre Autonomías (Madrid: Centro de Estudios Constitucionales, 1981);

Acuerdos Autonómicos firmados por el Gobierno de la Nación y el Partido Socialista Obrero Español el 31 de julio de 1981 (Madrid: Servicio Central de Publicaciones de la Presidencia del Gobierno, 1981).

12. Ivor Jennings, *The Approach to Self-Government* (1956) quoted by Lee C. Buchheit, *Secession. The Legitimacy of Self-Determination* (New Haven: Yale University Press, 1978), p. 9.

13. On the use of Basque see Euskalzanindia, Real Academia de la Lengua Vasca, *Conflicto lingüístico en Euskadi*, Informe SIADECO (Bilbao: Imprenta Industrial, 1979).

14. On the question of Navarra, see Juan J. Linz, "Peripheries within the periphery?" in *Mobilization Center-Periphery. Periphery Structure and Nation Building: A Volume in Commemoration of Stein Rokkan* (Bergen: Bergen Universitets Forlaget, 1982), pp. 335–380, see pp. 332–368.

15. On the Andalusian autonomist movement and post-Franco politics see Ulrike Liebert, *Neue Autonomiebewegung und Dezentralisierung in Spanien. Der Fall Andalusien* (Frankfurt: Campus, 1986); Antonio Porras Nadales, *Geografía electoral de Andalucía* (Madrid: Siglo XXI de España, 1985); Fernando Alvarez Palacios et al., *Andalucía dijo Si* (Sevilla: Augusto Lorca, 1980), on the February 28, 1980 referendum; Pilar del Castillo Vera, "Referendum en Andalucía en aplicación del artículo 151 de la Constitución," *Revista del Departamento de Derecho Político* (Universidad a Distancia), 6, 1980, pp. 175–179.

16. On the implications of bilingualism see Juan J. Linz, "Los jóvenes en una España multilingüe y de nacionalidades," in *Juventud española 1984*, Francisco Andrés Orizo et al. (Madrid: Ediciones SM, 1985), pp. 325–436.

The Law 7/1983 of April 18, Ley de Normalización Lingüística en Cataluña, which has served as a model for other bilingual communities, is the basic expression of the linguistic policy based on the Constitution and the Estatuto. Antoni M. Badía i Margarit, *Llengua i societat. Etapes de la normalització* (Barcelona: Indesinenter, 1982).

17. Michael Hechter, *Internal Colonialism. The Celtic Fringe in British National Development, 1530–1966* (Berkeley: University of California Press, 1975).

18. On the financing of the autonomies see José Juan Ferreiro Lapatza and Fernando Fernández Rodríguez, "La financiación de las autonomías," in *La España de les autonomiás*, Fernando Fernández Rodríguez, ed., pp. 447–473 (with basic bibliographic references); Ministerio de Hacienda, Secretaría General Técnica, *Ley Orgánica de Financiación de las Comunidades Autónomas, El debate en las Cortes Generales* (Madrid: 1982), which includes the text of the

LOFCA; Junta de Andalucía, Universidad de Sevilla, Universidad de Granada, *I Jornadas de Estudios Socioeconómicos de las Comunidades Autónomas. La hacienda de las Comunidades* (Granada, 1981).

19. Francesc Hernández and Francesc Mercadé, eds., *Estructuras sociales y cuestión nacional en España* (Barcelona: Ariel, 1986) is an excellent collection of papers on the social structure of all Spanish regions.

20. On the Constitutional Court, in addition to the studies of the Constitution, see Manuel García Pelayo (the first President of the Constitutional Court), "El 'status' del Tribunal Constitucional," *Revista Española de Derecho Constitucional*, I, 1981, pp. 11–34; Eduardo García de Enterría, "La posición jurídica del Tribunal Constitucional en el sistema español: posibilidades y perspectivas," in the same issue, pp. 35–131; and the special issue of the *Revista de Derecho Político*, 16, 1982–1983.

21. For the inequalities in economic development, population, occupational structure, unemployment, and so on, see Banco de Bilbao, *Renta nacional de España 1979 y su distribución provincial* (Zamudio-Bilbao: Banco de Bilbao, 1982). Because of the structural crisis of heavy industry (steel, shipbuilding, metal) and the impact of labor unrest and terrorism, the Basque Country, particularly Vizcaya, has slipped from its top position in GDP per capita. On immigrants in Catalonia see Esteban Pinilla de las Heras, *Estudios sobre cambio social y estructuras sociales en Cataluña* (Madrid: Centro de Investigaciones Sociológicas, 1979); Carlota Solé, *La integración de los inmigrantes en Cataluañ* (Madrid: CIS, 1981); Fausto Miguélez and Carlota Solé, *Classes socials i poder polític a Catalunya* (Barcelona: Promociones y Publicaciones Universitarias, 1987). For maps showing the concentrations of immigrants see Caixa d'estalvis de Catalunya, Ahorrobank, Servei d'Estudis a Barcelona del Banco Urquijo, *Atlas socio-económico de Catalunya* (Barcelona: Sirocco, 1980).

Commentary

Francisco Tomás y Valiente

Race

Spain is not a country of racial diversity. In fact, the gypsies are Spain's only ethnic minority, consisting of 500,000 people out of a population of almost 40 million. Although they do not suffer from discrimination, public opinion frequently rejects any movement toward their total integration into Spanish society. Such integration is greater in many towns of Andalusia, where the gypsies have settled down and have their own businesses or stable jobs. Many gypsy families remain nomadic, however, or live in the suburbs of large cities; they face the opposition of many Spaniards who are not willing to include them in their society. Such resistance was evident when the public authorities attempted to build cheap housing facilities in which the gypsies would live with other people and when the authorities tried to have gypsy children attend public schools with others.

In response to these events, the gypsy deputy of the Socialist party, Ramirez Heredia, voiced complaints in the Congreso de los Diputados (session of October 3, 1985). He suggested the creation of "an administrative body especially for the gypsy community" to encourage their social integration without sacrificing their "cultural autonomy." Although the Spanish Parliament approved his request with minimal opposition (225 votes in favor, 7 against, and 1 abstention), the noble goal envisioned by the Socialist representative will not be achieved through administrative steps alone. The administrative decrees and the constitutional imperative not to discriminate can, however, promote a change in the social attitude of Spaniards toward the gypsies.

Religion

A citizen's religious beliefs—membership in the Catholic Church or other Christian churches or belief in other religions, such as Islam or

Judaism—or lack of religious beliefs may not serve as a basis for discrimination and is not a socially relevant condition in Spain today. During the Second Republic, religious conflict, which meant being either for or against the Catholic Church, was one of the most important factors of tension and a catalyst of the uprising against the Republic; a half century later, this problem has disappeared.

The Catholic Church, which was allied with the Franco regime (*nacional-catolicismo*), and which knowingly served to legitimize that government, distanced itself from that regime in its last years with unsurprising ability. Some bishops, priests, and believers considered the renewed discussions of the Second Vatican Council incompatible with union of church and state. After the death of Franco, Cardinal Tarancón, president of the Episcopal Conference of the Catholic Church, publicly demonstrated his support for the transition to democracy. Since 1976, it has become clear that the Catholic Church would not be, and has not been, an obstacle to democracy. The Agreement with the Holy See of January 3, 1979, was signed by the minister of justice, Landelino Lavilla, a democrat and a Christian. This agreement, together with the ratification of the Spanish Constitution on December 27, 1978, demonstrated the sociopolitical changes that were taking place within Spain and the Vatican's acceptance of them.

The constitution contains fundamental rules in this area, as much in its emphasis on the freedoms of the citizen as in its treatment of the relationship between the state and religious faiths. Article 14 of the Spanish Constitution prohibits discrimination among Spaniards because of religion. Article 18.1 "guarantees the freedom of ideology, religion, and worship of individuals and the communities," reinforcing it with the stipulation that "no one may be compelled to make declarations concerning his religion, beliefs, or ideology."

Article 18.3 mandates that "there shall be no state religion." This breaks the traditional association in Spain between the state and the Catholic Church, including that in the liberal state (under the Constitution of 1812). This association was broken only once before, with the Republican Constitution of 1931, the price of which has already been noted. The Catholic Church is, however, more deeply rooted in Spanish society than any other church (although unquestionably much less now than some decades ago). The constitution recognizes this social fact and grants the church a certain privilege compared with other religions. Article 18.3 provides that "the public authorities shall take the religious beliefs of Spanish society into account and shall maintain the consequent relations of cooperation with the Catholic Church and other religions."

But if the Catholic Church has a special status, the Law on Religious Freedom, signed on July 5, 1980, grants equal legal status to all churches, religions, and religious communities by requesting that they enroll in an ad hoc register, the purpose of which is to publicize their existence (Article 3 of the law). This law also created an Advisory Commission on Freedom of Religion, composed of representatives from the administration and the religions. They deal with everything referring to the enforcement of the Law on Religious Freedom, and they report on agreements signed with religions of "well-known influence in Spain" (Articles 7 and 8). This cooperation works.

Although no religion seems to be as influential as the Catholic Church, respect for individual and collective freedom of belief in another religion is undeniable. Non-Catholic churches, both Christian and non-Christian, can be found in any Spanish city. Synagogues are open for worship, and the number of Moslem Spaniards has increased in certain cities. The Moslems are even planning to build a mosque in Madrid. In spite of the peaceful and free coexistence of Jews, Moslems, and Christians, drastically different from centuries ago, a growing number of citizens practice no religion at all in a society in which religion has ceased being a *quaestio disputata* (disputed question). Although violently argued in the past, the religious question has evolved into a matter for private acceptance, rejection, indifference, or doubt.

The constitution as the highest judicial ordinance in Spain has forced the repeal, annulment, or adaptation of laws that regulate institutions or activities closely related to ideology and Catholic religious belief. Two specific areas are marital regulation and education.

In the Catholic Church, marriage is indissoluble. The last version of Spain's Civil Code before the adoption of the constitution established that canonical marriage must be contracted when at least one partner is Catholic; civil marriage was authorized only when neither partner was Catholic (Article 42 of the Civil Code, and Law of April 24, 1958). Since Article 52 of the Civil Code stipulated that "marriage becomes dissolved only when one spouse dies," civil marriage was also indissoluble. Article 32.2 of the Spanish Constitution provides, however, that the law regulates the form of marriage, the age and capacity of the contracting persons, their rights, and their duties, as well as "the grounds for separation and dissolution and their consequences." The constitution allows the dissolution of the marriage bond, that is, divorce. The Law of July 7, 1981, was reworded to adjust it to the constitution, particularly Articles 42–107 of the Civil Code pertaining to marriage, by including divorce *(divorcio vincular)*. Catholics and non-Catholics can now be married and divorced, facing only moral obstacles.

Freedom of ideology is recognized by Article 16 of the Spanish Constitution, freedom of education is intricately regulated by Article 27, and concurrent laws on education are based on them: the Organic Law on the Status of Educational Systems (LOECE) of June 19, 1980, and the prevailing Organic Law Controlling the Right to Education (LODE) of July 23, 1985.

Since the middle of the nineteenth century, the Catholic Church has maintained an almost monopolistic control over private education in Spain up to the university level. Resistance from the Catholic hierarchy was much greater to LODE than to civil marriage and divorce. Approved as law by the Cortes, the national parliament, the LODE was challenged by the church before the Constitutional Court, which declared on June 27, 1985, that the LODE conformed to the constitution with the exception of an article of secondary importance.

The LODE introduces a coordinated system of public schools, on the one hand, and private schools supported with public funds, on the other. It guarantees freedom of ideology for students and teachers. All private schools have the right "within the framework of the Constitution" to establish "their own character" with respect to their constitutional rights and freedoms. Private schools (religious or not, Catholic or non-Catholic) supported with public funds are accountable to a "participation group" composed of parents, teachers, and, depending upon the circumstances, students who control and manage the school's public funds. This plan increases the state's control over religious schools that the church has not always accepted, provides greater yield from public funds than could be derived from investment in building new educational centers, and guarantees ideological freedom to the school's officials, in addition to the teachers, parents, and students.

These laws of freedom recognized by the Spanish Constitution (primarily in Articles 16 and 27) can sometimes come into conflict, especially with private schools, on issues of ideology or religion. The citizen who believes his ideological and educational freedom has been violated can petition for the protection of his rights before the courts. If the citizen still believes his freedom has been denied, he can appeal again for protection before the Constitutional Court. One appeal of this type was presented by the public prosecutor against a ruling by the Supreme Court declaring null certain ministerial orders handing over public subsidies to private schools, because they violated Article 14 of the constitution. The Constitutional Court rejected his appeal. A teacher in a private religious school presented the other appeal of this type. He said that he was unjustly fired by the school's administration. The court accepted the appeal on the grounds that the dismissal was discriminatory and against the freedom of ideology. The court declared the dismissal void on March 27, 1985, and the school had to rehire the teacher.

There are no confrontations in Spanish society today over a person's having or not having religious beliefs. The relations between the state and religions are peaceful, notwithstanding disagreements arising from the Catholic Church's opposition to the divorce law, the LODE, and the law legalizing abortion under specific conditions. Spain's citizens have at their disposal efficient legal means to defend their freedom of ideology before the courts. In sum, one of the most feared ghosts of Spanish society has disappeared.

Language

Although Spain has a diversity of languages, one language is spoken by nearly all the citizens. Castilian is considered "the official Spanish language of the State" (Article 3.1 of the Spanish Constitution). Public measures have reinforced the growing predominance of Castilian over the centuries, at the expense of Basque and Gallego under the Crown of Castile. Concomitantly, with the Decrees of the New Plan (1707–1716) under Felipe V, the use of Catalan in Catalonia, Valencia, and Mallorca was overtly combated. More recently, Franco reinforced the elimination of Basque, Catalan, and Gallego as spoken languages. He used repressive means more efficiently and seriously before 1960 than later.

Nationalist movements identify emotionally with languages and seek to recover and extend their use. This is especially true in Catalonia, where writers and singers have succeeded in demonstrating not only that their language is alive but that it is valued as a cultural instrument. Basque linguists, associated with an active part of the Basque Nationalist Party (PNV), have set out to unify the Basque language and to show Basque cultural and scientific aptitude through their own active cultural centers. Freedom to change one's language, evident only during the latter part of Franco's regime, increased during the transition to democracy. It is evidenced in some of the "Estatutos de las Comunidades Autonomas" (Statutes of the Autonomous Communities) of Catalonia, Valencia, and Baleares (Catalan is spoken in these three regions), of the Basque Country and Navarra (Basque is spoken in both), and of Galicia.

The language issue is an important political problem, not only because of its emotional importance, but because of the various ways it is presented in each region. Catalan, for example, is uniformly diffused through all of Catalonia, but immigrants (from Andalusia, Murcia, and Castile), who make up almost half of the population, speak only Castilian; in Valencia, they speak Catalan in some areas but not in others; in the Basque Country, probably fewer than 800,000 people speak Basque, few read and write it, and only Navarra has Basque-speaking zones. Given this heterogeneity of language, the constitution cannot give detailed solutions for each region's problem. One solution, however, was adopted: the "co-officiality of languages."

Article 3 establishes Castilian as the official language throughout the state; all Spaniards have "the duty to know it and the right to use it." But Article 3.2 states that "the other languages of Spain shall also be official in the self-governing communities in accordance with their statutes." This radical change of political attitude toward language pluralism becomes evident in the last paragraph of this article: "the wealth of the different language variations in Spain is a cultural heritage which shall be the object of special respect and protection." Spain's language diversity, therefore, is no longer viewed as something negative that must be eradicated, but a cultural richness to be protected.

Although each region has its own language characteristics, the statutes of the six communities (the Basque Country, Navarra, Galicia, Catalonia, Valencia, and the Balearic Islands) agree on the following: (1) Castilian shall be official in all the communities; Basque in the Basque Country and Navarra; Gallego in Galicia; and Catalan in the other three regions. The Statute of Valencia, however, denominates Valenciano as the official language (a language scientifically established as a branch of Catalan). There is a certain emotional resistance to the official recognition of the latter in some political sectors of Valencia, which are inclined to reject whatever relationship Valencia may have with Catalonia. (2) No one may be discriminated against because of language. (3) A future law (one within each community) will regulate the standardization of the official use of language and of the teaching of any language that is not Castilian. Navarra's statutory law and the Statute of Valencia recognize the disproportionate use of Basque and Valenciano within their regions and therefore foresee a different treatment of their co-officiality.

Until now, Navarra has not initiated any legislation concerning Basque. The government of the Balearic Islands, however, presented a legal proposal to its parliament on April 1, 1985, to standardize the language, and other parliaments have approved standard language laws: in the Basque Country on November 24, 1982; in Catalonia on

April 18, 1983; in Galicia on June 15, 1983; and in Valencia on November 23, 1983.

These four laws regulate the following: the use of Basque, Gallego, or Catalan in the administration as well as the courts of justice; the right of children to receive teaching in their maternal language, whether Castilian or another official language; the use of a non-Castilian language for social communication; and the promotion of each community's own language by public authorities. The Valencian law regarding the use and teaching of Valenciano enumerates specifically the territories that are predominantly Valenciano-speaking and Castilian-speaking for the purpose of implementing their own laws. Generally the four laws contain provisional means of imposing its ordinances gradually, although with different thoroughness.

Can the language problem be considered solved? Though not fully resolving the problem, the law contributes to the improvement and pacification of the issue in a majority of the cases. The three ways the constitution deals with the language problem seem politically feasible: the respective statutes; the laws to standardize language use, including a variety of rational and adequate means; and the combination of general and specific precepts for each community. If these rules are applied prudently, moderately, and gradually over a long period, the linguistic problem will not have been resolved but directed and pacified, a significant accomplishment. Bilingualism appears to be gaining acceptance without serious tensions. The laws of the communities are enacted in two languages, and the official papers are published in two languages. Newspapers and literature, published in Catalan, are increasingly accepted as a normal and culturally positive thing, even by those who do not know the language, but this is less true of Gallego and even less of Basque. Radio and television programs are broadcast in Gallego and Catalan, and communities spread knowledge of their languages by teaching in them and about them.

There are no doubt problems, difficulties, and even mutual distrust. The constitutionality of three of the autonomy laws to standardize language (mainly in the Basque Country but also in Catalonia and Galicia) has been challenged by the national government before the Constitutional Court. If the public authorities of the affected communities try to defend their own languages, the national government will monitor their actions closely so that they do not challenge Castilian as the common Spanish language and the official language of the state. Castilian is not only a means of national cohesion but also an important cultural link to many countries in South America.

Nonetheless, the laws of language standardization are applied in each community. Perhaps the most delicate aspects pertain to teaching the language and to the prestige attached to knowing the official language of a community as an advantage to enter public service. Despite the problems, however, Spanish society seems to have recognized its language plurality, to have provided adequate judicial and political formulas and means to deal with it, and, above all, to be determined to resolve these problems peacefully, without altering the coexistence among those who speak languages different from the national one.

Nationalities

The most serious problem in democratic Spain is undoubtedly how to allow for the existence of autonomous governments of nationalities and regions without upsetting national unity. Inherited from previous regimes, it has deep roots in the historical composition of the Spanish nation. The difficulty of maintaining that equilibrium between the nation and nationalities becomes exacerbated by the terrorist activity of the Basque organization, ETA (Basque Homeland and Freedom), in the Basque Country. This adds to the complexity of the problem and spreads it over the entire Spanish political scene. Terrorism tempts the government to respond with force to counteract violence and provokes emotional reactions in the rest of the Spanish population against the Basque people in general (which is not always prudent or just). Obviously, the Basque and Catalan nationalities, and to a lesser degree the Gallegos, are committed to the defense of their nationalities and respective languages. Although these subjects are dealt with separately here, they should not be dissociated.

I agree with the fundamental lines of argument and almost all the assertions in Professor Linz's paper on the process of increasing the number of self-governing communities in Spain. Autonomy was at first intended only for Catalonia, the Basque Country, Galicia, and Navarra; afterward it was extended to thirteen other territories, for a total of seventeen Comunidades Autónomas. I also agree with his analysis of the Estado de las Autonomías. The following observations are, however, important.

1. The "autonomy map" was constructed mainly by the initiatives of Spain's nationalities and regions and was foreshadowed in the Spanish Constitution. In addition, each Comunidad Autónoma assumed more power in its own constitutional processes. But this method includes mechanisms for institutional correction and normative limits, all of which work to guarantee a minimum level of homogeneity among the communities, to provide fundamental rights

and common liberties to all citizens regardless of the community in which they reside (Articles 139.1 and 149.4 of the Spanish Constitution), and to ensure the primacy of the political integration of Spain given the movement toward regional autonomy. The Crown and the Constitutional Court also play a role as integrative factors in Spain. This role is established not only by certain rules (Articles 56.1 and 56.2 of the constitution, regarding the king; Articles 159 and 161 of the constitution; and Article 1.28 of the Organic Law of the Constitutional Court, regarding the Constitutional Court), but also by political reality, which reflects the unanimous acceptance of both the Crown and the Constitutional Court.

2. An important and complex factor is the tension among the Comunidades Autónomas. At times, problems arise among the people of adjacent communities, like Catalonia and Valencia, because of the ways the languages spoken in them are determined. The Constitutional Court has also heard two provinces, León and Segovia, which wanted to separate from Castile-León and establish their own communities. The court rejected the claim of the provinces in its rulings of September 29 and November 9, 1983. Perhaps the most profound and ambivalent tension concerns the existence of both Navarra and the Basque Country. The constitution (Provisional Ordinance 4a) anticipated the possible incorporation of Navarra into the Basque Country, provided that it was allowed in the autonomy statute of the Basque Country and, although attenuated, in the Statutory Law of Navarra (Article 70 of Additional Ordinance 2a).

The desire to include Navarra in the Basque Country is continually voiced by the Basque Nationalist Party and by radical Basque nationalists. They cite laws to try to make this integration possible through constitutional means. The first step in that initiative, however, would have to be taken by the parliament of Navarra. Although the majority of the people in Navarra appear not to support their incorporation into the Basque Country, their opinion does not discourage Basque nationalists. The official shield of the Basque Country is divided into four quarters, containing the emblems of Guipuzcoa, Vizcaya, Alava, and Navarra. When the community of Navarra contended before the Constitutional Court that its jurisdiction was in conflict with that of the Basque Country, the court's decision favored Navarra. Although it did not want to prejudice the community's possible future incorporation, the court stated that such integration had not yet taken place and that no entity except Navarra itself had the right to use and dispose of Navarra's symbol of identity. This ruling has been respected.

3. The Spanish electoral law provides that the parties in any

community (nationalist parties) may be represented by their deputies or senators in the Spanish parliament (Cortes Generales) if elected in general elections in their provincial districts. The law does not require a minimum of votes measured in proportion to the total electorate. This is an integrating factor, bringing the voice of regional parties to parliament. Today the primary Basque Nationalist Party (PNV) and the two most important parties in Catalonia (Convergencia i Unio and Esquerra Republicana) have deputies in Congress.

In general elections, the nationalist parties conflict with the majority party (Popular Alliance in Galicia) or popular minority parties (Socialist Workers' Party, or PSOE, in the Basque Country and PSC in Catalonia) in their communities because of their nationalism (Basque Country, Catalonia, Galicia). The regional elections of the Basque Country and Catalonia are, however, won by the nationalist parties (PNV and Convergencia i Unio, respectively). This situation generates a confrontational relationship between each of these communities and the central organs of the state. Sometimes the political tension rises dangerously, as in 1984 in Catalonia when the Attorney General of the state presented a complaint before the courts against the Banca Catalana. On another occasion in the Basque Country, the PSOE and PNV proposed a legislative plan involving both parties in a rapprochement.

4. Deep problems that underlie circumstantial situations episodically increase or decrease tensions. In Basque Country, ETA's terrorism creates tension intermittently, despite some success by the government in opposing it and trying to isolate ETA there. Former ETA members who have not been accused of life-threatening offenses and who renounce violence have been reintegrated into society, and cooperation has been gained in returning ETA fugitives from France. The primary problem in Catalonia is the budget for the provinces and the services transferred from the state to the community. A law of September 22, 1980, imposed a financial order on the Comunidades Autónomas, based on previous decrees. The first and second additional ordinances of that law, the Organic Law for the Financing of the Comunidades Autónomas (LOFCA), however, excluded the traditional system of privileges (fueros) for the Basque Country and Navarra. They demanded an increase in public spending, but the government has proposed to reduce the public deficit by cutting back on public expenditures in the communities and municipalities. Catalonia considers the budget system prejudiced against it and may want to obtain a flat-rate economic system similar to that of Navarra or the Basque Country. This belief can lead to feelings that the rest of the communities are unjust. Finally, there is a common underlying dilemma: Are all the Comunidades Autónomas equal or must prefer-

ences be granted to those with the greatest political weight given their history, language, and particular problems?

5. Leaving aside its political character and its undeniable importance to the monarchy, the Constitutional Court serves as an instrument of pacification by resolving the discord between the central organs of the state and the Comunidades Autónomas. A third of the verdicts of the court pertain to this problem area. Rulings with important political dimensions include those concerning the Organic Law for the Coordination for the Proceso Autonómico (LOAPA), the shield of Navarra, and the laws normalizing language.

Many different rulings resolve conflicts of authority between the central government and the autonomous public authorities, all of which are disputed and therefore subject to verdicts of the Constitutional Court. These disputes concern matters as diverse as school hours, the extraction of coral, health standards for food, public funding of the Cajas de Ahorros (savings accounts), tests for tour guides, reindustrialization, central control of highway transportation, public servants in city halls, registering property, varieties of fish, hydroelectric centers, and foreign publicity for tourism. The state's instruments of authority, previously uniform and powerful, are now distributed through the constitution and the statutes among the central bodies and seventeen communities. Perhaps through the solution of these difficult problems the current transformation of the state will be perceived clearly. With few exceptions, the rulings of the Constitutional Court have been immediately respected and implemented by all public authorities and have produced harmony between contending parties, cooled down tensions, and contributed to the construction of the Estado de las Autonomías.

Discussion

ROBERT GOLDWIN: In our discussion of Belgium, we had the example of a unitary, centralized state trying to move to some form of federalism. As Mr. De Bandt pointed out, it is an extremely difficult, perhaps impossible, task. Now we have the example of Spain, a centralized, unitary state, moving to a form called the state of autonomies. My question is, Why are the prospects more favorable in the case of Spain?

JUAN LINZ: When Franco died, the Spanish political system faced multiple challenges that had to be resolved. One of the most complex issues was regional or peripheral nationalism, as opposed to the Spanish state conceived as a unitary, centralist, Jacobin national state. Most Spaniards did not understand that problem. They were suddenly critical of administrative dysfunctions of the centralized state, but that was very different from the issue of the autonomists in the periphery. Why should such a challenge to the idea of a nation-state be so successful?

The Franco heirs who remained in power during the initial phase of the transition—and later Prime Minister Suárez, the first parliamentary prime minister of the new democracy—were not in a strong position to oppose certain trends that existed in the society. The Spanish Socialist party and the Spanish left, which had not been particularly favorable to the autonomies even during the republic, in this moment were carried away into an ultra-autonomist sentiment. In fact, in the congress of the Socialist party in December 1976, a resolution calling for the right of nationalities to self-determination was approved. Nobody, I think, knew exactly what self-determination meant, but it reflected the mood of the times.

To defend the unity of the state was, in a sense, to defend Francoism. The symbols of the Spanish state, like the flag, were rejected or doubted by the left. Only the Communist party, immediately after its legalization, suddenly accepted the Spanish flag and put it in a prominent place—something the Socialists did not do at that time. In this context of the left's rejection of everything that could be identified with Francoism, a large segment of the society that

315

supported the left was ready to accept this transformation of the autonomies. On the other side, the people in power were eager to neutralize as many conflicts as possible in the transition period. That is why they allowed the development of what were called the pre-autonomies, which in a sense prefigured the autonomy system that existed all over the country after the Constitution was approved.

These events were linked to the bringing back of Tarradellas, who was the last legal heir to the leadership of the republican autonomous government of Catalonia that had existed during the Spanish Republic under the 1931 Constitution. Tarradellas was a good, able Catalan politician, and, in a sense, he neutralized the danger of nationalist hostility to the Spanish state by first going to Madrid and meeting with the king and Suárez, thus legitimating the transition process from the Catalan perspective.

There was also Basque terrorism; the rapid construction of the autonomies, it was hoped, would finish terrorism, and so this was also an important element in facilitating the rapid acceptance of change.

On the other side, we have to look at the structural factors. First, Madrid is far away from the peripheral areas. The people in Madrid are not affected as much as Brussels is affected by the division of Belgium. Madrid is still the core of Spanish identity and the Spanish state for most Spaniards. To the extent that its political elite agreed to the autonomy changes, the rest of the society was ready to accept such change—especially because these changes seemed positive compared with the Franco period. The central government simply did not want more conflicts than necessary with the periphery. This mixture of structural and historical circumstances facilitated change.

JAVIER VALLE-RIESTRA: I lived in Spain for seven years as a political refugee, from 1969 until 1976. The downfall of the Franco dictatorship coincided with the fall of the dictatorship in Peru, and at that time I returned to my country, where I was a representative and am now a senator. Therefore, I have not lived through the constitutionalization process or through the construction of the state of the autonomies in Spain. Nevertheless, I have a strong sympathy with the wish to build a permanent, and not a transitory, democracy for Spain.

I prefer constitutions as statutes of human rights, rather than the sort of thing that was tried by Spanish politicians after the death of Francisco Franco. What was constructed in the 1978 Constitution is somewhat artificial, more the work of the political elite than of the Spanish people. The Spanish people did not have real leanings toward autonomy. The Basque problem arose only because of the fanatical minority that places itself above the rule of law. As Mr. Valiente says, only 800,000 people actually speak the Basque language, and only a minority of those 800,000 are able to read and write the language. In the French Basque country on the other side of the Pyrenees, the problem of autonomy and chauvinism disappears altogether. Young people over there do not want to speak Basque at all, thus showing that this is an induced problem.

Aside from the Basque problem then and to some extent the Catalonian problem, which the Constitution did, of course, have to recognize, the word nationalities in the Constitution is actually a euphemism. This ambiguous term nationalities leads some regions to claim that they are nations. This is happening in Valencia, and the community around Madrid also has pretentions to autonomy. These groups have national anthems and their own flags; I wonder, then, if the second chapter of this history, which started as a dramatic one, will not end as a comedy.

I am deeply disturbed by the second article of the Spanish Constitution, which reads as follows: "The Constitution is based on the indissoluble unity of the Spanish nation, which is the common and undividable nation of all Spaniards, and recognizes and guarantees the right to autonomy of the nationalities and regions that make it up." The Constitution of the 1931 republic simply said that the republic constituted an integral state that was "compatible with" the autonomy of municipalities and regions. That is to say, the statutes of 1931, which were put together by a number of brilliant men, did not use the type of childish language that is used today.

Nationalities "die" when they no longer have a reason for existing within a particular environment, and they survive as peoples. Only when peoples achieve a historical awareness do they become nations. The nationalities of Spain do not have a destiny within Europe. The autonomous community of Madrid, for instance, has no destiny within Europe or within the Spanish peninsula. So why have these nationalities been constructed? Why have they been constituted?

The Spanish nation is actually a cosmic and critical entity with a long and noble history. Its experience encompasses the reconquest of Spain, the discovery and conquest of the Americas, which was due to Spanish prowess; the struggle for independence in the face of Napoleonic invasion; the disasters of 1898; the fall of Alfonso XIII; the civil war, during which 1 million people died; and Franco. If during the course of these events over five centuries, a genuine nation has not been established, then I do not know what a nation is.

We have to bear all this history in mind, as well as the will for cohesiveness of the Spanish people, the will for united destiny.

Within Europe, Spain offers the least diversity. It has a geographical unity that can be claimed by few other European countries. Other than the temporary union with Portugal, Spain has maintained its geographical physiognomy much more than any other imperial or nonimperial entity in Europe.

Spain has racial unity. A Spaniard is recognizable on the street, whereas Canadians, Americans, or English are not as such. Racially speaking, there are few minorities in Spain. The number of blacks and Jews is so small that they could not in any way be considered a minority. As for religion, even Masonry was forbidden. The Catholic religion provides unity. Although Spaniards may have become somewhat agnostic, they are still formally Catholics.

When I read the statute on the autonomies, I feel torn asunder, because the nation has been torn apart to set up these different states. The part of the Constitution regulating the autonomies resembles the charters of some municipalities or local governments, but in no way does it appear to be a statute of a state or of a pseudostate.

What is the mission of the autonomous community, according to Article 148 of the Spanish Constitution? It includes organization of a self-governing institution, the alteration of municipal boundaries, the ordering of housing and urban territory, public works of interest to the community, and administration of municipal transport, tramways, sports stadiums, forestry projects, environmental projects, internal affairs, arts and crafts, museums, libraries, and social aid. Throughout the rest of the world these tasks are relevant only to municipal councils.

Rather than embarking on the autonomy process, the better thing would have been to decentralize the country on the basis of the municipality, which has historical power in Spain. In Spain the municipality precedes the state: it was the municipal power that actually conquered the Americas. During the Spanish war of independence, who rose in the face of the French invaders? It was the mayor of a small village near Madrid who declared the war on Napoleon. In the election of 1930, Madrid, Seville, and Barcelona voted against the king, forcing him to leave power.

The concept of municipality should have received the support of the Constitution. I am concerned to see that after 500 years of unity the autonomy movement may enable local imperialism. For example, Catalonia can require all officeholders to speak the Catalan language, thereby creating a hegemony based on language—and a language of noncommunication, an archaic language, at that. What we should seek instead is the universality of the Spanish people, which is in the

Spanish language. I sincerely believe that those elements of the statute of Catalonia are a danger for Spanish unity.

Perhaps the masses will save the situation. The impoverished masses of Andalusia and other provinces who go to the more developed, industrialized areas such as Catalonia to seek work will maintain the Spanish language, because they will not be assimilated. They are very powerful minorities who will be working in the local factories.

Those are my main criticisms of this fiction of autonomies and of this split-up, so dangerous for the destiny of Spain. This Constitution, which is the work of minorities and of intellectuals, should be rectified in the future. Reality will, after the initial rehearsal, oblige the country to go back toward a unitary but decentralized Spain.

HOWARD PENNIMAN: I am impressed by Professor Linz's statement that if a nation makes grants of political rights or political privileges in a period of weakness, those privileges will persist, and worse, they will multiply and spread throughout the country. In this case, I believe, seventeen divisions have grown out of grants only to the Basque region and to Catalonia. We in the United States had such an experience, which was considerably worse than Spain's. I do not know whether it was born of weakness so much as a desire to have a unified country two centuries ago, but we were justifiably and necessarily cautious in our Constitution in what we said about the question of slavery. We needed the thirteen states, not just half of the thirteen, to make a country. But because of this concession in a time of weakness, seven decades later we were faced with a civil war. And though that civil war solved the problem of slavery in one sense, it also left us with continuing problems, which lasted until at least a decade or two ago.

The problem in Spain is, as Professor Linz suggests, a great deal less dangerous than the one that the United States faced in the 1860s. Spain has no areas that can really be called separate and distinct regions with a claim to independence or autonomy from the government. It seems to me that one of the major advantages that Spain has at the moment, and is likely to continue to have, is that its parties, and particularly the Socialist Workers party of Spain (PSOE), draw strength not merely from Madrid or from isolated areas of Spain, but ultimately from the country as a whole. As a party with strength throughout Spain, it was able not only to come to power, but to rule with the moderation it has exhibited since 1982.

Therefore in spite of the problems that may have been created by the period of weakness at the time of the writing of the Constitution and the agreements that were made offstage, so to speak, I believe we are unlikely to continue to see serious problems save, perhaps, for the problems in the Basque region and, to a lesser extent, in Catalonia. Even in these cases, as, again, Professor Linz says, the Spanish language is spoken—a language that helps draw them to the larger entity. Although problems are unlikely to disappear altogether, those relating to language or to the autonomous states will probably remain at a minimum.

JOSEPH CROPSEY: One of the things that everyone has emphasized is that a group that can be identified or recognized as a minority in the politically relevant sense, however strong its feelings about itself, has no inclination to join some other national entity. The German speakers of Switzerland, for example, do not aspire to become Germans or Austrians. And the case was made with regard to Spain as well, that however strong the feelings about autonomy, nobody wants to change citizenship. A kind of centripetal tendency is evident in all of these nations where the problem of diversity has been recognized. I asked myself upon what grounds one could understand this impulse to unity, and I would recommend several possible answers for our consideration.

First, going back to the beginnings of reflection on political society, there is a hypothesis that expresses itself in the formula, "the natural sociality of man." Perhaps more modestly put, human beings tend to seek one another out and to find their well-being, their happiness, their prosperity in one another's company.

More than once, however, throughout the course of our speculations and ruminations, something has come to light that could be called historical conditioning. That is, those who are in the technical sense citizens of Belgium, for instance, or citizens of Spain, find that they are Belgians or Spaniards out of a kind of mindlessness. And they remain Belgians or Spaniards because they have always been Belgians or Spaniards, as were their forefathers. They have what could be called a conventional horizon, a boundary to their life that is not provided by nature. It does not grow out of natural sociality but out of the convention of history.

These two explanations are not necessarily incompatible, but they certainly differ. And if they were to be made compatible it would have to be on terms such as that the conventionality of the horizon of human beings exists within a matrix or a framework of nature, as if the two collaborate—the natural tendency and the evolution of a conventional horizon.

The notion of a conventional horizon is extremely grave. If it is taken seriously, it might prove tantamount to the proposition that human beings really have only a conventional or a political horizon, and that for every human being, the world is constituted by the constitution, or by the regime. In other words, this is the way we live, and it is the way we live because nature—however social it might make us in our disposition—does not provide us with the details of life. If it is in any respect true that Spaniards wish to remain Spaniards despite all the other possible forms of allegiance, then it appears that the horizon the political entity creates for human beings effectively becomes the sovereign fact of social life.

That is an interesting idea. If one were to say that the natural horizon of life is supreme in our affairs, then one would say that we are under the influence of something bigger than us all, as nature is. But if the political or conventional horizon is the decisive one for us, then something that is, to some degree, a matter of human production or of human cultivation, is decisive for the way in which we find our earthly salvation.

To go a step further: For better or worse, the same tendency to huddle, to stick together, that causes Swiss to desire to remain Swiss and so forth, is the same tendency that leads to the impulse for separation. The same thing that leads to unity on one level prompts a kind of disunity on another level. For another reason then, we cannot simply depend on the natural centripetal tendency that arises out of the natural sociality of man, because that tendency produces not only Swiss but also German-speaking Swiss, and so forth.

Spain did not evolve naturally. No modern country did. It might be that no country has ever evolved naturally. By naturally, I mean something like what was described as the natural growth of the *polis* or of the body politic in Book I of Aristotle's *Politics*. But no living city-state actually grew that way. The task therefore is for human beings to make out of their own resources that which nature does not provide them. Because the *polis* or the city does not grow naturally, it has to be constituted, and that is why we speak of constitutions. The constitution is the act by which the one is made of the many. It is an act of art by which the natural category of one out of many is brought into effect.

Although one says that the unity of the Swiss, the Belgians, the Canadians, and certainly the Spaniards is prompted by nature, one is also saying that it cannot be effected by nature; it must be produced by a human act. Is there some ground on which it is possible for us human beings to persuade ourselves that we ought to produce such a framework or such a horizon? I come back to the point I made earlier.

It is perhaps absolutely indispensable to the health of human beings that they have a solid horizon, that they have an identifiable, clear horizon to their lives.

Some sign of the truth of this can be seen if one imagines the state of mind of the citizens of an absolutely defeated country. What must it have been like to be a subject of the Japanese emperor in 1945 at the time that the Constitution of Japan was for all visible purposes destroyed? The framework of life must have looked to the Japanese as if it had dissolved. Life itself must have seemed absolutely threatened. It is for this reason that I emphasize the fact that the constitution of the state is, to some extent, also the constitution of the terms of human life.

To the extent that what we do when we constitute the regime is to constitute the conditions of human life, we are confirming to ourselves that the conditions of life are artificial. We are saying that the political task is a task of artifice. I could bore you to the limit of distraction by trying to confirm this in writings from Hobbes to Hegel, all of whom discussed the respect in which it was necessary to constitute political life in the teeth of nature. But I will not.

The reason that I mention this is that repeatedly—and in my opinion, absolutely validly—Mr. Goldwin has brought to our attention the question of the relationship between history and character, or history and ethos. This came strongly to our view in the interesting discussions about Switzerland, and how impossible it would be to imagine the transportation of the Swiss regime to a population that lacked those characteristics of spirit—what used to be called "virtues." I do not blush to use the word, because there is warrant for using it in, for example, Rousseau, who would tell you that democracy is the regime that makes the heaviest demands on the virtue of the population. If people are not equipped for autonomy, autonomy becomes either a travesty or a calamity.

That raises the question of the relation between character or virtue on the one hand and the regime on the other. As we think about what has gone on among us, we come closer and closer to the apparently illogical but nevertheless useful proposition that history produces character and character produces history. The way in which those two mutually supporting events occur is again excellently illustrated in the example of Switzerland. But I think it is illustrated in all human examples. I would like to accept that proposition and at the same time try to go one step beyond it. There is something unsatisfactory about this merely empirical proposition that history generates character and character in turn generates history. By the proposition that history generates character, I think one could mean, for our present purpose more exactly, that the constitution itself, the political order, tends to generate character. The political order is a teacher of virtue and is one of the reasons for the existence of political life.

But it must be clear to everybody that there is some limit to the efficacy of the political order in generating virtue. There are things that human beings subject to the political order are not prepared for or not equipped to receive. There is a training they cannot benefit from, and I think that is why the Swiss regime cannot profitably be exported with perfect success, nor can any other. I therefore propose the possibility of a third factor besides history or the political order on the one hand and character or virtue on the other. I would propose that there is some source from which the political order itself gets its inspiration. And that source is thought. That subject was raised earlier in discussions about reason and choice and whether mere experience will suffice or whether choice—that is, reason—is necessary.

I reflected on that and wondered what sort of reason could bring about a resolution of the relation between regime and character. And it occurred to me that there is such a thing as reason on a very high level. There is such a thing as reason about political affairs, about politics. Reason about politics at the highest level is called political philosophy. I was struck as I read from Professor Linz's paper, and also from the others, how far it is possible to go without referring to the figures who stand behind the formulations expressed in the constitutions.

How far is it possible to go on talking about the U.S. Constitution without invoking, for example, Montesquieu, without invoking Locke, and without invoking Hobbes? It is possible to go very far in discussion of the Spanish Constitution without invoking similar such political theorists.

But theoreticians and philosophers lie in the background of these things. They have been known as the teachers of the legislators. I would suggest that the prime movers, the movers who move the minds of legislators and eventually the minds of the people under the influence of the legislators, may be those remote figures who, in a certain way, stand in the same relation to political life as theoreticians of economics stand in relation to economics, as described by Keynes. He noted that people are absolutely unaware of those dead and obscure people whose influence is actually operating in their present day lives.

Otherwise, I have great difficulty understanding such things as the transformation of the Spanish regime since 1492, when the Jews were expelled: in the various constitutions of the middle of the nineteenth century, petitions were made repeatedly by the international community and the international Jewish community to lift the ban of expulsion on Jews and to permit the descendants of old citizens of Spain to return; then, in 1871 or so, notwithstanding the official pronouncements of the Constitution, the regime decided to be benign and allowed Jews and others who re-entered Spain to practice their religion in a modest way without being expelled again. I also have difficulty understanding the transition from 1870 until the period of the present Spanish Constitution, where autonomy is, if anything, carried to an unreasonable excess. I have trouble understanding these convulsions in the national ethos and must wonder if something arrived on the scene that went beyond the mere political horizon itself. Something must have liberalized the Spanish mind so that within the confines of those centripetal forces, there arose such a recognition of the centrifugal ones as could be explained only by the intrusion on the minds of men of some alien thought. I do not mean alien to Spain; I mean alien to the prevailing conceptions.

This is my reflection, based on things that have been said about all of the constitutions including the present one, but especially on what has been said with such learning, such reflection, and such originality about the Spanish Constitution.

MR. LINZ: I find myself in a somewhat difficult position, because my paper is based on the assumption of the multinational, multilingual character of Spain and a history of Spanish peripheral nationalism, which goes back to the nineteenth century. For instance, when we asked in a 1979 survey how people in the Basque country felt, we discovered that the desire for independence was very or fairly great in 35 percent of the population; fairly small in 15 percent; very small or none in 39 percent; and 6 percent had no opinion. When 35 percent of the Basque population say that they have a desire for independence and identify as more Basque than Spanish, that has to be taken into account in Spanish politics.

We looked at attitudes toward terrorism in 1982. Among those whose parents were born in Euskadi even after terrorism had shown its worst and ugliest face, 15 percent of the population still said the terrorists were patriots; 41 percent considered them idealists; 35 percent, manipulated; 28 percent, madmen; and only 25 percent described them as common criminals. Those numbers reveal some real reasons behind the multinational problem in Spain.

Certainly the nationalist sentiment in the Basque country could not be ignored, and it particularly could not be ignored because it was in the streets in mass demonstrations, in general strikes, in violence, and in support for a terrorist movement. Under Franco, that movement killed sixty-four people; in the transition year, seventeen; in the year that the constitution was being debated, sixty-five; in the year in which autonomy was granted, seventy-eight; and the year after autonomy, ninety-six.

It is certainly true that most of the rest of the Spaniards feel Spanish and nothing else. In that sense I agree fully that there is a considerable element of artificiality in the autonomy of Madrid, which is my home, and yet with which I feel no identification. But if we look at the distribution of attitudes on the complicated question of autonomy and centralism in the Basque country in 1978, centralism had the support of 18 percent of the population; autonomy, 45 percent; a more advanced form of autonomy, 17 percent; and independence, 15 percent. (Five percent had no opinion.) In Catalonia, autonomy was supported by 44 percent.

The reasons to extend the autonomy process to the rest of Spain are complex. On the one hand, it makes the privilege of the Basque country and Catalonia less of a privilege, and that has its political functions. The Basques are not federalists; their leadership is essentially nationalist and independent, although it accepts as a matter of practicality the existence of the Spanish state.

But this kind of federalization solution was on the one side a response to the problem of the Basque country and Catalonia, making it less apparent that we were breaking up Spain on the basis of nationalisms and autonomy of nationalities. They would not accept the word regions, and any kind of model of decentralization would have been absolutely unacceptable to Catalans and Basques. And on the other side, it obviously created a whole series of vested interests, particularly on the part of political parties, which thought that they could have the majority in some regions rather than others.

If we do not take that context into account, we cannot understand the progression of events. The referendum on the autonomy statute in the Basque country was barely passed, because so many Basques were against even that form of autonomy, wanting to go much further. In some ways the Constitution has been legitimated in the Basque country by the acceptance of the autonomy statute, rather than the autonomy statute deriving its legitimacy from the Constitution.

Contrary to the hopes that the concessions of autonomy would slow down the growth of regional nationalisms in the periphery and particularly in the Basque country, with each election the Basque nationalist parties have made more progress because they control more and more of the life of the society. If you want a loan from the savings banks, the savings banks are controlled by one of the Basque parties. If you want to be a professor, you had better be sympathetic to the Basque cause. Slowly the Spanish element, the Spanish bu-reaucracy that was transferred to the region, is opting to leave, and key positions in the judiciary, for instance, are not filled, partly because of the terrorism. There is a process of increasing segregation of two regions from the rest of Spain.

In the case of Catalonia, autonomy is not incompatible at all with the unity of Spain, because the Catalans say as long as they have a Catalan Catalonia within Spain, they can be Spaniards.

Meanwhile, nobody has paid much attention to the problem of mistreatment of immigrant minorities within the autonomies. It is, however, a serious problem. The central government does not defend those minorities for the simple reason that the central government wants the integration of the political system, and the center is far away. It does not affect them to give the Catalans total hegemony in Catalonia, though it certainly affects the immigrants who are in Cata-lonia. Among the problems of a multinational cultural society we perhaps need to see that decentralization, autonomy, federalization, and so on, might very well mean the sacrifice of the rights of the minorities within the minority. By solving the problem (that the Franco regime had exacerbated) of oppression of Catalan and Basque minorities within Spain, we are creating a problem of oppression of other minorities.

7
Unity and Diversity:
The Constitution of Malaysia

Visu Sinnadurai

Present-day Malaysia is a federation of thirteen states: Penang and Malacca (formerly called the Straits Settlements); Perak, Selangor, Negri Sembilan, and Pahang (formerly called the Federated Malay States); Kedah, Kelantan, Trengganu, Johor, and Perlis (formerly called the Unfederated Malay States); and Sabah and Sarawak (formerly called the Borneo States). The population of Malaysia, which is about 14 million, comprises three major races: Malays (and natives of Sabah and Sarawak), Chinese, and Indians.

Before gaining independence in 1957, Malaysia was under British rule, although some of the states had been at one time or another under Portuguese or Dutch rule. Before the British came to Malaysia, no uniform system of law was applicable throughout the country. Although Malay legal codes had existed since the fifteenth century, Malay customary law, mixed with Hindu law and Muslim law, was also in existence. These customary laws, however, were confined mainly to the Malays. Justice was administered by the sultans and their chiefs in a rather arbitrary manner.

When the British arrived, they organized a more systematic legal framework, because they saw a well-ordered judicial system as a necessary condition for open economic development and for large capital inflow into a country. In 1826, when the Straits Settlements was founded, English law was formally introduced throughout the settlements. As for the other Malay states, the sultans and rajas accepted British residents as "advisers" in all matters except Malay customs and religion. With the founding of the Federated Malay States in 1896, the British introduced English law and established a court system. The laws were soon extended to the Unfederated Malay States.

At this time the British also encouraged large-scale immigration of Chinese and Indian laborers to assist in the economic development of Malaya. The Indian immigrants were largely absorbed as laborers in rubber plantations, railways, public works, and local government. The Chinese, who came from the southeastern provinces of China, worked as laborers in mines and rubber plantations under very harsh conditions. As the Chinese and Indians came with their families, they brought with them their own culture and customs. Malaya, then, could be described as the epitome of a multiracial, multilingual, and multireligious country in which the major races had practically nothing in common. The philosophy, language, culture, religion, social behavior, and mercantile attitudes and practices varied enormously. Their only common element was that (except for the Indians) they had never lived under a European administration before.

Malaysia, of course, has always felt the influence of various religions and races. About the beginning of the Christian era, it came under the sway of Hinduism and Buddhism from India and China. Indian influence spread to the Malay states and affected political and social institutions. Hindu customs affected Malay life and society. Such influence can be seen today in certain customs of the court hierarchy and ceremonies and also in customary marriage rites.

By the fifteenth century, Islam had been brought to Malaysia and spread. Malacca, one of the Malay states, became an Islamic kingdom, and the rise of Islam ended the political control and cultural influences of the Hindu and Buddhist powers.

The Portuguese, the first Europeans to come to Malaysia, occupied Malacca from 1511 to 1641. Malacca then fell into the hands of the Dutch, who after occupying it for 130 years, surrendered it to the British in 1795. The Dutch reoccupied Malacca from 1801 to 1807, until it was finally ceded to the British in 1824. In the meantime, Penang had been ceded to the British in 1786. By 1824 the Straits Settlements was formed, comprising Penang, Malacca, and Singapore.

The Malay states came under British protection under different treaties with the various state rulers. In 1895 Perak, Selangor, Pahang, and Negri Sembilan joined to form the Federated Malay States. The other five states of Kedah, Perlis, Trengganu, Kelantan, and Johor remained outside this federation and were collectively known as the Unfederated Malay States. Each of these five states, however, had a British adviser.

In 1946 Malacca and Penang joined the other nine states, forming the Malayan Union. In 1948 the Federation of Malaya was established, and in August 1957 the Federation of Malaya became an independent sovereign country. In 1963 Singapore, Sarawak, and North Borneo joined the federation, and the new entity was collectively called Malaysia. Singapore separated from Malaysia in 1965, however, and today Malaysia is composed of the original eleven states of the federation together with Sarawak and North Borneo.

Constitutional Background

In 1957 Malaysia (then the Federation of Malaya) became an independent sovereign nation and was admitted as a member of the British Commonwealth.

Before independence, the Federated Malay States were British protectorates. Each of these states had a British resident who was in theory merely an adviser to the sultan (ruler) of the state. Although the Unfederated Malay States had a British adviser, the states remained under the direct control of the sultan of the state. Penang and Malacca were British colonies.

In 1946 the Malayan Union was formed, comprising the nine federated and unfederated Malay states, together with Penang and Malacca. This union was subsequently dissolved, and the Federation of Malaya was set up in 1948 by the 1948 Federation of Malaya Agreement between the British government and the sultans of each of the Malay states. A federal system of government was set up, with each constituent state having its own state constitution.

In 1963 with the signing of the Malaysia Agreement, the states of Sabah, Sarawak, and Singapore joined the federation, and Malaysia was formed. In 1965 Singapore ceased to be a member of the federation and became a fully independent republic within the Commonwealth.

Malaysia has a written constitution. It has a democratic system of government with a constitutional monarch (the Yang di Pertuan Agong), who is the supreme head of the federation. The federal Parliament, which is based on the Westminster model, comprises the House of Representatives (Dewan Rakyat) and the Senate (Dewan Negara). The Constitution of the Federation of Malaysia is the supreme law of the country, and any law which is inconsistent with the Constitution is void. In the tradition of all democratic nations, the doctrine of separation of powers is provided for: the legislative powers are vested in Parliament, the executive powers in the cabinet, and the judicial process in an independent judiciary (which is a source of great pride to all Malaysians). The ruling political party is the Barisan Nasional, which is a coalition party, generally comprising the three main ethnic-based political parties. In the political elections held since independence, the Barisan Nasional (Alliance) party has been elected successively by more than a two-thirds majority. The opposition is made up of a number of other political parties. Full parliamentary privileges are guaranteed to all members of Parliament.

The Legal System of Malaysia

The Malaysian legal system derives from the English legal system. In many areas, English law continues to play a prominent role in Malaysia. In recent years, however, much legislation passed by the federal Parliament has modified some of the English law. Legislation like the Criminal Procedure Code, the Penal Code, and the Essential (Security Cases) Regulations now govern criminal law and procedure in the country. The National Land Code, based on the Torrens system of registration, governs land tenure, while the Companies Act, based on the Australian Companies Act, governs corporate law. In certain branches of law where no legislation has been enacted by the federal Parliament, English law continues to apply. One such branch of the law is the law of torts. Such application of English law relating to the law of torts and certain other branches of the law is made possible by the provisions of the Civil Law Act. Section 3 of that act provides for the application of English law in Malaysia in cases where there is no specific local legislation on a particular matter. Section 5 of the same act is a specific provision for the application of English law in commercial matters where there is no specific legislation.

As the Malaysian legal system is based on English common law, the courts adhere to the doctrine of precedent. Case law, therefore, is another important source of law in Malaysia.

In a discussion of the laws of Malaysia, the application of Islamic law and customary law should not be overlooked. The application of these laws, however, is limited essentially to matters relating to marriage, inheritance, and succession. Muslim law is not applicable to persons not professing the Muslim faith, nor is it applicable in commercial matters.

Courts in Malaysia are generally classified as the subordinate courts (made up of the penghulu's courts, magistrate's court, or the sessions court), the High Court, and the Supreme Court (formerly the Federal Court). Until recently, final appeals were to the Judicial Committee of the privy council, though technically to the king, who then sought the advice of the Judicial Committee on the matter. Appeals to the Judicial Committee of the privy council on criminal and constitutional matters were abolished in 1979, however, and in 1985 all civil appeals to the privy council were abolished. The final court of appeal is now the newly structured Supreme Court.

The head of the Supreme Court is the lord president, and the head of the High Court is the chief justice. All judicial appointments to the High Court and to the Supreme Court are made by the king on the advice of the prime minister. To ensure the independence of the judiciary, the tenure of all judges is guaranteed by the federal Constitution. A stringent procedure is provided for the removal of judges. Since Malaysian independence, no judge has been removed from office. The Constitution also imposes certain restrictions on discussion in Parliament about the conduct of any judge.

The Constitution and Diversity

The extent to which the Malaysian Constitution deals with the diversity of the population in Malaysia, particularly concerning religion, nationality, language, race, and custom, will be considered here.

Article 8 of the Constitution expressly provides that "all persons are equal before the law and are entitled to equal protection of the law." This article further provides:

> Except as expressly authorised by this Constitution, there shall be no discrimination against citizens on the ground only of religion, race, descent or place of birth in any law or in the appointment to any office or employment under a public authority or in the administration of any law relating to the acquisition, holding or disposition of property or the establishing or carrying on of any trade, business, profession, vocation or employment.

It is important to bear this equality provision of the Constitution in mind when considering the constitutional protection granted to the various communities in Malaysia.

Religion. Article 3(1) of the federal Constitution provides as follows:

> Islam is the religion of the Federation; but other religions may be practised in peace and harmony in any part of the Federation.

Article 11, concerning freedom of religion, declares:

> Every person has the right to profess and practise his religion and, subject to Clause (4), to propagate it. No person shall be compelled to pay any tax the proceeds of which are specially allocated in whole or in part for the purposes of a religion other than his own. Every religious group has the right

(a) to manage its own religious affairs;
(b) to establish and maintain institutions for religious or charitable purposes; and
(c) to acquire and own property and hold and administer it in accordance with law.

State law and, in respect of the Federal Territory, federal law may control or restrict the propagation of any religious doctrine or belief among persons professing the religion of Islam. This article does not authorise any act contrary to any general law relating to public order, public health or morality.

These two provisions in the Constitution may give the impression that Malaysia is an Islamic nation. To understand this implication, however, particularly of Article 3(1), we must understand the circumstances under which this provision was inserted into the Constitution. For this purpose, it is essential to make reference to the *Report of the Federation of Malaya Constitutional Commission* (or the Reid Commission, so named for the chairman of the commission, the Rt. Hon. Lord Reid). This commission was established "to make recommendations for a form of Constitution for a fully self-governing and independent Federation of Malaya within the Commonwealth." In paragraph 169 of the report, the commission pointed out:

We have considered the question whether there should be any statement in the Constitution to the effect that Islam should be the State Religion. There was universal agreement that if such provision were inserted it must be made clear that it would not in any way affect the civil rights of non-Muslims.

There was, however, some difference in opinion among certain members of the commission as to whether a provision should be included in the Constitution declaring that "the religion of Malaysia shall be Islam." Various interested bodies also presented their views to the commission. But it was generally accepted that whatever the wording of the particular provision of the Constitution relating to Islam, the provision should be such so as not to "impose any disability on non-Muslim nationals professing and practicing their own religions and shall not imply that the State is *not* a secular State."[1]

It would appear that Article 3 of the Constitution was introduced in response to the dissenting view expressed by Justice Abdul Hamid of the West Pakistan High Court as a member of the Reid Commission. In pointing out that a provision should be included in the Constitution declaring Islam to be the religion of the federation and that other citizens of the country should not be prevented from practicing their own religion, Justice Hamid said:

> A provision like the one suggested above is innocuous. Not less than fifteen countries of the world have a provision of this type entrenched in their Constitutions. Thailand is an instance in which Buddhism has been enjoined to be the religion of the King who is required by the Constitution to uphold that religion (Constitution of Thailand, Article 7). If in these countries a religion has been declared to be the religion of the State and that declaration has not been found to have caused hardships to anybody, no harm will ensue if such a declaration is included in the Constitution of Malaya. In fact in all the Constitutions of Malayan States a provision of this type already exists. All that is required to be done is to transplant it from the State Constitutions and to embed it in the Federal.[2]

The position in Malaysia with regard to the rights of the minority peoples to practice their own religions may be summarized as follows:

• The Constitution guarantees the right of every citizen to practice his religion "in peace and harmony." This is an absolute right conferred by the Constitution [Article 3(4)].

• Every person also has the right to propagate his or her own religion (Article 11). This right, however, is subject to an exception as provided for in Article 11(4): The propagation of any religion among persons professing the religion of Islam may be restricted by state or federal law.

• No person shall be compelled to pay any tax, the proceeds of which shall be used for any religious purposes other than his own [Article 11(2)].

• The Constitution guarantees, as an absolute right, the right of every religious group to manage its own religious affairs and to establish and maintain institutions for religious or charitable purposes [Article 11(3)(a) and (b)].

• Every religious group has the absolute right to acquire and own property [Article 11(3)(c)]. In so holding and administering the property, however, the religious group must comply with any general law in force dealing with the holding and administration of property [Article 11(3)(c)].

• The Malaysian Constitution also confers the right of establishment of educational institutions by religious groups [Article 12(2)].[3]

• Article 12(3) expressly provides that no person shall be required to receive instruction in or to take part in any ceremony or act of worship of a religion other than his own.

The position of Islam under the Constitution is also relevant to an understanding of the constitutional rights of the minorities to practice their own religions. Islam is the religion of the majority in Malaysia. Article 3, in declaring that Islam is the religion of the federation, implied the following:

• In all state functions and ceremonies the principles of Islam shall be upheld. In compliance with this principle, therefore, the serving of alcohol is prohibited in state functions. In ceremonial functions, Islamic practices are adhered to whenever appropriate.

• In every state where there is a ruler, the ruler continues to hold the position as head of the religion of Islam in that state, and the ruler enjoys "all rights, privileges, prerogatives and powers" as the head of that religion. It necessarily follows that in these states, the state constitution requires the ruler to be a Muslim.

• As mentioned above, the propagation of any religious doctrine or belief among the Muslims may be restricted by law.

• The establishment and maintenance of Islamic institutions and the assistance for providing instruction in the religion of Islam may be provided for by the federation or the state from public funds [Article 12(2)].

Finally, it should be pointed out that by virtue of Article 8(2) of the Constitution there is no discrimination concerning the holding of any office or employment under public authority on the grounds that a person does not profess the Islamic faith. Therefore, in the appointment of the prime minister, ministers of the state, chief ministers, judges, and other senior federal or state posts (except in certain states where the state secretary is required to be of the Malay race and professing the Muslim religion), there is no requirement that such persons profess the Islamic faith.

Race. Article 8(1) of the Constitution provides that all persons are equal before the law and entitled to equal protection of the law. Article 8(2), provides that:

There shall be no discrimination against citizens on the ground only of religion, race, descent or place of birth in any law or in the appointment of any office or employment under a public authority or in the administration of any law relating to the acquisition, holding or disposition of property or the establishing or carrying on of any trade, business, profession, vocation or employment.

This provision against discrimination is not absolute, however. The article provides that this right is subject to other provisions of the Constitution that expressly authorize discrimination. The main exception, so to speak, provided for by the Constitution, allowing discrimination on grounds of race, is Article 153, which, among others, provides as follows:

(1) It shall be the responsibility of the Yang di Pertuan Agong to safeguard the special position of the Malays and natives of any of the States of Sabah and Sarawak and the legitimate interests of other communities in accordance with the provisions of this Article.

(2) Notwithstanding anything in this Constitution, but subject to the provisions of Article 40 and of this Article, the Yang di Pertuan Agong shall exercise his functions under this Constitution and federal law in such manner as may be necessary to safeguard the special position of the Malays and natives of any of the States of Sabah and Sarawak and to ensure the reservation for Malays and natives of any of the States of Sabah and Sarawak of such proportion as he may deem reasonable of positions in the public service (other than the public service of a State) and of scholarships, exhibitions and other similar educational or training privileges or special facilities given or accorded by the Federal Government and, when any permit or license for the operation of any trade or business is required by federal law, then, subject to the provisions of that law and this Article, of such permits and licenses.

This provision of the Constitution has been subject to much controversy, principally caused by the lack of understanding of the scope and intention of this article. It is therefore necessary to understand the background against which this provision was added to the Malaysian Constitution.

It is no doubt true that Article 153, in so granting special privileges to the Malays and the natives of Sabah and Sarawak, appears to create an anomaly regarding the "equality before the law" provision in Article 8(1). It is also difficult to reconcile Article 153 with the basic aspirations of the freedom fighters in the struggle for an independent Malaya (as it was then):

A common nationality was the basis upon which a unified Malayan nation was to be created and that under a democratic form of Government it was inherent that all the citizens of Malaya, irrespective of race, creed or culture, should enjoy certain fundamental rights including equality before the law.[4]

Indeed, the representation made to the Reid Commission by all interested parties was that there should be no discrimination among the various races in Malaysia. The Alliance party, in fact, made the following representation: "In an independent Malaya all nationals should be accorded equal rights, privileges and opportunities and there must not be discrimination on grounds of race and creed."[5]

Their highnesses the Malay rulers also expressed the view that they "look forward to a time not too remote when it will become possible to eliminate communalism as a force in the political and economic life of the country."

Why then was such a provision introduced into the Malaysian Constitution? What is the background of the "special position" of the Malays? The answers to these questions lie in the various arrangements made by the British with the Malay rulers for the conferment of certain rights and privileges to the Malays. These arrangements existed long before Malaysia gained independence from the British, and it appears that they were part of the *quid pro quo* for British administration in the various states. In fact, in the 1948 Federation of Malaya Agreement, there was an express provision that made the British High Commission responsible for safeguarding the special position of the Malays and the legitimate interests of the other communities. There were four main areas in which the special position of the Malays was recognized and safeguarded. One area concerned land that had been specially designated as Malay reservation land, while another concerned quotas for admission to certain sectors of the public services. In this regard, it should be pointed out that:

> Until 1953 admission to the Malayan Civil Service was only open to British subjects of European descent and to Malays but since that date there has been provision for one-fifth of the entrants being selected from other communities. In other services in which a quota exists the rule generally is that not more than one-quarter of new entrants should be non-Malays.[6]

A third area concerned the issuance of licenses and permits for the operation of certain businesses. The main reason for this was that "in the past the Malays have lacked capital and have tended to remain on the land and not to take a large part in business, and that this is one method of encouraging the Malays to take a larger part in business enterprises."[7] The last area concerned scholarships and other forms of educational assistance:

> The reason for this appears to be that in the past higher education of the Malays has tended to fall behind that of the Chinese, partly because the Chinese have been better able to pay for it and partly because it is more difficult to arrange

higher education for Malays in the country than for Chinese in the towns.[8]

It is in the light of these socioeconomic problems faced by the Malays that the Reid Commission itself recommended that the special position of the Malays should be continued for a period of time. As such, the commission made the following recommendation for the incorporation of a provision in the Constitution for the continued safeguard of these rights:

> We are of opinion that in present circumstances it is necessary to continue these preferences. The Malays would be at a serious and unfair disadvantage compared with other communities if they were suddenly withdrawn. But, with the integration of the various communities into a common nationality which we trust will gradually come about, the need for these preferences will gradually disappear. Our recommendations are made on the footing that the Malays should be assured that the present position will continue for a substantial period, but that in due course the present preferences should be reduced and should ultimately cease so that there should then be no discrimination between races or communities.[9]

The Reid Commission itself did stipulate a time limit of fifteen years for the continuance of these privileges.[10] When the *White Paper on the Constitutional Proposals for the Federation of Malaya*[11] was presented as the final proposal, however, a number of changes were made to the recommendations of the Reid Commission Report. One such change concerned the period of review:

> The Commission recommended that their proposal for continuing the present preference should be reviewed after 15 years. This recommendation was given careful consideration but it was not considered necessary to include such a provision in the Constitution. It was considered preferable that, in the interests of the country as a whole, as well as of the Malays themselves, the Yang di Pertuan Agong should cause a review of the revised proposals to be made from time to time.[12]

It should be emphasized that the responsibility of the king under Article 153 is to safeguard not only the special position of the Malays and the natives of Sabah and Sarawak (now referred to collectively as *bumiputras* or "sons of the soil") but also the "legitimate interests of other communities." As there are more positive steps taken or provided for in the Constitution itself for the discharge of the responsibility of the king to safeguard the interests of the *bumiputras*, the constitutional responsibility of the king to safeguard the interests of the other races has not been fully appreciated and as such has often been overlooked. As a result, Article 153 is often misinterpreted to mean that it merely provides for the safeguarding of the privileges of the *bumiputras* alone by the king. As Professor Hickling points out,

> There has been a curious lack of any judicial discussion or interpretation of what is perhaps the most critical article in the Constitution, Article 153. That Article is not, after all, such a generous boon to the *bumiputra* as many suppose: for it seeks, to the best of its intent, to balance the interests of all races in Malaysia in as equitable a manner as conditions may admit.[13]

The Constitution of Malaysia grants equal protection by way of rights to all persons irrespective of race or creed. To safeguard the "special position" of the *bumiputras*, however, Article 153 spells out certain privileges that may be granted to a particular race alone, that is, the *bumiputras*. These privileges are provided for by the Constitution itself, and, as such, in all other matters not covered by the Constitution there can be no discrimination in favor of or against a particular race. The special privileges spelled out by Article 153 of the Constitution in favor of the *bumiputras* concern: (1) positions in the public service; (2) scholarships, exhibitions, and other education and training; (3) permits and licenses for the operation of any trade or business; and (4) entry into educational institutions, including universities.

The granting of these privileges to *bumiputras* is subject to three requirements: first, the king must give general directions (presumably by way of an order) to the relevant authorities concerned to ensure that *bumiputras* obtain these special privileges; second, the king may direct that only a proportion and not all of such privileges be accorded to the *bumiputras*. This would necessarily mean that none of the special privileges spelled out in Article 153 are granted to the *bumiputras* to the exclusion of all other races. Therefore, persons from all races are able to enjoy these benefits, although in different proportions. Third, the king may not, in the exercise of his powers to safeguard the special position of the *bumiputras*, deprive any person of any such privilege that he holds or enjoys, including the holding of a post in the public service, the continuance of a scholarship, or the enjoyment or renewal of a permit or license.

Language. In Malaysia, a pluralistic society, a number of different languages are spoken by the different races. By far, Malay (the national language) is the most widely spoken and used language in the country. Chinese dialects in great variety, however, are used by the vast Chinese community. The other language, Tamil, is used by the Indian community. As in any other multiracial country, the minority races perceive the use of their own language as a means of identifying and maintaining their own communal background. In contrast, the government of the country considers language an instrument of assimilating the various races in the country. Against this background, the Reid Commission had to consider the nature and scope of the provision that was to address this issue in the draft proposal on the federal constitution. The commission pointed out,

> After giving full consideration . . . we have decided to recommend that Malay should be the national language. . . . We do not recommend that any other language should become an official language. This has not been found necessary in the past and we think that it might lead to great inconvenience.[14]

The commission's recommendation that for a period of ten years after independence the use of the English language should be permitted in Parliament, in the legislative assembly of the state, and in courts and that all bills and acts of Parliament should be in English was not accepted. Instead, in the final proposals on the Constitution,[15] these changes in the recommendations of the Reid Commission Report were made:

> First, it is proposed to provide that no person shall be prohibited or prevented from using (otherwise than for official purposes) or from teaching or learning any language. Secondly, it is proposed that the Federal and State Governments shall have the right to preserve and sustain the use and study of the language of any community in the Federation. Thirdly, it is proposed not to accept the recommendation of the Commission that for a period of ten years there should be a limited right to speak in a legislature in a Chinese or Indian language.[16]

Article 152 of the federal Constitution was therefore introduced in the following terms: "The national language shall be the Malay language and shall be in such script as Parliament may by law provide."

For our purposes, the proviso to Article 152(1) and clause 6 are relevant. The proviso reads as follows:

Provided that:
(a) no person shall be prohibited or prevented from using

(otherwise than for official purposes), or from teaching or learning, any other language; and

(b) nothing in this Clause shall prejudice the right of the Federal Government or of any State Government to preserve and sustain the use and study of the language of any other community in the Federation.

Clause 6 to Article 152 reads: "In this Article, 'official purpose' means any purpose of the Government, whether Federal or State, and includes any purpose of a public authority."

For a long time it was thought that by virtue of the proviso, the use of the Chinese and Indian languages was permitted for all purposes (other than for official purposes) including teaching and learning. The federal court, however, in the case of *Merdeka University Berhad* v. *Government of Malaysia*[17] held that the teaching in Chinese, or in any language other than Malay, in a university was prohibited by Article 152. The court held that since every university in Malaysia has to be by law a statutory authority exercising powers vested in it by federal law, it was therefore a public authority.[18] Universities, therefore, being public authorities, had to use the national language, that is, the Malay language, and no other language, for conducting their business. Since the official purpose of the universities was teaching, all teaching had, it followed, to be in Malay.

The federal court, however, in so deciding that all teaching in universities had to be in the national language, did point out that no person should be prohibited or prevented from using the Chinese language (or any other minority language) for nonofficial purposes and that no person should be prohibited or prevented from teaching or learning the Chinese language (or any other language). It was, however, the restrictive interpretation of the word "using" in the proviso to Article 152(1) that caused concern. The majority view of the federal court was that "using" cannot also be interpreted to mean "teaching in" a particular language. The interpretation so given by the federal court, therefore, would mean that "using" is only limited to speaking or as a medium of expression or communication within the language of the ethnic group concerned. It is indeed surprising that the judgment of the majority in the federal court gave such a restricted interpretation to the scope of the proviso to Article 152(1). It is even more surprising when one considers the fact that it went into the background of Article 152 and yet arrived at an interpretation so obviously not intended by the drafters of the constitution. From the passages quoted from the Report of the Reid Commission and the *White Paper*, it is clear that the drafters never intended the proviso merely to spell out the obvious, that is, to provide that the other minority races were allowed to speak their own languages in social settings or at family occasions only. What was intended was that in the conduct of any business with the government or any other administrative body, all administrative matters, such as correspondence, notices, meetings, and other related matters, should be in Malay. Where no official purpose is involved, the use of any other languages for any other purposes was not to be prohibited.

Although one may be legalistic and take to task the views expressed by the federal court in the *Merdeka University* case, the decision is readily acceptable from a policy point of view:

> Bearing in mind the history of education in this country and the divisive results of allowing separate language schools and the lesson learned from the experience of our neighbour with a private university and the determination of Parliament to so regulate schools and universities and education generally as an instrument for bringing about one nation out of the disparate ethnic elements in our population, we have no choice but to hold, as we have already held, that MU if established would be a public authority within Article 160(2) of the Constitution and that accordingly teaching in Chinese there would be use of that language for any official purposes, which use may be prohibited under Article 152.[19]

Be that as it may, the decision of the federal court does not in any way affect the teaching or learning of Chinese or any other language. Together with this right, the minority ethnic groups are permitted to use their own languages for nonofficial purposes.

Nationality and Citizenship. Even before the country gained independence in 1957, the question of citizenship had posed some difficulties to the government in power. When the formation of the Malayan Union, comprising the nine Malay states and Penang and Malacca, was first proposed in 1946, the British government attempted to introduce the concept of uniform local citizenship laws in Malaya. It was proposed that citizenship should be granted to all persons born in the union and to all persons born in Singapore. It was also suggested that citizenship ought to be granted to all persons who had been residents in the Malayan Union or Singapore for ten out of the fifteen years preceding 1942.

The effect of these proposals would have been to accord political rights to practically the entire non-Malay population of the union. The Malays completely rejected these proposals for fear of non-Malay domination in the political arena. Hence these proposals were not implemented.

The British government then abandoned the proposals and initiated fresh talks with the Malay rulers with the view to the establishment of a new political unit, the Federation of Malaya. The Federation of Malaya was then set up following the 1948 Federation of Malaya Agreement.

Citizenship was deemed an essential part of the policy for the establishment of the Federation of Malaya, and as such it was proposed to create a common form of citizenship for all those who regard Malaya as their real home and as the object of their loyalty. The committee created to make proposals for the establishment of the Federation of Malaya found that the question of citizenship was the most "difficult and delicate" issue.

In an attempt to reach a compromise between the deep resentment felt by the Malay population throughout the Malay States with the creation of the status of Malayan Union citizens, on the one hand, and the policy of the British government to grant citizenship to the non-Malays "who regarded Malaya as their real home and as the object of their loyalty," on the other, the committee recommended that federal citizenship should be granted to "any subject . . . of His Highness the Ruler of any State." Basically, "subject of His Highness the Ruler of any State" was defined to mean any person who: (1) belonged to an aboriginal tribe resident in that state; (2) was a Malay born in that state; (3) was a Malay born outside the Malay state of a father who was a subject of the ruler of that state; or (4) was a person naturalized as a subject of that ruler under any law. Besides the subjects of the rulers, federal citizenship was also to be conferred on: (1) any British subject born in either of the settlements who permanently resides in the federation; (2) any British subject born in the federation whose father was either born in the federation or, at the time of birth of such British subject, was a permanent resident; (3) any person born in the federation who habitually speaks the Malay language and conforms to Malay customs; (4) any person born in the federation, whose parents were also born in the federation and were permanent residents in the federation; and (5) any person whose father is a federal citizen. Provision was also made for the acquisition of federal citizenship by application: any person who was born in the federation and had been resident there for ten out of the fifteen years preceding his application or any person who had resided in the federation for fifteen out of twenty years preceding his application might apply for citizenship. Minor children of such persons who are also residents in the federation would also be granted such citizenship.

It must be emphasized that federal citizenship at this stage was "not a nationality; neither could it develop into a nationality. It would not affect or impair, in any respect whatsoever, the status of British subjects in the Settlements or the status of subjects of the Rulers in the Malay State. It is an addition to, and not a subtraction from, nationality and could be a qualification for electoral rights, for membership of Councils and for employment in Government service."[20] From the point of view of international law, federal citizens born in the Straits Settlements remained British subjects.

It must also be pointed out that the 1948 Agreement did not take into consideration the existing laws relating to state nationality. As mentioned above, as early as 1904 the four states of the Federated Malay States had introduced their own nationality laws. Even though none of the Malay States had any legislation defining the status of a subject of a ruler, it was the practice to classify all non-Malays who were born and resident in a state as a subject of the ruler by the principle of *jus soli*. This principle was also accepted by the courts. In the case of *Chik Kwan* v. *The British Resident, Selangor,*[21] it was held that a Chinese born and resident in a Malay State became a subject of the ruler of that state according to the general principle of international law. It was by virtue of this practice that the non-Malays, particularly the Chinese, were regarded as British-protected persons. Furthermore, the British Protectorate, Protected States and Protected Persons Order of 1949 provided that British-protected persons were those who were declared citizens or nationals of any state by any law of that state. In the absence of any such law, all persons born in the protected states would be treated as British-protected persons. Since the federation by itself was not considered to be a separate legal entity and therefore not a protected state, federal citizenship did not bestow the status of a "British-protected person" on a federal citizen. State nationality laws were still relevant in determining a British-protected person. Therefore, the Chinese who at this stage were subjects of the rulers by the local laws and British-protected persons by international law were not subjects of the rulers for the purpose of federal citizenship.

The Reid Commission recommended that all persons who had rights of citizenship before Merdeka (Freedom) Day should continue to have such rights and that all persons born in the federation on or after Merdeka Day should be citizens by operation of law (that is, without the need to make any formal application). It was also recommended that citizenship be obtainable without due difficulty by those born in the federation before Merdeka Day who were then resident in the federation.

In 1957 when the Constitution of the Federation of Malaya was introduced, many of the recommendations of the Reid Commission were accepted. Every person born in the federation on or after Merdeka Day became a citizen by operation of law. This unqualified principle of *jus soli* was applied in the federation for the first time. In 1962 the principle of *jus soli* as embodied in Article 14(1)(b) was constitutionally amended. The new amendment provided that children whose parents were not citizens of the federation or permanent residents would not become citizens by operation of law even if they were born within the federation. This provision applied to all persons born within the federation after September 1962. If these qualifications could not be fulfilled and, as a consequence, the child would be stateless, however, then such a child could become a citizen by operation of law. As pointed out by the solicitor general, "This amendment curbed resort to the malpractice of a woman entering into the Federation merely to give birth to a child to have it acquire the status of a Federal citizen."

Citizenship laws in Malaysia, then, are embodied in the federal Constitution, and three methods are prescribed for the acquisition of citizenship: operation of law, registration, and naturalization.

Operation of law. All persons born within the federation of Malaya acquire citizenship by operation of law, by the principle of *jus soli*, only if they were born between August 31, 1957, and October 1962. The *jus soli* principle as embodied in the 1957 Constitution is now confined to persons born after September 1962. Such persons become citizens of the new federation by operation of law only if at the time of their birth one of their parents is either a citizen or a permanent resident of the federation. Furthermore, persons born after September 1962 would also become citizens by operation of law if they were not citizens of any other country by birth. The latter provision and the one whereby citizenship is granted to any person born in the federation, even if neither of his parents is a citizen but only a permanent resident, are consequences of the amendment made to the *jus soli* principle as embodied in the 1957 Constitution.

Similar provisions, as embodied in the 1957 Constitution, exist for persons born outside the federation before Merdeka Day. Such persons acquire citizenship if their father was a citizen of the federation at the time of their birth and was either born in the federation or was in service under the federation or state government. If the father of such person does not satisfy either requirement, then that person can become a citizen by operation of law only if his birth had been registered at a consultate within a year.

The provisions relating to persons born after Malaysia Day are similar to those relating to persons born after Merdeka Day. All persons born after Malaysia Day can acquire citizenship only by operation of law depending on the status of their parents; if the individual was born within the federation, one parent must be a citizen or permanent resident, and if the individual was born outside the federation, then the father must be a citizen. He must also satisfy one of the following three requirements: (1) he must have been born in the federation; (2) he must have been in the service of the federal or state government; or (3) his birth must have been registered at a consulate. Any person born within the federation and not born a citizen of any other country, however, also becomes a citizen of the federation by operation of law.

Registration. Wives of citizens (but not husbands of citizens), certain classes of children born in the federation, and other persons born in the federation are entitled to be registered as citizens of the federation only if they satisfy certain residential qualifications and show an intention to reside permanently in the federation.

Naturalization. Persons who were not born in the federation but who have resided in the federation for a number of years may, upon application, be granted a certificate of naturalization. Unlike an applicant who applies for citizenship by registration, an applicant who intends to become a citizen by naturalization is not *entitled* to be granted such status even if he satisfies all the necessary requirements. Wide discretionary powers are given to the federal government as to whether to grant citizenship status to a person born outside the country.

The Constitution also provides for the different circumstances under which a person may be deprived of his citizenship. Article 24 provides that if the federal government is satisfied that any citizen has acquired by registration, naturalization, or other voluntary and formal act the citizenship of any *other* country, the government may by order deprive such person of his citizenship. Furthermore, if the federal government is satisfied that any citizen has voluntarily claimed and exercised in a foreign country any rights available to him under the law of that country, such rights being accorded exclusively to citizens of that country, then an order may also be made to deprive such person of his citizenship.

Clause 3(A) provides that the exercise of a vote in any political election in a place outside the federation shall be deemed a voluntary claim and exercise of a right available under the law of the place. Furthermore, any citizen who, after October 10, 1963, applies for the issuance or renewal of a passport to the authorities of a country outside the federation or uses a passport issued by that country may also be deprived of his citizenship under Article 24.

If the federal government is satisfied that a woman who is a citizen by registration under Article 15(1) has acquired the citizenship of any country outside the federation by virtue of her marriage to a person who is not a citizen, the federal government may by order deprive her of her citizenship. In addition, Article 24 does not require that before an order of deprivation is made the federal government be satisfied that it is contrary to the public good that the person's citizenship in the federation continue, as do the other provisions dealing with the deprivation of citizenship status.

Article 25 provides that the federal government may by order deprive any person who is a citizen under Article 16A or 17 or by naturalization of his citizenship if the government is satisfied: (1) that the citizen has shown himself to be disloyal or disaffected toward the federation; (2) that he has, during any war in which the federation is or was engaged, unlawfully traded or communicated with any enemy; (3) that he has, within the period of five years beginning with the date of the registration or the grant of the certificate of naturalization, been sentenced in any country to imprisonment for a term of more than twelve months or to a fine of more than $5,000; (4) that he has, without the federal government's approval, accepted, served in, or performed the duties of any office, post, or employment under the government of any country outside the federation or any political subdivision thereof or under any agency of such a government where an oath, affirmation, or declaration of allegiance is required to hold the office, post, or employment; (5) that any such citizen has been ordinarily resident in countries outside the federation for a continuous period of five years and during that period has not, at any time, been in the service of either the federation or an international organization of which the federal government is a member, or has not registered annually at a consulate of the federation his intention to retain his citizenship; and (6) that the citizen had obtained the registration or certificate of naturalization by means of fraud, false representation, or the concealment of any material fact or that the registration had been effected or granted by mistake.

The federal government may also by order deprive any woman who is a citizen by registration under clause (1) of Article 15 of her citizenship if satisfied that the marriage by virtue of which she was registered has been dissolved otherwise than by death within the period of two years beginning with the date of marriage.

No person shall be deprived of his citizenship under Article 25, 26, or 26A unless the federal government is satisfied that it is not conducive to the public good that he should continue to be a citizen.

Neither can an order for deprivation be made on certain of the above grounds if, as a result of such deprivation, the person would not be a citizen of any country.

The procedure for deprivation is also spelled out in Article 27 of the Constitution.

Conclusion

Among all the fundamental rights that any minority group would clamor for would be the right to belong to a particular country that it can call home. More than any other right, citizenship rights confer a sense of security and belonging. Together with such a right also comes the right to education, free movement, employment, and property ownership. It follows that, since a high premium is placed on citizenship status, the motive for the acquisition of such status may be purely economic or political, with no deeper sense of belonging or commitment. Naturally, therefore, the granting of such status should be well guarded so as not to affect adversely those who have a rightful and genuine claim to it. The Malaysian citizenship laws attempt to do this. On the one hand,

> the policy must be broad enough to enable those who have attachments of birth and/or a suitable resident period to become citizens. On the other hand, this basis should be limited in order that the interests of the Malays (and the natives of Sabah and Sarawak) be protected as persons who have no alternative home and allegiance.[22]

The Malaysian constitutional provisions attempt to strike a balance between these two principles. To this extent, then, there is much to be said for having the citizenship laws embodied in the Constitution. The intention of the drafters of the Constitution to embody these provisions so as "to allay fears that they would be amended if they had been enacted as ordinary legislation" has, to this extent, been achieved. In fact, the provisions relating to citizenship are "entrenched" under the Constitution. Article 150(6A) provides that even if a proclamation of emergency is declared by the Yang di Pertuan Agong under Article 150, no law shall be passed that is inconsistent with the provisions of the Constitution relating to citizenship. Furthermore, by virtue of the Sedition Act, it is an offense to question the provisions of the Constitution relating to citizenship.

Notes

1. See representation made by the Alliance party, referred to in paragraph 169 of the Commissioner's Report.

2. Paragraph 12 of the "Note of Dissent" by Justice Abdul Hamid.

3. See views on this provision by Ahmad Ibrahim, "The Position of Islam in the Constitution," in *The Constitution of Malaysia*, Suffian et al., eds., p. 52.

4. Paragraph 163 of the Reid Commission Report.

5. Ibid.

6. Ibid., paragraph 164.

7. Ibid.

8. Ibid.

9. Ibid., paragraph 165.

10. Ibid., paragraph 167.

11. Cmnd 210.

12. Paragraph 55 of the *White Paper.*

13. R.H. Hickling, "Constitutional Changes in Malaysia: 1957–77," in Suffian et al., eds., pp. 18–19.

14. Paragraph 170 of the Reid Commission Report.

15. *White Paper.*

16. Ibid., paragraph 61 of the *White Paper.*

17. [1982] 2 MLJ 243.

18. See definition in Article 160.

19. At page 262.

20. *Constitutional Proposals for Malaya: Report of the Working Committee*, Malayan Union Government Press.

21. [1932] 1 MLJ 99.

22. Per Tan Sri Salleh Abas, "Federation in Malaysia," in Suffian et al., eds., p. 179.

Commentary

Teh Boon Eng

A nation's constitution can best be appreciated in the light of its historical background. Professor Sinnadurai has provided a comprehensive background of the Constitution of Malaysia.

The Reid Commission, which made recommendations for the Malaysian Constitution, was fully cognizant of the diversity that exists in Malaysian society. It is believed that the commission adopted many of the recommendations of the Alliance party, which were the product of intensive negotiations among the components of the Alliance party, a coalition of three parties representing the three major races in the country.

The basic provisions of the Constitution commented upon by Professor Sinnadurai—those respecting religion, race, equality, language, and citizenship—reflect a legislative desire to provide for exigencies in a society peopled by different races. The balance of power between the Malay and non-Malay peoples embodied in the Constitution is a precarious thing. The quest for a national identity and the desire to assimilate one race within the boundaries of another are objectives fraught with danger.

Race

Article 153 makes preferential treatment based on race constitutional. The head of state is entrusted with the responsibility "to safeguard the special position of the Malays and natives of any of the Borneo States." This is a controversial provision in the Constitution, affecting racial sensitivities very strongly. To dissuade public comment and disaffection, Section 3 of the Sedition Act prohibits such comment. That prohibition will be dealt with later.

Although the provisions of Article 153 create a serious inroad into the equality provision of the Constitution, this is the price to be paid to redress the all-too-well-known economic imbalance that exists between Malays and others. Article 153 can best be understood as an attempt to balance the interests of all races in Malaysia in as equitable a manner as conditions may admit. The granting of special rights, however, sets those with such special rights in opposition to those without them.

The non-Malay peoples of Malaysia have often viewed Article 153 and other government-initiated economic programs and policies as vehicles to further redress the economic imbalance but without a corresponding sharing of political power with themselves.

Religion

Article 3 of the Constitution declares Islam the religion of the federation. The Constitution then prohibits the promotion of any other religion among persons professing the religion of Islam, but the same protection is not extended to persons professing other religious beliefs. Quite apart from the declaration that Islam is the religion of the federation, Malaysia remains a secular state.

Language

The preeminence of the Malay language as the national language of Malaysia has been taken a step further by the federal court of Malaysia (which is the highest judicial forum) in the celebrated case of *Merdeka University Berhad* v. *Government of Malaysia.* The federal court's interpretation of Article 152 has had the effect of restricting the use of minority languages to domestic and social confines, an interpretation that certainly does not augur well for a pluralistic society. Proviso (a) to Article 152 (1) says that "no person shall be prohibited or prevented from using, teaching, or learning any other language (otherwise than for official purposes)." The court's restrictive interpretation of this provision dilutes an otherwise clear safeguard envisioned by Article 152 for the use of non-Malay languages in an unofficial environment.

Previously, apart from national schools (which are fully government aided and where the Malay language is the medium of instruction), there existed schools established and promoted by missionaries. There were also vernacular schools, promoted and funded by various ethnic organizations, in which the languages of ethnic minorities were used. It is now no longer possible to establish missionary or vernacular schools. The very existence of these schools (as opposed to the national schools) is uncertain.

Political Rights

The legislative power in Malaysia is vested in a parliament consisting of the head of state, the Senate, and the House of Representatives. Election to the House of Representatives is by universal adult suffrage and is ordinarily held once in five years. An election commission is established by the Constitution, whose responsibility among others is to review the division of the federation into election constituencies. The provisions of the Constitution relating to the definition of constituencies superficially encourages the popular notion of "one man, one vote." The Thirteenth Schedule of the Constitution, Part 1, Section 2(c), however, provides that:

> The number of electors within each constituency in a State ought to be approximately equal, except in regard to . . . disadvantages facing rural constituencies; a measure of weight for area ought to be given to such constituencies.

Because rural constituencies in Malaysia are constituted predominantly of a particular ethnic group, this constitutional provision may well encourage gerrymandering and manipulation of the numerical possibilities between "rural" and "urban" constituencies for political advantage. It is, indeed, interesting to note that the Constitution itself does not define either a rural or an urban constituency.

Personal Laws, Customs, and Culture

The personal laws, customs, and cultural practices of the diverse racial groups in Malaysia have been preserved in the Constitution. A wide body of customary laws pertains to marriage, divorce, inheritance, and property. In recent times, however, there has been much legislative activity in these areas to bring local customary law practices in line with modern thinking. While the (Marriage and Divorce) Law Reform Act has taken away the right to polygamous marriages by non-Muslims, the status of Muslim polygamous marriages has not been disturbed. Notwithstanding the Law Reform Act, the Chinese and the Hindus may celebrate a marriage in accordance with their customary laws, but such marriages are deemed monogamous by the act.

While the Constitution is silent on the matter of culture, many have been very dissatisfied with government policy encouraging a "national culture" based on Malay culture. In justification of this approach, the government has contended that common cultural values are the best way to integrate nationally the several ethnic groups in Malaysia. Opposition to this approach can still be felt, however, because the non-Malay peoples of Malaysia strongly desire to keep their cultural indentities intact.

Federal-State Relationship

Malaysia was constituted as a federation in 1963 with the admission of Sabah, Sarawak (the Borneo States), and Singapore. With the admission of these states into the enlarged federation, provisions had to be made in the Constitution to take into account their ethnic composition vis-à-vis the federation.

The Borneo States (predominantly native) and Singapore (predominantly Chinese) were granted special status in the federation. An important aspect of this special status is evident in the immigration and employment laws enacted for the protection of ethnic groups in these states. Whereas unrestricted movement and equal employment opportunities prevailed in the original eleven states of the Federation of Malaya, in the Borneo States and Singapore restrictions on entry and employment existed against citizens of the other states. Such restrictions persist in the Borneo States, but, of course, Singapore withdrew from the Federation of Malaysia in 1965.

The Constitution accords additional protections for the Borneo States. These protections are embodied in Article 161, A–E. The most significant protection (owing to the diversity in the population) is an extended time period for the use of English and the native languages [Article 161(1)].

Emergency Powers

Under Article 150, if the yang di pertuan agong is satisfied that a grave emergency exists, he may issue a proclamation of emergency. Upon such a proclamation, the government is able to exercise a wide range of extraordinary executive and legislative powers. While such a proclamation is in effect, emergency legislation is valid even if inconsistent with any provision of the Constitution [Article 150 (b)]. The government's wide-ranging emergency power to legislate contrary to the Constitution, however, is inapplicable to the constitutional provisions on religion, citizenship, and language [Article 150 (6) (A)], which are sacrosanct in the multiracial society of Malaysia.

Diversity in population and constitutional provisions designed to strike a balance in the competing claims and interests of diverse groups in the population are only one side of the constitutional coin.

Emotions and sensitivity normally run high when topics of race, religion, culture, and creed are discussed. To stifle animosity leading to violence on sectarian grounds, provisions of the Sedition Act proscribe, on pain of penal consequences, utterances of a seditious tendency.

Section 3(1) of the Sedition Act defines a seditious tendency in the following way:

1. to promote feelings of ill-will and hostility between different races or classes of the population of Malaysia
2. to question any matter, right, status, position, privilege, sovereignty, or prerogative established or protected by the provision of Part 111 or Articles 152, 153, or 181 of the Federal Constitution

Part 111 of the federal Constitution is the chapter on citizenship; Article 152 prescribes the Malay language as the national language of Malaysia, and Article 153 provides for the special position of the Malays and natives of the Borneo States. The prohibitions cited above apply equally to members of Parliament, acting in accordance with normal parliamentary procedure, who address the House of Representatives in such a manner as to question those protected subjects [Article 10(4)]. Statements or utterances that point out errors or defects in the implementation of the articles of the Constitution referred to, however, are permissible.

It is not difficult to see the wisdom of the prohibitive provisions of the Sedition Act in the context of a nonhomogenous society, but whether such a gag on discussion will work to achieve the tolerance and acceptance looked to in Article 153 is speculative.

Citizenship

Citizenship is an important matter in Malaysia. Under the original Constitution every person born within the federation on or before August 31, 1957 (the date of independence), was, subject to certain exceptions, a citizen by operation of law. In 1962, a small but significant amendment was made to the citizenship laws. As amended, the law now states that a person born in the federation does not gain citizenship unless one of his parents is, at the time of his or her birth, either a citizen of or a permanent resident in Malaysia. Non-Malays viewed this amendment with alarm.

Although the citizenship provisions of the Constitution enable noncitizen wives of citizens to be registered as citizens of the federation (on fulfillment of residential requirements), the common complaint of non-Malay citizens with foreign wives is that the delay in obtaining approval is inordinately slow. That the right of citizenship is something to be jealously guarded and reluctantly given is the attitude of a government that perceives political power to be the domain of a particular race.

One must caution against the practice of viewing every political or socioeconomic issue through racial spectacles, however. A national constitution with provisions that protect diverse ethnic groups entails the risk of perpetuating divisiveness in the populace.

Diversity in the population provides a great temptation to those less imbued with a sense of constitutionalism to discriminate against the minority. Such diversity, therefore, should never be an excuse or justification for the existence of a Constitution that infringes traditionally accepted basic rights cherished by all regardless of race, color, or creed.

Discussion

ROBERT GOLDWIN: Malaysia is different from the other nations we have discussed in several important respects.

First, the diversity of the population is not a territorial diversity. The one territorial concentration of race that did exist, Singapore, is no longer part of the Malaysian federation. There can be, therefore, no territorial arrangement—no federal structure or "autonomies"—to deal with the Malaysian problem of diversity.

Second, unlike most other nations we have discussed, Malaysia has held an explicit assimilationist goal: "the integration of the various communities into a common nationality."

Third, the differences of race, religion, language, and nationality are not cross-cutting as, for instance, to some extent they are in Switzerland, where some German speakers are Catholic and some are Protestant, and some French speakers are Catholic and some are Protestant. In that sense, the Swiss differences are cross-cutting. In Malaysia, they are all reinforcing; people of one race are also of the same religion, language, and nationality.

Fourth, the community with majority political power, the Malay or *Bumiputra* community, is economically disadvantaged, and those with economic power lack political power.

Finally, the special preferences designed "to redress the imbalance" are for the benefit of the majority group, not a minority as, for instance, in the United States, where affirmative action is designed for racial and ethnic minorities.

All these features make Malaysia distinctive, even unique, among the nations we have discussed so far. In the face of these unusual characteristics, is the task of reconciling unity and diversity merely more formidable in Malaysia, or is it impossible?

VISU SINNADURAI: I must congratulate Robert A. Goldwin for so ably summarizing the whole paper and understanding the whole environment in Malaysia.

MR. GOLDWIN: It was very easy. I had the instruction of your paper, and I once spent two days in Malaysia. [Laughter]

MR. SINNADURAI: To answer your question, one has to understand the background and the circumstances under which the Constitution itself was implemented. We have talked about the intention of the drafters in a number of sessions during the past few days. But the Malaysian Constitution, which was first drafted in 1957 and subsequently revised in 1963, was in fact a joint effort by the British government and the Malay rulers. It is important to take into consideration the role of the Malay rulers; those representatives of various communities who sat around the table to discuss the formulation of the provisions were either Malay, Chinese, or Indian.

At the time the Constitution was drafted, political power was solely in the hands of the Malays; that is, they considered themselves the natives of the country. The Chinese and Indians were largely immigrants brought in by the British, and yet, having stayed in the country for a number of years, many did not look upon China or India as the motherland. The Constitution itself was in fact negotiated almost like a barter trade. The Chinese gave up some of their rights; in return the Malays were willing to give up some of theirs. One of the biggest threats, of course, was the fact that out of the eleven states existing in 1957, nine had hereditary Malay rulers. Those rulers looked upon any kind of independence as a threat to their power, because as Malays and heads of the Muslim faith, they had to depend on the Malays, to a very large extent, for their support. The question of nationality thus posed one of the most difficult issues with which the drafters had to deal. After much negotiation, it was decided that nationality would be granted to anyone who had been born in the country or who had been living there for a number of years, in return for a certain price.

This was the background against which Article 153 of the Malaysian Constitution was drafted. Article 153 basically gives special privileges to the Malays, or what are now called the *Bumiputras*. Upon a close reading of Article 153, however, one would notice that the so-called special privileges given to the Malays or the *Bumiputras* are not exclusive to them, because the king of the country is also under a duty to safeguard the interests of minority groups. The extent to which this has been achieved over the years is subject to some discussion and probably some doubt, because many of the positive actions taken by the ruling government party and in Parliament in pursuance of Article 153 have in fact been for the sole benefit of the Malays.

In our present situation admissions to the university are based essentially on quotas, and job opportunities have all been biased in favor of the Malays. This arrangement was designed to redress an economic imbalance that developed over the last few years before independence. At the time independence was granted, political power was in the hands of the Malays; economic power was in the hands of the Chinese. Politically powerless, the Indians and others were in no position to bargain.

After the formation of Malaysia in 1969, a racial riot followed on the heels of the general elections in which the Chinese won a number of parliamentary seats. This made the Malays wonder whether their grip on political power was also now threatened by the minority. Subsequently, the government has taken positive actions to ensure an economic redress and a political redress.

The impression one gets of Malaysia, of course, is that Article 153 gives advantages to the majority race rather than to a minority race, a most unusual situation compared with most of the other constitutions we have discussed. But when we talk about the majority race in Malaysia, we have to bear in mind the two states of Borneo, Sabah and Sarawak, which were brought into Malaysia at the same time as Singapore in 1963. Many of the communities in Sabah and Sarawak are not necessarily Muslim or Malay; they are in fact Christian or are generally regarded as native. (I use the word native deliberately, because the constitution uses that word.) The word *Bumiputra* includes Malays as well as the natives of Sabah and Sarawak, and it is only with these other groups that the *Bumiputras* form a majority.

Although attempts to assimilate the different peoples or to bring about unity have not in fact been altogether successful, none of the communities has made any attempt or has expressed any aspiration to break away from the federation as such, except for Singapore, as pointed out. The various religious, language, or racial groups are dispersed throughout the country, thereby precluding a move by any one of them to build an autonomous state.

The question of assimilation has been raised particularly with the issue of language. English, which was very commonly used before, has been relegated to a second language, and Malay is now the official language. This is one of the few steps the government has taken to assimilate the various peoples. The situation was such that, for example, a Chinese from Penang and a Chinese from Perak or Malacca could not converse in any language because the dialect varied. Even among the Indians this was true, because the Indians spoke different dialects. So it was felt a common identity could be brought about through a uniform language.

The language issue has been addressed quite satisfactorily; all instruction in schools and universities is in English and Malay now, with English being used as a second language. One must address the larger issue, however: how can one bring about assimilation in a country with such a diverse population? The background of the various races is quite instructive. The Chinese, for example, depend to a very large extent on strength in the business and commercial sectors. They know that probably nowhere else could they have things any better than in Malaysia. They have lost all links with China. The Indians probably feel the same. Their ties with India or Sri Lanka are largely lost. To them Malaysia is a country with great potential. This is the reason why the status quo is maintained in the country.

With the Malays themselves, a great imbalance in economic power and education exists, particularly because many rural areas have had no schools at all. In the university where I teach, for instance, the faculty of engineering has been 99 percent Chinese for the past twenty-five years. In the medical schools, until the past five years, about 95 percent were Chinese. This is the imbalance the government is attempting to overcome by providing special privileges. Now in fact there is a quota basis for university admissions. Special privileges are granted for scholarships, education, and the like, so that Malays, Chinese, and Indians will at one stage, sooner or later, come to a level where the differences will not be so obvious.

Unity then is not impossible. It may sound a bit formidable at this stage, but I think with some of the measures being taken, it can be accomplished.

TEH BOON ENG: The Constitution as framed takes into account and recognizes diversity, and many of its provisions were indeed designed to encourage and foster unity among the diverse races in Malaysia. For instance, in the articles of the Constitution that pertain to religion, Islam is proclaimed as the national religion of the country, but a corresponding provision allows other religions to be practiced, in recognition of the presence of other races in the country. The language provision of the Constitution designates Malay as the national language of the country, but then it proceeds to guarantee the use of the languages of the other races.

As Professor Sinnadurai explained, Article 153 of the Constitution was required because the Malays, even during British rule, enjoyed preferential treatment. Such special status could not be taken away at the time of the federation of the eleven states.

The real question is, of course, whether, given the diversity in Malaysia, unity among the races is possible. From the progress of the country since its independence in 1957, one can see that it is doing relatively well, despite the pull of conflicting forces in many directions. We see, for instance, that the ruling party is composed basically of a coalition of parties based on racial lines. Thus since independence the ruling party has always been a coalition of Malays, Chinese, and Indians. Contentious issues pertaining to race relations have, most of the time, been resolved by the ruling party and have generally been accepted by the population. Even the pattern of voting in parliament does not indicate voting along racial lines. On bills in parliament impinging on minority rights, the votes of members of parliament belonging to the coalition government have always been unanimous. This, then, is one factor that has enabled the containment of racial issues in Malaysia—that is, a political resolution of these issues by the leaders of the coalition government.

The black mark for the country, of course, was the riots in 1969. These, however, did not reflect any weaknesses in the Constitution. It was only a question whether those born after independence were prepared to honor the agreement reached in 1957, regarding the various privileges that were granted to the majority races, in return for which citizenship was obtained by the Indians as well as the Chinese.

The challenges to unity the government now faces emanate from a different source altogether. Muslim fundamentalism, which arose in Iran, has, of course, spread to Malaysia. And the Pan-Malaysian Islamic party, advocating a government on that basis, competes with the ruling party, which nonetheless has, so far, remained in favor with the Malays. The government faces the dilemma therefore of how to improve the status of the Malays without encouraging further growth of the Pan-Malaysian Islamic party and without making the Chinese and the Indians uncomfortable. Although clearly at various times in the country's history issues have tended to pull the country in different directions, nevertheless a Malaysian identity of sorts has surfaced. To be sure, action initiated by the government for the creation of a national identity initially met with opposition and misgivings. Today schools in Malaysia use Malay as the medium of instruction, so that the standard of spoken English has declined and teachers from England must be brought into the country to teach English.

The other kind of action initiated by the government has been to foster a common culture. As things are now, the three main races in the country live within their own cultures. Government attempts to fashion a national culture reflecting that of the Malay race have, of course, resulted in much dissension. And in the face of such dissension, the government has backpedaled on such efforts.

It would not really be wrong, however, to say that, despite the presence of the three major races in Malaysia, unity is not an illusory goal in the country. As long as the government in power comprises the three major parties, I think the progress of Malaysia toward unity is ensured. The fact that the coalition government has stayed in power for the twenty-eight years since independence speaks quite well for the political views of the people in Malaysia. I would join Professor Sinnadurai then in predicting that unity in the face of diversity is not an unattainable goal in Malaysia.

EDWARD BANFIELD: My answer to the chairman's question, Can diversity and unity be made compatible in Malaysia?, is the typical Yankee one: yes and no. In my first reading of these papers, I concluded that Malaysia was a hopeless case. Here there seemed to be three gods, three laws. This seemed to be really an insoluble problem. But in the spirit of Goldwin, I thought of a modest proposal: call back the British civil servants who have an extraordinary talent for running things and for running them with fairness and justice. The British are now unemployed. One might think there were opportunities enough for the exercise of these skills in Britain, but, alas, having withdrawn from their colonies, they seem to have been demoralized. I think this would be good for some of the other excolonies. We could use a few in Philadelphia.

After a second reading of the papers, however, it came to my attention that the Malaysian arrangement was devised by an alliance; that is to say, the three major groups together came to the conclusion embodied in the Constitution. These cultures were not unable to reach some kind of compromise. These are, as far as I understand them, essentially gentle peoples. We should not assume that they will set about cutting each other's throats, in the literal sense of the word. And it occurred to me that maybe, in fact, there are not three gods, but really one, as there is, in my opinion, in Switzerland and, for that matter, in the United States—Mammon. Mammon has made his appearance in Malaysia. As we see in the history of the United States, he was welcomed here with open arms as the least objectionable of the possibilities open to man, constituted as he was.

Adam Smith gave one of the clearest and earliest statements of the prospect that commercial society opened for mankind: conditions now would allow for civilization, justice, law, order, and high culture. That the pursuit of wealth, the bettering of one's condition materially, was the most common and vulgar of pursuits was a fact that would be accepted as long as the payoff in the long run was the existence of a stable, orderly society in which higher things would be made possible.

It seems to me that the commercial society may serve that purpose in Malaysia. Therefore, I see the role of the Chinese in a different light, perhaps, from what I would if I were a non-Chinese Malaysian.

To have a part of the population supremely talented at entrepreneurial and commercial undertakings is a great national asset. It is an asset for everybody in this society. It creates the material conditions of life under which other people can do other things. It may be that the Indians in Malaysia and the Malays will find eventually that they are the beneficiaries of Chinese economic preeminence.

Meanwhile, however, there are clearly real injustices in these arrangements, and it is clear that there are dangers of worse to come. The position of the Indians now, I gather from other sources, is in some ways comparable to that of the free blacks after the American Civil War. In Philadelphia, for example, there was a class of black professionals and skilled artisans who had not been flayed for generations in some cases but who—in the racial animosity directed against them after the Civil War—lost their professional status and became a proletariat. They were demoralized by this, and only recently has their status in our society been reconstituted. That seems to be happening, as I understand it, to a great many Indians, the smallest of the small minorities—10 percent of the population or so—in Malaysia at the present time. It may be that the Indians who are now being proletarianized by prejudice or disadvantages imposed on them constitutionally will, in a later society, be restored to their professions.

I am concerned, too, about the dangers of radical Muslim fundamentalism in a country that is officially Muslim. It seems to me the radicals may have an advantage that they do not have in other Muslim countries or that they would not have if the country were not officially Muslim. It is not clear yet, however, that the Muslim world will be entirely radicalized. Perhaps I am worrying about something that I needn't.

Finally, a great deal will turn upon whether the officially dominant Malay culture proves to be a respectable one and whether it is a culture that the Chinese and the Indians can come to identify with, or at least not hold in contempt. At the moment, this is apparently not the case. According to a newspaper account, the educated Chinese and Indians are openly contemptuous of Malay culture, which an Indian professional described to a reporter as "a couple of folk dances." By culture the reporter may have had in mind high culture, but what I have in mind is the moral basis of the society. The moral basis of a society need not necessarily be represented by ballet dancers, of course; folk dancers will do. The question is, What is perceived by the Malays, by the Chinese, and by the Indians as the central moral content of their common life and culture?

KOH ENG TIAN: As Mr. Goldwin pointed out, Malaysia is a unique situation, where special rights and privileges are conferred by the

Constitution on a majority of the population. Article 153 was no doubt necessary at the time the Constitution was formulated and was politically acceptable to the Malays and non-Malays. One may wonder whether, as a result of the passage of time, the circumstances have so changed that today there would be a need to review Article 153. Of course, as my friends from Malaysia pointed out, the Malaysian Sedition Act prohibits any questioning of Article 153.

As for assimilation through the use of the Malay language, the designation of Malay as the sole official language in Malaysia appears to have accomplished its purpose. Most of the non-Malays in Malaysia today can speak Malay with proficiency. There may, however, be some adverse consequences from this policy. The use of English has declined, causing a decline in the standard of English among the younger generation in Malaysia. And English, of course, is an international language. Many non-Malays in Malaysia tend to send their children abroad in order to study English, a practice that could result in a brain drain from Malaysia.

In my view the important thing in Malaysia is not what is to be included in or excluded from the Constitution, but how effectively the government can deal with communal problems and prevent a recurrence of the racial strife that occurred in 1969. Up to now the government appears to have been successful in dealing with such problems and has managed to prevent them from getting out of hand. The Malaysian Constitution has managed to sail through some stormy waters in the past, thanks to the effectiveness of the government in dealing with communal issues.

CELIO BORJA: I noticed in these two excellent papers some positive elements for building unity in Malaysia.

First, all races are attached to the land. And more important, the Constitution itself is the product of negotiation among the several races that inhabit the country. The will to stay together, I think, is there. The disparate groups have decided to live on the same land, in the same country, although they have probably built up their defenses against one another. But the will to stay together is a fundamental element for a modern nation to exist.

The element that is not conducive to building national unity is the fact that the Constitution itself discriminates in certain ways against some of the parties involved in that negotiation. This is an effort to redress a material imbalance. The Malays have fewer schools and less access to universities and professional schools, but these inequalities could be overcome by administrative means and ways. As a legislator, I would try to find the means to overcome the imbalance between races, but this requires, I think, administrative means, not the establishment of different treatment of the parties involved as a universal rule. Let's be frank: in our own countries we have always had disadvantaged minority groups. What do we do? We simply create means to overcome the imbalance existing between them.

BARRY STRAYER: In our discussion of the Malaysian Constitution we have seen that, at the time of its drafting, the minority had a certain dynamism and momentum that were seen as threatening in various ways to the existence or the identity of the majority. In Quebec this has been dealt with, mostly through language legislation, on the whole successfully. It has been painful to some people, but now, after some years of difficulty and with the unfortunate emigration of a certain number of Anglophones from Quebec, those who remain are living in harmony with the majority better than they were before. And the majority now feels self-confident enough that it can take a more liberal view toward the minority.

I now have a question about the provisions respecting the nonestablishment of religion. The Constitution seems to guarantee on the one hand that no citizen shall be obliged to pay taxes to support a religion not his own. But on the other hand Article 12 seems to allow for the state—either the federal government or the individual states—to provide some sort of tax support or financial support to the Muslim religion. I would like to hear some explanation and reconciliation of those two provisions.

THOMAS PANGLE: The papers hinted at deeper, graver, even dangerous potential problems that were not really addressed. One of those was that provision forbidding the discussion of one of the most socially and politically important articles of the Constitution. This article is an anomaly; a majority is guaranteed discriminatory privileges against minorities in a constitution that, at the same time, attempts to be fundamentally democratic and egalitarian. In other words, although the Constitution is not explicitly aristocratic, and not explicitly elitist, it nonetheless has this powerful inegalitarian provision.

What allowed men of good will to come together and agree to what is, in the twentieth century at least, a rather anomalous constitution? Isn't the situation more fragile than it appears in these papers? How do these minorities tolerate a constitution that discriminates against them in the name of the majority? They went into the streets in 1969; why aren't they in the streets now? Why is there nothing like the feeling among the Basques or like what once existed among the

363

French Canadians or like what existed among the English once the French Canadians got their provincial control? The English began leaving by the thousands.

Perhaps the reluctance of the minorities has something to do with the economic situation. In Malaysia the minorities were economically advantaged and powerful. They knew that, once the British left, they were in trouble, because they were sitting on top of a majority, or at least a potential majority, that was disadvantaged. The fact that, in this case, the minorities were economically better off made it possible for them to give in, so to speak.

But what did they hope would result from this? Why did they think this would be any more than a temporary solution? I presume that the most thoughtful of them were hoping that this majority would become more like them—entrepreneurial or commercial. In other words, they were not hoping that the country would become more Islamic, for example, or more distinctively Malay, but more homogeneously modernized, perhaps. Of course, if so, then it seems as though the minorities were counting on a real diminution of the influence of religion in the national life. And that means that, as Professor Banfield indicated, the rise of Muslim fundamentalism raises very serious questions about what must have been the long-range plan of the leaders of the minorities, when they made this agreement.

The secession of Singapore, which was not really discussed, raises the question, Why did one of the most powerful and economically advanced sections of the original country decide that it had to get out? I would have assumed that the Singapore community was an important part of the minority that agreed to make the original constitutional compromise; that is to say, the entrepreneurial Chinese and Indian classes must have been, if not concentrated in Singapore, at least sympathetic with the Singapore situation. For the Chinese and Indians, therefore, the secession of Singapore must have been somewhat discouraging, particularly because of this plan that, I hypothesize, might have been in the minds of those who made this compromise.

TEH BOON ENG: One of the main factors that brought about the departure of Singapore from the federation was the participation of a Singapore political party, namely, the People's Action party, in the 1964 general elections in Malaysia. This was considered to be such a destabilizing force within Malaysia that the Federation of Malaysia requested Singapore to leave.

FALI SAM NARIMAN: I am a bit pessimistic with regard to the situation in Malaysia, especially because of the lack of constitutional safeguards. I mention this particularly because of my experience with the working of the Burmese Constitution, which led ultimately to vast numbers of Indians, who contributed to some degree to the economic prosperity of that country, to come back to India. I am reminded that the three principal ways of dealing with minorities—decimate them, assimilate them, or tolerate them—are not necessarily the only approaches. They may be treated in two additional ways. One is to encourage them, when they are not seen as a threat to the majority, as in India. The other is to contain them—and that seems to be the Malaysian situation—when they are considered a distinct economic threat to the majority community.

The absence of a common culture is a very important problem in Malaysia, which requires very great effort on the part of the community to stick together as a nation. What contributes to nationhood in Malaysia is the economic necessity for the minority communities to live together with the majority. As we have heard, the Chinese cannot go back to the mainland; they have no other home. The Indians can "go home," but they would not be as prosperous in India as they are in Malaysia. These, then, are the constraints of economy, which are nonetheless a rather poor way to maintain the unity of a nation.

As for the question of sedition, I became acquainted with it in a somewhat different context. I belong to an organization, a council member of which has just been hauled up for sedition in Kuala Lumpur. He is a prominent member of the Malaysian bar council, who happened to comment on the conviction of a particular minister. The minister was ultimately reprieved by the king through exercise of his powers of clemency. At the same time, another man, who was caught for drugs, was sentenced to death, and his sentence was not commuted. My friend mentioned in a statement that this sort of attitude on the part of those granting clemency would make people believe that it is only the high and mighty who are able to exercise influence in the corridors of power. For this seemingly innocuous statement he has been charged with sedition. The penalty entails imprisonment for around three to seven years. The problem of sedition, then, raised by Professor Pangle, is more serious than people may think.

Sedition has two aspects. In British India, want of affection for the government was defined as sedition and was penalized as such. Fortunately, our Supreme Court, after independence, took the view that this was not the correct definition. It followed an earlier judgment of its own, in which it said that sedition is accompanied by a plea for violent disorder; a mere spoken word would not constitute sedition. In the context of the Malaysian law as it stands today, however, it appears that no arguments can be raised with regard to this provision in the Constitution. No amendment therefore could be proposed with regard to it. This is surely a peculiar way of maintaining the unity of the nation.

MR. SINNADURAI: I may have been somewhat misleading in my paper. Article 153 in fact specifies only four areas in which special privileges are granted to the *Bumiputras* or Malays: positions in public services, scholarships and educational training, permits and licenses, and entry into educational institutions. The arrangements for the public service positions resulted from give-and-take between the British and the Malay rulers originally. The British agreed to give special privileges to the Malays; in return, the Malays agreed to surrender some control over the public service to British advisers.

As far as businesses are concerned, there are, in fact, hardly any restrictions on non-Malays opening up businesses. A misunderstanding arose during the period when independence was granted to the effect that the Chinese were holding the economic power of the country. This was not true.

In point of fact, 70 percent of the wealth at the time of independence was foreign owned, essentially British, not Malaysian. All rubber plantations at the time were British. Of course, the Chinese participated in this process, giving the impression that they had control over the economy. This is the reason for the hard negotiation that went on.

As we have noted, neither the Chinese nor the Indians for that matter have a home country. They want to be in Malaysia. They find the country attractive, and they have opportunities. This may help explain the ready acceptance by the Chinese and the Indians of some of the provisions in the Constitution, discriminatory as they are. As far as they could see, probably, it is better to have something than nothing. This was, in fact, a compromise, because they could not go anywhere else.

During this period Communist activities were also rampant. Just before independence, the country was under emergency rule, with Communist activities everywhere. In fact, one of the high commissioners was murdered. Every Chinese was under suspicion of being a Communist. Both sides feared what would happen. To my mind, at least this was why the Chinese and the Indians were willing to negotiate and accept these conditions.

366

As for the influence of Islam on the Malays, Islamic values were not greatly emphasized in their lives just before independence. The major reason for emphasis on Islam was political: the sultans of the nine states believed that their positions as leaders of the Muslim faith conferred upon them some power in the colonial arrangement when the federation was formed. The Constitution emphasized Islam to please the nine hereditary rulers.

With its awakening throughout the world, of course, Islam is now playing a more important role than was probably envisaged. As rightly pointed out, the Pan-Islamic party—one of the radical or fundamentalist parties that enjoys some power in the poorer states on the east coast—has now been able to play a major role in the country through Iranian influence. This situation poses a great threat to the government itself. Although the government is Islamic and the majority of the members of the Malay party are Muslims, they do not share in toto the principles of the fundamentalist movement. The fundamentalist groups, which have been gaining popularity, have accused the present government of being infidels and the Constitution of being un-Islamic.

It is a delicate situation. If the ruling Malay party gives too much to the non-Malays, then its survival is threatened, because the Malays will then throw their support to the fundamentalist groups or elsewhere. If the party does not give enough support to the Chinese and the Indians, again, the imbalance might encourage the Communists in the country.

This is the background for some of the issues raised about support for religious institutions *versus* religious toleration. Recently, because the government wants to show that it is also Islamic, the number of Islamic institutions and mosques set up with state funds is increasing. During British rule, every village or town had to have a chapel or a cathedral. To show that we are an Islamic country, why should we not now have a mosque in every village or housing estate?

As for citizenship, one of the problems under the present Constitution is that a person, one of whose parents was a citizen, is thereby entitled to citizenship. The majority of the Chinese in Malaysia had parents born there; the peculiar problem arises with the Indians. They want to have the best of two worlds; that is, they regard India as their motherland to a certain extent. Any conflict between the Sikhs and the Hindus in India is echoed by a small riot in Malaysia. When India and Malaysia play a football match, the Malaysian Indians support India. Many small traders—newspaper vendors, bakers, and the like—still go back to India to find their brides. Sometimes they have more than one wife, one in Malaysia and one in India. The problem arises with the children who are not born in Malaysia. When the wives are brought back, the whole family comes back—perhaps ten children. The government must face this difficulty with citizenship. Approving citizenship is therefore a very delicate matter with the government. I think, however, that only a very small percentage are not citizens.

As for the Sedition Act, the reasons for it are, I think, obvious. One very volatile factor in the country has always been race. In the universities, for example, there have been a number of riots completely along racial lines. Among the students there is more polarization than ever because of the provisions in the Sedition Act. Although I am not trying to justify the sedition provision, I think one has to understand the background against which it was, in fact, drafted.

For these reasons the government deemed that the Sedition Act—which is very broadly worded, I must admit that—should protect the safety and security of the country. When the Sedition Act was introduced, the prime minister assured the House that the act would be carefully implemented and that there would be care that it not be applied discriminately.

WALTER BERNS: I offer an example of a certain subject that could not be discussed in the United States and, in fact, could not be discussed in the Congress. We once had what was called a gag rule on the subject of slavery. At a certain point, the Congress of the United States was not permitted to discuss that subject. Southern states adopted laws forbidding the very discussion of slavery, manumission, emancipation, and the like. At one time in the 1830s, the national government passed a law making it a federal crime to place antislavery newspapers, propaganda, and literature in the mails of the United States. So we in the United States have a precedent for this. Our history shows that the subject could not be suppressed.

8

How Political and Constitutional Institutions Deal with a People of Ethnic Diversity: The Yugoslav Experience

Vojislav Stanovcic

The Character of Diversities

A story among students in Yugoslav studies has been told over and over. Although many elements in it have changed, its original meaning is still applicable. It is about the influential chief of the British and Allied mission to the Yugoslav partisans, Sir Fitzroy Maclean, intimate friend of Winston Churchill. After World War II, Maclean once spoke to a select political audience in London about Yugoslavia. Someone in the audience interrupted Maclean's address with a question: Why did he try so hard to make his thoughts on Yugoslavia known? Sir Fitzroy answered unhesitatingly: "Because this is an unusual and complex country, which is apparent from the fact that it has six republics, five nations, four languages, three religions, two alphabets, and one party that ensures the unity of all these diversities."

Anecdotes, of course, simplify things to emphasize the message. This picture of Yugoslavia, however, no matter how true it might have been at the time, is even more true today. The social and political life of Yugoslavia has grown even more complex and intricate. First, today we can speak of eight federal units, six nations, two nationalities, and other diversities that have become prominent and that should be given due attention within the framework of the constitutional system and life. Second, the party—which has served as a unifying factor, though never the only one—has lost much of its ability to integrate.

The first change is the result of the sociopolitical and demographic process. It is partly related to the transformation of

Yugoslavia from a patriarchal-agrarian society to an urban-industrial society, which was facilitated by the creation of greater opportunities for free expression of individual pursuits brought about by the development of self-management in both the general economy and local enterprises. All the political, constitutional, and legal solutions to problems then had to be adapted to real life.

The second change was simply caused by the new focus of the federally organized party on identification with local, regional, and, above all, national (that is, the nations') interests in making and pursuing appropriate policies. This change occurred because the struggle for power within the party leadership led to requests for support and mobilization, and even for new foundations for the legitimization of power at the national and regional levels.

The complexity of Yugoslav society has required permanent adjustments to avoid sharp social and political conflicts. When its older and its more recent history are taken into account, together with its population composed of various nations, religions, and cultures, it is easy to conclude that Yugoslavia's condition is ripe for conflict. The price Yugoslavia has paid to have its numerous and diverse interests and views gratified has been economic difficulty, especially during the 1980s.

Since 1918 Yugoslavia has had six constitutions (1921, 1931, 1946, 1953, 1963, 1974). In the time between any two successive constitutions, the existing constitution was changed either by force (1929) or by constitutional amendment or act. Decisions of the wartime AVNOJ (the Antifascist Council of the National Liberation of Yugoslavia) antifascist assembly in 1943 should be included in the list of changes affecting Yugoslavia. Those decisions are extremely significant because, among other things, they laid the first foundations for the federative order of the future state. We cannot say, however, that coping with diversity was the only cause of these constitutional changes. Serbia, the first of the Yugoslav countries to acquire independence (in the nineteenth century) is composed of one nation; yet, in a period of less than a century, it had eight different constitutional systems.[1]

What were the causes, motives, and reasons for these frequent changes in Yugoslavia? The change, instability, and uncertainty did not come only from the population's diversity. It is hard to understand the present Yugoslav situation and its problems without considering the historical circumstances. Apart from the diversities, which in the Middle Ages and even under foreign occupations helped to force recognition of the rights of autonomy (such as those of the church, nations, and regions) and some privileges or monopolies (over salt, overseas transportation lines), the country's strategic geographic position, constant wars, prevailing authoritarian political culture, deep-rooted patriarchal relations, and the long lasting influence of different traditions all played major roles in the changes and instability. The historical struggle for power and territory that had been waged within the framework of this political culture was extremely cruel, leaving deep scars in the popular memory, and becoming, as expressed in the folk epics, part of the consciousness of every succeeding generation. Brutal methods of war (for instance, the blinding of tens of thousands of prisoners) and sadistic executions of overthrown rulers in Byzantium (who had a "second showing" in Belgrade in 1903); family wars within the Serbian and other dynasties; murders by pretenders to the Turkish throne of all other pretenders, usually their own brothers—all of this encouraged endeavors, beginning as early as the Middle Ages, to regulate social life through legal codes.

The oriental tradition, in the form of Byzantine and, later, Turkish despotism, had its own domestic followers. The technique of ruling and maintaining despotism by beheading the most prominent citizens—about which Plato and Aristotle wrote on the basis of Herodotus' notes on the counsel one Greek tyrant, Thrasybulus, gave to another, Periander[2]—was still being practiced during the nineteenth and twentieth centuries in Yugoslavia.[3]

In short, the history of the Balkans has nurtured an authoritarian political culture. The hope that it has been outgrown is constantly accompanied by skepticism and fear that it might be resuscitated, all the more so because the relations among diverse groups, unless adequately regulated, create tensions that easily give rise to violent conflicts. For these reasons diversity should be addressed in such a way that the autonomy of some groups does not come into conflict with the autonomy of others. That diverse groups frequently draw closer together and cooperate with each other within a constitutional framework, without any administrative pressure for unification, also should be considered, but the right relationship between the parts and the whole is not easy to find.

In area (255,804 square km.) and population (22,424,711 inhabitants according to the 1981 census), Yugoslavia is a medium-sized European country; however, except for the Soviet Union, which is a Euro-Asian country, it is the most complex. Its complexity is reflected not only in the diverse ethnicity and religions of the population, but also in differences of historical heritage, culture, and tradition.[4] The historical and cultural factors that have influenced the region have left traces on its cultural patterns, behavior, and perspectives on various issues. Historical diversity has led to distrust, and a variety of viewpoints and interests have taken root. Without resorting to statistics one may notice big differences in the levels of economic development—as, for instance, between the most developed Republic of Slovenia and the least developed federal unit, Kosovo.[5] The population of each lived under different political and cultural systems and therefore inherited different, though commonly authoritarian, political cultures.

It could be said that northern and southern Yugoslavia have separate cultures. The same is even more true in the east and west. In many respects, Yugoslavia is an example of the French proverb, "the dead bind the living." The division that the Roman emperors Diocletian and Theodosius the Great made several centuries before the Slavs came to the Balkan Peninsula, delineating the western and eastern Roman Empires, was drawn right through the middle of present-day Yugoslavia. It was around this border that the division between the western (Roman Catholic) and eastern (Orthodox) churches, which emerged as separate entities immediately after the division of the empire (although the schism between them occurred in the year 1054) would fluctuate. On Yugoslavia's soil, the eastern and western traditions and two cultures have come perpetually face to face in conflict. Vatroslav Jagic, a Croatian Slavicist of world renown, has written that in this region "the West fights with the East for predominance," in the same way that Rudyard Kipling expressed in his famous verses the view that East is East, and West is West, and the two shall never meet until Judgment Day.[6] The old lines of division that intersect in modern Yugoslavia should be kept in mind in contemporary controversial discussions not only about the division of Europe into spheres of interest after World War II and the Moscow and Yalta conferences, but also about the idea of dividing Yugoslavia itself into spheres of interest.

In a nonpejorative sense, Yugoslavia is a mishmash of opposites. From the Adriatic coast, with its many examples of Romanesque and Renaissance architecture and culture and the remains of Roman palaces and aqueducts, to the Bosnian-Herzegovinian hinterland one sees both Christian and Moslem monuments and great variety in the ways the people dress, live, and behave.[7] Sarajevo is unique in Europe in this regard.[8] Traveling by road, one sees famous Bogomil (a pagan-Christian sect that lived on the territory of today's Bosnia in the tenth and eleventh centuries) tombstones, exceptionally decorated large stone blocks that are considered distinct pieces of European folk art, the origin of which is uncertain. The fate of the people living on that ground, a blend of Christians, Moslems, and Jews, was unusual and unpredictable.[9]

The creation of the first Yugoslav state in 1918 was a development long aspired to by all of these and other peoples. Movements organized in the nineteenth century promoted the Yugoslav idea of national liberation and union. Questions about the character of the newly created state, as well as about how to unite it, however, spread seeds of discord among the nations. As a result, figuratively put, it was a badly performed delivery of a long-awaited child.

The union was not entered into according to the principle of equality, since the participants were unequal, both factually and legally, and the various religious, cultural, and historical differences among the populations were not taken into account. More than a thousand years ago, diverse parts of the population were Christianized (the eastern regions from the Byzantine, adopting at the same time a modified Greek alphabet, and the western regions from the Roman missionaries under the Franks, adopting simultaneously the Latin alphabet), but in spite of their common Christianity, their differences led to religious intolerance, which characterized the period after the great schism between the western and eastern Christian churches. The divisions deepened because the western regions, especially some parts of Croatia and Slovenia, had social, economic, and cultural bonds with German and Austrian lands, while parts of Croatia were bound to the Austro-Hungarian political and governmental matrix. Slovenia was influenced significantly first by German feudal lords and later by Hapsburgs, while Croatia had a limited autonomy that decreased or increased depending on a range of circumstances.

These conditions were reflected in legal accords and produced several forms of statehood for Croatia. For the most part, however, the conditions of limited statehood were not considered at the time of Yugoslav unification, in part because parts of the future Yugoslavia found themselves on opposite sides during World War I. Serbia and Montenegro, as independent states before the war, were on the side of the Entente, while Slovenia, Croatia, Bosnia and Herzegovina, and Vojvodina, though unwillingly, were on the side of the Central Powers, which lost the war. The greatest mistake made during unification was not considering proposals of the political parties for a federal structure among the states. The imposition of a centralization- and unity-minded plan, which most suited the forces supporting the dynasty, caused great damage to the political development of Yugoslavia in the period that was to follow.

Differences in historical development, customs (partly connected to religion), and social systems led to the creation of several legal regimes that continued to function after unification.[10] By introducing dictatorship in 1929, the king also introduced legal uniformity under the guise of equalizing the legislature.

In Yugoslavia today, the population's membership in religious denominations has not been counted. A variety of religions influenced the historical shaping of individual ethnic groups and cultural-traditional habits and behaviors. Many conflicts, including bloody clashes, took place between religious groups, and religious diversity still plays a significant role in Yugoslav development.[11] The intermingling of the population, together with migrations and influences from the past (and even from our own times) has also contributed to diversity. In addition, governmental-legal, religious, and ethnic identities did not emerge all at the same time. All groups have only a few traits in common, although every trait may be characteristic of at least several groups.

Geographic conditions, too, contribute to diversity. Yugoslavia has three climatic zones in a small area (mediterranean, alpine, and continental). The traits of highlanders (some Montenegrin and Albanian tribes, for instance) differ from those of inhabitants of coastal regions (such as Dalmatia or the Bay of Kotor) or from those who live in the Vojvodina plain.

The Yugoslav Constitution contains many ideological explanations rather than precise constitutional regulations. These explanations frequently touch on the mutual relations between nations and even more frequently on socioeconomic relations and views of the future. The Constitution is understood not only as an instrument for the legal regulation of existing conditions, but also as a framework for directing society toward its goals. It should be understood that the paragraphs dealing with relations among the Yugoslav nations arise from long experience with a very sensitive issue. This is why the writing of the Constitution had to begin with issues that are beyond the law. The paragraphs that comprise the second group of explanations, which make this Constitution one of the longest in the world, address the intense dynamics of change in the contemporary world. Thus, certain organizational solutions and principles have led to a parceling of the Yugoslav economic domain into narrow political units.

The problem of constitutionally responding to diversity, guaranteeing the preservation of diverse groups, and bringing them into accord is considered here with respect to: (1) the problem of ethnic and national identity and status, self-determination, and its limits and possibilities, and how the present Yugoslav Constitution attempts to solve them with new principles and institutional and legal foundations; (2) "pluralism of interests" as an ideological device expressing and legitimizing diverse social, cultural, economic, and political groups, as well as its articulation and coordination within the framework of constitutional solutions based on decentralization; (3) how ethnic groups and regional interests are represented, the influence of diverse groups on the system, and principles of decision making; and (4) the framework provided by the Constitution for solving the problems of social and economic development among the ethnic and sociopolitical communities.

Ethnic and National Identity

The Yugoslav experience may serve as a textbook example of the extent to which the delicate question of nations and nationalities is conditioned by historical processes and circumstances. The problem of national identity of the largest Yugoslav populations—Serbs, Croats, and Slovenians—was shaped by their struggle for autonomy and statehood and for liberation from foreign dominance. Although national loyalty and certain elements and symbols of identity were long present, the presumption of politicians at the beginning of unification was that a single nation with three names was the issue. The Communist Party of Yugoslavia (CPY), whose later positions on the national question greatly influenced the present constitutional solution, first adopted the view that Yugoslavia was a single nation with three names and that the national question was a constitutional question.[12]

The idea of Yugoslavia as a melting pot was present at its creation. This idea was reflected in some acts of the transitional government, in some manipulations within the Constitutional Assembly (1920), and in the so-called Vidovdan Constitution (1921). The framers of that Constitution ignored all ideas about federalization of the country, although such ideas were raised not only by Croatians and Slovenians, but also by a host of Serbian, Moslem, Montenegrin, and Vojvodinian representatives. The 1921 Constitution included nothing about the rights of nationalities (that is, ethnic groups) because it rested on the theory of one nation with three names. Instead of using the former, traditional, though ethnically mixed, provinces as territorial-political units, it tailored new regions so that members of a single nationality would not live in a single region (a region numbered only 800,000 inhabitants). The process of gerrymandering was used abundantly to dissolve ethnic groups by decreasing their concentration within territorial-political units.

Because of the discord over national policies, the left-wing faction of the CPY addressed the Communist International. At its Fifth Congress (Moscow, June–July 1924) it adopted a resolution on the national question in Yugoslavia that determined the position of the CPY on this issue for the next decade. The position was that Yugoslavia was an "artificial creation of Western European imperialism" and that it should be broken up. Croatia, Slovenia, and Macedonia, it held, should be separated out of it.[13] This position changed only after a decision was made in 1935 to establish popular fronts as an obstacle to the fascist threat.

Not until the 1926 Congress, for instance, did the CPY first mention the Macedonian national question (the Montenegrin question was mentioned much later, in 1940). Thus, one may conclude that one radical opposition party (the CPY)—which was theoretically guided by a doctrinal position on national self-determination (the position adopted in 1923) only slowly reached an understanding of the individual nations, their status, and their identity in general. In the late 1920s, the national question intensified as relations between the Serbs and the Croats became strained. In a highly tense atmosphere of accusations and counteraccusations in the Parliament in 1928, a representative made an attempt on the lives of several members of the Croatian Peasants party (which in the meantime had recognized the monarchy and had dropped the word "republican" from its name). Popular party leaders, the Radics, and another representative were killed, and two party leaders were wounded. This incident provided the king with a good excuse to introduce his dictatorship in 1929, to abolish the Constitution, and to ban all political organizations and associations active in "tribal-religious" matters along with all national coats of arms, banners, and symbols. Soon the country was divided into nine regional administrative units (*banovina* is the Serbo-Croatian term), and the gerrymandering system became even more evident.

In 1939 a Serbo-Croatian accord created the regional unit Banovina of Croatia, which obtained autonomy greater than the other regional units. Nevertheless, popular demands were not satisfied by this accord, and Yugoslavia collapsed in the face of the fascist powers' attack in April 1941 in accordance with Hitler's directives on destruction of Yugoslavia as a state.

Soon after the German occupation and the creation of the Independent State of Croatia (ISC), *Ustashis* (Croatian nationalist units formed in the mid-1930s in replication of the Nazi SS) began persecuting the Serbian population, driving them out of Croatia, Bosnia and Hercegovina, and other regions that came under the ISC's jurisdiction (1,900,000 Serbs had found themselves in ISC territory). Mass extermination of the Serbian population began, together with forced conversion to Roman Catholicism in certain regions. The Serbs mounted an armed resistance, and the population was taken away to death camps. The victims were Serbs, Jews, Gypsies, and any Croats and others who disagreed with the so-called regime of quislings that had been established. It is considered that in the biggest camp alone, Jasenovac, 500,000 to 600,000 men, women, and children were killed, while some estimates reach up to 700,000. Of the 1,706,000 Yugoslav victims in World War II, a large number were killed in fratricidal fighting over nationalistic and religious convictions. Serbian nationalists (Chetniks) started to kill Moslems and Croatians. The clashes featured the typical elements of religious warfare.

The forming of national identities for individual Yugoslav nations took place during the National Liberation War (World War II). The decisions made at the second session of the AVNOJ antifascist assembly (November 29, 1943) are considered to have formed the foundation of present-day Yugoslavia. Among them was the decision to establish Yugoslavia's federative order, although the decision to have five nations and six federal units had been made earlier. The basic principles of the new Yugoslavia were equality and national self-determination, including the right to secede. Representative legislative bodies and governments of individual federal units to enforce the new principles and relations were established during the war.

The Constitutional Assembly elected in 1945 established the Assembly of Nations as the second house along with the Federal Assembly. The 1946 Constitution transformed the two assemblies into two councils: the Federal Council and the Council of Nations. The Constitution in its entirety, and in particular the institutions designed to solve the national question, were inspired by the 1936 Soviet Constitution. Later the constitutional system and the federalism it introduced were evaluated as promoting centralism under the guise of federalism. The shortcomings of this system were first observed not in the area of federal institutions and their relations, but rather in the relationship between government and society.

When analysis and criticism of the system began, federalism and the way it addressed the national question were set aside. In that period, the national question was thought to have been solved by the established structure of power and the inclusion of the national republics as states. The governments turned most of their attention to industrialization. Administrative centralism deprived the federal units of influence in the most substantial sectors of the economy, leaving them control over the less important projects of the republican and local economies. Thus the central government disposed of the largest part of the national income, both directly (by management through appointed directors and officials) and indirectly (by means of laws and regulations). It might be said that a federal shell was established within which administrative centralism operated.[14]

The late 1940s saw adoption of decentralization and the introduction of self-management, thus greatly changing societal relationships.[15] Those changes did not, however, substantially affect the federal system itself, the question of statehood for different nations within the country, or other issues of status and symbols of national identification. The decentralization process gave the regions some autonomy in solving their own problems and increased their freedom of expression.

When the Constitutional Law was passed in 1953, self-management acquired a constitutional and legal foundation. The Council of Nations, along with the establishment of national republics, was considered to be one of the most important ways for different groups and nations to have expression in Yugoslavia and anticipated the guarantee of national equality. Its status changed in 1953: its representatives were included in the general, political Federal Council, except on matters of national equality when it would act separately. This arrangement was retained in the 1963 Constitution of the Socialist Federal Republic of Yugoslavia (SFRY). Accordingly, the Council of Nations became almost inactive and did not meet in special session except to consider changes in the Constitution. The Yugoslav constitution makers seem to have considered the national question resolved. They believed that other governmental bodies, more capable of effectuating the functional aspects of federalism, should be included in the process of decision making. This view also has been expressed by Yugoslav political leaders.

The program of the LCY (League of Communists of Yugoslavia), developed in 1958, dealt less with federalism and the national question than with other issues. Chapter VIII of the program is subtitled, "The Federation and Relations among the Nations of Yugoslavia." It emphasized "principles of recognizing individuality, equality, and the right to self-determination of all Yugoslav nations as well as their unity, based on the federal governmental structure." Five nationalities, ranked according to their populations, are mentioned individually: Serbs, Croats, Slovenians, Macedonians, and Montenegrins. (Moslems were not yet mentioned as a nationality.) According to the program, "the unity" of Yugoslavia is only possible if based on the free development of nations and on the full equality of all nationalities and national minorities. This is the reason why socialist Yugoslavia came into being, why Yugoslavia could have been created only as a federal state of equal and sovereign nations, and why the rights of all nations in Yugoslavia are ensured by the "status of national republics and other institutions of the federal state."[16] In supporting Yugoslav socialist patriotism in conjunction with democratic national consciousness, the program stated that the "creation of a single new Yugoslav nation to replace existing nations is not the issue. . . . In Yugoslavia today, the national question does not concern a problem of national hegemony or of the oppression of nations."[17]

The transformation of the Yugoslav Federation in the late 1960s, which has been called the "dismantling of the Federation," was influenced by several factors. Certainly, issues of the status and identity of nationalities played a role in this process. In 1966 the question was raised of identifying Croat as a separate literary language, as was the problem of restricting the rights of Albanians and other minorities in Kosovo in light of the secret police's special role. A question also was raised regarding the role of federal institutions in the flow of income from more developed to less developed (or "favored") regions. This latter question centered on the right certain national communities might have to dispose of their own income. Also raised was the question of the national structure of the decision-making bodies, of governmental and party administration, and of the system of decision making in general. Among the factors usually ignored was the struggle for power within the various circles of leading officials, although it preceded the demands related to the status and symbols of group identity and the economy.

The freedom to use the mother tongue in education and in matters before government institutions has always been very important in those areas with mixed populations. For centuries, language was a means not only of communication but also of identifying individual nations, and the struggles for the right to use a national language took numerous victims. We can recall here the advice Jean-Jacques Rousseau gave to the Poles: If a nation refuses to accept the language of its occupiers, the intruders will never be able to conquer that nation.[18] This is why in many regions many people who can understand a second particular language will engage in conversation only in their own or even in a third language.[19]

Yugoslav circumstances would not be as complicated as they are if the language question resulted solely from relations between the speakers of the Serbo-Croatian language (spoken by over three-fourths of the population) and the members of smaller ethnic groups who speak other languages. But because of the intense rivalry between the Serbs and the Croats, especially after unification, and the intolerance that was instigated partly by the churches to which each belonged, major arguments flared over the relationship between what some contended were two languages: Serbian and Croatian.[20]

The use of a mother tongue in education and communication is an issue closely related to the basic rights of national minorities. The equality of languages of Yugoslav nations was proclaimed as early as 1943 in a decision made at the second AVNOJ session. Basic rights in this regard were guaranteed by all Yugoslav constitutions after World War II, but because the realization of these rights depends on the availability of significant financial resources, in some cases economic potential and local circumstances determined the language actually used. A brief survey of how the 1974 Yugoslav Constitution addresses diversity of language follows.

Article 170 of the 1974 Constitution guarantees every citizen freedom to proclaim adherence to a nationality, the freedom to participate in one's national culture, and the freedom to use one's own language and alphabet. A citizen is not obligated to declare the nation or nationality to which he or she belongs, nor to declare a membership in only one nation. Every act of propaganda, of implementing a policy of national inequality, and of inflaming national, racial, or religious hatred or intolerance is punishable.[21] Members of nationalities have, in accordance with the Constitution and the law, the right to use their own language and alphabet in the exercise of their rights and duties, as well as in procedures before government institutions. Members of nations and nationalities of Yugoslavia, in the territory of each individual republic (autonomous region) have the right to be educated in their native languages.[22]

In line with traditional demands that nations should be organized and defined as political entities in the form of "national states" (regardless of the trend to transcend regionalism), the fact that republics within the Yugoslav federation are defined as states is of particular importance. To be defined as a state each must include more than one nation, though nationalists, as a rule, have opposed this view. This is important because, as mentioned above, not one Yugoslav republic, except for Slovenia, has a homogeneous national structure.

The federal units (socialist republics) are defined as state communities of multiple ethnic groups. This definition might seem meaningless to someone not informed about the Yugoslav situation. Its importance, however, can be seen from the discussions on constitutional amendments in 1971. At that time nationalists claimed that each republic should be defined as a national state of a single nation. This upset the additional nations living in a republic because of what they had experienced in the not-so-distant past—pressure applied to force emigration, "ethnic counting" when people apply for jobs, the favoring of a single nationality in the labor force, and advocacy of the "ethnic purity of a territory," thereby denying other ethnic groups the opportunity to claim their rights as ethnic groups. For these reasons the Constitution of Bosnia and Herzegovina, for instance, defines a republic as a "socialist democratic state," and defines its national structure as "nations of Bosnia and Herzegovina and members of other nations and nationalities." Under the term "nations of Bosnia and Herzegovina," three nations are mentioned: Moslem, Serb, and Croat. These three nations are mentioned every time in varying order, so that every nation has its turn at the beginning, middle, and end of the list.[23]

The constitution of the Socialist Republic of Croatia states that it is the "national state of the Croatian nation, the state of the Serbian nation in Croatia, and the state of nationalities living within it."[24] The preamble of that constitution begins: "By means of the revolutionary struggle of workers, peasants, and all progressive people of Croatia during the national liberation war and the socialist revolution, the Croatian nation, in a brotherly union with the Serbian nation in Croatia and all nations and nationalities of Yugoslavia. . . ." The meaning of this ideological exposition can be understood only in the light of history. The Croatian nation struggled for over a thousand years to preserve its national identity and to establish the legal foundation of its statehood within the broader, imperial structures of the Hungarian and Hapsburg monarchies; the Croatian intellectuals were the first to propose the Yugoslav idea, which the people accepted very willingly, though unification after World War I seemed to negate Croatia's governmental-legal tradition and identity. Since its beginning, the national movement and the Croatian national question together have been one of the fundamental issues in Yugoslavia. To these historical facts one must add the experience of the Serbs in Croatia under the notorious "government of quislings," the Independent State of Croatia (1941–1945).

In the early 1970s, nationalist activity in Croatia began anew. The nationalists, with their extremism and exclusiveness, provoked great concern among the Serbian population whose number in Croatia, according to the 1981 census, was 531,000 compared with 3,454,000 Croats.[25] In 1971 the scope of that concern was demonstrated by the

Serbian population in certain regions of Croatia who began to arm themselves and who posted guards around their settlements, an action that Tito himself warned against.[26]

Croatian nationalists proposed that the constitutional definition contain the term "Serbs in Croatia" so that the Serbs would be considered as individuals rather than as a group. The term "Serbian nation in Croatia," they thought, expresses the idea that "Croatia is the homeland of this part of the Serbian nation, that the Serbs are natives of this land, and that nothing is temporary."[27]

The constitution of the Socialist Republic of Serbia also defined Serbia as a "state of the Serbian nation and parts of other nations and nationalities living and exercising their sovereign rights within it."[28] Republics are defined similarly in other constitutions.[29]

Each Yugoslav republic has its own coat of arms and flag. Croatia is the only one with its own national anthem. The content and use of these symbols and emblems are regulated by the constitutions and laws. There are few problems in this regard. The authorities insist that the signs of nationalities be used on public occasions in such forms as are determined by the constitution or the law, that is, alongside the federal flag or coat of arms and the five-pointed star as symbols of the new postwar state. On the occasion of their own celebrations, however, the nationalities use the same national flags and colors without these emblems. It is not the "socialist" character of these emblems that is in question, but the tokenism of recognizing or not recognizing the country's federal statehood and its constitutional forms. Concerning the use of national anthems, problems have arisen only on occasions of international character when they replace the Yugoslav federal anthem. In practical terms, this has meant that particular national anthems may be used on national (republican) occasions, but on international occasions only after the federal anthem or not at all. The issue of the flag used by the Albanians in Yugoslavia is still unsettled. They use a flag identical to that of the neighboring Socialist Republic of Albania (a red field with a black eagle in the middle). In the Yugoslav republics in which Albanians live, the sociopolitical organizations insist that such a flag include an emblem (a miniature coat of arms or a small Yugoslav flag in the corner, for instance, as used by other Yugoslav republics), so that it can be recognized that Albanians using it live within the borders of Yugoslavia and recognize its sovereignty.

The importance of religion for national and other identification is a question that has been discussed extensively in Yugoslavia. Since constitutions divide church and state authority, they do not include religious adherence as an element of identification or national statehood, as was the case in some Yugoslav nations in the past. Following one's religion is considered a private matter and is not banned, but the Constitution and laws say that in following one's religion one may not use it for political purposes.

The Pluralism of Interests

In the development of Yugoslavia, and in efforts to systemically and constitutionally address diversity, a particular role was played by what is now referred to as "self-management pluralism of interests," which originated in the policy of decentralization. This was the first noncentralist, even anticentralist, course in the history of Yugoslavia. In its development during the period from 1950 through the late 1960s, when the polycentric statism of the federal units suppressed and "organized" the expression of various interests, pluralism represented one consistent alternative to the preceding administrative centralism. Centralism failed to control the conflicts that resulted from contradictory interests and was extremely dangerous for Yugoslavia in the prewar and postwar periods. Pluralism made the formation of large factions on ethnic, religious, or administrative bases very difficult.

Yugoslav political scientists, sociologists, law specialists, economists, and others still debate whether the constitution-making leadership deliberately chose atomization for the society in order to mitigate conflict and to contribute democratically to meeting the needs and interests of diverse groups and to creating the framework for their autonomy. Foreign observers, not bound by any need for ideological rationalization, see it simply as a technique for controlling conflict. Jack Fisher, an American specialist in the study of urbanization in Yugoslavia and the system's approach to regional differences, formulated this conclusion in the early 1960s:

> The Yugoslavs attempted to restrict conflict and ensure progress by including mass participation of the country's citizens in both local and administrative organs of their communities and the governing institutions of the enterprises in which they worked. The Yugoslav goal was to obtain integration through controlled differences or ordered local diversity under an indirect mechanism of federal supervision.[30]

The Yugoslav leadership began looking for a democratic alternative to authoritarian socialism after a conflict with the Informbureau and the Soviet leadership was subjected to investigation and analysis.

Stalin's tendency to dominate other parties, movements, and countries was related to the bureaucratic and authoritarian character of his regime.

The first major step in paving the Yugoslav way to socialism was the introduction of worker self-management. Changes in the relations between the government and the self-management leadership were frequent, and the government bureaucratic and political elites have remained a dominant force for self-management to this day; direct management was entrusted to the employed, while the most important financial-monetary, investment, and personnel decisions were retained by the government and the party administration. Despite these restrictions, self-management yielded many positive consequences. From the beginning it presumed the legitimacy of a pluralism of interests and the potential for democratic expression, even though pluralism did not obtain full ideological legitimacy until the late 1960s.

The policy of the four Ds—democratization, decentralization, debureaucratization, and destatization—as well as worker self-management, has been implemented through local self-management agencies since the mid-1950s. Instead of state control and management by appointed state officials, forms of social management were soon introduced in the social services, education, health, and the sciences, through bipartite or tripartite councils to which representatives of the employed, representatives of consumers, or concerned groups of citizens (such as parents, students, and the like), as well as representatives of society from various associations, institutes, and universities were elected.

It became clear to Yugoslav politicians and theorists that the new system could not function if, in the one-party system, the party held all the levers of power and influence. The agenda of constitution-making discussions included the issue of changing the party's role, its reform and internal reorganization. But "Damocles' sword" was hanging over the head of those who wanted such change. They were accused of reformism, of "liquidatorship," or of transforming the party into a debating club, all of which were, since Lenin's times, serious charges against those who questioned the rigorous organizational structure of the party, despite the fact that the structure led to oligarchic tendencies in both the party and in society. As emphasized above, though, the political party in Yugoslavia was the very element that integrated diverse social groups in a noninstitutionalized way. Indecision about this matter characterized the entire development of Yugoslavia that followed.

At the Sixth Congress of the Communist Party of Yugoslavia

(Zagreb, 1952), the leadership proposed that self-management would require a different role for the party. The presumption was that bureaucratic tendencies, apparent in the history of socialism and in postrevolutionary regimes, were related to the role ascribed to the ruling party. It was proposed that the CPY should express the change in its role symbolically by changing its name to the League of Communists of Yugoslavia (LCY).

A system based on pluralism and decentralization was an implicit criticism of the centralistic model of society, and this criticism related especially to the role and position of the Communist party. This is why such a conception elicited sharp criticism from the communist parties in power. The criticism waxed and waned, depending on relations with foreign countries and international developments. It was mitigated during Khrushchev's and Bulganin's visits to Belgrade in 1955. Relations became strained, however, after the 1956 events in Hungary and Poland and in 1957 when the LCY refused to take part in the Moscow gathering of twelve Communist and workers' parties of socialist countries. The criticism directed at Yugoslav politicians and the Yugoslav system was extremely sharp because of allegations of "revisionism" and other "deviations." The LCY leadership's explanation of its views focused on the problems connected with the evolution of socialism. It prepared a draft program of the LCY and prepared to adopt it at the Seventh Congress of the LCY (Ljubljana, 1958) after public discussion. The Soviet leadership of that period viewed the draft (published in several foreign languages) as a model of socialism presenting an alternative to the Soviet model. This provoked a series of arguments and efforts to postpone the adoption of the program.[31]

In Yugoslavia there also were attempts to give up, change, or treat the program as outdated, but arguments that the program include basic ideas and tenets of the "Yugoslav way to socialism" prevailed.[32] These ideas form the foundation upon which the social, political, and constitutional systems are built. Although this document is not constitutional in character, the evaluative system upon which social and cultural pluralism developed—one that enables expression of differences within a society and provides for the adjustment of legal and institutional approaches to them—cannot be perceived fully without taking this program into consideration.

The program placed the individual before all institutions and organizations, and even before the government and the party. It proclaimed that socialism may not subordinate an individual's happiness to some "higher goals," since the highest goal of socialism is the "happiness of individual men," and the "restriction of the freedom to work necessarily leads to the distortion of socialist relations."[33] The conclusion drawn on that basis was that the development of democracy and the establishment of institutions should "guarantee an individual the right to independence and the freedom to express his or her thoughts, that is, religious and other convictions, and to join economic, political, social, cultural, professional, scientific, sporting, or other associations, for the protection of human dignity."[34]

Reality, of course, is never as beautiful as the programmatic vision of the future, but the commitments of the program did play a role in constituting the political and legal institutions. Another important position in the document rejects, on the ideological level, a monopoly over truth:

> The LCY as a whole, and in its particular sections, does not consider itself the final arbiter in the field of Marxism-Leninism or in the area of the social sciences and humanities. Science is its own judge, and the crucial criterion of the objectivity of truth in the area of the social sciences can only be whether the results of an inquiry correspond or not to reality, which is determined by the social scientific practice itself.[35]

The first part of this quotation implies the human being's right to pursue his or her happiness and the right to reject the advice of the government or a social authority as supposedly in the individual's best interest. The second part of the quotation refers not only to the autonomy of science, but also to the right of each person to doubt and test all that used to be considered ideologically taboo as well as to consider new ways of solving social problems. Various schools of literature, arts, and philosophy have emerged, as have theoretical concepts and views on social issues, without which it would be impossible for groups to express their diversity.

A certain pragmatism in the approach to social problems is contained in the frequently quoted final paragraph of the program, according to which every dogma is subject to criticism. It says, too, that "nothing created can be so sacred to us that it cannot be superseded by something even more progressive, more free, and more human!"[36]

The program was instituted in the middle of the decade between the passing of the Constitutional Law (1953) and the Constitution of the SFRY (1963). To resolve the problems of diversity in Yugoslav social life these two constitutional acts emphasized local adjustment and functional interrelations. Federalism has played an important role in this, though not a dominant one.

The problems to be settled in the course of decentralization were understood as communal, local, sectional, professional, regional, and developmental or as the social problems of specific categories of persons (lower paid workers or children whose parents perished in wartime, for instance). But problems relating to individual nationalities were thought to be only secondary.

Politics has included for over a millennium the practice of increasing the number of factions to mitigate conflict. The price of using this remedy can be high in the face of demands posed by modern technology and economics for integration into ever larger entities. James Madison's advice in *The Federalist* (numbers 10 and 51), however, is well known. He saw a "republican remedy for the disease most incident to Republican Government," that is, against factional tyranny, by finding a way to "secure the public good, and private rights, against the danger of such a faction," and to "guard one part of the society against the injustice of the other part." He contended that this can be done "by creating a will in the community independent of the majority" and by allowing for as many different interests as possible so that their mutual competition would restrict and neutralize them, providing space for liberty and the protection of rights. To achieve this goal, "ambition must be made to counteract ambition."[37]

We also can see the idea of competing interests leading to neutralization in Rousseau's writings. He cited Machiavelli and provided the examples of Solon, Numa, and Servius: If societies are already divided, then it is politically wise to multiply the number of divisions in them, so that each faction will be in an equal position in regard to the others.[38]

On the role of interests in the political process, one scholar, Miroslav Pecujlic has said, with reference to Shan-Yan, that a "ruling political and economic system produces the interests that serve the reproduction of its power."[39] The "interests produced by the ruling system appear as the working people's own interests (i.e., of the world of work), even though their dependence is thus renewed." He cites two examples. The first is the principle of "bureaucratic collectivism" or of a "political corporate system" based on two opposing characteristics: "the atomization of the working classes and their simultaneous integration forced by the bureaucratic authority which determines and defines the common interest." We also can cite the views of Chinese legists on this from the ancient book by Shan-Yan. A ruler is counseled to weaken his people in order to strengthen the state by breaking the community up into small groups that will watch over one another and by breaking off communications between them. The bureaucracy would then come forth to integrate this shattered community by means of its uniform views and administrative methods.[40]

When the population is divided, it is easier to manipulate. Divisions also can be provoked by creating political entities; once they obtain their autonomy it is difficult to convince them that they should reunite. John Adams, in *A Defence of the Constitution of Government of the United States of America*, published in London in 1787–1788, discusses the discord in ancient democratic republics, but he begins the discussion with the following:

> In the year 1774, a certain British officer, then at Boston, was often heard to say, "I wish I were Parliament: I would not send a ship or troop to this country, but would forthwith pass a statute, declaring every town in North America a free, sovereign, and independent commonwealth. This is what they all desire, and I would indulge them; I should soon have the pleasure to see them all at war with one another, from one end of the continent to the other."[41]

The other method by which the system relies on local interests for a strengthening of its structures, according to Pecujlic, is through the preoccupation with consumer goods. The people strive to satisfy their increasing needs and, by racing after social status and its symbols, take on patterns of behavior that maintain the social hierarchy. Pecujlic dealt with these mechanisms in a general way, though his implication is that they found application in Yugoslav society.

From the above, one might conclude that the division, as well as the decentralization, of the population can be used to promote human freedom and the participation of individuals in the affairs of the community in the same way that it was conceived by James Madison and many others who have contributed to the theory of democracy.[42] The conclusion that can be drawn, based on an analysis of the complexity of Yugoslav society and the achievements of pluralism during the 1950s and the 1960s, is that intrinsic economic, ideological, cultural, and (indirectly) political pluralism are not only social facts of life, but also indications of the level of freedom enjoyed by Yugoslav citizens. It is possible that the atomization of society was a "lesser evil," chosen because it prevented potentially destructive confrontation between the larger population blocs. Creating new diversity probably had an economic price; nevertheless, with other safety valves in the system, it helped prevent sharper conflicts among social groups and between nations (except in Kosovo, where tensions have been smoldering since 1945, with eruptions in 1968 and 1981).

What would be the method of integration according to this conception? At the time, the role of promoting integration was assigned to the party and to "self-management integration." In order to integrate and direct the society the party was to distance itself from everyday politics and the details of administration. Steps in that direction were taken as early as the late 1960s, but in practice other tendencies prevailed.[43]

When the communal system of local autonomy was introduced, Edvard Kardelj said: "Our previous goal was to have our society become an organic 'national community' of communes, not, therefore, a federation of communes, but a single organism in which individual cells live their full lives by drawing their strength from the society as a whole and their own initiative."[44] The ideas that gained constitutional-legal expression in 1963 had to do with the functional connections among the individual areas of social life, ranging from the smallest community to the Federation. The result of these concepts was a complex structure of the representative body at the federal level, with five (six, if the Council of Nations is taken into account) councils for various fields such as economy, education and health. Some writers see Yugoslavia as a federation of municipal or communal administrations; the idea of communal federalism has remained attractive to this day.[45]

Representation of Ethnic Groups and Regional Interests

Statistical data, political opinions, and retrospective criticisms of the state of things in the early 1960s revealed that dispersion to communes of either political power or material (financial) means had never prevailed in practice. Problems were also perceived in the succession to power, in decision making, and in the relationships among the political centers in the post-Tito period.[46] The constitutional solution to these problems led to a new distribution of power between the Federation and the federal units, the reorganization of the Federation's agencies, the adoption of consensus and cooperative federalism, the establishment of a collective head of state which, after President Tito's death, replaced the former office of the president of the republic, and a range of other solutions.

During the late 1960s, political elites, who had ensured their new positions through the process of amending the constitution, realized that their power was being diminished by the market economy and its autonomy. Two economic reforms in Yugoslavia in 1961 and 1965 failed because of internal resistance from the same persons who had adopted them or from those who were supposed to implement them.

In 1966 forces in the party and government ruling circles, which were judged to be statist and centralist, were defeated politically and pushed into the background. But the development of self-management, the market-oriented economy, and the democratization of society did not make progress to the extent expected. Indeed, instead of a single, statism-oriented federal center dominating the economy and social life, eight political centers were constituted among the federal units. These centers duplicated former statist relationships, but on another level. The idea of national statehood and national sovereignty in political and economic issues, as well as in national culture, language, education, information media, and other issues, became the basis of legitimacy for the regional political elites.

Several changes were carried out according to two bases of legitimacy. The first was the realization of national equality; the second was the promotion of self-management so that it would become the dominant, ruling system of relationships within the economy and society.

The difference between the terms "nations of Yugoslavia," which numbered five (and later six) nations of Slavic descent, and "national minorities" has existed since the Second World War (that is, since the second session of the antifascist assembly (AVNOJ) in 1943). The difference between the rights of these groups has never been related to their members' individual rights, but rather to the character and scope of their collective rights to organize into distinct political communities. The rights of the two kinds of groups were made equal in principle by the nineteenth constitutional amendment (1968). National minorities were given the opportunity through the Constitution to become—by virtue of their residence in their autonomous regions—constituent parts, not only of their republics, but also directly of the Federation. Not long afterward, the autonomous regions became elements of both the Federation and the Federal Republic of Serbia. This duality in the status of the autonomous regions is a subject of frequent discussions in the organs of the Socialist Republic of Serbia today, the title of which does not state explicitly that it is federally structured, although actually it is. Because of the existence of two regions within the framework of the Socialist Republic of Serbia, many ill-defined issues became apparent in the system's solutions to problems.[47]

As discussed above, the Council of Nations was established beginning with the Constitutional Assembly of 1945 to guarantee national equality. Its responsibilities were somewhat reduced by the regulations in the 1953 and 1963 constitutions. In the process of amending the 1963 Constitution, however, the Council of Nations went through a transformation. First, its importance as a council was re-established (Amendment I, 1967). In 1968, the council became the most important council representing the republics and regions (Amendments VIII and IX). Finally, its name was changed by the third series of amendments to the Council of the Republics and Provinces, and it acquired the status of a federal house, even though it lost its role of representing the nations and ethnic groups. (This change, however, should be viewed in light of the fact that, except for Slovenia, no federal unit is nationally homogeneous. Not even the delegations in the former Council of Nations consisted of nationally homogeneous representations.) Therefore, the federal units were represented at the federal level through their delegations in the Council of the Republics and Provinces. Technically, this mode seemed to be the only one possible. Some large groups remained without a "delegation," however, while others were even denied the status of a nationality—those, for instance, who declared themselves Yugoslavs.[48]

In the distribution of power that took place between the mid-1960s and the mid-1970s, the fundamental source of power passed from the Federation to the federal units.[49] This was reflected in the role of the presidency of the SFRY, in the character and position of the Council of the Republics and Provinces, as well as in the methods by which the council is elected and makes decisions. The 1974 Constitution abandoned the principle of two houses for decision making in the SFRY Assembly, thus increasing the role of the Council of the Republics and Provinces. The most important matters of concern to the federal units are now addressed by this council. These are not political, but economic matters.

The Council of the Republics and Provinces consists of twelve delegates from each of the assemblies of the republics, plus eight from each of the assemblies of the autonomous provinces, but these delegates retain their positions in the assemblies of their respective republics or provinces.[50] The delegates' continuing role in their home provinces is especially important because the basic constitutional role of the Council of the Republics and Provinces is to ensure consensus among the assemblies of the republics and provinces in the areas in which federal laws and other general acts are passed by mutual agreement (Article 286, 1974). The process of reaching agreement is very complicated and usually takes a long time. When the council decides on such matters the voting is done by delegation, and a law is adopted only when all the delegations vote in favor of it (Article 295, 1974). In addition, all the delegations are required to represent the views of the assemblies of their respective republics and provinces.

In this way, the federal units now take part in the process of decision making and in the determination of policies of the Federation agencies. In practical terms, this means that each federal unit has a veto power in the legislative body of the Federation. This power can be mitigated, however, by "temporary measures" effective for one year. In addition, the federal units may reach bilateral and mutual agreements, without the Federation agencies' participation, on a range of matters within their jurisdiction, in order to determine the so-called common interest. Finally, several interrepublican committees coordinate the views of the republics on certain issues.

One of these changes dealt with the problem of defining democracy itself and the process of democratic decision making. For about two decades after World War II, democracy in Yugoslavia was defined as majority rule. Democratic theories concerning the rights of minorities and certain principles and rules that could not be changed by the majority were neglected. Suddenly there was a complete turn of events. Discussion began about the dangers of majoritarianism, and the possibility that it could produce violations of the inalienable rights of minorities. At the time, only two areas existed in which Yugoslav constitutional provisions and judicial practice provided protection for minorities: the identification of ethnic minorities and federal units (as important creations for national relations) and the institutional guarantee that decisions on their substantial interests and rights could not be voted on by majority rule.

Therefore, the Jacobin principle of the organization of power and society was accepted earlier, although it was incompatible with authentic federalism and local autonomy—that is, incompatible with the autonomy of diverse groups existing in Yugoslav society, and with the autonomy of nations in particular. Since many issues involve national feelings, pride, prestige, and even national interests, decisions that affect one or a few groups cannot be made by a majority vote of the members of other ethnic groups in the broader community without producing undesirable effects and discontent.[51]

The Assembly of Yugoslavia does not decide all issues by consensus. The Constitution enumerates the issues on which decisions are to be made in this manner. Usually, these issues fall within the jurisdiction of the Council of the Republics and Provinces. In certain cases, in order to avoid major economic or other consequences resulting from the irreconcilability of views, the Council of the Republics and Provinces, on the recommendation of the presidency of the SFRY, may adopt temporary measures by a two-thirds majority vote.[52]

The principle of equal representation does not apply to the legislative body alone. As the collective head of state, the presidency of the SFRY plays the role of "taking account of the consensus on the common interests of the republics and autonomous provinces, with the objective of assuring the equality of nations and nationalities" (Article 313, 1974). It is made up of one representative from each federal unit elected for a five-year term and of one person who performs the functions of the president of the presidency of the League of Communists of Yugoslavia (LCY) (Article 321, 1974). The presidency of the SFRY has certain rights concerning its relation to the legislative body (the Assembly of the SFRY) and the government (the Federal Executive Council). The Federal Executive Council—that is, the administration—is established on the principle of equal representation of the federal units; other officials in the state administration also are elected and appointed on the principle that the representation of various nationalities, republics, and provinces must be taken into account (Article 348, 1974).

This last requirement is called the "personnel key." This "key" means, in effect, that all major political bodies and federation agencies must include equal representation from each federal unit. The national structure must be taken into account in the representation principle for the governing bodies. This approach is in accord with the principle of national equality in a multinational country. It provides the federal units with a new instrument of influence and strengthens certain elite interests relevant to the federal unit in question.

Nevertheless, this solution contains a number of disadvantages. First, there are cases when regional loyalty takes precedence over the ability to perform a given task, which can lower the quality of performance. Second, the Constitution says that federal officials who are members of the Federal Executive Council and officials of the federal administration and organizations "cannot receive directions and orders from the organs and officials of other sociopolitical communities, or act according to their directions and orders" (Article 362, 1974). In fact, though, this regulation has not been followed, since survival at a given position and promotion to a higher one depends on the support of the official's federal unit. Another disadvantage of the personnel keys is the difficulty of ensuring democratic elections, and a frequently made argument against candidate lists is that candidates belonging to a particular nationality might be dropped from the race, possibly disturbing the necessary balance in the composition of official personnel.

The last objection to the concept of personnel keys, but not the least important, is that such a system may lead to the inequality of both individuals and national groups within the population of certain federal units. Individuals may find that a given official position is more easily accessible to those belonging to smaller ethnic groups, where competition based on ability is far less intense than in larger ones. It has already become proverbial that a capable assistant or colleague must be found for every incapable official. The latter comes to the position through the "key," while the former does the job of both of them. Populations of different regions have found themselves in unequal positions, since the smallest republic, with fewer than 600,000 inhabitants, is entitled to the same rights as the most numerous republic with over 9 million.

The federal units are provided with a major veto power, though an absolute veto does not really exist. A federal unit can resort to it as an instrument of bargaining. The Constitutional Court of the SFRY (made up of two members from each republic and one member from each province, according to Article 381, 1974), the Federal Court (Article 370, 1974), and other organs are established according to the principle of equal representation.[53]

The complexity of the Yugoslav federal system extends beyond the process of decision making. Because it has to ensure the participation of the diverse parts, groups, and various interests in Yugoslavia, the process of reaching consensus becomes intricate and, at times, very long. Once a decision is made, however, the complex process of implementation begins. In order to implement federal regulations, some federal units pass their own laws, while others implement the federal acts directly. Problems arise when federal acts conflict with local interests. In those cases the organs that are supposed to put the law into effect yield to the local interests and end up either not implementing the law or implementing it incompletely or incorrectly. Frequently, local courts, inspectors, and other organs must decide whether to support and enforce the law, as prescribed by the Constitution and laws, or to support the local interests. Recent analyses have demonstrated that a large proportion of the failures in implementation are due to local pressures. Achieving economic stabilization and ensuring the citizens' legal security have become practically impossible. In yielding to local interests, one frequently sacrifices those of the general public.

Solving the Problems of Social and Economic Development

In dealing with the status of nations and the relationships between individual nations and nationalities, Yugoslav politicians and humanities specialists have always paid particular attention to the so-called material foundations of equality. They employed the traditional Marxist perspective of viewing social problems through relationships within the sphere of material production and the distribution of income and placed primary importance on the conditions in which individual Yugoslav ethnic groups lived until the end of World War II. Speeding up their economic development was one of the most important elements in solving the national question.

Another problem became apparent much later—the emergence of "economic nationalism" among the more developed Yugoslav nations. They resisted the system of redistributing income from more developed to less developed regions. In the late 1960s they expressed their economic nationalism in a series of demands, a great number of which were met.[54] Later the 1974 Constitution made it impossible for the Federation (the federal administration) to form on its own any kind of financial reserves, as it had done before. During the discussions of the amendments, agreement was reached that only the Fund for the Development of Insufficiently Developed Provinces and the Autonomous Province of Kosovo should remain at the Federation level.

The federal units, and the nations and nationalities within them were sensitive to the previous mechanics of the Federation that enabled income to flow from one region to others. The goal could have been attained by economic policy measures such as credit policy, tariffs, import-export measures, and price policy. It would have been sufficient, for instance, to maintain prices of agricultural products and commodities at a low level with some regions negatively affected, and others (whose industrial products, for instance, would be protected by a high tariff and tax barrier) favored.

Dissatisfaction also was provoked by some of the Federation's investments. The last big investment project financed by the Federation's funds was the Belgrade–Bar railroad, which was 300 miles long and built in extremely mountainous terrain, making construction very expensive. But its construction could be justified by economic and other reasons, among them that the railroad provided Serbia, Macedonia, Kosovo, and Montenegro (where the railroad ends) their first direct acccess to a port on the Adriatic Sea. While almost half the country benefited from the railroad, however, the ports and railroads previously built in the other half of the country lost significance and their use has decreased. Similar issues arise when, for example, several federal units need and want to construct short roads through their territories, but none want to invest in a road connecting the northwestern parts of Yugoslavia with the southeastern, that is, Austria with Greece. It has been on such issues that nationalism has acquired its economic roots.

Constitutional regulations (1971, 1974) abolished independent funds for the Federation and its ability to engage directly in investment projects. A system of decision making was established that gave the federal units the right to determine Federation policy. According to an accord reached by the various assemblies of the republics and provinces, the Council of the Republics and Provinces can pass acts, primarily in the area of the economy, to adopt social planning projects for directing national income; to govern monetary, credit, and foreign currency systems; to determine the income of the sociopolitical communities, which is realized through taxation of products and services; and to define the system and the sources of the federal administration's income. The council also may determine the scope of expenses in the Federation budget, although specific decisions on the budget are made by the Federal Council (Article 286, 1974).

One of the effects of the constitutional changes in the early 1970s was the establishment of the economic sovereignty of the republics under the pretext that it is, in fact, a form of *national* economic sovereignty. Some of the principles that had been elaborated during self-management development were expanded to relations between nations. Those principles constitute a part of the national question by themselves. One principle is the inalienability of income from those who earn it. For instance, the abolition of exploitation, a principle on which the system of values and the range of institutional provisions in Yugoslavia are partly based, was extended to the relations between nations. Here is how Edvard Kardelj viewed the necessity for extending the validity of this principle from relations within the self-management enterprises to relations among the political communities:

> Our present practice of integration abounds in the forms of the centralization of income and of funds outside of the work organization and the economic units, as well as in the excesses of income among them. This can only be viewed by the worker as a limitation on his self-management rights, and even as expropriation of income that is rightfully his to manage. . . . If this matter is not resolved more successfully in practice, every large concentration of "capital" within the framework of the large and composite organizations of associated labor will be proclaimed as an instrument of extracting income from another national economy (within Yugoslavia), and the political factors in that other republic always will pose this question even if (or, perhaps, even though) the workers themselves do not.[55]

Such an argument supported the demand for the inalienability of income from either the worker or the regional districts (federal units). The effect of the constitutional regulations that met this demand was to enclose the economies within the boundaries of republics and autonomous provinces. Thus, the economic transfers between republics and provinces were cut, and the possibility for circulating funds was reduced to the area of a single sociopolitical community. The logic of enclosing the economies was further applied from the republics and provinces to municipal administrations, since they were not willing to have their incomes flow out of their jurisdictions either. The greatest effects of the regulations concerning the inalienability of income were experienced in the strengthening of polycentric statism and the effort of eight federal units to enclose their respective economies. The resulting duplication of production capacities in several republics and the making of investment decisions without economic rationale or consideration of market criteria contributed to the economic crisis in Yugoslavia.

There were other problems with the economic foundations of national equality. The Federal Fund for the Development of Undeveloped Regions allotted funds mainly to political communities, the leaderships of which were given control over expenditures. Their uneconomical investment of these funds, often in luxurious, unproductive buildings, created demands for the funds to be allotted to enterprises that would invest in projects in insufficiently developed regions. These demands appear to have been economically justified, although they were opposed by local political officials who preferred funds with an undefined purpose to investment-directed funds over which they had no control.

Regional differences in per capita income and the unemployment rate reveal enormous economic differences. The most developed Yugoslav republic (Slovenia) and the largest (Serbia) have the lowest and highest unemployment rates in Europe respectively. The 1985 unemployment rate in Slovenia was 1.3 percent, while in Serbia it was 18 percent.

Certain regions have specific problems of their own. In some, agriculture has been abandoned as the population has flowed into cities and industrial areas. This is why entire areas have become sparsely inhabited. In others, the population density has increased so greatly that, with employment opportunities reduced, serious economic problems and problems of social progress have emerged. The Kosovo region is characteristic of this. Until recently, its leadership and representatives did not want to accept the fact that the demographic explosion has been a factor in its slowed development. They believed regional development would cause the unemployment rate to fall as in any other developed industrial society.[56]

Conclusions

In Yugoslavia today, the theoretical concept of unity in diversity has been used frequently.[57] It presupposes that the deeply rooted population melange should not be suppressed and that the society cannot be made uniform using administrative instruments alone because the society as a whole would be greatly damaged. This has been shown in the experience of Yugoslavia since its beginning. Anyone who would try to replace Yugoslavia's ethnic and cultural color with administrative "grayness" would be met by resistance from local interests and would tread on national pride and religious beliefs. In Yugoslavia, the existing diversity is as accepted as the abundance of tradition and experience. In the distant and more recent past, efforts to homogenize the population in terms of religious and ethnic affiliation have failed, but they have also caused great human loss. Yugoslavia today is seeking ways to maintain the autonomy and colorfulness of its parts, while simultaneously ensuring its unity and vitality as a whole. This is not an easy task to achieve. Frequent constitutional changes in Yugoslavia have been instituted as ways to find the appropriate relations between the whole and its parts. These changes are indicators of the difficulty of achieving that goal. The changes that were carried out could be compared figuratively with participation in a bicycle race: changes in one's position, while moving, are required in order not to fall and to remain in the race; and structural shortcomings in the whole make progress by the parts difficult.

Awareness of common interests and emotional ties, due to the similarity of fates and historical experiences of Yugoslav nations, is of much greater political significance than is sometimes considered. With this in mind, Miroslav Krleza saw the inevitable connections between Yugoslav nations:

> The fate of these nations on the Danube and of the Balkans has been at stake from time immemorial. Not a single generation has plowed a furrow that the wheels of foreigners' cannons did not cross between two harvests. Successes or failures in such circumstances, where brutal forces have crushed even the most innocent manifestations of the people's subjective will, are so fateful that the individual human being surrenders to them in weak resignation, unable to profit from any opportunity of one's own advantage whatsoever. Regardless of centuries-old efforts, when entire tribes were killed in Jacqueries and in guerrilla fighting, foreign forces were so prevalent that the people's life, with a

lasting clanking of arms, did not have an opportunity, even for a moment, to develop the conditions which would bring them the most minimal chances for the development of civilized circumstances. . . . Our people are not so un-learned that they would not be able to distinguish a volcanic, blind and cruel reality by which they are surrounded, from their own warm shelter.

One can always point to nearsightedness, strict adherence to local and regional interests, national and religious blindness and intolerance, and the bickering of elites about power as factors contrib-uting to discord and decay in political experiments. But there is one thing in Yugoslavia today in which all should be equal: the attainment of a high rate of economic development and prosperity. Yugoslavia is a prime example of how increasingly difficult it is to reach this goal if everyone pursues individual goals without regard for the problems of general industrial and social growth. Economic nationalism (es-pecially of small nations), leading to economic enclosure and protec-tionism, brings little economic prosperity in the long term.

Two major mistakes were made in constructing the Yugoslav constitutional system from the viewpoint of integrating Yugoslav society, achieving harmony in the relations of the parts, and creating conditions for bringing diverse groups closer. First, the important constitutional idea was not realized: that the Yugoslav community should form an autonomous and loosely connected society without political over-mediation. The second mistake was systemic: The Yugoslav Federation was not conceived or constitutionally founded in a way that would enable it to perform the minimal functions entrusted to it and through which consensus is reached. Because of this mis-take, disintegrative tendencies surfaced in the process of implement-ing joint decisions.

Nationalism, as Carl Freidrich once wrote, is probably the most powerful force in the contemporary world. Unless equality is en-sured, and the conditions necessary for social and democratic de-velopment are provided, nationalism can be a disintegrative force. The so-called theory of a socialist nation has always been rejected in Yugoslavia. The only alternative seemed to be the theory that placed the development of society and the individual's growth ahead of the strengthening of the state. But political reality has taken another course.

The constitutional and sociopolitical system of Yugoslavia is based on the accepted distinction between the society and the state. This concept is a part of the Yugoslav democratic alternative to au-thoritarian socialism. What has prevailed in the theory is that the state is but one among several social agencies and that its activity should be narrowed as much as possible and placed under the control of society so that the society can develop freely. The government's striving for constant expansion of its control has been observed not only on the global-historical level, but on the domestic level as well. The policy of destatization required that the economy and other areas of human activity such as science, education, and health be freed from the government's tutelage. But the bureaucracy has shown itself to be resistant and vital in Yugoslavia. It became an indispensable instrument in the hands of the new national elites. They stamped out the federal administration's influence by taking over the majority of its former functions and establishing so-called polycentric statism.

In polycentric statism eight "national" economies are established, following the logic of Keynesian economic theory or the logic of "state socialism." Each territorial-political unit creates an enclosed economic system, which tends to become an autarchic entity in which political principles dominate and edge out economic and market criteria, rationales, and logic. Of course, some say that this system is exactly what favors development of regional, national, or religious autonomy. This is partly true, especially if "autonomy" is understood as it is, for instance, by the leaders of present-day Albania; but the general and primary economic effect of such mini-states is weakness. On the political level, in multinational communities, weakness can lead to confederal forms, which might be a source of political instability; at the same time, it might lead to authoritarian power on the regional level, which some Yugoslav writers have termed "feudalization" or "refeudalization."

Such a trend is a matter of fact, as opposed to ideological commitments and constitutional regulations. One of the characteristics of Yugoslav constitutions is that they are never simply governmental-legal acts, but social charters as well. Every sociopolitical community in Yugoslavia—and this holds for the Federation as a whole—is defined as a state (the Federation and the republics), according to the elements of power, and as a democratic community of citizens, producers, nations, and nationalities. The essence is that the mechanisms of power—government organs, the administration—were given a status in which they would serve the society, and not the converse. The aim was to free the society as much as possible from unnecessary intervention by the government. All diverse groups were to flourish and to constitute a community through free associations, independent from territorial-political borders between the federal units or municipal districts.

This orientation was contained in the 1963 Constitution and was more broadly detailed in the 1974 Constitution. Yugoslavia is defined as (1) a "federal state having the form of a state community of voluntarily united nations and their Socialist Republics, and of the Socialist Autonomous Provinces of Vojvodina and Kosovo, which are constituent parts of the Socialist Republic of Serbia . . ." and (2) "a socialist, self-managed, democratic community of working people and citizens and of nations and nationalities having equal rights."[58]

The ten-year period after the adoption of the 1974 Constitution reveals that Yugoslavia and its constituent parts developed in a way that emphasized the first part of this definition. Mechanisms of government control and decision making were developed, paralleled by the growth of an administrative apparatus. Both developed together, however, into an obstacle to free commerce between the federal units. The second part of the definition, to develop a democratic society in spite of, and independent of, national statehood, has been realized only to a very small extent. The development of self-management has therefore lagged since it falls more within the social than the governmental sphere. This applies even more to science, culture, education, and social and professional associations. The individual citizen, being a natural carrier of the idea of the community, has been given a restricted role, while the corporations, organizations, and controlled associations have acquired a primary one.

Applying the categories developed by French sociologist Emile Durkheim, one could say that in Yugoslavia a lower or mechanical form of "communality" and solidarity has been prevalent. This form is based on common political frameworks and, therefore, more on external, and sometimes imposed, factors and forms of "gathering." The individual and citizen and his free associations and needs are in this case subordinated to governmental mechanisms operated by the administrative apparatus. In this context, the advancement of communality is a very slow process that can be perceived only over a long period.

The second form of communality treated by Durkheim is "organic" solidarity. The communality here evolves on the foundation of economic and cultural bonds and developed needs, which help intensify communication without government mediation; on the basis of the division of labor, the satisfaction of needs of the members of such a community is facilitated by bringing them into mutual relationships.[59] Since in Yugoslavia territorial-political boundaries and mediation by elites have tended to diminish economic, scientific, cultural, and other exchanges, not only among the federal units but among municipal administrations as well, the possibility for functional federalism is very restricted; the forms of territorial-political organizing have prevailed, especially in the name of national state-hood, which fits the forms of the operation and organization of power rather than the development of community and communality.

Prevailing Yugoslav policy preserves within the area of ethnicity all that has been inherited from tradition and history and at the same time changes the relationships and forms in all other areas. This found noticeable expression in constitutional and legal institutions. The ensuing contradiction between tradition and modernization increases the tendency toward economic and cultural exclusivity, internal unification, and the development of "enclosed consciousness," be it nationalistic or bureaucratic-dogmatic. To overcome this situation, more democracy, more self-management, more rationality, and more moral autonomy are needed.

Notes

1. After the first successful efforts of the Serbian people in their struggle, which began with a general insurrection against Turkish occupation in 1804, two conflicting factions were active among the insurrectionists: one supported the absolutist aspirations of the "leader" *(vozd)*; the other, supported by popular leaders and representatives, wanted both to participate in power and to restrict that of the prince, who always displayed a tendency toward absolute power no matter who he was. Later, the political movements (for example, the Constitution Defenders) and political parties developed various ideas about the content of the Constitution, and the prince, who would later hold the royal title, had a decisive influence on constitutional development. As in other cases where liberal and authoritarian currents meet, constitutions frequently changed in Serbia. In its one hundred years it had lived under the following constitutions: in 1811; in 1835, the liberal, so-called Sretenje Constitution (to which the Serbian Orthodox holiday is attributed), written under the influence of the ideas of Montesquieu, and the one that the prince was forced to accept (though the great powers of the period—Austria, Russia, and Turkey—opposed its liberal regulations and found reasons to try to abolish it); in 1838, the constitution offered by the Turkish Sultan in the form of an edict; in 1869, the first constitution passed by the Serbian authorities themselves, providing for the dominance of the prince over the Parliament; in 1888, the most liberal constitution, which the king abolished in 1894 to reinstate the 1869 Constitution; in 1901, the King's Bestowed Constitution; and in 1903, the reinstated and amended 1888 Constitution, following a forced change of dynasty.

2. See Plato, *Republic*, 567; Aristotle, *Politics*, 1313 b; and Herodotus, *Historiae*, vol. V, p. 92.

3. The immediate reason for the so-called First Serbian Insurrection against Turkish power (1804), described by Leopold von Ranke as the "Serbian Revolution," was the Turkish governors' decision to behead all prominent Serbian captains in order to maintain the governors' tyranny. They

succeeded in beheading a number of them before the rest, who learned of the fate ahead of them, fled to the woods as outlaws. A few years later (1822), Turkish authorities judged that the state of things in Bosnia was "anarchic" and the Sultan's envoy resorted to the well-known technique for control of Turkish captains: he called them for a consultation in Travnik (a Bosnian town) and beheaded them "in order to prevent future rebellions."

4. The large majority of the Yugoslav population consists of six nations of Slavic descent: Serbs (8,140,452), Croats (4,228,005), Moslems (1,999,957), Slovenians (1,753,554), Macedonians (1,339,729), and Montenegrins (579,023) (according to the 1981 census). There are also two major nationalities: Albanians (1,730,364) and Hungarians (426,866). These nationalities, like other smaller nationalities such as Bulgarians, Czechs, Italians, Romanians, Ruthenians, Slovaks, Turks, et al., were treated according to international standards as "national minorities" after World Wars I and II. In Yugoslavia, because of the sizes of some of these groups, and in order to indicate the full equality of all ethnic groups no matter how big or small they were, the terms "nation" and "nationality" were introduced (*The Constitution of the Socialist Federal Republic of Yugoslavia*, Belgrade, 1974, English Edition, p. 51). In everyday language these terms are synonyms, but in Yugoslavia they have acquired different particular constitutional-legal meanings.

The registering of nationalities is done on the basis of the citizens' own declarations. Interestingly, according to the Constitution, citizens do not have to declare a nationality (but there are only 46,698 citizens who have chosen not to make a declaration). 1,219,045 Yugoslav citizens have declared themselves as Yugoslavs; in the official statistical data, however, they are not recorded as a "nationality," but as those who "declared themselves as Yugoslavs." There were public arguments on this issue. These citizens are most frequently children of mixed marriages, citizens who have changed the place of their residence in the course of recent decades, or those who, in the rise of new nations, simply remained undeclared as to any of those new nations.

On the occasion of unification into one state, the prevailing opinion was that there would be one nation with three names (Serbs, Croats, and Slovenians); thus, the first name of the state was the "Kingdom of Serbs, Croats, and Slovenians." Even the newly founded Communist Party of Yugoslavia (1919) accepted that view, which might be evaluated in retrospect today as a unity-minded underestimation of the national question. In the resistance to the unity-minded monarchist regime, it became evident quickly that there are, in fact, three nations.

5. A rough indicator of differences in the levels of development is the fact that the ratios between the poorest administrative communities and a number of more affluent administrative communities, measured by per capita income, can range from 1:6 to 1:52. See *Statisticki godisnjak Jugoslavije 1984* (1984 Statistical Yearbook of Yugoslavia), hereafter referred to as *1984 SYY*. Tables on population and national income by administrative communities are found on pp. 614–623 and 634–643.

6. "Oh East is East, and West is West, and never the twain shall meet, Till

Earth and Sky stand presently at God's great Judgment Seat." Rudyard Kipling, "The Ballad of East and West" (1899).

7. For a very good description of diverse customs, folklore, and monuments in Yugoslavia, see Rebecca West, *Black Lamb and Grey Falcon* (New York: The Viking Press, 1943).

8. A recently published facsimile edition of the *Sarajevo Haggadah*, a valuable testament to Jewish culture in the Spanish provenience (dating from the 13th or 14th century), was awarded the first prize at a book exhibition in Jerusalem, Israel. Only a few members of the Sarajevo Jewish community survived World War II. They either fled abroad early enough or joined the partisan troops. This cultural treasure was preserved because it was hidden in time, thanks to a Moslem priest, among others.

9. Some of the people from this region were made immortal by Yugoslav Nobel Prize winner Ivo Andric in his novel *Na Drini cuprija* (The Bridge on the Drina). In Yugoslavia today, there are families in which brothers born to the same mother and father belong to three different nationalities. It would not be difficult to find, for instance, a Moslem family with several children each of whom declares himself a different nationality. This is possible because there are Moslems who consider themselves Serbs, Croats, Yugoslavs, Montenegrins, or Macedonians. Such a case is likely to occur when, having pursued jobs and education, they have settled in different regions.

10. Particular legal regimes were in force in Serbia and Montenegro (whose independence was recognized in 1878 by several European powers and Turkey), which had passed civil codes as early as 1844 and 1888. In Slavonia and the parts of Croatia belonging to Austria, a separate legal regime was in force, and an 1811 civil code containing numerous innovations was applied in these territories. Even though they belonged to Hungary, Croatia and Slovenia enjoyed a great deal of autonomy, each having its own governmental council and governor who served as executive officer. These territories completely lost their autonomy when they became included within Yugoslavia. Vojvodina belonged to Hungary where the Hungarian civil code was in force. Bosnia and Herzegovina, which Austria occupied in 1876 and annexed in 1908, were formerly under Turkish power. From 1910 till 1918 they had their own constitution and autonomy, similar to Croatia, but only until 1918. Moslem religious law continued to be applied in certain cases, such as family relations, inheritance matters, etc. In Dalmatia, especially on the islands, a manorial system based on the old Venetian law had been preserved.

11. See *1984 SYY* and Branko Petranovic, *Istorija Jugoslavije 1918–1978* (History of Yugoslavia, 1918–1978) (Belgrade: Nolit, 1980), pp. 32–35. According to the data from the 1921 census, the first census taken after World War I, of the 12,545,000 inhabitants, 5,593,057 inhabitants (44 percent) declared themselves Christian Orthodox; 4,708,657 (37 percent) Roman Catholic; and 1,345,271 (10.7 percent) followers of Islam. The demographic changes of the populations of these three denominations had different rates, which we will not detail here. During World War I, the nations of the present-day Yugoslavia lost 1,900,000 people, which is even more than during World War II when 1,706,000 people perished. It also takes second place on the list of

victims in World War II, with losses of 11.8 percent (immediately after Poland, with 17.3 percent, but before the Soviet Union, with 11.4 percent). With the exception of Jews, the Christian Orthodox suffered more than other denominations.

12. See S. Markovic, *Ustavno pitanje i radnicka klasa* (The Constitutional Question and the Working Class) (Belgrade, 1923); and *Nacionalno pitanje u svetlosti marksizma* (The National Question in the Light of Marxism) (Belgrade, 1923). Markovic, then secretary of the CPY, was "liquidated" in the USSR in 1939, only to be resurrected later in public memory by the Soviet judicial authorities.

13. See *Pregled istorije Saveza komunista Jugoslavije*, A Survey of the History of the League of Communists of Yugoslavia (Belgrade: Institute for Studies in the Labor Movement, 1963), pp. 125–26.

14. In his book, published after Yugoslav federalism began its journey to authentic federalism, Carl J. Friedrich called Yugoslav federalism "facade federalism." Carl J. Friedrich, *Trends of Federalism in Theory and Practice* (London: Pall Mall Press, 1968).

15. This was by virtue of The Law on the Management of State Economic Enterprises and Higher Economic Associations by Work Collectives, June 27, 1950.

16. See *Program SKJ* (The Program of the LCY) (Belgrade: Komunist, 1965), pp. 145–46.

17. Ibid., pp. 148, 150.

18. Jean-Jacques Rousseau, *Considerations sur le gouvernment de Pologne*, in *The Political Writings of Jean-Jacques Rousseau*, edited by C.E. Vaughan (Cambridge: 1915), Vol. II.

19. The language issue was a subject of sharp political conflicts in the nineteenth century, when the literary Serbo-Croatian language was created. The struggle for a popular language was fought in Croatia in the tenth century against the Pope's effort to make Latin the only accepted language of religious service.

20. Some maintain that Serbo-Croatian is a single language with a number of dialects; others maintain that every nation should have its own language and therefore that these are two languages. In Vienna in 1850, Serbian and Croatian scholars agreed that Serbo-Croatian is a single language. In the 1960s, however, some literary authors began to call that agreement into question in order to compile a handbook of contemporary language and to prepare a more practical dictionary. In 1967 a group of Croatian writers published *Declaration on the Language*, which a group of Serbian authors answered with a proposal of their own. The two documents and the activity surrounding them were viewed as nationalistic. See: "Deklaracija o nazivu i polozaju hrvatskog knjizevnog jezika" (Declaration on the Name and Position of the Croatian Literary Language), *Vjesnik* (Zagreb daily), March 19, 1967.

Three days later, on March 22, 1967, *Vjesnik* published the view of the Executive Committee of the Central Committee of the League of Communists of Croatia on this Declaration. It held that the language issue should be discussed among the experts within the framework of interrepublican cooperation and in the spirit of mutual understanding, with full political and social responsibility and respect for public opinion.

All of this indicates the nationalistic trends in political and cultural life, which had strengthened noticeably in the late 1960s, peaking by the early 1970s. Miroslav Krleza, a prominent twentieth-century Yugoslav-Croatian author, said concisely and accurately: "This is one language, which Serbs call Serbian and Croats Croatian." The difference (or similarity) is comparable to that between "British English" and "American English."

21. Article 170. These matters are addressed in the same way in the individual constitutions of all federal units.

22. Article 171. The constitutions of individual federal units put different emphasis on this matter since the situation regarding languages is not the same everywhere, though the basic principles are. The position everywhere is that there is no official language. Nationalities have their own press and other information media.

23. See USTAV SR Bosne i Hercegovine (1974), Preambula, Osnovna nacela, clanovi 1, 2 i 3. (The 1974 Constitution of the Socialist Republic of Bosnia and Herzegovina, Preamble, Basic Tenets, Articles 1, 2, and 3.) See also Gaso Mijanovic, "Osnovne specificnosti ustaynog uredjenja SR Bosne i Hercegovine" (Basic Specificities of the Constitutional System of the SR of Bosnia and Herzegovina) in *Specificnosti republickih i pokrajinskih ustava od 1974* (Specificities of the Constitutions of the Republics and Provinces as of 1974), in Borislav Blagojevic, ed. (Belgrade: Savremena administracija and Institut za uporedno pravo, 1976).

24. Ustav SR Hrvatske (1974), clan 1 (the 1974 Constitution of the Socialist Republic of Croatia, Article 1).

25. *1984 SYY,* p. 349. It is interesting to note that according to the 1971 census there were more Croats (3,513,000) and Serbs (626,000) in 1971 than in 1981 (See *1977 SYY,* p. 377). Apart from migrations, this change is due primarily to the great number of persons who, in an atmosphere of intolerance in 1971, declared themselves Croats or Serbs, and who, in 1981, made use of the constitutional provision and declared themselves Yugoslavs, so that this latter category grew in number from 84,000 in 1971 to 379,000 in 1981.

26. Tito issued this warning on July 4, 1971, at the meeting of the Executive Committee of the Central Committee of the League of Communists of Croatia. The CC of the LCC, "Izvestaj o stanju u Savezu komunista Hrvatske u odnosu na prodor nacionalizma u njegove redove" (Report on the State of Things in the LCC in Regard to the Penetration of Nationalism into its Ranks), *Zagreb,* 1972, pp. 82–88.

27. Cedo Grbic, "Osnovne specificnosti ustavnog uredjenja SR Hrvatske" (Basic Specifications on the Constitutional System of the Socialist Republic of Croatia), in Blagojevic, *Specifications of the Constitutions.*

28. Ustav SR Srbije (1974) clan 1 (the 1974 Constitution of the Socialist Republic of Serbia, Article 1).

29. Borislav Blagojevic, ed., *Uporedni pregled republickih i pokrajinskih ustava*

1974 (A Comparative Survey of the 1974 Constitutions of the Republics and Autonomous Provinces) (Belgrade: Institut za uporedno pravo, 1974), pp. 16–17.

30. Jack C. Fisher, *Yugoslavia—a Multinational State: Regional Differences and Administrative Responses* (San Francisco: Chandler Publishing Co., 1966). This author also concludes that local autonomy was ensured, though at the expense of economic efficiency.

31. Notes taken by a perceptive observer, participant, and analyst, speak about the changes in bilateral relations and the nature of the "response" to these events. Veljko Micunovic, *Moskovske godine 1956–1958* (Moscow Years, 1956–1958) (Zagreb: Liber, 1977), especially the parts dealing with the LCY program.

32. An American edition of this program was published under the title, *The Yugoslav Way* (New York: F. Praeger, 1959). Another American edition is *Yugoslavia's Way* (New York: All Nations Press, 1959).

33. *Program SKJ* (1958) (The 1958 Program of the LCY) (Belgrade: Komunist, 1964), p. 107.

34. Ibid., p. 139.

35. Ibid., p. 179.

36. Ibid., p. 200.

37. James Madison, *The Federalist*, No. 51. This sounds like a paraphrasing of Montesquieu's "Le pouvoir arrête le pouvoir" (Montesquieu, *De l'Esprit des Lois*, I, liv. XI, ch. IV).

38. Jean-Jacques Rousseau, *Du Contrat Social*, liv. III, ch. II.

39. In connection with the following discussion, see Miroslav Pecujlic, "Interesi i politicki proces" (Interests and the Political Process) from a discussion organized by the Marxist Center of the League of Communists in Belgrade, and published in the journal, *Marksisticka misao* (Marxist Thought), no. 4, 1984, pp. 212–214. The motive for the discussion was the publication of an inspirational book by Najdan Pasic, *Interesi i politicki proces* (Interests and the Political Process) (Belgrade: Komunist, 1983).

40. Shan-Yan, *Knjiga vladara oblasti San* (The Book of the Ruler of the Shan Region) (Belgrade: BIGZ, 1977), p. 153.

41. John Adams, *A Defence of the Constitution of Government of the United States of America*, vol. I (New York: Da Capo Press Reprint Edition, 1971), p. 286.

42. Edvard Kardelj, a major contributor to all of the Yugoslav constitutions in the period from 1943 to 1974, supported on several occasions (when local autonomy and worker self-management in large economic organizations was discussed) the thesis that larger population blocs should be divided into smaller ones in a manner that facilitated direct participation in decision making by the people.

43. Some writers still focus on self-management integration of the society, while others provoke arguments on the elaboration of such concepts. See, for instance, Predrag Vranicki, *Marksizam i socijalizam* (Marxism and Socialism) (Zagreb: Liber, 1979), and Jovan Miric, *Sistem i kriza* (The System and Crisis) (Zagreb: CEKADE, 1984).

44. Edvard Kardelj, "Ekspoze povodom donosenja Opsteg zakona o ured-jenju opstina i srezova" (Exposé Given on the Occasion of the Passing of the General Act on the System of Municipal and District Administration), June 1955.

45. See William Dunn, "Communal Federalism: Dialectics of Decentraliza-tion in Socialist Yugoslavia," *Publius,* vol. 5, no. 2 (Spring 1975).

46. Little has been written on this subject in Yugoslavia. At the Tenth Congress of the League of Communists (1974), Tito stated that the basic causes of the factional struggles that shook the League in the period preced-ing the Congress were varied, but that the principal cause was the struggle for power. See Joseph Broz Tito, "Borba za dalji razvoj socijalistickog samoupravl-janja u nasoj zemlji i uloga Saveza komunista Jugoslavije" (The Struggle for Further Development of Socialist Self-Management in Our Country and the Role of the League of Communists of Yugoslavia), Referat na Desetom kongresu SKJ (Report at the Tenth Congress of the LCY), Belgrade, May 27, 1974.

47. For example, representatives (or delegates) from the two regions take part in the process of passing laws in the Assembly of the Socialist Republic of Serbia, even when a law is not relevant to the regions but only to the inhabitants of so-called narrow Serbia; representatives from the territory of narrow Serbia do not, however, participate in passing laws that are relevant only to the regions.

48. This group is statistically important: According to the 1981 census, their number totaled 1,219,000. There was an argument in the press as to whether this group can be called a nationality. There are those who are disturbed by the higher numbers of this group because their ideological commitments are called into question.

49. For a description of the character of this change, the conflicts that accompanied it, its influence on the methods of decision making, and several structural shortcomings in the constitutional solutions addressing these is-sues see Jovan Miric, *Sistem i kriza* (The System and Crisis) (Zagreb: CEKADE, 1984); Steven L. Burg, "Ethnic Conflict and the Federalization of Socialist Yugoslavia: The Serbo-Croat Conflict," *Publius,* vol. 7, no. 4, 1977; and Steven L. Burg, *Conflict and Cohesion in Socialist Yugoslavia: Political Decision Making Since 1966* (Princeton: Princeton University Press, 1983).

50. Ustav SFRJ (1974), clan 292 (The 1974 Constitution of the SFRY, Article 292).

51. This can be seen in Canada where the problems of Quebec cannot be discussed exclusively as a matter of the relations between national and local values and interests. See H. G. Thorburn, "Ethnic Pluralism in Canada," in St. Ehrlich and G. Wooten, eds., *Three Faces of Pluralism (Political, Ethnic and Religious)* (Westmead, 1980). The author argues that federalism presupposes not only certain political and legal conditions and institutions, but also eco-nomic and sociological conditions. It could be added that the political culture of a society modifies all established institutions, and thus federalism as well.

52. In the first house of the Assembly of the SFRY, the Federal Council, which primarily makes decisions on political issues, foreign policy, defense,

international relations, etc., the decisions are made, as a rule, by majority vote without a consensus of the assemblies of the relevant republics and provinces (except in a small number of cases when changes in the Constitution are at issue). Increasingly, however, the practice of this Council, the composition of which is based on an equal representation of the republics (30 delegates each) and the provinces (20 delegates each), is to request the reaching of consensus among the assemblies on its positions. In this way, the principle of consensus is extended to areas of decision making that were not anticipated by the Constitution. Moreover, the "consensus among the assemblies of the republics and provinces" is practically reduced to approval by a small group of the highest executive officials from each federal unit.

53. Frequently, foreign authors writing about Yugoslavia consider this entire mechanism of equal representation not to be of major importance, because all of these questions are dealt with in a centralized way through party bodies, especially the Central Committee of the League of Communists of Yugoslavia. But the dispersion of power in the late 1960s within the state administration occurred within the League of Communists as well. Its most important organs are established on the principal of equal representation of the individual leagues of the republics and provinces, and this also applies to the presidency of the LCY, numbering twenty-three members (three from each republic, two from each province, and one from the Yugoslav People's Army). It is also important to note that the League's congress only confirms the election of members of the Central Committee, while the last word in the election is pronounced by the federal units without whose consent no official delegated by them can be dismissed. In this manner, officials are exclusively and entirely bound by and responsible to the forums of their own federal units.

54. For a description of these demands see Burg, *Conflict and Cohesion.*

55. Remarks given at the Second Congress of Self-Managers of Yugoslavia, Sarajevo, May 1971.

56. In the Kosovo region in 1948 (the first postwar census), there were 733,000 Albanians; according to the latest census (1981), the number is 1,584,000. This demographic explosion in one of the least developed regions of Yugoslavia was accompanied by migration from rural to urban areas. In 1948 the share of agrarian population of the total inhabitants was 81 percent, while in 1981 it was only 25 percent. Of the total population, only 23.8 percent are economically active, so that for every active inhabitant there are 3.2 publicly supported ones. This makes the economic and social situation rather complex. An average household in the Kosovo region has almost seven members, and the region's rate of unemployment is 30 percent. See Milos Macura, "Problem radjanja na Kosovu" (The Problem of Childbirth in Kosovo) reported at the symposium *Naucna istrazivanja Kosova* (Scientific Research of Kosovo), Serbian Academy of Sciences, Belgrade, March 1985.

Macura assumes that part of the reason for the high rate of childbirth can be found in the culture and ethnic and group traditions. He states that women interviewed from that province claimed to have wanted birth control, but that the conservative institutions, including the local religious servants, exerted pressure on them to give birth to as many children as possible. The political organs of this province have long opposed family planning as a part of their economic and social planning project.

For an explanation of the above data in relation to other factors contributing to the problem of economic development of the province, see Kosta Mihailovic, "Ekonomski razvoj Kosova" (Economic Development of Kosovo), delivered at the same symposium.

Sharp discussions took place at the symposium cited above and in the Yugoslav press following its closing. Since Kosovo has only 28 percent of the average Yugoslav social product per capita, the question keeps arising as to what extent the demographic explosion has been a factor in the economic slowdown, and how high the rate of economic growth ought to be to produce the effects birth control and family planning would have produced. (See *NIN* weekly magazine, Belgrade, March 10, 24, and 31, 1985.) Demographic trends in Yugoslavia as a whole are very complex and are still not studied sufficiently. In addition to other characteristics of migration, ethnic grouping on a territorial basis can also be observed.

57. This term was used right after World War I by Serbian politician Stojan Protic. He proposed federalism for Yugoslavia in the name of the principle, "Unity in diversity and diversity in unity, but never, and at no price, unity in uniformity." See Branko Petranovic, *Istorija Jugoslavije 1918–1978* (History of Yugoslavia 1918–1978) (Belgrade, Nolit, 1980), p. 52.

58. The Constitution of the SFR of Yugoslavia, Article 1.

59. See Emile Durkheim, *De la division du travail social* (Serbo-Croatian translation) (Belgrade: Prosveta, 1972), pp. 111–240. The lower or mechanical form is based on common political and legal frameworks, which Durkheim analyzes primarily through the conditions of enforcing the criminal law and administering punishment. Apart from external frameworks, this "communality" relies on "organized beliefs" (which today increasingly take the place of political ideologies). The creation of larger and stronger entities under these circumstances requires the growth of "organized consciousness" in which the collective consciousness entirely represses the individual. Such a "communality" assumes that people are alike. The organic or higher form of solidarity presumes that they differ. "The former form is only possible," says Durkheim, "to the extent to which the individual personality fits the collective personality; the latter is only possible if everyone has his own field of activity, that is, if he or she has a personality " (Ibid., pp. 160–61).

Commentary

Milan Matic

It would be useful, at the outset, to say something about the invisible side of the Constitution, that is, about the influences of political culture and traditions on the political inclinations, views, and behavior of people in Yugoslavia. The authoritarian component is usually stressed and is undeniably present in the tradition, though it is not the only component, nor is it generally characteristic of the political culture in Yugoslavia. Analysts such as Wahl, Beer, and others identified deep schisms in the political cultures of other great European countries such as the "red" and "black" tradition in France and the south and north contrasts of Italy. Similarly, the political culture of Yugoslavia has diverse and divergent tendencies and components and is far more complex than a first impression of Yugoslavia's "authoritarian" political tradition would indicate. For instance, let us not forget the relatively early development of great feudal states in what is today Yugoslavia, such as the Croatian medieval state, the Serbian state, Bosnia, etc. The advent of these great feudal sovereignties as early as the ninth and tenth centuries made possible accelerated civilizational change, as seen in the progressive achievements of the social and political traditions from that period such as the Code of Dusan and feudal charters. These trends, however, were interrupted by the Turkish invasion and the enslavement of the people who inhabited the southeastern parts of what is today Yugoslavia. Later, other parts of the Yugoslav territory came under the sovereignty of neighboring Ottoman, Venetian, Hapsburg, and Napoleonic empires for several centuries.

The loss of united statehood and several centuries of enslavement meant not only a slowdown in organized social development for the Yugoslav peoples, but also repression of productive civilizational debate. Under those circumstances, the fundamental goal becomes the liberation of one's country from foreign authority and the preservation of the national being in the face of pressure from various proselytizing churches, cults, and the like. In comparison with some West Euro-

411

pean countries such as England, where class and social debates continued throughout the Middle Ages, terrible battles for mere self-preservation were waged by the Yugoslavs. The heroes of the folk epics and literature of the Yugoslav peoples are not crusaders for rights of the poor, but primeval types who performed heroic wonders in struggles against superior foreign enemies. In such historical circumstances, internal social divisions were no longer important; national unity was, and at any price, for the purposes of resistance against foreign authority and the struggle for freedom. Religion, the church, and various pagan traditions served as guardians of national unity, collective memory, and freedom in the absence of political institutions. The mobilization of these ancient collective forces within the political tradition dates back to the great battles fought against the Turkish aggressor in the fourteenth century and continues in later phases of historical development to the present day.[1]

Various church divisions and conflicts, multitudinous divisions and migrations of peoples, and aspirations for the conservation of the language, culture, and tradition of the past even in diverse ethnic environments had an influence in preserving archaic elements in political culture. Research shows that archaic folk traditions can be important factors in political mobilization, tending to revive national identity, and that such revitalization of archaic passions and energies gives greater power to collective resistance and freedom-loving movements, so much so that they remind one of religious wars.

A more detailed analysis of the political culture in Yugoslavia uncovers a dualism between a tradition of freedom-loving nationalism (with archaic and pagan roots) and another tradition which could be designated as a nationally constructive civilizational tradition.

The freedom-loving nationalist tradition represents a kind of "last bastion" mentality, for which ancient mythical and ethnic identities and emotions are mobilized for the purpose of self-defense and national self-preservation. It is the last reserve of the national strength in its struggles for freedom and independent collective existence, imbued with a readiness for sacrifice and suffering. But this same line of tradition is frequently and destructively manipulated by rationalized ruling political elites, and this has led, in the near and far past, to bloody misunderstandings and clashes. This tradition is also problematic because it is condemned to decline in the face of civilizational progress and the rationalization of cultural values, but at the same time it is necessary as an instrument of mobilization in threatening situations. Finally, this tradition sustains narrow, parochial cultural orientations, is permeated with negative experiences, and is suspicious of various forms of central power, which have most frequently been foreign. It is insufficiently participative and activist and fuels the friction among various nationalistic and ethnic sensitivities.

The nationally constructive civilizational tradition is more modern and rational, but at the same time it is authoritarian. Its authoritarianism comes from the experience with foreign domination, which proved so unpleasant that *any* native government, no matter how bad otherwise, enjoyed complete legitimacy.[2] But in contrast to other multinational, complex states, which tended to become more homogenized and centrally directed, Yugoslavia became more diversified and decentralized.

Yugoslav constitutional developments since 1974, reflecting powerful aspirations of various peoples toward affirmation and identity and their traditional aversion to any form of central domination, resulted in the triumph of diversity and the right not only of nations and nationalities, but also of ethnic groups and other collective entities to express idiosyncrasies and identity. After the signing of the Constitution of 1974, the general trend toward decentralization, regionalization, and emphasis of national differences went much further than constitutional intent, resulting in regional isolation and "national economies"; this in turn significantly hindered national development and the process of integration. Constitutional emphasis on narrow regional and "national" interests encouraged other developments: (1) regional inequalities increased as the more developed areas tried to retain and gain an even greater advantage in degree of development, while the lesser developed tried to preserve the privileges connected to particular sources and funds for financing their development; (2) regional elites worked to retain leadership in representing the regional and "general-nation" interests of their communities, which is a safer and "easier" base of legitimacy than the more complex process of broader association and cooperation; (3) investment expansion occurred in all regional levels in the second half of the 1970s, encouraged by world credit market conditions and other opportunities for acquiring and spending the means for investment and development, leading to a temporary hegemony of politics and regional influences over economics and social association; (4) crisis tendencies intensified in the economy, and various forms of primary, as well as national, identifications were strengthened; (5) new foundations and institutions of social integration developed, relying not on state and centralistic mechanisms, but on local and regional forces and factors.

Under contemporary conditions, the constitutional concept of unity in diversity is being realized insufficiently, whether from the standpoint of the real content of these diversities or from the standpoint of the degree of association and unification of social forces necessary for a dynamic and equal joint development and modernization. The question of democratic and self-management integration of economic and other joint forces in Yugoslavia becomes important in this context; it is one of the key questions in current debates on the functioning and improvement of the Yugoslav political system. The sentiment of the broad masses favoring greater unity is indisputably an important factor in today's climate in Yugoslav society; this momentarily exceeds the possibility of systemic cohesion, as was demonstrated by J. Seroka in one of his papers on political systems of Mid-Eastern Europe.[3]

A third point: Professor Stanovcic raises an interesting question about the character of the "pluralism of self-management interests" in Yugoslavia's contemporary constitutional system. National and ethnic pluralism is one of the sources from which this concept originated to denote room for free expression and the coordination of interests of freed social factors and active political forces in society. Ethnic diversities, however, are not the only source of this new type of pluralism, nor are they (especially in present practice) a sufficient framework for expressing the democratic potential of that pluralism.

This pluralistic concept may be a synthesis of all elements of revolutionary and democratic change in Yugoslav society to the present day—the emancipation of the new political subjectivity of the citizens and communities to which they belong; opposition to Stalinism, bureaucratic blandness, nonproductivity, and dogmatism—political leveling of all types. Regardless of how much that concept is realized, as an expression of new and fundamental rights and new social positions of man (who is at the same time the bearer of work management and property and the expropriator of the fruits of his labor), it should represent the strategic direction of future transformations of Yugoslav society.

Today all nations are aware of just how deep the penetration of the state is into the former domain of political and social pluralism; conditions are such that the creative mixing of social forces is displaced by biased political control and étatistic technologies of political rule in the East, and in the West. We also know that even Aristotle linked the concept of the existence of politics (as a democracy) to the question whether there is in any society that free and relatively independent social and political space that provides life to constitutional institutions and creates the conditions for fruitful political synthesis and decision making. Basing associated labor and self-management in Yugoslavia on the pluralism of interests is an attempt to establish an alternative form of democratic and direct social plu-

414

ralism and to thwart the forces of biased state or party control, which limited and blocked the development of creative social forces and society as a whole.

Thus, when we read Professor Stanovcic's comments about the decline of the former integrative role of the party in the Yugoslav political system, we must remember that in the current constitutional system of self-management the party will play a different role. The party, the state, self-management, free-trade regulations, and other complex coordinating mechanisms coexist in a type of reciprocal balance. It is dangerous when one of these factors, even self-management (which in today's contradictory times must be supplemented and protected by an appropriate role for the state) becomes a monopolistic or exclusive mechanism of economic and social regulation. This is where a significant role should be played by citizens and social groups, the communities to which they belong, and other forms of free association and organization. They must have a greater role in the institutions and public life of the society, while applying increasing pressure toward the formal synthesis of diverse interests.[4]

National and ethnic freedom, equality, and identity, which are guaranteed in the contemporary Yugoslav Constitution, are certainly among the more significant components of this new concept of the pluralism of self-management interests, because they express an important dimension of social diversity. But as we previously pointed out, expressing national diversities as elements of pluralism of self-management interests can lead to problems. Yugoslavia today belongs to a relatively small group of medium-developed nations that must try to establish internally a rational balance between diversity and the sort of social integration that furthers modernization and progress. According to the current state of constitutional interpretation and practice, this balance has shifted in favor of the interest of the parts, at the expense of common interests and the whole. The question is, how much does the federal structure of republics and provinces express the authentic diversities and interests of the national parts?

We encounter today this characteristic paradox: the pluralism of interests of republics and provinces is overemphasized in relation to the broader community and the federation, while within these units, on the contrary, there appears a homogenization and a limitation of pluralism. This reflects the administrative-political competition (and insufficient democratic cooperation) among the nations who tolerate only with difficulty social differentiation and pluralism within their borders. Thus the pluralization of the Yugoslav system (along national and ethnic lines), *via facti* also represents a form of limitation of

415

the real *social* pluralism. A nation that lacks within itself mechanisms for differentiation and reward according to the real contributions made by the people toward joint labor and progress enables significantly different people to become equal: workers and idlers, parasites and creators, exploiters and exploited. We thereby risk suppressing that which is most progressive in the nation and encouraging that which is not, thus condemning the nation to stagnation. For this reason, we must evaluate carefully the effort to realize national and ethnic diversities in light of other even more significant social diversities, because national diversities may paradoxically produce political monopolism and homogenization.

The course of decision making within the Yugoslav federation then affirms national diversities on the one hand and on the other confirms that overemphasizing national diversities gradually suppresses other social diversities which, in relation to further development, are no less significant than national diversities.

It should be noted, finally, that republics and provinces have great meddling power in the sphere of the economy, which practically ensures their domination here. They enjoy broad authority over price fixing, foreign currency policy, taxation policy, reallocation of resources (in cases where self-management organizations come to no accord), extended reproduction, coverage of losses, credit policy, and finally, personnel policy.

Associated labor, which by the Constitution of the SFRY is defined in principle as the mainstay of economic integration in the country, does not have a council in the Federation, even though such a council exists in the communes, provinces, and republics. The delegates on the federal council who formally represent associated labor are not chosen in associated labor organizations, but rather in communes, and function along with delegates from territorial self-management organizations (local communities). The Federal Executive Council, however, cannot interfere in economic issues, only in general political ones. This council functions on the principle of parity, and the dependence of its members on the republics and provinces is great. The important point, however, is that significant economic (associated labor) decisions, which according to the Constitution should be considered within the context of a united national market, are nonetheless made by those same republic and provincial organs. Therefore, there are territorial political interventions into the sphere of association of labor and economic development that are, according to basic constitutional principles, matters of free union and association of the economic factors involved, regardless of territory.

More than economic factors, however, lie behind so-called polycentric étatism, which favors the interests of the units at the expense of the whole and whole "national" interests at the expense of the common and social interests of associated labor throughout the Yugoslav nation. Further causes include the vested interests of managing structures in republics and provinces. This polycentric étatism appeared on the margins of reform of the centralistic federation, which was deprived of much authority and sources of economic power; this reform, however, did not bring about a reallocation of power in favor of self-management, but once more in favor of independent centers of political decision making in republics and provinces, which was not the intent of the Constitution of 1974. The formation of decentralized étatism in Yugoslavia occurred in the second half of the 1970s in such a way that the intended de-étatization was checked at the stage of decentralization. During this period, after constitutional changes, the newly formed political centers and the nationalized banks incurred foreign debts to finance development. Labor investments were initiated, regardless of the consequences for the common interests of the whole country. Spectacular results in economic development and other modes of consumption, even personal, were temporarily achieved in this investment boom, strengthening the position of polycentric étatism in republics and provinces.

Decision making based on the common interests of the Federation was for a period in second place because of the possibility of solving development problems by credit within the republics and provinces. In the early 1980s, when symptoms of an economic crisis became evident, problems of decision making at the Federation level once again became urgent, but this decision making continued in harmony with previously formed relations and aspirations about economic matters, which went into a phase of nonproductive investment expansion. Attempts to solve development and economic problems at the expense of other interests caused increased conflicts in the process of decision making at the level of the Federation. These same causes led to resistance against implementing the comprehensive program of economic stabilization, which attempts to solve development and economic problems by united efforts across the country. For many reasons, this strategy upsets vested interests. The more developed endeavor to sustain their advantage over the underdeveloped, the underdeveloped to acquire a greater share of federal funds for aid. These competing factions involve national development issues far too much in politics and political compromises, when they should be solved according to a truly national view of the economy and economic association. The resulting tensions within federal institutions fosters the application of consensus decision making in areas where such a process has no constitutional foundation.

In the above-mentioned essay by J. Seroka on the systems of Middle and Eastern Europe, which also covers Yugoslavia, Seroka notes that in the areas of economics, population, industrialization, and urbanization those countries have reached the point at which they must address this key dilemma: either increase growth even at the price of inequality in society, or preserve the values of equality at the price of slowed growth and relative stagnation. For Yugoslavia, this dilemma has a unique twist. It is no longer a question of accepting certain inequalities and differences in order to accelerate growth (because, in fact, they already exist in society and among regions), but of determining on what foundations certain inequalities came to be and what enables a quicker rate of growth for some and a slower rate for others. The Constitution of 1974 assumed that one's social and political condition (from the individual to the community) should depend solely on work for and contribution to the production of the whole country. The principle was one of equality of opportunity, not of guaranteed equal economic results. Various interests and processes of decision making do, however, work toward ensuring equal positions or privileges for political reasons, regardless of the effect on productivity growth. Within the process of decision making, political considerations dominate economic ones and concentration of competitive political power is encouraged at the republican and provincial levels. Treating national diversities as absolute absorbs and suppresses all other basic social diversities. The power of polycentric étatism and the prevalence of administrative-political competition over economic considerations at the federal level (instead of productive cooperation) significantly impair essential developmental, economic, planning, and other federal functions and decision making. These functions are a vital aspect of central regulation, which is in turn an essential element of every system and the prerequisite for rapid development and the harmonious functioning of all parts. Theorists frequently demand more direct representation of the economy (associated labor) in the federation and the creation of institutions for technological development and opportunities to eliminate uncontrolled development and the transfer of technology. A greater role for the Federal Executive Council within the Assembly of the SFRY and a strengthening of the democratic role of the assembly are also called for. With regard to the composition of the Federal Executive Council, there is a need for greater independence of federal functionaries from influence by the republics and provinces. A number of other reforms are also suggested, but they all stem from the realization that the one-sided expression of diversities by the republics and provinces departs from an essential constitutional principle: that working people and citizens, united in self-management communities and organizations, are the fundamental factor of social and economic development and that insufficient realization of this basic constitutional diversity among people and communities led to difficulties for overall economic development. In this respect, certain positive changes have been made, proof of which is found in the latest material on reforms within the political system.

Notes

1. On the role of religion in the war of liberation of the nations and nationalities of Yugoslavia from 1941 to 1945, see, for example, Vladimir Dedijer's *New Supplements to the Biography of Josip Broz Tito* (Rijeka-Zagreb, 1981), book II, pp. 569–83.

2. See our book *Myth and Politics* (Belgrade, 1984), chapter 10.

3. J. Seroka, "Problems of Integration, Economic Growth, Demographic Change, and Political Pluralism in East Central Europe." Paper presented at the Congress of the World Political Science Association, Paris, July 1985.

4. Some Yugoslav political theoreticians, operating within the context of the democratic pluralism of the self-managing interests, create drafts of new human and collective rights, in which the rights to self-management and the rights to work with social means are developed. Such rights are, for example, the right of diversity and differences; the right to form a union; the right to form communes; initiatives; freedom of communication; the rights to truth, tolerance, and innovation; freedom from mystification and fetishism of personality, institutions, and ideas; etc. Whether or not any of these new rights will be incorporated in future constitutions depends, of course, on the general direction of constitutional development and democratic change in Yugoslavia. See Jovan Djordevic, *Socialism and Freedom* (Belgrade: Kultura, 1982).

Discussion

ROBERT GOLDWIN: When we discussed the papers on India, we focused on characteristics peculiar to the Indian nation and ended with the question, What holds India together as one nation? The essay on Yugoslavia quotes Sir Fitzroy Maclean's description of Yugoslavia as an unusual and complex country, with "six republics, five nations, four languages, three religions, two alphabets, and one party that ensures the unity of all these diversities." Mr. Stanovcic tells us things are actually more complex than that—today there are eight federal units, six nations, two nationalities, and other diversities that Sir Fitzroy did not know about. Furthermore, he says that the party—which had served as a unifying factor, though never the only one—has lost much of its integrative force. So to bring these sessions full circle, I ask the same question with which I started the first one: what holds Yugoslavia together? What accounts for whatever unity it may have? How can we explain that it is still one nation?

VOJISLAV STANOVCIC: In Yugoslavia the idea prevails that the diversities can create a great richness for certain countries under certain conditions. The chief condition, of course, is sufficient unity: that we can invent or devise a political system by reflection and choice able to keep all elements together, making harmony out of differences. In my paper I quoted a Yugoslav politician from the period after World War I, who put it nicely: "Unity of diversities, yes; diversities in unity, yes; but under no condition, unity in uniformities." As Blaise Pascal, a French philosopher of the seventeenth century, put it: "Pluralism without unity is a cause of anarchy; while unity without pluralism is despotism or tyranny." In my view, the art of constitution making and the idea of constitutionalism itself are to create working political and legal institutions that avoid the two extremes of anarchy and despotism.

I do not argue in my paper that we have succeeded in doing that in Yugoslavia, although we have made sincere efforts. That is why we have changed our constitution several times. But the Yugoslav people, even in the Middle Ages, realized that disunity endangered their existence. Despite this experience, however, the Yugoslav people still did not know how to save their unity. They did learn something from the past, though. They experienced foreign domination, which lasted for a long time and was very ruthless. The Turks ruled over the Serbs for five hundred years, for instance, and the Hungarians over the Croats for a thousand years. For even a longer period the Slovenes were under German, and later Austrian, rule.

In the nineteenth century then the region's best minds—mainly intellectuals from Serbia, Croatia, and Slovenia, meeting abroad usually in Czechoslovakia, in Vienna, or in Paris—launched the idea of a joint Yugoslav state, a state of south Slav nations. This idea was very strong, motivating the intellectuals and other people during uprisings in the nineteenth and twentieth centuries. As a matter of fact, the Communist party won popular support during World War II, in my view, not on any platform of communism or socialism but on the basis of Tito's slogan, "Unity and fraternity of all Yugoslav nations." But Tito was very wise to add that the new state would differ from the previous one in the freedom of all nations within it and in the social liberties of the society.

That was the period Sir Fitzroy Maclean spoke of and the role that the party played. I suggested in my paper that the party has now lost much of its unifying role and ability but not all of it. Still, some other unifying elements are not stressed very frequently in Yugoslavia, because, I think, some party leaders prefer to claim that the unity of the new Yugoslavia results from their political devices or political wisdom. For example, besides the historical experience, the fact is that over 90 percent of the Yugoslav population are of Slav origin, and although they belong to five or six different nationalities—Macedonians, Serbs, Muslims, Croats, Montenegrins, and Slovenians—they still have a language with a common origin. And, with some difficulties, they can understand one another. It is frequently said that the differences among our languages are not larger than differences among French dialects or among German dialects in the nineteenth century. Three quarters of the population speak the same language— Serbo-Croatian. Some people will argue, particularly nationalists from both sides, that these are two different languages, but the difference between them is not greater than the difference between American English and British English.

The economies of these regions are quite complementary as well, and that also helps explain why the populations of these regions are striving for unity.

Finally, I should say something about the population of Yugoslavia. In the past several years a situation has developed in which the population on the one hand and the political leaders on the other are more and more removed from each other. The present-day situation in Yugoslavia really results from the dealings of political leaders who, in the struggle for power, seek to mobilize support on a regional basis and have thereby brought the country very near to a system of confederation. It is wisely said in Yugoslavia that if the people at large were allowed to exercise more effective influence on their representatives, they would use that pressure to decrease their animosities and increase their willingness to deal with one another.

I see three ways of fostering unity that have been neglected in Yugoslavia but that many Yugoslavian intellectuals are trying to develop further. First, we have proceeded too long under a system in which government dominates society completely—economy, press, intellectuals, universities, opinion, everything. We believe that if we develop what is called civil society—and that includes autonomy of the economy, of the press, of universities, of intellectuals, of different scientific institutions, and so on—a common language will develop more easily than if we leave it to politicians. When directors of economic enterprises meet, they very easily reach agreements, even though they are from different republics. And very frequently when they return to their nations, they are reproached and prevented from doing what they jointly already agreed to do.

Second, we must develop the role of citizen. In Yugoslavia it has diminished to an unbelievable degree. We call him a mini-citizen, because he can deal only in local affairs; the electoral system is an indirect one. We can elect only our local representatives, and they elect further communal, republican, and federal representatives.

Third, we must try to remedy the defects or shortcomings of the Yugoslav federal system. The chief shortcoming is that even for the limited number of federal functions—and I am in favor of limiting federal government—the government cannot apply its own laws; it has neither financial nor personal nor organizational means. All laws are applied by local governments, rendering the federal government completely powerless. So I suggest not that we increase the competence of the federal government but that it should have the means to use what powers it has.

EDMUNDO VASQUEZ MARTINEZ: Several interesting problems are apparent in these papers on Yugoslavia: ethnic and national identity problems, the variety of interests, and, something very interesting, the policy of the four Ds—democratization, decentralization, debureaucratization, and destatification. About this last, my question is, To what point are these four Ds reflected in reality, and is there, in fact, any contradiction among those four concepts?

Another of the problems is the representation of ethnic groups and regional interests. That raises the issue of what is called the "personnel key," which says that all major political bodies and federal agencies must employ representatives of the various nations on an equal basis. It would be interesting to have a more detailed explanation of this provision.

Finally, I would like to see some discussion of the material foundations of equality.

DANIEL ELAZAR: I commented earlier on a paper on Switzerland—a country that, with all its difficult history, has had one of the more felicitous historical experiences in Europe—and now I am commenting on a paper on a country that has had one of the most difficult and tragic historical experience in Europe. Whatever the limitations and whatever the problems of Yugoslavia, the experience of the past generation of Yugoslavs in the direction of free constitutional government has been more extensive than that region has ever experienced before, with the possible exception of some of the Adriatic republics.

I suggested earlier that there were three or possibly four approaches to protecting diversity while maintaining unity. The Swiss emphasized the federalist approach, combined with the local liberties approach: every valley with its traditional liberties forming a commune, then the cantons, and so forth. Contrasted to that, to some extent, is the individual rights approach combined with federalism as seen in Canada and even more pronounced in the United States. I suggested that there is perhaps yet another approach: namely, the communal liberties approach. Yugoslavia, I believe, is an example of that approach to maintaining or protecting diversity while maintaining unity.

The problem of unity was to transform the nineteenth century nationalism of the several nations of Yugoslavia into a willingness to settle for "communal liberties." This in itself was a major problem of transformation, one that may or may not have been completed at this point. Nationalism as it developed among the south Slavs and related peoples of Yugoslavia in the nineteenth century was as exclusivist as any other nationalism in that part of the world, or for that matter, in most other parts of the world. It was romantic, based on the notion of the nation-state, but a nation-state in the eastern and southern European mold. That is to say, because the nation preexisted the state, the problem was to create a state and establish its borders in such a way that it would embrace only one nation. And if there should be some pockets of other nations, they should be either driven out or at some point perhaps even exterminated. This certainly was the thrust of

423

nationalism in the part of the world that is now Yugoslavia, no less than it was in Poland or in Hungary.

Although we should not neglect the importance of external circumstances—the USSR, in this case—we have something more than external circumstances here. Undiluted nationalism has been transformed into a commitment instead to "communal liberties." That transformation was in part generated by the ideological momentum that accompanied Tito and the League of Communists in World War II. I do not know that this role has been properly investigated. I have heard any number of stories about why Tito adopted a federal solution, the most prominent of which is that he was persuaded by his advisers to do so because the Soviets had adopted a federal solution as well. In the end, however, this situation illustrates the interaction of the approaches described above. A federalism developed that proved to be increasingly successful in practice in guaranteeing the basic needs of the national groupings. It permitted, encouraged, or fostered the transformation of romantic nineteenth century nationalism with its exclusivist character into a commitment to communal liberties but nothing beyond.

Professor Stanovcic appropriately points out that Yugoslavia today is really more like a confederation than a federation; that in itself reflects the strength of the communal liberties approach and the fact that it is still closely tied to old nationalism. It is a confederation that seeks to stay together, not to pull apart, however; it is not a way station to something else, in which case I think we have an important lesson to learn from the Yugoslav experience.

MR. STANOVCIC: As to the question about how far the policy of the four Ds has been expressed in practice and the possibility of contradiction among them, the four Ds have been combined so that one D supports the other D: democratization, decentralization, debureaucratization, and destatification are mutually reinforcing. The problem is that in Yugoslavia this policy was not implemented for some time, not until about the second half of the 1960s. Then another trend developed—polycentric statism. The authoritarian government we shared in the beginning, in 1945, was dissolved in the 1960s, and power was transferred to the republics and autonomous provinces, with the intention that this process of the four Ds would go farther within these units. But this process was reversed, in what I sometimes call in Yugoslavia a new policy of the four Rs: repression, restrictions, reductions, and regression.

The communal liberties Professor Elazar describes thus had important effects. More and more scholars and even politicians in

Yugoslavia are talking about how the republics and autonomous provinces have deprived not only citizens but also local communities and self-managing enterprises of liberties.

As for the "personnel key," referred to by Mr. Martinez, that means that someone can hold a job, particularly with the federal government, simply on the ground that he belongs to a certain nationality and, it used to be, regardless of qualifications. Some criticisms were made of this arrangement, however, so the republics are now required to select persons for federal offices on the ground of their skill and ability, not only on national qualification. This "personnel key" is also frequently criticized because it can put in office an unqualified politician; then a skilled and qualified deputy must be found. Sometimes conflicts and animosities develop between the politician and the deputy, preventing certain offices from functioning properly.

It also happens, particularly in the army, that of two men with equal seniority, one will get a higher rank simply because he belongs to a smaller nationality. Montenegro, with 500,000 people, is entitled to the same number of members of parliament, of the central committee, of ambassadors, and of generals as is Serbia, with a population ten times larger. So the equality of groups creates inequality of individuals.

As for the material bases of equality, regional differences among parts of Yugoslavia are tremendous. Between Slovenia and Kosovo, the ratio of national income per capita is 6.5:1, while between some smaller units and communes the ratio is 1:14 or 1:16. More developed republics are not eager to contribute money for the development of underdeveloped regions. This was one of the bases for nationalism in the 1960s, that is, an "ism" of nationality, particularly Slovenian and Croatian nationalism. Slovenia is the most developed of all Yugoslav republics. The rate of unemployment there now is only 1.3 percent, which is lower, they say, than in any other European country. In Serbia, meanwhile, the rate of unemployment is 18 percent, higher than in any other European country. At Kosovo, it is 26 percent. Selfishness, then, is one of the bases for nationalism, and that also explains why the nationalities all wanted their own republics to preserve their own national economies as closed entities.

They are ready to give *some* money for the development of underdeveloped regions through a federal fund for the purpose. But that is just a certain percentage. They were very strongly opposed to any federal shifting of money from one region to another. Thus, according to the Constitution of 1974, the federal government is not authorized to make any investment of any kind. All economic investments and decisions about investments have to be done by republics. Under-developed areas are complaining that the ratio of inequality is enlarg-ing, while the more developed complain that the money they gave was spent on useless projects. One of the reasons for Croatian na-tionalism is the Croatians' complaint that their money is taken and spent in underdeveloped regions, peopled by different nationalities.

We frequently hear the term "Lebanonization" in discussions about Yugoslavia. At this time we are far from that degree of disunity, although that might be the "final solution" if the system breaks down. We know, however, that the great powers are very concerned about this, because Yugoslavia occupies an even more sensitive geographic position than Lebanon does. Both great powers restrain their allies from putting forward any territorial request, and we enjoy good relations with almost all our neighbors. In a certain way, Yugoslavia is also kept from falling apart by pressures from the outside.

One must always take into account that in Yugoslavia we have had experience with centralism and unitarism of two different kinds. One, the monarchy before World War II, led Yugoslavia to a tragedy, to a collapse in the war in 1941. The other experience was with what is called Socialist administrative centralism in the period after World War II. We found both of them were unsatisfying, at least in part because they could lead Yugoslavia to the same kind of crisis Hungary experienced in 1956 or Poland in 1981. That is why Yugoslavia em-barked on this policy of decentralization, to accommodate the system to different local needs.

To return to Professor Elazar's question about communal liber-ties, it is true, perhaps, that Yugoslavia is a case where traditional nationalism had to be transformed into something else, because all Yugoslav federal units, except Slovenia, have a heterogeneous popu-lation. All have strong minorities. Some republics comprise several nationalities, like Bosnia with the Muslims, Serbs, and Croats. Thus the nation-state in the purest sense cannot be realized.

Regarding the source of Tito's idea for a federal Yugoslavia, some notions about arranging Yugoslavia along federal lines existed even before Yugoslavia was created, particularly in Croatia and Slovenia. Some in Communist circles were interested in organizing Yugoslavia as a federal state before World War II. It was clear the direction was toward some kind of regionalization.

EDWARD BANFIELD: Could you discuss the role of the police in Yugoslavia? When I was in Belgrade twenty years ago, there appeared to be a lot of policemen in evidence.

MR. STANOVCIC: The police are mainly in the hands of local communities or communes. I am sure that there are no fewer today than twenty years ago, but they are less powerful. Twenty years ago a big change took place. The police forces, which were very centralized at the time, were seriously criticized for misusing their power and intruding too deeply into the lives of the citizens. In response to the criticism, the minister of police was removed.

In Yugoslavia it is possible for any citizen to sue in court any government body, the police, or any other administrative agency. For a long time, this right existed only in Yugoslavia, out of all the Socialist countries of Eastern Europe—although I think now that Poland has it, too. Before that right was introduced, the assumption was that government agencies could not make a mistake in relation to citizens, and if such mistakes were made, it was left to the higher authorities to remedy the complaint. Now that we can sue government in court, it is a very widespread practice.

As for whether some of the causes that favored a united Yugoslavia in 1918 still stand, I think they do, although much more strongly among the population than among political leaders. While the party has lost its unifying ability, it is still a strong unifying force, because of the fresh memory of its role during the war and in the postwar period.

In addition, no other alternative is presented or is appealing. There are many nationalistic causes, to be sure. Many movements would like to see Yugoslavia disintegrate. Serbian nationalists, for example, are working for an independent Serbia. Montenegrin nationalists would like to see an independent Montenegro. During the war Croatian nationalists created a so-called independent state of Croatia under the protection of Nazi Germany, while Macedonia was annexed by Bulgaria.

Today there is a movement for an independent Macedonia that would unite Yugoslav Macedonia with Bulgarian and Greek Macedonia. There are even Muslim fundamentalists who would like to see Bosnia and Hercegovina as a purely Muslim state, which would involve throwing out more than 50 percent of the population. But none of these movements enjoy widespread popular support.

MR. GOLDWIN: Am I wrong in thinking that there is a very powerful natural limit to the possibilities of unity for Yugoslavia? On the one hand, is it not true that even a very powerful government, using as much force as it thought necessary, would probably fail to achieve more unity because of the historical experiences described—that is, would it not only intensify the resistance of the various national groups? On the other hand, would not a looser, more liberal sort of government only give free rein to the expression of all these national tendencies and sentiments? In other words, does not any effort at governing Yugoslavia have to start from an assessment of the natural limits to the degree of unity in a nation composed the way Yugoslavia is?

MR. STANOVCIC: That is correct. Our experience for the past sixty years or so since Yugoslavia was created tells us that when we try stronger government to control all these diversities, it is a tragedy for Yugoslavia. That approach does not solve any one of our problems. What we really need to do is to learn how to live together, with all these diversities. We cannot abolish them, and nobody believes that we should. But what we are forever trying to do is to design a political system that can accommodate all those diversities and still maintain an overall unity. This unity would not be the uniformity we tried after World War I, but a unity that would, while maintaining the diversities, accommodate individual regions or nationalities.

9
Final Thoughts and Questions

ROBERT GOLDWIN: We should now attempt some summarizing: the expression of final thoughts, attempts at reaching general and generalizing concepts, ideas for future research, and identification of problems that we touched on but did not formulate very well, where you think additional work would be necessary. To help us make the most of this final session, let me state a question, a long question but, I hope, a helpful one.

During and after World War II—although perhaps these thoughts have a much longer history than that—there was an expectation, or maybe just a hope, among decent-minded people in the world that we were coming to a new time when the differences and boundaries that had separated mankind would somehow be diminished in importance. The phrase that was used constantly to characterize that idea was the hope for "one world." That summed it up. Many things were written, either scientific or pseudoscientific, arguing that there are no races, that mankind is one, and that we are all brothers. You are all familiar with that writing and thinking, and one still hears sentiments of that sort in international gatherings.

Today, however, all over the world, we in fact see increased emphasis on smaller groups and the divisions that separate mankind, one group from another. We cannot fail to be impressed by the terrible power of those forces that somehow bind together groups of people who feel a similarity based on nationality or language or race or religion. These bonds are apparently more powerful than the bonds of nation-states or aspirations toward even larger groupings such as a united Europe, not to speak of one world.

In the philosophies of modern democratic liberalism going back to the teachings of John Locke and similar writers, there is a determined effort to universalize the principles of government, by emphasizing the principles of human nature that are common to all and that transcend particular nations or groups or nationalities. In a certain sense, the same can be said of Marxism: very simply, the working man has no country. Here we have the two dominant systems of political thought and yet the contrary evidence before our eyes of a problem that is universal, that exists everywhere: the problem of powerful particulars. Nothing in John Locke helps us to think about this problem or to know what to do when faced by it. And the same is true of Marxism.

Here, then, is one problem for further consideration, respecting unity and diversity: the need for a systematic effort to think about and to deal with this powerful force loose in the world that is affecting the lives of hundreds of millions of people. It is causing deaths and the destruction of civil life in many places all over the world. Yet we do not have a way of thinking about it well, let alone a way of doing something about it.

Are the divisions among individuals and groups increasing and intensifying? And if so are there constitutional remedies? That is an example of the sort of question that I hope we will now strive to formulate and discuss.

JACQUES VANDERLINDEN: I believe it is essential to maintain our historical perspective. For instance, although many people were talking about world government after 1945, we should remember that in 1918 we tried the League of Nations. After any such huge conflict there is an impetus toward world government.

What about the centralized state and its unity and diversity? Again we have to look at it in the perspective of the flow of history. After all, when did the centralized state come to Germany? Not so long ago. If we look at, say, Bavaria in the late nineteenth century and Bavaria today, I am not sure that things have changed dramatically. How the period of centralization will appear in the broader course of history—it may be only a parenthesis—we do not know.

At any rate, we need to scrutinize the birth of the centralized state. Why did it appear? Was it the high point of unity to that moment? Was it not a creation of the mind, an ideal, an artificial construct of thinkers who persuaded lawyers and constitutionalists that it would help overcome fundamental social problems?

JUAN LINZ: It might be helpful to undertake in the future some sustained reflection on the conceptual categories, unity and diversity. What I have in mind is not some kind of linguistic analysis but rather some historical reflection on when and where the concern for diversity arose. Here I go back to some comments made by Professor Belz, who pointed out that—although the concern for unity is as old as political life—the concern for diversity dates only from the eighteenth century. I do not believe a single political thinker of the first rank before Montesquieu ever expressed a concern for preserving diversity. The reason was, as Professor Belz noted, that the world was all too diverse already and the chief problem was unification. It would therefore be helpful to reflect a little about what makes diversity such a deep, heartfelt concern in politics and such a subject of theoretical fascination in modern times. It obviously has deep connections with nationalism, which is also a new and modern phenomenon.

The very fact that diversity is an extraordinarily parochial concern—a concern only of the past two centuries and mainly among Western thinkers—may be a hint that its roots in political reality are somewhat shallow. It may be a reaction against the excessively "universalizing" intellectual imperialism of a certain late stage in Western political thought, the kind of universalism that has some very healthy but also some unhealthy manifestations. A healthy manifestation would be, for example, the notion of human rights. An unhealthy manifestation might be some of the uglier features of capitalism. But modern Western culture has an awesome, homogenizing power, and the concern for diversity is a kind of late reaction to that. So further reflection about the roots of these fundamental categories might be profitable. We need to keep distinct the problems of state building or empire building, on the one hand, and the building of nations, on the other. To some extent we have tended to confuse these notions, but not every nation is able to or should be a state, and not every state should be conceived as a national state.

A second vital distinction is that between the rights of individuals and the rights of groups. We have not always been clear whether we want to guarantee the freedom of individuals or the rights of groups. We have two kinds of situations: groups that have a clear, well-defined territorial basis and groups that are intermingled territorially. When groups are intermingled, the problem of defining rights and protecting minorities becomes particularly acute, and territorial decentralization of power, democratization, and representation of groups become extremely complicated.

Furthermore, we are dealing with two kinds of processes: one in which social groups or territorial units are uniting into larger bodies, as the Americans went from a confederal to a federal structure; the other in which an existing centralized structure is being dismantled. The latter instance, as in Spain or Belgium, poses problems quite different from those that come from a heterogeneous society. Furthermore, it is important to remember that federalism in the United States, Germany, and to some extent Italy functions in the context of relatively homogeneous national cultures. The moment you introduce distinctive linguistic, ethnic, religious, or cultural minorities with territorial bases, federalism assumes functions other than those it has in the United States or in the later Germany. Therefore, the problems we are dealing with, though formally similar, are not the same, if we keep these various distinctions in mind.

We have to try to harmonize democratic principles, which always presume a sense of collectivity or community in which democratic decision making and legal authority are established, with the problem of liberties and of representation of particular areas, interests, groups, and communities. Democracy serves very well to paper over, to resolve, or to integrate class conflict, even in political systems that are not particularly wealthy. But the problems derived from ethnic, linguistic, cultural, and religious heterogeneity, built on strong territorial bases, are different. Unless the larger unit has some cultural, historical, and mythical legitimacy, democratic processes are not very effective in resolving differences of this sort, and we have to turn to "modifying" the majority in ways that are, from the democratic point of view, very dubious.

That was the case in Yugoslavia, where federalization and the representation of regions and nationalities have been handled well; but they have forgotten to create a central assembly in which Yugoslavs are represented directly, without the mediation of all these other structures, and where the government is accountable in one way or another to the collectivity. We should focus on how it is possible within the framework of autonomies and federalisms to create a responsible, responsive, and accountable central government that will be accepted as legitimate by all citizens.

KEITH KYLE: I would like to make three points. First, how permeable is the membrane of sovereignty? Bodin's principle of sovereignty, we must remember, has not ruled forever. It was developed only toward the end of the Middle Ages, or indeed at the time of the Renaissance. That principle is now being challenged in Britain by her membership in the European Community. The European Community, in relation to a limited number of functions, abolishes the classic distinction between foreign and domestic affairs. The institutions set up by the Treaty of Rome are at some midway point between diplomatic negotiation and political process. Insofar as the European Commission can be regarded as a protogovernment, it bears a distinct resemblance to the Swiss Federal Council, which we discussed earlier, although the presidency of the commission does not rotate every year.

The most distinctively federal element in these institutions is the European Court of Justice, which is going about interpretation of the letter and spirit of the Treaty of Rome as if it were a full-fledged, written constitution for Western Europe—including Great Britain, which until now has had an "unwritten constitution." There is the separate matter of the European Convention on Human Rights, which is prior to and not connected with the European Economic Community. This proclaims a bill of rights to which Britain adheres, and the pronouncements of the commission and court that sit at Strasbourg have been accepted as binding on Britain in respect to those matters covered by the convention.

The sovereignty of Britain and the sovereignty within Britain of the British Parliament are said to remain intact because it would be constitutionally valid to withdraw from these commitments. The subject has recently aroused attention in politics because the social Democratic party is committed to enacting the European Convention on Human Rights into British statutory law, with a clause that would instruct judges to interpret all subsequent legislation in accordance with the bill of rights, except where the subsequent legislation explicitly provides otherwise. That would mark a very considerable change in our way of doing things. So much for the membrane of sovereignty.

My second point concerns a distinction that needs to be made between a claim for minority rights and a claim for equality of status. There is a fairly established corpus of legal and constitutional rights and safeguards that can be applied to a situation in which an ethnic or other clearly defined group in a country requires something special to be done to prevent its culture from being overwhelmed by the predominant community—guarantees about the use of minority language, safeguards for minority religion, provision of minority schools, sometimes even special political representation.

It is an entirely different matter, however, in Cyprus and Sri Lanka. It is particularly difficult when the less numerous group claims to be on an equal initial footing with the more numerous group in founding the political society, if there are only two units, as in Cyprus. The way of a two-unit federation is very hard, because it does not have one kind of majority offsetting another kind.

The third point follows Mr. Linz's contributions: Somehow a constitution has to be found for those societies where, because of the intermingling of groups, it is impractical to run the society by means of straight majority voting, or democracy. A body of writing beginning within the last decade of the Austro-Hungarian Empire addresses this issue, with what is called the consociational approach. Its characteristics, however, were those of power sharing, compulsory coalition, the making of compromises essentially between elites. We saw, when we were discussing the Yugoslav Constitution, to what difficulties this gives rise, by alienating the political class from the people.

We face the question with this sort of society: how high a price is it prepared to pay to keep the political society together? The record of this form of organization has not been good. This question is being asked about the Greeks and Turks who are still trying to negotiate some kind of settlement in Cyprus other than complete partition. It has come up already in Lebanon, which is trying to establish some form of constitutional settlement to replace the national pact that worked very well for a number of decades but has now fallen to pieces. South Africa will confront this problem once the white minority faces up to the implications of the fact that apartheid will not provide any sort of long-term solution.

The challenge is felt very much by the United States, Britain, and others who are concerned and considering putting pressure on South Africa. It is a moral challenge to us to say what sort of constitution would work in South Africa, supposing it abandoned apartheid. It is quite natural for the African National Congress to opt for the Westminster model: one man, one vote, and the winner take all. Does anyone think that a successful society could exist in South Africa on that basis? But, then, what basis is best?

FALI NARIMAN: I would like to bring into the discussion something that has not been addressed: not diversity, not unity, but constitutionalism, which I think is extremely pertinent. We have now seen, though briefly, the workings of eight constitutions. A constitution, in my view, is no respecter of persons or of particular parties. It is not built around a person or amended for the benefit of the person. But we must not overlook one important fact: more than half the countries in the world today are governed by a form of constitution that is not in the spirit of constitutionalism. More than half the countries are dictatorships. They have constitutions of a sort but not the sort one means when one speaks of constitutionalism. The spirit of constitutionalism is extremely important for all of us to remember.

I remember a story told by a brave and famous judge of Bangladesh, the man who received the Nobel Peace Prize on behalf of Amnesty International. He told us that when democracy had failed within a year and a half of independence in Bangladesh and the new leader emerged as a dictator, he was summoned by the new leader, because they had been in college together, and was asked to draft a new constitution. The reply the judge gave was very significant. He said, "You remember when we were in Calcutta in college together and there were two famous actors and all the plays there were fashioned to fit the peculiar characters of the actors. Now you want me to write a constitution of that nature." Only the judge's close friendship with the president saved his life.

I mention this because there is of course a need for constitutional and institutional safeguards in every country, not only to protect diversity and to foster unity but to preserve the rule of law. This is an aspect of constitutionalism that must pervade every constitution that would truly be a basic document governing a people.

MR. GOLDWIN: When I planned this conference, I had to reflect on the issue of constitutions that lack the spirit of constitutionalism. Suggestions were made to me about including country X, country Y, or country Z—countries whose constitutions lacked the spirit of constitutionalism—simply on the ground that they did have a written constitution. So I made a very precise, very "scientific" division of constitutions into two categories. In the world there are honest constitutions and dishonest constitutions, and I made a rule that we will study the honest ones and disregard the dishonest ones.

Not all honest constitutions are good constitutions, but they do affect directly the daily life of the citizen. It is, for instance, possible under an honest constitution for a citizen to go to court and get some redress of grievances, even against government officials.

DANIEL ELAZAR: I agree absolutely with the earlier remark that we must distinguish between state and nation. The main reason for the development of the state as a political unit is that human beings are, as Aristotle says, political beings, beings who try to collaborate. Collaboration requires some kind of control or some kind of order. Because human beings are always trying to collaborate on a higher level, we are always searching for some kind of control on a higher level. For this reason the concept of sovereignty was absolutely appropriate for the nineteenth century and at least the beginning of the twentieth century, but it may not be the concept of the future: sovereignty may be limited because we are working toward further international collaboration.

By that I mean not a world state but further international collaboration. At the same time sovereignty may—let me be provocative and use Lenin's words—wither away, to give some diversities or groups more specific rights.

With regard to group rights, we are still on the level of Locke's concept of individual rights. It is wonderful that we now have this idea of individual rights, but at the same time we must find a constitutional concept that permits groups—families, local authorities, local communities, or national groups—certain kinds of rights, so that people can feel at home not only in their state but also in their smaller environment.

P. K. TRIPATHI: What I have learned from these discussions has helped me formulate my views on the problem of diversity in a particular way. I would not go so far as to say that the problem of diversity is nothing but the problem of individual liberty, but there is a very intimate relation between the problems of diversity and the problems of individual liberty. Wherever individual liberty has not been secured in fact and in action, the problems of diversity have become very acute and poignant, and vice versa. Where individual liberty is properly protected, the edge is taken off the problems of diversity.

The individual's liberty includes, of course, the liberty of forming associations. But if an association claims more rights than other groups do, it might create the same kind of problem as when the group feels it is not being given equal protection or equal rights. As Professor Glazer pointed out, even when the individual is protected from the states, that is not enough; sometimes he must be protected from the group.

In India particularly we have the experience of group rights or group privileges beginning to cut into individual liberty. The difficulties we had about quotas or reservations of legislative seats for certain groups is a fitting example. Every individual in the backward community must of course have the same rights as every other citizen. But the moment this group begins to ask for more than the individual's share of the cake because of backwardness or whatever criterion, it immediately begins to cut into the rights of other individuals and cause dissatisfaction and tension.

These are not the days to talk of natural law and universal principles. But we did not reject the universal principle theory on the ground that it was universal. We rejected it on the ground that it was not based on facts and observation. It discouraged taking into account the facts of life, and it tried to formulate regulations for all times and all people. But if we observe in actual life some kind of universal experience, then just as we have universal medicine, we can also have some universal remedies for social problems. More than ever I am affirmed in my belief that when individual rights are protected— preferably through judicial intervention, as they are under the Bill of Rights in the United States and the Chapter on Fundamental Rights in India—serious tensions, hatreds, and dislikes between groups are less likely to arise.

This is the reason group relations have not taken that shape in the United States. I am not saying there is no group strife in the United States, but group strife there can be seen as stemming from the failure to give the individual the rights to which he is entitled under the Constitution. At least that is one way to consider the struggle of blacks, for example, for equality. Ultimately the Supreme Court, the Congress, and the people of the United States saw the problem in that way. They did not so much act for the group as to give relief to the individual from a denial of rights.

Mr. Goldwin: That fits perfectly your formulation at the beginning: When black citizens were able to win their cases in court, it was not because they were black but because they were citizens and persons and because all the assurances given in the Constitution to persons and to citizens were said to apply to them. This so-called group right was satisfied on the basis of individual rights.

Jacob Landau: We need to consider those countries that do not have written constitutions. They may be divided into two groups. On the one hand, we have such countries as Saudi Arabia and Libya, which do not have written constitutions because they maintain that the Koran is their written constitution. I submit that this is an even more rigid form of constitution than, say, one written in 1813 in Belgium.

On the other hand, we have such countries as Great Britain, New Zealand, and Israel. Even if they do not have full, written constitutions, they do have a number of documents, some of which serve as a very good criterion to measure citizens' rights. Parts are missing from those constitutions because the people responsible for their drafting could not agree what should be prescribed for their society in certain areas. In Israel there are eight basic laws, which form part of the future constitution. One of the missing chapters is about the relations between the secular and religious parts of the population, a basic issue and a cardinal one in matters of diversity.

It may be worth examining those countries that do not have written constitutions and considering their merits relative to one another and to those countries that do have written constitutions.

Michel Troper: How can we distinguish between honest and dishonest constitutions? We notice that some constitutions, though beautiful on paper, are not properly implemented while others are. Therefore, perhaps the distinction should be between constitutions that are really implemented and those that are not, that are not effective.

If the constitution is not to remain merely a beautiful piece of paper, we need some device to ensure its effectiveness. The one that comes most often to mind is a judicial body and system of legal procedures that will enable citizens to secure their rights. But this concept is a modern one, and in many cases it leads to the transfer of the power of an arbitrary legislature to an arbitrary system of courts. Another device, however, which was developed in the eighteenth century, can be at least conceptually opposed to the system of courts: a system of checks and balances between the legislative organs of the state. In the context of our problem of unity and diversity, some minorities could play parts in the legislative process, within the system of checks and balances.

WALTER BERNS: It is indeed foolhardy to suppose that the judiciary can secure individual rights against a majority that is permitted to manifest itself, to organize itself, and to govern on a national level. In the United States, for example, the Supreme Court has played a major role in securing individual rights against the states. *Wisconsin* v. *Yoder* is one such case, and *Brown* v. *Board of Education* is another major illustration. One could indeed say that the federal judiciary has played *the* indispensable role in securing rights against the states.

The other part of the story, however, is that the Court has played almost no role whatsoever in securing individual rights against the national government. Indeed, for the first 135 years of our national existence—until 1925, when the Court began applying rights to the states—there were only fifteen cases involving the Bill of Rights. We enjoy freedom of speech in this country, for example, but not until 1965 did the Supreme Court of the United State enforce the First Amendment provision protecting freedom of speech against the national government. We enjoy freedom of religion in this country, but not until 1971, if then, did the Supreme Court enforce the First Amendment provision protecting freedom of religion against the national government. So one does indeed have to pay some attention, when writing a constitution, to the internal structure of the government. Although a judiciary is probably indispensable in a federal system, it is probably inadequate in a unitary system.

MR. GOLDWIN: So your point is that the Constitution did something to fashion the structure of the society and *that* is what has been securing rights down through the decades, rather than court action as such.

MR. BERNS: It *is* an interesting fact that the Constitution of the United States as it came out of the Philadelphia convention did not have a bill of rights. It is also interesting that the word "right" in any of its forms appears only once in the Constitution, as you have pointed out; there is no mention of property rights or free speech, and so on. The only time the word "right" appears in the unamended Constitution is in Article I, section 8, describing the powers of Congress. There it refers to the right of inventors and authors, which Congress has the power to protect through the copyright law. If one asked the Founding Father par excellence, James Madison, how this constitution would secure rights, the answer is provided in *Federalist* 51: there he says that civil rights are to be secured through a multiplicity of interests, religious rights through a multiplicity of religious sects. We have organized the government and representation in such a way as to allow those people to be manifested in their multiplicity. That is the way one secures rights against an oppressive government.

MR. GOLDWIN: Just to complete the record, when public demand for a bill of rights—or at least demand from politicians in the states, began to increase, Madison and Alexander Hamilton were at first opposed. Hamilton wrote the formulation, which Madison also used, that this Constitution does not need a bill of rights, because the Constitution, properly understood, is itself a bill of rights. When, in the end, Madison proposed a bill of rights, he excluded from it everything that might alter the institutions of government or the structure of society.

ROBERT VIPOND: Throughout these sessions we have probably done a better job of understanding diversity than unity. We might understand unity if we think of it as having something to do with democratic government, a system of making intelligent choices. The obverse of Mr. Berns's point, then, is that diversity makes it difficult in certain circumstances for modern democratic governments to make the sort of decisions that need to be made—that it places a certain handicap on democratic decision making, which ought to be factored into the calculation when one is trying to balance these two forces. We have seen several examples in these sessions.

The one with which I am most familiar, the Canadian example, seems to me to be a very good one. Precisely because of the strength of provincial governments and regional sentiment, it is very difficult for the national government in Canada to take the actions that would be necessary to address some of the important problems that have arisen throughout the West in the past ten years. Huge budgetary deficits are only the first in a long string of problems that have been left unresolved. Part of the problem is that provincial governments are so strong that, even if the federal government had the will, it would be very difficult to take concerted, coherent action to meet these problems. Part of the problem also is a party system that attempts to paper over as many of the regional differences as possible; in many ways this contributes to the unity of the country, but it also makes democratic decision making in the face of important economic and political problems more difficult.

The dispersion of power that one finds in the American political system—which, as Professor Berns points out, is linked to an understanding and an appreciation of diversity—has had the same effect. A common theme of most political science analysis is that it is very difficult to get a Congress composed of two houses, together with a president, a judiciary, a bureaucracy, various interest groups, and all the other interests that feed into the political system, to agree on action that will solve, for instance, the problem of huge budgetary deficits.

We have seen this in Switzerland as well, where there has been tremendous economic centralization but without a similar political centralization to act as a counterpoise, especially in the case of the banks. Of course, in Malaysia we saw perhaps the best example: the appreciation of diversity or sensitivity to race takes certain questions off the political agenda altogether and makes them "undiscussable."

When we try to understand the ways in which diversity and unity interact and the tensions to which they lead, it is important to view the problem in light of the ability of democratic governments to make hard decisions. In the past few years it has been very fashionable in this country as well as others in Western Europe to talk about the "overload" of the system and to argue that governments simply face too many problems. They raise expectations and then are unable to satisfy those expectations, giving way to cynicism or discontent among citizens. Perhaps this conference suggests that the problem is one not simply of political overload but of diversity overload. As important as protecting that diversity is, it nevertheless has costs that must be calculated as well.

RUTH BADER GINSBURG: The U.S. Constitution has been much discussed in these meetings. I am glad that I live and work under that Constitution. Professor Henry Steele Commager wrote on this subject that the Founding Fathers, in their fifty-two word Preamble, made the most satisfactory statement of the purpose of government ever written.

The United States falls notably short, however, in one area: we have not yet been willing to join even the most loose confederation with respect to international accords on human rights. We have certainly internalized those norms, but we have avoided speaking in unison with other nations to promote respect for human rights worldwide. Perhaps we will make a beginning soon by joining the conventions against genocide and against torture.

To comment briefly on a second point: we have seen in many nations, and markedly in the United States within the past fifteen or so years, progress toward a full voice in the political community for a once silenced (disenfranchised) majority—women. Opening the political arena and diverse occupations to women adds diversity, sharpens or deepens perspectives, and will make a most positive contribution as we move forward in the management of our world.

ENOCH DUMBUTSHENA: Although we did not speak much about unity, unity within a nation may come about because the citizens feel they *belong* to the nation. They have pride in it. Regardless of the nature of our Constitution, I belong to Zimbabwe. I cannot tell you why I am proud of belonging to Zimbabwe, but the Constitution does not enter into it. The unity of the people of Zimbabwe is brought about because we belong together and live together in one country, regardless of the kind of constitution we have.

Perhaps this is why different kinds of constitutions have succeeded in different countries and why, for instance, in India, Switzerland, and even Malaysia we have successful democracies in spite of the many diversities of nationalities within the boundaries of one country. This is why the Chinese and the Indians of Malaysia, who are in terms of their Constitution deprived of some of their educational and economic rights, nevertheless remain in that nation and are still proud to be Malaysians. There is something beyond the Constitution of that country that binds them together.

This helps explain why constitutions cannot be exported. Nigeria tried it, first with the British model and then with the U.S. model, which after a few years it also abandoned. It has not yet come across a solution that suits the nature or the temperament of its people.

JOSEPH CROPSEY: I have been trying to arrange in my own mind or to detect for my own purposes the unity that should arise out of the diversity of our various views on the subject, and I am having some difficulty. I altogether agree with Mr. Nariman's statement regarding the relationship of constitutionalism to the problem of diversity and unity. The so-called problem of constitutionalism is not determined or defined by the disjunction of unity and diversity. We can see this in the following way: What is primary in constitutionalism is rights. The primacy of rights in constitutionalism appears, at least at the outset, to be in conflict with the concept of sovereignty, and sovereignty is close to the problem of unity.

Historically speaking, we can see how the principle of sovereignty and the principle of rights converged in the seventeenth century and especially in the work of Hobbes, which is as much an analysis of rights as it is of sovereignty. To understand how the divergence occurs, we must look at the history of the theory of politics in the centuries after the seventeenth, where we see the evolution of the doctrine of rights departing from the evolution of the doctrine of sovereignty. In what sense is this relevant?

We have been told repeatedly that the question before us could be reduced to or translated into the question of the rights of individuals and the rights of groups. It has also been shown that that disjunction may be dissolved. Mr. Goldwin made a special point of how the rights of blacks as a group in this country may properly be understood as the rights of individual blacks, who may litigate and bring action for remedy of particular abuses or violations of their rights. But to dissolve the tension between the rights of groups and the rights of individuals on some less casual or less empirical ground—that is to say, on some more systematic ground—one could perhaps apply the following formula: if individual human beings were to think of themselves as men rather than as members of some group, they would conceive their rights to be the rights of men rather than the rights of groups. That seems to make the solution of the problem of unity and diversity quite simple: convert the thinking of men from the plane of group to the plane of individuals. As soon as one converts the question into a problem of how men think about themselves, however, one realizes that to some extent we have entered the realm of the translegal or the transpolitical.

It is clear to every modern person that how men think of themselves is to some extent determined or at least affected by what the government wants them to think about themselves. Vast propaganda machines grasp little human beings and indoctrinate them in some view of themselves. For example, the notion of the "new Soviet man" has been proclaimed and is in some sense accepted by the denizens of the Soviet Union. But human beings think about themselves in some respect that is independent of politics, of government, and even of the category that goes most systematically with thinking, and that is reason.

How men think about themselves is not determined simply by government within the realm of politics, nor is it determined simply within the realm of reason. How men think about themselves is very much affected by their religious affiliation. Could one say that the difficulties encountered by—if one wanted to be provocative, one would say the failure of—constitutions in some parts of the world, say, for instance, in Malaysia or even to some extent in Yugoslavia, are failures of the way in which men think about themselves? Perhaps the answer to that is yes, that they think about themselves in ways that are not conducive to their life in an orderly, problem-free community.

Is there, to use the formulation of Mr. Tripathi, a universal solution to this? Is there some solution that is common to all mankind? My feeling, as a result not only of what has gone on in this conference but also of what I have learned elsewhere, is that there is no universal solution to the problem of how men think about themselves. Following the indication of Chief Justice Dumbutshena, it is probably true that now and forever men will think about themselves in ways that escape the government of thought and reason. There is something, in other words, transpolitical and transrational invested in the way human beings think about themselves.

My conclusion from this is that mankind is destined—one might say, perhaps, doomed—to continue its efforts to solve the problems of unity and diversity on a highly empirical plane. There will be infusions of reason and there will be infusions of politics, but there will always be a residue; there will be a residual, impervious area in which men will continue to work out their destiny within politics but distinctly without reference to a universal principle. In other words, the solution of the human problem is impossible within the bounds of politics.

I do not think that is a gloomy conclusion, because it indicates that as long as there are human beings trying to live together, there will be a scope for the human activity that will always be imperfectly consummated but that will always elevate men. If there were some device by which politics could be extinguished among men, that device would be tantamount to the extinction of their humanity.

Mr. Goldwin: On that note, which Professor Cropsey does not consider "a gloomy conclusion," we come to the end of our deliberations with much more to think about than when we began. My heartfelt thanks to all of you for your patience and your diligence.

Contributors

ROBERT A. GOLDWIN (United States) is resident scholar and director of Constitutional Studies at the American Enterprise Institute. He has served in the White House as special consultant to the president of the United States and, concurrently, as adviser to the secretary of defense. He has taught at the University of Chicago and Kenyon College, and was dean of St. John's College in Annapolis, Maryland. He is the editor or coeditor of more than a score of books including *A Nation of States, How Democratic Is the Constitution?, How Capitalistic Is the Constitution?, How Does the Constitution Secure Rights?,* and *How Federal Is the Constitution?;* and the author of many articles including "Of Men and Angels: A Search for Morality in the Constitution," "Rights versus Duties: No Contest," and "Why Blacks, Women and Jews Are Not Mentioned in the Constitution."

ART KAUFMAN (United States) is research assistant in the Department of Government, Georgetown University. He has served as acting director of educational programs, Commission on the Bicentennial of the U.S. Constitution; assistant director of constitutional studies, American Enterprise Institute; program officer, Institute for Educational Affairs; and assistant editor, *The Public Interest* magazine. He is the coeditor (with Robert A. Goldwin) of several volumes on constitutional subjects, including: *Separation of Powers: Does It Still Work?, How Does the Constitution Protect Religious Freedom?,* and *Slavery and Its Consequences: The Constitution, Race, and Equality.*

WILLIAM A. SCHAMBRA (United States) is resident fellow at the American Enterprise Institute, on leave for government service. He was, until recently, codirector of constitutional studies at AEI. He is coeditor, with Robert A. Goldwin, of *How Democratic Is the Constitution?, How Capitalistic Is the Constitution?, How Does the Constitution Secure Rights?,* and *How Federal Is the Constitution?*

EDWARD C. BANFIELD (United States) is George D. Markham Professor of Government Emeritus at Harvard University. Previously, he was

William R. Kenan, Jr. Professor of Political Science and Policy Studies at the University of Pennsylvania, Henry Lee Shattuck Professor of Urban Government at Harvard University, and associate professor of political science at the University of Chicago. He has written extensively on American politics, especially on the problems of American cities and political party reform. His books include *The Moral Basis of a Backward Society* (with Laura Banfield), *Political Influence*, *City Politics* (with James Q. Wilson), *Big City Politics*, *The Unheavenly City*, *The Unheavenly City Revisited*, *The Democratic Muse*, and, most recently, *Here the People Rule*.

HERMAN BELZ (United States) is professor of history at the University of Maryland. He has written extensively on the subject of civil rights law and policy. He is the author of *A New Birth of Freedom: The Republican Party and Freedmen's Rights, 1861–1866* (1976) and *Emancipation and Equal Rights: Politics and Constitutionalism in the Civil War Era* (1978). He is the coauthor of *The American Constitution: Its Origins and Development* (6th ed., 1983), and is most recently author of *Affirmative Action from Kennedy to Reagan: Redefining American Equality* (1984).

WALTER BERNS (United States) is John M. Olin University Professor at Georgetown University and an adjunct scholar at the American Enterprise Institute. A political scientist, he is the author of a number of books and articles having to do primarily with the Constitution of the United States; his most recent book is *Taking the Constitution Seriously.* He is a member of the National Council on the Humanities and has served on the American delegation to the United Nations Commission on Human Rights.

ALBERT P. BLAUSTEIN (United States) is professor of law at Rutgers University. He has served as a constitutional consultant and legal adviser to governments and liberation movements in Liberia, Cambodia, Bangladesh, Peru, Zimbabwe, Uganda, Niger and others. Dr. Blaustein is the author or coauthor of more than twenty books, including *Constitutions of the Countries of the World* (18 volumes, 1971–), *Constitutions of Dependencies and Special Sovereignties* (7 volumes, 1975–), *Independence Documents of the World* (2 volumes, 1977), and *Human Rights Source Book* (1987). He is chairman and president of Human Rights Advocates International and is chairman of the Committee on the Influence of the U.S. Constitution Abroad for the League of Human Rights, World Peace Through Law Center.

CELIO BORJA (Brazil) has been a Supreme Court justice since April 1986, and was, prior to then, an adviser to the president of Brazil and a professor of constitutional law, State University in Rio. He has served as federal deputy of the Liberal Front party of Rio, speaker of the Chamber of Deputies, and was a member of the Constitutional Committee that prepared and presented a draft constitution to the Constituent Assembly.

HUMBERTO BRICENO SIERRA (Mexico) is vice-president of the Mexican Bar Association and teaches at Iberoamericana University. He has served as judge in the third court of the Mexican federal court system, and is the author of thirteen books, including two on constitutional issues. He was legal manager of the Mexico City Chamber of Commerce and is the president of the Pan-American Institute of Procedure Law, practices law in Mexican courts, and is an arbitrator in the national and international legal field.

JOSEPH CROPSEY (United States) is distinguished service professor of political science at the University of Chicago. He has taught at the City College of New York and at the New School for Social Research. He has twice been named a Rockefeller Foundation Fellow in Legal and Political Philosophy. Dr. Cropsey is the author or editor of several books (and numerous articles) on political philosophy, including *Polity and Economy: An Interpretation of Adam Smith* (1957), *History of Political Philosophy* (3rd ed., 1987) (coeditor with Leo Strauss and contributing author), *Ancients and Moderns: Essays on the Tradition of Political Philosophy in Honor of Leo Strauss* (editor and contributing author), and *Political Philosophy and the Issues of Politics* (1977).

JEAN-PIERRE DE BANDT (Belgium) is senior partner in the firm of de Bandt, Van Hecke, & Lagae. From 1962 to 1968 he was a lecturer at the Hoger Instituut voor Bestuurswetenschappen (Antwerp). He received his education at the University Faculty of Namur, the University of Louvain and at Harvard Law School. He is a member of the Executive Committee and is secretary of the American Chamber of Commerce in Belgium. He is president of the Coudenberg Group, a study group on federalism.

ENOCH DUMBUTSHENA (Zimbabwe) is the chief justice of Zimbabwe. Previously, he served as acting chief justice of the Supreme Court, judge president of the High Court, and a High Court judge. He has taught at several schools in Zimbabwe and South Africa and is the author of *Zimbabwe Tragedy*. He was educated at Marshall Hartley Mission and Waddilove Institute in Zimbabwe, Adams College in South Africa, and the University of South Africa and Gray's Inn, London, England.

Daniel J. Elazar (United States) is professor of political science and director of the Center for the Study of Federalism at Temple University. He has written and edited numerous books on American federalism, including *The American Partnership: Federal-State Relations in the Nineteenth Century* (1962), *American Federalism: A View from the States* (3rd ed., 1984), *Cities of the Prairie* (1970), and *Exploring Federalism* (1987). Dr. Elazar is editor of *Publius: The Journal of Federalism* and is Senator N. M. Paterson Professor of Political Studies, and head of the Institute of Local Government at Bar-Ilan University in Israel. He is also president of the Jerusalem Center for Public Affairs.

Thomas Fleiner (Switzerland) Dr. honoris causa is director of the Institute of Federalism at the University of Fribourg, and professor in public law and general theory of the state. Previously, he was dean of the faculty, president of the legal department, and assistant professor at Fribourg. He has taught at the Hebrew University of Jerusalem, the University of Rouen, France, and the University of Belgrade. He is the author of *Recht und Gerechtigkeit* (1976), *Droit et Justice* (1979), *Grundzuge des Allgemeinen und Schweizerischen Verwaltungsrechts* (2nd edition, 1980), *Allgemeine Staatslehre* (1980), and *Théorie Général de l'Etat* (Paris 1986).

Ruth Bader Ginsburg (United States) is a judge on the United States Court of Appeals for the District of Columbia Circuit. Prior to her appointment to the bench in 1980, she was a professor of law at Columbia University (1972–1980), and at Rutgers University (1963–1972). She has taught at Harvard Law School, New York University Law School, at the law faculties of the Universities of Amsterdam, Leyden, and Strasbourg, and at the Salzburg Seminar in American Studies. She is on the Council of the American Law Institute and is a fellow of the American Academy of Arts and Sciences. She has been a fellow at the Center for Advanced Study in the Behavioral Sciences (Stanford, California) and is secretary and member of the Executive Committee of the American Bar Foundation. Judge Ginsburg has published extensively on judicial systems, civil procedure, conflict of laws, and constitutional law.

Nathan Glazer (United States) is professor of education and sociology at Harvard University, and coeditor of *The Public Interest* magazine. He has taught at the University of California at Berkeley, Bennington College in Vermont, Smith College, the Salzburg Seminar in American Studies, and the Ecole des Etudes en Sciences Sociales in Paris. He is the author of numerous books and articles, among them:

American Judaism, The Social Basis of American Communism, Beyond the Melting Pot (with Daniel P. Moynihan), *Affirmative Discrimination: Ethnic Inequality and Public Policy,* and *Ethnic Dilemmas, 1964–1982.* Most recently, he is editor of *Clamor at the Gates: The New American Immigration* (1985). He has received several presidential apppointments, and has served on the Task Force on Urban Affairs (1964 and 1972), Task Force on Education (1980), and, since 1980, Board of Foreign Scholarships.

OTTO KONSTANTIN KAUFMANN (Switzerland) is former president of the Swiss Federal Court (1983–1984). He served as a judge on that court, and as rector and professor of law at the Saint Gall Graduate School of Economics and Social Sciences. He has studied law at the universities of Zurich and Rome, at Yale University, and at Georgetown University.

KOH ENG TIAN (Singapore) has been solicitor general of Singapore since 1981. Before this he was senior state counsel, assistant parliamentary counsel, deputy parliamentary counsel, and parliamentary counsel. He has been involved since 1965 in the drafting of legislation. He has represented Singapore in a number of international conferences, including the United Nations General Assembly.

KEITH KYLE (United Kingdom) is special assistant to the director of the Royal Institute of International Affairs in London. He has served as meetings secretary of the Royal Institute, and has been a member of the staff of the Institute since 1972. Prior to this, he worked for BBC Television in the United States, the Middle East, the European Economic Community, and Northern Ireland. From 1967 to 1968 he was a fellow of the Institute of Politics at the John F. Kennedy School of Politics, Harvard University. Earlier, he was the Washington correspondent for the *Economist* and a free-lance writer for the *Atlantic Monthly,* the *Christian Science Monitor,* the *New York Post* and other publications. Mr. Kyle has published a monograph on the Cyprus problem for the Minority Rights Group (1984). His study of the Suez conflict is scheduled to be published in 1988.

JACOB LANDAU (Israel) is professor of political science at the Hebrew University of Jerusalem, with special reference to the politics and governments of the Middle East. He has taught at Brandeis University, the University of California at Los Angeles, Wayne State University, Columbia University, Ankara University, Candido Mendes University (Brazil), and the University of Utah, and has been a resident fellow at the Netherlands Institute for Advanced Study in the Humanities and Social Sciences. The author of several books and over 400 articles in specialized journals, Professor Landau is an editorial adviser to, or a member of, the editorial boards of numerous periodicals, including *Plural Societies* (Holland), *State, Government, and International Relations* (Jerusalem), and *Asian and African Studies: Journal of the Israel Oriental Society.*

JUAN JOSÉ LINZ (Spain) has taught since 1968 at Yale University, where he is the Pelatiah Perit Professor of Political and Social Science. He has also taught at the Universidad Autonoma de Madrid, Columbia, Stanford, Heidelberg, and other universities, and is a member of the American Academy of Arts and Sciences, of the board of the Committee on Political Sociology of the International Sociological Association, and of the International Political Science Association. Professor Linz served as president of the World Association of Public Opinion Research and as chairman of the Council for European Studies. In 1987 he was awarded the Premio Principe de Asturias prize in the social sciences. He is the author of *Conflicto en Euskadi,* coauthor of the *Informe sobre el cambio político en España,* 1975–1978, and coeditor of *Crisis y cambio: electores y partidos en la España de los años ochenta* and other books. He also wrote *Crisis, Breakdown and Reequilibration,* the first volume of a series he coedited, *Breakdown of Democratic Regimes.* His book-length essay "Totalitarian and Authoritarian Regimes" appears in *Handbook of Political Science.*

AFAF M. MAHFOUZ (Egypt) is professor of international law and political science, University of Helwan, Cairo, and is chairman of the Department of Law and Political Science. She also is a scholar at the American Research Center in Egypt, having served as a member of the Cairo Advisory Board at the Center in 1982 and 1983, director of research at the centre de documentation et d'études économiques, juridiques et sociales (Franco-Egyptian Center of Technical Cooperation, CEDEJ), and is a member of Conseil Scientifique of CEDEJ. She has served as cultural counselor at the Egyptian Embassy in Washington, D.C., as Egyptian representative on the Arab Cultural and Information Committee, and as director of research at the Center for Strategic Studies, Al-Ahram, Cairo. She is the author of, among other publications, *Socialisme et Pouvoir en Egypte,* "Le Changement Fondamental des Circonstances: l'article 59 du Projet de la Commission de Droit International" in *l'Egypte Contemporaine,* and "The Afro-Asian Struggle" in *Al Siyasah al Dawliya.*

TERENCE MARSHALL (United States) is maitre de conferences at the University of Paris X (Nanterre). Previously, he was associate professor of juridical and political sciences. He has taught political science at the University of Pennsylvania, North Carolina State University, the University of Paris I (Sorbonne-Pantheon), and L'Ecole Normale Superieure. His publications include "Leo Strauss, le Philosophie et la Science Politique" in *La Revue Française de Science Politique*, "John Locke et la Philosophie Constitionnelle," in *Synthèse, Vie et Institutions Politiques des Etats-Unis*, "Rousseau Translations: A Review Essay," in *Political Theory*, among many others. He is currently preparing a two-volume study in French on American constitutional theory and practice.

MILAN MATIC (Yugoslavia) is vice dean of political science faculty at the University of Belgrade. He is the author of many publications, including *Political Representation, Political Thought of C. W. Mills*, and *Self-Management and the Socialization of Politics*. He is author most recently of *Myth and Politics* (for which has was awarded the October prize by the City of Belgrade for achievement in the field of social sciences).

FALI SAM NARIMAN (India) is a senior advocate of the Supreme Court of India. He has been practicing law for over thirty-eight years and is a member of the International Commission of Jurists and a member of the International Council for Commercial Arbitration. He has been the vice-president of the Bar Association of India for over ten years and has recently been appointed as a member of the London Court of Arbitration. He was Additional Solicitor-General of India from 1972 to June 1975 when he resigned in protest at the declaration of emergency. From 1985 to 1987 he was president of LAWASIA (Law Association of Asia and the Pacific) and was founder and cochairman of LAWASIA's Permanent Committee for Human Rights from 1976 to 1986.

THOMAS L. PANGLE (United States) is professor of political science and chairman of the American Studies committee at the University of Toronto. He has taught at the University of Chicago, Dartmouth College, and Yale University. He serves on the editorial boards of the journals, *Polis* and the *Review of Politics*. He has served as an adviser to the National Endowment for the Humanities and currently serves as an adviser to the National Public Television Series, "Visions of the Constitution." He is the author of *The Laws of Plato* (translation and interpretive study) (1980), *Montesquieu's Philosophy of Liberalism* (1973), and *The Spirit of Modern Republicanism* (1988). He is also the author of numerous published articles, including "Virtue in the Thought of the Leading Federalists," in *This Constitution,* and "Rediscovering Rights," in *The Public Interest* magazine. He is coauthor of "The Philosophic Foundation of Human Rights," in *Human Rights in Our Time* and "Restoring the Human Rights Tradition" in the journal, *This World.*

HOWARD PENNIMAN (United States) is an adjunct scholar at the American Enterprise Institute. He is general editor of AEI's *At the Polls* series describing national elections in some twenty-five democratic countries around the world. He has been an election consultant to the American Broadcasting Company since 1968. Previously, he served with the U.S. Department of State, the U.S. Information Agency, and the Pscyhological Strategy Board. He taught political science at Georgetown University from 1957 to 1980. He was elected delegate to the Maryland Constitutional Convention in 1967–1968 where he chaired the Committee on Style, Drafting, and Arrangements. Dr. Penniman served as a consultant to the team of observers sent to Vietnam by President Lyndon Johnson for the 1967 elections in South Vietnam. He also served as a member of the Freedom House teams that observed the elections in Zimbabwe in 1979 and 1980, on the official U.S. observer team for the 1982, 1984, and 1988 elections in El Salvador, and on the observer team for the 1985 constituent assembly elections in Guatemala, Philippines, 1986 and Taiwan, 1987.

VISU SINNADURAI (Malaysia) is the dean of the faculty of law and a professor of comparative law at the University of Malaya, and is former advocate and solicitor of the High Court of Malaya. He is editor-in-chief of the *Journal of Malaysian and Comparative Law,* and editor of the *Survey of Malaysian Law.* He is the national representative to the governing council of the ASEAN Law Association, and is the author of *Law of Contract in Malaysia and Singapore: Cases and Commentary, Judgments of Sultan Azlan Shah: Cases and Commentary* (forthcoming), *Hundred Years of Privy Council Decisions from Malaysia and Singapore, 1882–1982* (in preparation), "Citizenship Laws of Malaysia," in *The Constitution Of Malaysia: Its Development, 1957–1977,* "Rights to Education under the Malaysian Constitution," in *The Constitution of Malaysia,* and many other publications.

JOHN S. SORZANO (United States) is former deputy U.S. permanent representative to the United Nations with the rank of ambassador extraordinary and plenipotentiary (1983–1985). Prior to that, he served as ambassador and U.S. representative to the United Nations Economic and Social Council (1981–1983). He is president of the Cuban American National Foundation, an independent, nonprofit organization which gathers and disseminates data about Cuban economic, political, and social issues. He is also associate professor of government at Georgetown University where he has taught since 1969 in the School of Foreign Service, the Graduate School, and the College of Arts and Sciences. From 1976 to 1978, Ambassador Sorzano served as a Peace Corps country director in Colombia. He has held fellowships with the Organization of American States, Georgetown University, and the University of Michigan.

VOJISLAV D. STANOVCIC (Yugoslavia) has been professor of political theory, faculty of political science, at the University of Belgrade since 1968. He has served previously as managing editor of *Our Reality*, a monthly review of social science, and editor of *Socialism*. He has written and edited three editions of *Political Encyclopedia*, and is preparing a fourth edition. He also has edited the 1,159-page *Theory and Practice of Self-Management*. Among his other publications are: *Industrial Democracy, Utopian Theories of Society*, "Territorial and Functional Federalism," "Social Role, Ethical, and Political Teachings of the Founders of Great World Religions," "On the Character and Political Ideas of *The Federalist* Papers," as well as many other articles on federalism, human rights, political parties, and other subjects. Dr. Stanovcic has translated *The Federalist* papers into Serbo-Croation.

BARRY L. STRAYER (Canada) is a judge of the Federal Court of Canada. He was appointed Queen's Counsel (Canada) in 1974. Previously, he was professor of Law, College of Law, University of Saskatchewan, and assistant deputy minister of justice in the government of Canada. He is the author of many publications, including *The Canadian Constitution and the Courts.* He served as a constitutional adviser to the government of Seychelles in 1979 during the drafting of their new Constitution. Judge Strayer was involved in the constitutional reform process in Canada for over twenty-two years, first as an adviser to the Saskatchewan government and then to the government of Canada. He participated in 1971 and 1980 in Canadian-British discussions on patriation of the Constitution. He has served as counsel for the attorney general of Canada in the Court of Appeals of Newfoundland and in the Supreme Court of Canada in litigation over proposals for constitutional reform. A former visiting scholar at the Center for

International Affairs at Harvard University, Judge Strayer also sits on the Court Martial Appeals Court of Canada.

Ismail Suny (Indonesia) is professor of constitutional law and legal theory and department chairman at the University of Indonesia, and is a consultant to the National Defense and Security Council of the Republic of Indonesia. Previously, he was rector of the University of Muhammadiyah in Jakarta; a member of the People's Congress (Parliament) (1967–1969); professor of government at the National Defense Institute, Department of Defense and Security; and vice chairman of the National Legal Reform institute, Department of Justice. He is the author of *State Power Division: A Comparative Study in British, United States, Soviet Union, and Indonesian Constitutional Law; The Shifting of Executive Power: A Comparative Study in Constitutional Law;* and *The Mechanism of Pancasila's Democracy.*

Teh Boon Eng (Malaysia) is advocate and solicitor, High Court of Malyaysia. Having received his legal education (with honors) from the University of Malaya in 1976, he was admitted to the Malaysian Bar in 1977.

Francisco Tomas Y Valiente (Spain) is judge and chairman of the Constitutional Court of Spain. He was appointed to this position by the Spanish Congress of Deputies in 1980 and reappointed in 1983. He has been successively professor of legal history at the University of La Laguna, University of Salamanca, and at the University of Madrid. He is a member of the councils of editors for the *Annual Review of Spanish Legal History,* the *Spanish Review of Constitutional Law,* and the *Review of Agriculture and Society,* among others. He is also the author of six books on legal history and many articles in professional journals.

P. K. Tripathi (India) is professor of law and dean of the Law School, University of Delhi. He served twice as a full-time member of the Law Commission of India and has taught at the University of Melbourne (Australia), the University of New South Wales, Sydney, the University of Singapore, and at the University of Allahabad in India. He was a K. T. Telang Memorial Lecturer at the University of Bombay (the first academic lawyer to do so), a Baldev Sahai Memorial Lecturer at the University of Patna (the first to do so under the trust), a National Professor of Law, and he delivered the Dr. Rajendra Prasad Memorial Lecture to the nation by radio in 1976. He also delivered the Anundoram Borooah Lecture in Gauhati organized by the honorable chief justice of the Gauhati High Court. Among his publications are: *Spotlights on Constitutional Interpretation, Some Insights into Fundamental Rights, Bharatiya Samvidhan ke Mool Tatva* (a volume that has been awarded a prize for the best book on law published in the decade 1972–1982 in Hindi), and numerous articles in foreign and Indian journals.

MICHEL TROPER (France) is professor of law at the University of Paris X (Nanterre). He previously taught at Rouen Law School, Paris Law School, and the University of Lyon Law School. He has been director of the Center of Legal Theory at the University of Paris (Nanterre) since 1978, and director of public law studies since that time. He has taught abroad in Brazzaville; Southampton, U.K.; Annaba, Algeria; Lodz, Poland; Boston; Bologne; and in Mexico. In addition to numerous articles, he is the author of *La Separation des Pouvoirs et l'Histoire Constitutionelle Française* and coauthor of *Reinventer le Parlement*.

JAVIER VALLE-RIESTRA (Peru) is a member of the Senate of Peru and president of the Senate Human Rights Commission. His term of office runs until 1990. Previously, he was a member of the Peru Chamber of Deputies where he served as president of that body's Human Rights Commission. He is past president of the Executive Committee on Human Rights of the Lima Bar Association, vice-president of the Latin American Association for Human Rights, and a former member of the Commission to Draft Human Rights Legislation. Educated at the Universidad Catolica and Universidad Compultense de Madrid, he is also a former member of the Lima City Council.

JACQUES VANDERLINDEN (Belgium) is professor of law and former dean of the Faculty of Law at the University of Brussels. He is currently teaching at the University of South Carolina in the United States for the second time. Previously, he has taught in Paris, London, and Wroclaw, as well as at the universities of Abidjan and Edinburgh. He has served as a visiting professor at the newly created Law Faculty in Addis Ababa and at Kinshasa in Zaire. He is the author of many articles and books, mostly on African affairs.

EDMUNDO VASQUEZ MARTINEZ (Guatemala) is former rector of Guatemala's San Carlos University and currently serves as a member of Guatemala's Civilian-Military Council. He has served in the past as the representative for professional schools to the Council of State. He is a past president of the Guatemalan Bar Association as well as of the Superior University Council of Central America.

ROBERT C. VIPOND (Canada) is assistant professor of political science at the University of Toronto where he teaches courses in Canadian and American politics and American constitutionalism. He received his bachelor of arts and master of arts degrees from the University of Toronto, and his Ph.D. from Harvard University.

A Note on the Book

This book was edited by the
publications staff of the American Enterprise Institute.
The text was set in Palatino, a typeface designed by Hermann Zapf.
Coghill Book Typesetting Company, of Richmond, Virginia,
set the type, and Edwards Brothers Incorporated,
of Ann Arbor, Michigan, printed and bound the book,
using permanent, acid-free paper.